MULTIDIRECTIONAL MEMORY

Cultural Memory
in
the
Present

Mieke Bal and Hent de Vries, Editors

MULTIDIRECTIONAL MEMORY

*Remembering the Holocaust in the
Age of Decolonization*

Michael Rothberg

STANFORD UNIVERSITY PRESS
STANFORD, CALIFORNIA
2009

Stanford University Press
Stanford, California

© 2009 by the Board of Trustees of the Leland Stanford Junior University. All rights reserved.

Chapter 4 was originally published as "W. E. B. Du Bois in Warsaw: Holocaust Memory and the Color Line, 1949–1952," *The Yale Journal of Criticism* 14, no. 1 (2001): 169–89. © Yale University and the Johns Hopkins University Press. Reprinted with permission of the Johns Hopkins University Press. Parts of Chapter 5 were originally published as "Writing Ruins: The Anachronistic Aesthetics of André Schwarz-Bart," *After Representation? The Holocaust, Literature, and Culture*, ed. R. Clifton Spargo and Robert Ehrenreich. New Brunswick, NJ: Rutgers University Press, 2009. Reprinted by permission of Rutgers University Press. Chapter 6 was originally published as "The Work of Testimony in the Age of Decolonization," *PMLA* 119, no. 5 (2004): 1231–46. Reprinted by permission of the copyright owner, the Modern Language Association of America. Chapter 7 was originally published as "Between Auschwitz and Algeria," *Critical Inquiry* 33, no. 1 (2006): 158–84. Reprinted by permission of *Critical Inquiry* and the University of Chicago.

This book has been published with the assistance of the Program in Jewish Culture and Society at the University of Illinois at Urbana-Champaign.

No part of this book may be reproduced or transmitted in any form or by any means, electronic or mechanical, including photocopying and recording, or in any information-storage or -retrieval system without the prior written permission of Stanford University Press.

Printed and bound by CPI Group (UK) Ltd, Croydon, CR0 4YY

Library of Congress Cataloging-in-Publication Data

Rothberg, Michael.
   Multidirectional memory : remembering the Holocaust in the age of decolonization / Michael Rothberg.
      p. cm.—(Cultural memory in the present)
   Includes bibliographical references and index.
   ISBN 978-0-8047-6217-5 (cloth : alk. paper)
   ISBN 978-0-8047-6218-2 (pbk. : alk. paper)
   1. Holocaust, Jewish (1939–1945)—Historiography.   2. Holocaust, Jewish (1939–1945), in literature.   3. Decolonization—Historiography.   4. Decolonization in literature.   5. Collective memory.   6. Collective memory in literature.   I. Title.   II. Series.
D804.348.R67   2009
940.53'18072—dc22

2008041759

Yasemin'e—aujourd'hui et demain

Contents

List of Illustrations   xi
Acknowledgments   xiii

1 Introduction: Theorizing Multidirectional Memory in a Transnational Age   1

PART I: BOOMERANG EFFECTS: BARE LIFE, TRAUMA, AND THE COLONIAL TURN IN HOLOCAUST STUDIES

2 At the Limits of Eurocentrism: Hannah Arendt's *The Origins of Totalitarianism*   33

3 "Un Choc en Retour": Aimé Césaire's Discourses on Colonialism and Genocide   66

PART II: MIGRATIONS OF MEMORY: RUINS, GHETTOS, DIASPORAS

4 W. E. B. Du Bois in Warsaw: Holocaust Memory and the Color Line   111

5 Anachronistic Aesthetics: André Schwarz-Bart and Caryl Phillips on the Ruins of Memory   135

PART III: TRUTH, TORTURE, TESTIMONY: HOLOCAUST MEMORY DURING THE ALGERIAN WAR

6 The Work of Testimony in the Age of Decolonization: *Chronicle of a Summer* and the Emergence of the Holocaust Survivor   175

7 The Counterpublic Witness: Charlotte Delbo's
  Les belles lettres   199

PART IV: OCTOBER 17, 1961: A SITE OF HOLOCAUST
MEMORY?

8 A Tale of Three Ghettos: Race, Gender, and
  "Universality" After October 17, 1961   227
9 Hidden Children: The Ethics of Multigenerational
  Memory After 1961   267

  Epilogue: Multidirectional Memory in an Age
    of Occupations   309

  Notes   315
  Index   365

Illustrations

1	André Fougeron, *Atlantic Civilization* (1953).	35
2	Boris Taslitzky, *Riposte* (1951).	68
3	Photograph by Israel Gutman of the ruins of the Warsaw Ghetto in July 1945.	123
4	Marceline, Rouch, and Landry discuss racism and anti-Semitism in the rooftop restaurant of the Musée de l'Homme. Jean Rouch and Edgar Morin, *Chronique d'un été* (1961).	185
5	Marceline recounts the story of her deportation while walking through the Place de la Concorde. Jean Rouch and Edgar Morin, *Chronique d'un été* (1961).	186
6	The November 9, 1961, cover of *France-Observateur* featuring Marguerite Duras's "Les deux ghettos."	238
7	Georges and Anne argue about their missing son while the television news reports on the Abu Ghraib torture scandal. Michael Haneke, *Caché* (2005).	284
8	Hidden children. Pierrot and Majid's son on the bottom left of the school steps. Michael Haneke, *Caché* (2005).	291
9	Elie Kagan's photograph, taken from the metro, of Algerian demonstrators attacked by police in the Concorde metro station.	302
10	Elie Kagan's photograph of a young man assisting an Algerian demonstrator who has been bloodied by the police in the Solférino metro.	303

Acknowledgments

Multidirectional Memory brings together Holocaust studies and postcolonial studies for the first time in a book-length work. It seeks to reconstruct the relations between at least three primary archives that span transnational cultural spaces. It combines consideration of black Atlantic and French-Algerian contact zones, and it reads both of these formations across and through diasporic Jewish history. Drawing on the resources of these unusual conjunctions, this book seeks to change thinking about collective memory and its relation to group identity. It does so in two ways: by interrogating the logic of dominant accounts of memory and identity—a logic I see defined by competition and the zero-sum game—and by uncovering a countertradition in which remembrance of the Holocaust intersects with the legacies of colonialism and slavery and ongoing processes of decolonization. The countertradition I uncover continues to this day, but it has its roots in generations of activists and intellectuals who are now passing from the scene and whose example inspired this book. Some of these figures are well known in the contemporary academy; some should be better known. They include several who died during the writing of *Multidirectional Memory*—Aimé Césaire, André Mandouze, Jean Rouch, André Schwarz-Bart, and Pierre Vidal-Naquet—as well as several who passed away in earlier decades, including Hannah Arendt, Charlotte Delbo, Marguerite Duras, and W. E. B. Du Bois. I am convinced much remains to be learned from them, as from those figures who are still very much active, such as Didier Daeninckx, Michael Haneke, Caryl Phillips, and Leïla Sebbar.

Working at the intersection of two fields and several national contexts means that I've incurred many personal and intellectual debts during the last years of work on this project. I'm grateful to the editors, anonymous readers, and editorial collectives of three journals for helping make several chapters of this book stronger (and for permission to reprint them in revised form): *Critical Inquiry* (Chapter 7), *PMLA* (Chapter 6), and the *Yale Journal of Criticism* (Chapter 4). Part of Chapter 5 is to appear in a volume edited by R. Clifton Spargo and Robert M. Ehrenreich and to be published by Rutgers University Press and the United States Holocaust Memorial Museum. At Stanford University Press, I was fortunate to find Emily-Jane Cohen, whose enthusiasm for the project has been gratifying. Thanks also to Ariane De Pree-Kajfez at Stanford for helping me navigate the treacherous waters of permissions and rights, and to Sarah Crane Newman, Tim Roberts, and Alex Giardino for their help in getting the manuscript into shape and into the world. Andreas Huyssen, whose work on memory has inspired me from the beginning, provided a supportive and helpful reader's report, as did another, very generous anonymous reviewer for the press. I couldn't imagine a better home for the book than Mieke Bal and Hent de Vries's series "Cultural Memory in the Present."

A number of colleagues invited me to present portions of this work in a series of stimulating venues. Eleanor Kaufman organized what turned out to be a particularly lively exchange at the University of Virginia early in the project. A seminar and conference at the U.S. Holocaust Memorial Museum provided another early venue for this work, as did conferences organized by David Bathrick at Cornell and Marianne Hirsch at Dartmouth. Participating in Dirk Moses's important "Genocide and Colonialism" conference at the University of Sydney was an especially significant experience. In the summer of 2004 I worked on this project as a fellow of the Simon-Dubnow Institute for Jewish History and Culture, and I am grateful to its director, Dan Diner, for a warm welcome in Leipzig. I got to try out versions of the thesis of this book in a couple of invigorating dialogues with the delightfully skeptical Walter Benn Michaels, once during a seminar organized by graduate students at the University of Illinois at Chicago and once during a conference organized by my colleague Gordon Hutner. As I was nearing completion of the project, I had the good fortune of participating in a seminar in Berlin on Holocaust literature and narrative theory hosted by Jakob Lothe, James Phelan, and Susan Suleiman and in the 2007 conference of the Post-45 collective hosted by J. D. Connor and Amy Hungerford at Harvard. Erica Lehrer's invitation to give the Annual Public History Lecture at Concordia University in Montreal (an

Acknowledgments xv

invitation from one nonhistorian to another!) provided an occasion that proved to be both fun and invigorating.

Beyond my home base in Champaign-Urbana, many colleagues and friends have contributed in innumerable ways to this project. New York will always be home away from home; thanks to Beth Drenning and Neil Levi, Jeffrey Escoffier, Matthew Lore, Carine Montbertrand, Helen Roth, and Jennie Uleman for hospitality, friendship, and toleration of our outrageous epicurean demands. Beth and Neil have also helped this project evolve from its earliest moments to its latest. Nancy K. Miller has been an inspiration and supporter since I entered the profession. Gary Weissman is always a challenging interlocutor, not to mention an expert CD-burner. Russ Castronovo is a fine reader and even finer friend. The Summer Institute crowd continues to be an audience I value: Liz Blasco, Susan Hegeman, Caren Irr, Carolyn Lesjak, Chris Pavsek, Rob Seguin, and Phil Wegner. Recently I've had the good fortune to meet a number of people pursuing exciting related projects, including Stef Craps, Debarati Sanyal, Max Silverman, and Estelle Tarica. Philippe Mesnard and Carola Hähnel-Mesnard have been generous and engaging friends in Paris, as have been Andrés Nader and Agnès Benoit-Nader in Berlin. A number of other colleagues from far and wide influenced this work in various ways—by responding to parts of the book, by providing references, or simply through the example of their own scholarship: Leslie Adelson, Lauren Berlant, Bryan Cheyette, Sam DiIorio, Sidra Ezrahi, Marianne Hirsch, Irene Kacandes, Jean-Louis Jeannelle, Dominick LaCapra, Darrell Moore, Dirk Moses, Sam Moyn, Debbie Nelson, Bruce Robbins, Ronnie Scharfman, Cliff Spargo, Dan Stone, Susan Suleiman, and Jürgen Zimmerer. Although he certainly doesn't know it, Manthia Diawara had a profound influence on the shape of this book when he presented his film *Rouch in Reverse* at the School of Criticism and Theory in 2002.

The vast majority of this book has been written amidst the vibrant intellectual community that is the humanities at the University of Illinois at Urbana-Champaign, a community enhanced by the generous institutional support for research that has been a proud tradition here. I would like to acknowledge the Campus Research Board for helping to provide necessary time for writing and for funding a research trip to Paris that proved essential to this book's completion. A Mellon Foundation Faculty

Fellowship administered by the university also provided welcome time off. In addition, I benefited from the stimulating environment provided by the Illinois Program for Research in the Humanities, and I'm indebted to then-director Matti Bunzl as well as Associate Director Christine Catanzarite. Dennis Baron and Martin Camargo, the two heads of the English Department during the course of my writing, helped to facilitate this institutional support, as did the excellent English Department staff.

Such material support is crucial, and to be defended by any means necessary, but, above all, what has made the Illinois flatlands such an inviting place to live and work is the generosity of the colleagues here. Two chapters of this book benefited from readings by the Americanist group in the English Department: Nancy Castro, Chris Freeburg, Bill Maxwell, Justine Murison, Bob Parker, Naomi Reed, and Julia Walker. Special thanks to Bill, for understanding the stakes, and to Bob, for his commitment to good prose. I've had the enormous fortune of directing the Unit for Criticism and Interpretive Theory the last five years, and I'm grateful to all the colleagues and students who have collaborated with me and taken part in our events. The challenging interdisciplinary dialogues that take place at the Unit have left their mark everywhere in this book. The same should be said for our Program in Jewish Culture and Society, another interdisciplinary home base that has provided essential intellectual and material support. An incomplete list, as we say here, of the many colleagues and friends in and around Illinois who have enriched my work (sometimes without knowing it) through their conversation, commentary, and general camaraderie includes: Anustup Basu, Manisha Basu, Jodi Byrd, J.B. Capino, Tony Clark, Ramona Curry, Jonathan Druker, Jed Esty, Maggie Flinn, Melissa Free, Peter Garrett, Zsuzsa Gille, Lauren Goodlad, Andrea Goulet, Jim Hansen, Matt Hart, Brett Kaplan, Suvir Kaul, Ania Loomba, Harriet Murav, Adlai Murdoch, Jan Nederveen Pieterse, Cary Nelson, Bruce Rosenstock, and Renée Trilling. Manuel Rota and Nora Stoppino came late to this project, but contributed more than a little in the way of sustenance, fun, and lively discussion. Dara Goldman makes friendship autochthonous, wherever she is. Matti Bunzl deserves a category of his own, one that would capture his energy, intelligence, and generosity. Lilya Kaganovsky and Rob Rushing's contributions defy categorization (but should definitely be filed under good times).

I'd like to acknowledge the support of my family, especially my mother Sondra Rothberg, my father Joseph Rothberg, my sister Madeleine Rothberg, and my brother-in-law Dylan Jones. My niece Shuli is a voracious reader, and I hope one day she'll find some inspiration here—although she may want to wait for the French translation!

This book is dedicated, once again, to Yasemin Yıldız. Without her love, intelligence, support, and acute editorial skills, I literally don't know where I'd be.

1

Introduction: Theorizing
Multidirectional Memory
in a Transnational Age

Beyond Competitive Memory

In a characteristically provocative essay on the relationship between racism and anti-Semitism in contemporary America, the literary critic Walter Benn Michaels considers the seemingly incompatible legacies of slavery and the Nazi genocide in the United States:

> Why is there a federally funded U.S. Holocaust Museum on the Mall in Washington, DC? . . . The difficulty of coming up with a satisfactory answer to this question has produced a certain exasperation among African Americans, memorably expressed by the notorious black racist Khalid Muhammad when, in the wake of a visit to the U.S. Holocaust Memorial Museum, he told an audience at Howard University on 3 April 1994 that "the black holocaust was 100 times worse than the so-called Jew Holocaust. You say you lost six million. We question that, but . . . we lost 600 million. Schindler's List," as Muhammad put it, "is really a swindler's list." The force of these remarks consists not in the absurd Holocaust denial but in the point—made precisely by his visit to the Holocaust Museum—that commemoration of the Nazi murder of the Jews on the Mall was in fact another kind of Holocaust denial. Why should what the Germans did to the Jews be treated as a crucial event in American history, especially when, given the absence

of any commemoration of American racism on the Mall, what Americans did to Black people is not?[1]

In this passage Michaels takes up one of the most agonizing problems of contemporary multicultural societies: how to think about the relationship between different social groups' histories of victimization. This problem, as Michaels recognizes, also fundamentally concerns collective memory, the relationship that such groups establish between their past and their present circumstances. A series of questions central to this book emerges at this point: What happens when different histories confront each other in the public sphere? Does the remembrance of one history erase others from view? When memories of slavery and colonialism bump up against memories of the Holocaust in contemporary multicultural societies, must a competition of victims ensue?

Michaels's stance toward his example in his essay on anti-Semitism and racism is somewhat cagey; he acknowledges Muhammad's racism and the "absurd" nature of his Holocaust denial, yet he seems simultaneously to embrace a fundamental feature of Muhammad's argument. Like Muhammad, Michaels implies that collective memory obeys a logic of scarcity: if a Holocaust Museum sits on the Mall in Washington (or just off of it, as is the actual case), then Holocaust memory must literally be crowding the memory of African American history out of the public space of American collective consciousness. There are plenty of legitimate ways to engage critically with the fact and function of the U.S. Holocaust Memorial Museum, and there is certainly a great need to engage with the ongoing fact of American racism, but Michaels's argument begs some important questions: Does collective memory really work like real-estate development? Must the claims of memory always be calculated according to their relevance for national history? Is "commemoration of the Nazi murder of the Jews" really a form of "Holocaust denial"?

Although few people would put the matter in such controversial terms, many other commentators, both inside and outside the academy, share the understanding of memory and identity articulated by Michaels. This study is motivated by a sense of the urgency of the vexing issues that Michaels raises, but it challenges the widely held ideas about the nature of collective memory and its links to group identity that undergird Michaels's provocations. Like Michaels and, indeed, Muhammad, many people assume that the public sphere in which collective memories are articulated is a scarce resource and that the interaction of different collective memories within that sphere takes the form of a zero-sum struggle for preeminence. Because many of these same commentators also believe that a direct line runs between remembrance of the past and the formation of identity in the present, they understand the articulation of the past in collective memory as a struggle for recognition in which there can only be winners and losers, a struggle that is thus closely allied with the potential for deadly violence. While there can be no doubt that many manifestations of contemporary violence, including war and genocide, are in part the product of resentful memories and conflicting views of the past, I argue that the conceptual framework through which commentators and ordinary citizens have addressed the relationship between memory, identity, and violence is flawed. Against the framework that understands collective memory as *competitive* memory—as a zero-sum struggle over scarce resources—I suggest that we consider memory as *multidirectional*: as subject to ongoing negotiation, cross-referencing, and borrowing; as productive and not privative. This shift in perspective allows us to see that while Muhammad and Michaels both speak of Holocaust memory as if it blocks memory of slavery and colonialism from view (the model of competitive memory), they actually use the presence of widespread Holocaust consciousness as a platform to articulate a vision of American racism past and present. This interaction of different historical memories illustrates the productive, intercultural dynamic that I call multidirectional memory.

In focusing on the politics of commemoration, Michaels criticizes the role memory plays in public discourse about the past and its impact on the present. As its title indicates, this book also places memory at the center of analysis, although it adopts a less skeptical position toward its object of study than does Michaels. But what is memory? And why does it feature so prominently in this book? These are crucial questions that I will return to below and throughout this study. The literature on memory is enormous and continues to grow at a staggering rate—a growth that has itself become an object of study![2] For now, let me note the useful minimalist definition from Richard Terdiman that orients this book: memory is the past made present. The notion of a "making present" has two important corollaries: first, that memory is a contemporary phenomenon, something that, while concerned with the past, happens in the present; and second, that memory is a form of work, working through, labor, or action.³ As Alon Confino and Peter Fritzsche write, "Memory [is] a symbolic representation of the past embedded in social action"; it is "a set of practices and interventions."⁴ *Multidirectional Memory* considers a series of interventions through which social actors bring multiple traumatic pasts into a heterogeneous and changing post–World War II present. Concerned simultaneously with individual and collective memory, this book focuses on both agents and sites of memory, and especially on their interaction within specific historical and political contexts of struggle and contestation. Making memory the focus of this work allows me to synthesize concerns about history, representation, biography, memorialization, and politics that motivate many scholars working in cultural studies.⁵ Not strictly separable from either history or representation, memory nonetheless captures simultaneously the individual, embodied, and lived side *and* the collective, social, and constructed side of our relations to the past.

In both its individual and collective versions, memory is closely aligned with identity, one of the most contested terms in contemporary debate. What is the relation between memory and identity? As readers familiar with the writings of Walter Benn Michaels will know, his purpose in propounding an implicit theory of competitive memory is not in any way to valorize memory or collective identity. Indeed, much of Michaels's work has offered a thoroughgoing critique of both memory and identity and what he sees as the straight line that connects them in mutual confirmation. This attitude certainly differentiates him from Khalid Muhammad, who enters the arena of competitive memory in order to stake out a claim for a militant black identity. My perspective differs from both of these polarized positions. Unlike Michaels, I don't see all claims of memory or identity as necessarily tainted; instead, I see such claims as necessary and inevitable. But unlike Muhammad, I reject the notion that identities and memories are pure and authentic—that there is a "we" and a "you" that would definitively differentiate, say, black and Jewish identities and black and Jewish relations to the past. I differ from both of these positions because I reject two central assumptions that they share: that a straight line runs from memory to identity and that the only kinds of memories and identities that are therefore possible are ones that exclude elements of alterity and forms of commonality with others. Our relationship to the past does partially determine who we are in the present, but never straightforwardly and directly, and never without unexpected or even unwanted consequences that bind us to those whom we consider other. When the productive, intercultural dynamic of multidirectional memory is explicitly claimed, as it is in many of the cases I discuss in this book, it has the potential to create new forms of solidarity and new visions of justice.

The understanding of collective remembrance that I put forward in *Multidirectional Memory* challenges the basic tenets and assumptions of much current thinking on collective memory and group identity. Fundamental to the conception of competitive memory is a notion of the public sphere as a pregiven, limited space in which already-established groups engage in a life-and-death struggle. In contrast, pursuing memory's multidirectionality encourages us to think of the public sphere as a malleable discursive space in which groups do not simply articulate established positions but actually come into being through their dialogical interactions with others; both the subjects and spaces of the public are open to continual reconstruction. Equally fundamental to the conception of competitive memory is the notion that the boundaries of memory parallel the boundaries of group identity, as we've seen with Michaels and Muhammad. As I struggle to achieve recognition of *my* memories and *my* identity, I necessarily exclude the memories and identities of others. Openness to memory's multidirectionality puts this last assumption into question as well. Memories are not owned by groups—nor are groups "owned" by memories. Rather, the borders of memory and identity are jagged; what looks at first like my own property often turns out to be a borrowing or adaptation from a history that initially might seem foreign or distant. Memory's anachronistic quality—its bringing together of now and then, here and there—is actually the source of its powerful creativity, its ability to build new worlds out of the materials of older ones. Finally, those who understand memory as a form of competition see only winners and losers in the struggle for collective articulation and recognition. But attention to memory's multidirectionality suggests a more supple social logic. The struggle for recognition is fundamentally unstable and subject to ongoing reversal, as Hegel recognized with his famous "Master/Slave dialectic": today's "losers" may turn out to be tomorrow's "winners," and "winning" may entail learning from and adopting the rhetoric and images of the other. Generally speaking, moreover, the examples of multidirectional memory explored here are much too ambivalent and heterogeneous to reduce too quickly to questions of winning and losing—which is not to say that there is little at stake in articulations of collective memory, for quite the contrary is true.

In order to demonstrate the stakes of the past in the present, *Multidirectional Memory* takes remembrance of the Holocaust as its paradigmatic object of concern. Michaels's and Muhammad's choice to stage the problem of the stakes of memory and identity in relation to the Nazi genocide of European Jews is not accidental. Indeed, there is probably no other single event that encapsulates the struggles for recognition that accompany collective memory in such a condensed and global form. While, as historians have demonstrated in multiple national contexts, public Holocaust memory only emerged belatedly as a widespread collective form, the last half-century has seen such memory move toward the center of consciousness in many Western European, North American, and Middle Eastern societies—and significant inroads have been made throughout the rest of the world as well.[6] The spread of Holocaust memory and consciousness across the globe sets the stage for and illustrates perfectly the multidirectional dynamic I draw attention to throughout this book.[7] I argue that far from blocking other historical memories from view in a competitive struggle for recognition, the emergence of Holocaust memory on a global scale has contributed to the articulation of other histories—some of them predating the Nazi genocide, such as slavery, and others taking place later, such as the Algerian War of Independence (1954–62) or the genocide in Bosnia during the 1990s. Because of the Holocaust's salience to the relationship of collective memory, group identity, and violence, an exploration of its ongoing public evocation in multiple national contexts stands as the central example of this book's exploration of multidirectional memory.

But multidirectional memory, as its name implies, is not simply a one-way street; its exploration necessitates the comparative approach I adopt here. My argument is not only that the Holocaust has enabled the articulation of other histories of victimization at the same time that it has been declared "unique" among human-perpetrated horrors (a point to which I return below). I also demonstrate the more surprising and seldom acknowledged fact that public memory of the Holocaust emerged in relation to postwar events that seem at first to have little to do with it. Here, we can observe that Michaels's and Muhammad's staging of Holocaust memory in competition with the memory of slavery, colonialism, and racism is also not accidental. As a series of case studies treating intellectuals and artists ranging from Hannah Arendt and W. E. B. Du Bois to French anticolonial activists and experimental documentarians will demonstrate, early Holocaust memory emerged in dialogue with the dynamic transformations and multifaceted struggles that define the era of decolonization. The period between 1945 and 1962 contains both the rise of consciousness of the Holocaust as an unprecedented form of modern genocide and the coming to national consciousness and political independence of many of the subjects of European colonialism.[8] This book argues that far from being an arbitrary conjunction of two separate histories, this observation about the early postwar period contains an important insight into the dynamics of collective memory and the struggles over recognition and collective identity that continue to haunt contemporary, pluralistic societies. The fact that today the Holocaust is frequently set against global histories of racism, slavery, and colonialism in an ugly contest of comparative victimization—as is the case in Muhammad's infamous speech and in the pronouncements of many "defenders" of the Holocaust's uniqueness—is part of a refusal to recognize the earlier conjunction of these histories that I explore in *Multidirectional Memory*. But the ordinarily unacknowledged history of cross-referencing that characterizes the period of decolonization continues to this day and constitutes a precondition of contemporary discourse. The virulence—on all sides—of so much discussion of race, genocide, and memory has to do, in other words, partly with the rhetorical and cultural *intimacy* of seemingly opposed traditions of remembrance.

From Uniqueness to Multidirectionality

One of the major stumbling blocks to a recognition of the interactions that take place among collective memories is the belief that one's own history, culture, and identity are "a separate and unique thing," to adopt a phrase that W. E. B. Du Bois uses critically and that I discuss further in Chapter 4. This is especially true when it comes to thinking about the Nazi genocide of European Jews. Along with its "centering" in public consciousness in the last decades, the Holocaust has come to be understood in the popular imagination, especially in Europe, Israel, and North America, as a unique, sui generis event. In its extremity, it is sometimes even defined as only marginally connected to the course of human history. Thus, Elie Wiesel has written that "the Holocaust transcends history," and Claude Lanzmann has claimed that "there is an unbreachable discrepancy" between any of the Holocaust's possible historical causes and the ultimate unfolding of the events.[9] Even arguments for uniqueness grounded in history sometimes tend toward ahistorical hyperbole. In an essay that seeks to differentiate the Nazi genocide from "the case of the Native Americans," "the famine in the Ukraine" under Stalin, and "the Armenian tragedy," Steven Katz argues that the "historically and phenomenologically unique" character of the Holocaust ensures that the Nazi genocide will differ from "every case said to be comparable to" it.[10] Initially, asserting the uniqueness of the Holocaust served to counter the relative public silence about the specificity of the Nazi genocide of Jews in the early postwar period that many historians of memory and students of historiography have described. Such assertions thus played a crucial role in fostering understanding of the genocide and generating acknowledgment and study of its horrific particularities and traumatic legacies. Although one of my purposes in *Multidirectional Memory* is to complicate this view of the early years of silence by drawing attention to articulations of Holocaust memory that have remained absent from the standard corpus, I certainly agree that in the first postwar decades there was a necessity to assertions of the Holocaust's specificity.

But, even if understanding of that specificity has not become universal today (and what historical understanding ever does?), by the time Wiesel, Lanzmann, and Katz were writing, acceptance of the uniqueness of the Holocaust was widespread. At the same time that this understanding of the Nazi genocide emerged, and in direct response to it, intellectuals interested in indigenous, minority, and colonial histories challenged the uniqueness of the Holocaust and fostered research into other histories of extreme violence, ethnic cleansing, and genocide. Many of these latter intellectuals have argued that, while it is essential to understand the specificity of the Nazi genocide (as of all events), separating it off from other histories of collective violence—and even from history as such—is intellectually and politically dangerous. The dangers of the uniqueness discourse are that it potentially creates a hierarchy of suffering (which is morally offensive) and removes that suffering from the field of historical agency (which is both morally and intellectually suspect).[11] This critique of uniqueness discourse undergirds Michaels's and Muhammad's complaints about the place of the Holocaust in U.S. public culture.

Despite their obvious intellectual and political differences, however, many proponents and critics of uniqueness share the model I'm calling competitive memory: that is, both groups tend to understand memory of the Holocaust as taking part in a zero-sum game of competition with the memory of other histories. Thus, on the one hand, the proponents of uniqueness assiduously search out and refute all attempts to compare or analogize the Holocaust in order to preserve memory of the Shoah from its dilution or relativization. Deborah Lipstadt, one of the leading scholars studying Holocaust denial, suggests links between those who relativize the Holocaust through comparison and analogy and those who deny its very existence; both groups, she argues, blur the "boundaries between fact and fiction and between persecuted and persecutor."[12] Blurring is also the concern of literary critic Richard Golsan. In a discussion of the trial of Maurice Papon, a French police secretary-general during the Vichy period who will play a key role in this book, Golsan worries that comparison between French complicity in the deportation of Jews and French persecution of Algerians during decolonization, which Papon was also involved in, "could only deflect the focus from the Vichy past and, more significant, blur the specificity of the Final Solution."[13] On the other hand, critics of uniqueness or of the politics of Holocaust memory often argue, as do Michael and Muhammad, that the ever-increasing interest in the Nazi genocide distracts from the consideration of other historical tragedies. For instance, in his study of the creation of the U.S. Holocaust Memorial Museum, Edward T. Linenthal expresses a concern that "official Holocaust memory may also function as a 'comfortable horrible' memory, allowing Americans to reassure themselves that they are engaging profound events, all the while ignoring more indigestible events that threaten Americans' sense of themselves more than the Holocaust."[14] In one of the more extreme versions of this argument, David Stannard asserts that the uniqueness argument "willingly provides a screen behind which opportunistic governments today attempt to conceal their own past and ongoing genocidal actions."[15]

There is, of course, some truth in both of these views. Relativization and banalization of the Holocaust do take place, although perhaps more frequently at the hands of a culture industry that seeks to exploit its currency than among marginal or oppositional intellectuals and activists. Conversely, undue stress on the singularity of the Holocaust at the expense of its similarities with other events can block recognition of past as well as present genocides, if not generally with the full intentionality implied by Stannard. The fact of such a blockage of recognition is one of the lessons of Samantha Power's convincing study *"A Problem from Hell"*. In summing up her account of American response to the threat and actuality of genocide in the twentieth century, Power writes that "perversely, America's public awareness of the Holocaust often seemed to set the bar for concern so high that we were able to tell ourselves that contemporary genocides were not measuring up."[16] Memory competition does exist and sometimes overrides other possibilities for thinking about the relation between different histories.

The existence of such contradictory and intractable positions on the uniqueness of the Holocaust suggests that the controversy is not an empirical, historical one. Rather, as Fredric Jameson has argued with respect to the related and more general issue of historical periodization, such controversies always turn on the deployment of narratives, and not on facts that can be objectively adjudicated: "The decision as to whether one faces a break or a continuity—whether the present is to be seen as a historical originality or as the simple prolongation of more of the same under different sheep's clothing—is not an empirically justifiable or philosophically arguable one, since it is itself the inaugural narrative act that grounds the perception and interpretation of the events to be narrated."[17] If the place and status of the Holocaust is not determined purely through recourse to the historical archive, as Jameson's argument implies, then getting beyond the deadlock characteristic of the uniqueness debates requires thinking about the work of memory and representation—the consequential arenas in which narrative acts shape understanding.[18] The competitive memory model functions something like what Michel Foucault, in the introduction to his *History of Sexuality*, calls "the repressive hypothesis." Foucault argues that the popular notion of sexual prohibition in the Victorian age should not be made "into the basic and constitutive element" in a history of sexuality because "negative elements" were "only component parts that have a local and tactical role" within a larger incitement and dissemination of discourses on sexuality.[19] Similarly, I would argue that the negative elements of the competitive memory hypothesis are only component parts of a larger dissemination of memory discourses.

An overly rigid focus on memory competition distracts from other ways of thinking about the relation between histories and their memorial legacies. Ultimately, memory is not a zero-sum game.[20] Instead of memory competition, I have proposed the concept of multidirectional memory, which is meant to draw attention to the dynamic transfers that take place between diverse places and times during the act of remembrance. Thinking in terms of multidirectional memory helps explain the spiraling interactions that characterize the politics of memory—the fact, borne out by Muhammad's reference to the "black holocaust," that the use of the Holocaust as a metaphor or analogy for other events and histories has emerged precisely because the Holocaust is widely thought of as a unique and uniquely terrible form of political violence.[21] Assertions of uniqueness thus actually produce further metaphorical and analogical appropriations (which, in turn, prompt further assertions of uniqueness). However, such moments coexist with complex acts of solidarity in which historical memory serves as a medium for the creation of new communal and political identities. It is often difficult to tell whether a given act of memory is more likely to produce competition or mutual understanding—sometimes both seem to happen simultaneously. A model of multidirectional memory allows for the perception of the power differentials that tend to cluster around memory competition, but it also locates that competition within a larger spiral of memory discourse in which even hostile invocations of memory can provide vehicles for further, countervailing commemorative acts. The model of multidirectional memory posits collective memory as partially disengaged from exclusive versions of cultural identity and acknowledges how remembrance both cuts across and binds together diverse spatial, temporal, and cultural sites. While I hold that understanding memory as multidirectional is ultimately preferable to models of competition, exclusivity, and exceptionality, I also consider cases in this book where memory's multidirectionality functions in the interests of violence or exclusion instead of solidarity.

Rethinking Screen Memory

Some critics targeting the Holocaust's alleged domination of the spheres of collective memory adopt a psychoanalytic terminology and describe remembrance of the Holocaust as a "screen memory" (*Deckerinnerung*). According to this Freud-inspired argument, memory of the Holocaust doesn't simply compete with that of other pasts, but provides (as the arguments of Linenthal and Stannard alluded to above suggest) a greater level of "comfort" than confrontation with more "local" problems would allow. Thus, in a sophisticated version of this argument, film scholar Miriam Hansen speculates that "the popular American fascination with the Holocaust may function as a 'screen memory' in the Freudian sense, covering up a traumatic event—another traumatic event—that cannot be approached directly. . . . The displaced referents . . . may extend to events as distant as the genocide of Native Americans or as recent as the Vietnam War."[22] While Hansen's argument echoes Michaels's, her emphasis on displacement—as opposed simply to silencing—opens up a potentially more productive approach to the relation between different traumatic events. *Multidirectional Memory* incorporates psychoanalytic insights, such as Hansen's, but my reading of Freud shows that his understanding of screen memory approximates the multidirectional model I develop here rather than the model of competition: the displacement that takes place in screen memory (indeed, in all memory) functions as much to open up lines of communication with the past as to close them off.[23]

Memory is, as Freud recognized, primarily an associative process that works through displacement and substitution; it is fundamentally and structurally multidirectional, even though powerful forces are always trying to shape it according to more or less rigid psychic or ideological parameters.[24] In the 1899 essay "Screen Memories" and again a decade later in *The Psychopathology of Everyday Life*, Freud tries to understand why some memories from childhood are preserved and some are not. In particular, he asks why "the content of some people's earliest memories consists of everyday impressions that are of no consequence and could not have affected the child emotionally, but were nonetheless noted in copious detail . . . whereas other, roughly contemporaneous events are not remembered, even though the parents testify that the child was profoundly affected by them at the time."[25] Pursuing networks of associations between the particularities of a memory and other events in an individual's life, Freud determines that the banal memory of the everyday is in fact a *screen memory*, "one that owes its value as a memory not to its intrinsic content, but to the relation obtaining between this content and some other, which has been suppressed" ("Screen" 19). Despite its apparent innocence, screen memory stands in or substitutes for a more disturbing or painful memory that it displaces from consciousness. (Note that the screen memory is at some level authentic, according to Freud; it is not a mere fantasy.) The mechanism of screen memory thus illustrates concretely how a kind of forgetting accompanies acts of remembrance, but this kind of forgetting is subject to recall.[26]

As Freud clarifies in "On Childhood Memories and Screen Memories," a chapter in *The Psychopathology of Everyday Life*, the content of the screen memory has a variety of "*temporal* relation[s]" with "the subject it has screened out." He distinguishes between "retrospective," "anticipatory," and "simultaneous" screen memories in order to clarify that the content of a screen memory can be formed by projections from repressed memories that happened after, before, or at the same time as the remembered events.[27] Noting the temporal complexity that Freud finds in childhood memories (and pointing out that the memories at stake in "Screen Memories" are probably Freud's own), Hugh Haughton writes that "the notion of the 'screen' or 'cover' becomes increasingly many-layered and multidirectional."[28] The English translation of *Deckerinnerungen* (literally, "cover memories") as "screen memories" is thus apt, if not literal, since such memories do encapsulate two notions of the "screen": they serve both as a barrier between consciousness and the unconscious, and as a site of projection for unconscious fantasies, fears, and desires, which can then be decoded. Consequently, screen memory is, in my terminology, multidirectional not only because it stands at the center of a potentially complex set of temporal relations, but also—and perhaps more importantly—because it both hides and reveals that which has been suppressed. The example of screen memory—which as with so many concepts in Freud begins as a special case but ends up seeming to encompass almost all acts of remembrance—suggests the limits of the model of memory as competition. While screen memory might be understood as involving a conflict of memories, it ultimately more closely resembles a remapping of memory in which links between memories are formed and then redistributed between the conscious and unconscious. To be sure, the truths of memory are often in tension with the truths of history; as with many of the multidirectional exchanges that I consider here, the "motives" of screen memory are "far removed from the aim of historical fidelity" (Freud, "Screen" 21). Yet both screen memories and multidirectional memories provide access to truths nonetheless, truths that produce insight about individual and collective processes of meaning-making. Thinking about screen memories and multidirectional memories as less "pathological" than "normal" proves to be a boon to interpretation.[29] Awareness of the inevitability of displacement and substitution in acts of remembrance points toward the need both to acknowledge the conflicts that subtend memory and work toward a rearticulation of historical relatedness beyond paradigms of uniqueness.

If multidirectional memory functions at the level of the collective as screen memory does at the level of the individual, there remain obvious difficulties with moving from Freud's model to a discussion of the intersection of memories of the Holocaust and colonialism. First, while screen memory is individual and biographical, multidirectional memory, as I use it, is primarily collective and historical, although it is never divorced from individuals and their biographies either. Additionally, while screen memory replaces a disturbing memory with a more comforting, everyday scene, the multidirectional memory explored here frequently juxtaposes two or more disturbing memories and disrupts everyday settings. These are important distinctions, but further reflection also helps to modulate the apparent starkness of the differences between screen and multidirectional memories.

Let's take these difficulties one at a time, beginning with the question of what we mean by collective memory. The work of the French sociologist Maurice Halbwachs is crucial here since it helps to break down the commonsense opposition between individual and collective memory. For

Halbwachs and the tradition that has emerged from him, all memories are simultaneously individual and collective: while individual subjects are the necessary locus of the act of remembrance, those individuals are imbued with frameworks common to the collectives in which they live.[30] The frameworks of memory function something like language—they provide a shared medium within which alone individuals can remember or articulate themselves. The philosopher Avishai Margalit's distinction between two forms of collective memory, common and shared, helps clarify further how memory operates beyond the individual: "A common memory . . . is an aggregate notion. It aggregates the memories of all those people who remember a certain episode which each of them experienced individually. . . . A *shared* memory, on the other hand, is not a simple aggregate of individual memories. It requires communication. A shared memory integrates and calibrates the different perspectives of those who remember the episode . . . into one version. . . . Shared memory is built on a division of mnemonic labor."[31] The memory at stake in multidirectional memory, and indeed in most collective memory today, resembles Margalit's shared memory. When we talk about collective Holocaust memory or about collective memories of colonialism and decolonization, we are talking primarily about shared memory, memory that may have been initiated by individuals but that has been mediated through networks of communication, institutions of the state, and the social groupings of civil society.

In contemporary societies, mediascapes of all kinds play a predominant role in the construction of the memory frameworks described by Halbwachs. While global media technologies make possible a new kind of common memory, via the creation of global media events that all might witness simultaneously, the lack of an Archimedean point of reference ensures that even memory of such events (like the attacks of September 11, 2001) will ultimately more closely resemble shared memory with its division of labor and calibration of different perspectives. Both Halbwachs and Margalit, however, seem to overestimate the degree to which collective memory will converge into "one version." Multidirectional memory is collective memory insofar as it is formed within social frameworks; it is shared memory insofar as it is formed within mediascapes that entail "a division of mnemonic labor." Yet the concept of multidirectional memory differs from both of these others because it highlights the inevitable displacements and contingencies that mark all remembrance. Collective memory is multilayered both because it is highly mediated and because individuals and groups play an active role in rearticulating memory, if never with complete consciousness or unimpeded agency. Competitive scenarios can derive from these restless rearticulations, but so can visions that construct solidarity out of the specificities, overlaps, and echoes of different historical experiences.

The other difference between screen memory and multidirectional memory concerns the question of the affective charge of the memories at issue. For Freud, screen memories stand in for and distract from something disturbing—either a traumatic event or an illicit, unacknowledged desire. As we have seen above, many critics think that memories of the Holocaust function this way, at least in places like the contemporary United States that are temporally and spatially far removed from the events of the Nazi period. What is odd about the case of Holocaust memory, however, is that such memory hardly seems innocent or comforting. And yet, as the concept of screen memory reveals, the content of a memory has no intrinsic meaning but takes on meaning precisely in relationship to other memories in a network of associations. My interest in multidirectional memory takes off from this insight to complicate assumptions about what in memory is "innocent" and what is "disturbing," about what serves as a necessary screen for the projection of memories and what as a barrier to remembrance. Looking at particular cases leads me to conclude (in the spirit of Freud, but sometimes with opposite results) that one cannot know in advance how the articulation of a memory will function; nor can one even be sure that it will function only in one way. The concept of multidirectional memory holds memory open to these different possibilities, but does not subscribe to a simple pluralism, either. While a given memory rarely functions in a single way or means only one thing, all articulations of memory are not equal; powerful social, political, and psychic forces articulate themselves in every act of remembrance.

On Comparison and Justice

Because of the complex psychic demands that Freud identified, individual memory emerges and recedes in fits and starts—especially when the memory of traumatic events is at stake. The same holds true for collective memory. When we look at collective memory historically, one thing we notice is how unevenly—and sometimes unexpectedly—it develops. Memories of particular events come and go and sometimes take on a surprising importance long after the materiality of the events remembered has faded from view. An important epistemological gain in considering memory as multidirectional instead of as competitive is the insight, developed here through historical case studies, that the emergence of memories into the public often takes place through triggers that may at first seem irrelevant or even unseemly. Thus, to give a concrete example that will prove significant for this book, the practice of torture seems like an unlikely trigger for Holocaust memory—for how could a practice as widespread, if repellant, as torture conjure up the extremity of genocide? But in France during the Algerian War of Independence many observers understood the French state's widespread use of extrajudicial violence as just such a reawakening of the past. As I discuss in Chapters 6 and 7, some survivors of the Nazi camps, such as the Austrian/Belgian writer Jean Améry, even cite the discussion of torture as one of the impetuses for their own public articulation of Holocaust memory. But this is not the end of the story. For a practice that triggered memory of Nazism at one moment could later serve as a trigger in France for memory of the Algerian War itself—a war that had for almost four decades seemed to be blocked from view even as, in its wake, Holocaust consciousness experienced an incredible growth. Thus, the turn of the millennium in France (and elsewhere) has seen renewed debates about torture, renewed interest in the connections between the Holocaust and the Algerian War, and a sense—expressed in Michael Haneke's film *Caché*, among other places—that post–9/11 policies in the United States echo older histories of imperial and fascist violence.[32] It is precisely that convoluted, sometimes historically unjustified, back-and-forth movement of seemingly distant collective memories in and out of public consciousness that I qualify as memory's multidirectionality. As these examples, which will be pursued at much greater length later in this book, begin to suggest, thinking of memory as multidirectional instead of competitive does not entail dispensing with a notion of the urgency of memory, with its life-and-death stakes. Rather, these examples alert us to the need for a form of comparative thinking that, like memory itself, is not afraid to traverse sacrosanct borders of ethnicity and era.

The shift in the conceptualization of memory from competition to multidirectionality that this book advocates has methodological implications for comparative thinking and study. A central methodological problem and opportunity concerns the constitution of the archive for comparative work. Far from being situated—either physically or discursively—in any single institution or site, the archive of multidirectional memory is irreducibly transversal; it cuts across genres, national contexts, periods, and cultural traditions. Because dominant ways of thinking (such as competitive memory) have refused to acknowledge the multidirectional flows of influence and articulation that collective memory activates, the comparative critic must first constitute the archive by forging links between dispersed documents. As this book demonstrates, there is no shortage of cross-referencing between the legacies of the Holocaust and colonialism, but many of those moments of contact occur in marginalized texts or in marginal moments of well-known texts. The evidence is there, but the archive must be constructed with the help of the change in vision made possible by a new kind of comparative thinking. The greatest threat to the visibility of this marginalized archive of Holocaust memory in the age of decolonization is the kind of zero-sum thinking that underwrites the logic of competitive memory. The greatest hope for a new comparatism lies in opening up the separate containers of memory and identity that buttress competitive thinking and becoming aware of the mutual constitution and ongoing transformation of the objects of comparison.[33] Too often comparison is understood as "equation"—the Holocaust cannot be compared to any other history, the story goes, because it is unlike them all. This project takes dissimilarity for granted, since no two events are ever alike, and then focuses its intellectual energy on investigating what it means to invoke connections nonetheless.[34] The logic of comparison explored here does not stand or fall on connections that can be empirically validated for historical accuracy; nor can we ensure that all such connections will be politically palatable to all concerned parties. Rather, a certain bracketing of empirical history and an openness to the possibility of strange political bedfellows are necessary in order for the imaginative links between different histories and social groups to come into view; these imaginative links are the substance of multidirectional memory. Comparison, like memory, should be thought of as productive—as producing new objects and new lines of sight—and not simply as reproducing already given entities that either are or are not "like" other already given entities.

Emphasizing the dimension of imagination involved in acts of remembrance should not lead to assumptions of memory's insubstantiality. Remembrance and imagination are material forces as well as fundamentally human ones. They cannot be wished away, nor, I believe, should they be. Despite the plentiful evidence of violence and willed oblivion that can accompany hegemonic (and sometimes even subaltern) acts of remembrance—and despite this book's predominantly dark subject matter—*Multidirectional Memory* has been written under the sign of optimism. Because the structures of individual and collective memory are multidirectional, they prove difficult to contain in the molds of exclusivist identities. If memory is as susceptible as any other human faculty to abuse—and here again Muhammad's speech serves as a convenient example, although only one of many—this study seeks to emphasize how memory is at least as often a spur to unexpected acts of empathy and solidarity; indeed multidirectional memory is often the very grounds on which people construct and act upon visions of justice.

A theory of multidirectional memory can help us in the task of "reframing justice in a globalizing world," to cite the title of a relevant essay by political philosopher Nancy Fraser.[35] Fraser argues that today's debates about justice—which she defines as "parity of participation" (73)—need to move beyond the "Keynesian-Westphalian frame" that has defined them for most of the post–World War II era. By this she means that the acceleration of globalization creates injustices that a previously taken-for-granted nation-state framework based on a national citizenry can no longer solve (if it ever could). For Fraser, drawing attention to the way capitalism, migrations, and other transnational forces break the nation-state frame also brings into view a third dimension of justice beyond economic redistribution and cultural recognition that theorists need to account for, a dimension she associates with questions of political representation: "Whether the issue is distribution or recognition, disputes that used to focus exclusively on the question of *what* is owed as a matter of justice to community members now turn quickly into disputes about *who* should count as a member and *which* is the relevant community. Not just the 'what' but also the 'who' is up for grabs" (72). Additionally, addressing the issue of the subjects or "who" of justice entails, Fraser argues, thinking about the procedures or "how" of justice (84). The matters of "who" and "how" point toward what she calls "meta-political" issues concerning the "framing" of disputes over justice. Framing entails decisions about who is permitted to claim the right to speak about issues of injustice affecting them. In a globalizing world, in which transnational factors (such as flows of capital and ecological degradation) coexist with or even predominate over national factors, debates about framing become unavoidable elements of a quest for justice. As Fraser sums up the political force of her argument, "Struggles for justice in a globalizing world cannot succeed unless they go hand in hand with struggles for *meta-political democracy*. . . . [N]o redistribution or recognition without representation" (85–86).

As my opening example of Michaels and Muhammad illustrates, debates about collective memory and group identity are primarily struggles over injustices of recognition, over whose history and culture will be recognized. Such injustices are real, but the rethinking of the relation between memory and identity can contribute to a rethinking of cultural recognition beyond zero-sum logic.[36] Fraser helps us see that part of the problem may lie in the assumed nation-state framing of the problem of recognition, although she also recognizes, as I do, that the nation remains a significant player in questions of recognition, redistribution, and political representation. Despite Michaels's and Muhammad's desire to fix the memory wars to the landscape of the Mall in Washington, the articulations of cultural recognition and collective memory I consider in this book do not remain tied to the fetishized sites of the state—which doesn't mean that they ignore the salience of state spaces either. Such articulations also allow us to supplement Fraser's account.[37]

In *Multidirectional Memory* I reveal how memory of the Nazi genocide and struggles for decolonization have persistently broken the frame of the nation-state during the entire period of Keynesian-Westphalian dominance. Fraser admits that there have been exceptions in the postwar period to the framing of justice on the terrain of the nation-state, but she doesn't consider in a substantive way what such exceptions might contribute to reframing justice: "Occasionally, famines and genocides galvanized public opinion across borders. And some cosmopolitans and anti-imperialists sought to promulgate globalist views. But these were exceptions that proved the rule" (69–70). *Multidirectional Memory* focuses on just such exceptional views and makes visible a countertradition that not only foregrounds unexpected resonance between the Holocaust and colonialism but also can provide resources for the rethinking of justice. In addition to moving the logic of recognition beyond identitarian competition, the theory of multidirectional memory and the countertradition it helps expose can contribute to what Fraser calls "the politics of framing": "Focused on the issues of who counts as a subject of justice, and what is the appropriate frame, the politics of framing comprises efforts to establish and consolidate, to contest and revise, the authoritative division of political space" (80). A work of scholarship does not intervene directly in the materiality of political space, although many of the intellectuals I address were actively involved in political struggle. Rather, I undertake an archaeology of the comparative imagination in the hopes that documenting these earlier attempts to reconceptualize the subjects of justice can inspire our present and future projects to remake political space.

Argument and Outline of the Book

In *Multidirectional Memory*, I put forward arguments that are theoretical, historical, and—in a world not yet free from colonialism or genocide—inevitably political. Let me reprise them while also outlining the scope and trajectory of the book. At the level of theory, I rethink the conceptualization of collective memory in multicultural and transnational contexts. Fully cognizant of the differentials of access and power that mark the public sphere, I nevertheless provide a framework that draws attention to the inevitable dialogical exchange between memory traditions and keeps open the possibility of a more just future of memory. I identify the misrecognition of collective memory as a zero-sum game—instead of an open-ended field of articulation and struggle—as one of the stumbling blocks for a more inclusive renarration of the history of memory and a harnessing of the legacies of violence in the interests of a more egalitarian future. Several of the chapters of *Multidirectional Memory* also suggest the need to think outside the universal/particular opposition that marks much discussion of the politics of identity and cultural difference. Many of the writers, intellectuals, and activists considered here point us instead toward a multidirectional ethics that combines the capacious open-endedness of the universal with the concrete, situational demands of the particular. An ethics of multidirectional memory involves creating fidelity (in the sense given that term by Alain Badiou's *Ethics*) with the multiple events and historical legacies that define any situation.[38] A politics built on that ethical foundation will require a notion of transnational, comparative justice that can negotiate conflicting and sometimes mutually exclusive demands made on unstable and shifting terrain.

At the historical level, *Multidirectional Memory* uncovers a marginalized tradition that has implications both for Holocaust studies and postcolonial studies—and can serve to stimulate the kinds of ethical and political thinking I call for here. Drawing on this tradition of Jewish and non-Jewish writers, artists, and political figures, I renarrate the received history of Holocaust memory. I demonstrate, first, that the early postwar period is richer and more complex than earlier studies, with their stress on a period of silence and repression that lasts until around the time of the Eichmann trial in 1961, have allowed. Shifting attention to unexpected texts, such as the writings of Du Bois on the Holocaust, or underexplored contexts, such as André Schwarz-Bart's engagement with the Caribbean diaspora, reveals both more Holocaust remembrance than we've been led to expect in this era and markedly more comparative forms of memory than would come to predominate in later decades. My renarration of this early postwar period reveals, additionally, that the emergence of collective memory of the Nazi genocide in the 1950s and 1960s takes place in a punctual dialogue with ongoing processes of decolonization and civil rights struggle and their modes of coming to terms with colonialism, slavery, and racism. Tracing events and reading texts from the late 1940s to the beginning of the twenty-first century, I make the case for a long-term minoritarian tradition of "decolonized" Holocaust memory.

This new approach to Holocaust memory has implications, in turn, for those concerned primarily with the varied experience of decolonization and the aftermaths of colonialism. Postcolonial studies can learn from the history of Jews and anti-Semitism in Europe in a number of ways. In particular, the experience of Jewish difference within modern Europe—and the frequently violent reaction Jews confronted—foreshadows many of the debates and problems faced by postcolonial societies and by postcolonial migrants in contemporary Europe.[39] Even if the histories of Jews and formerly colonized peoples diverge significantly, Europe's ambivalent memory of the Nazi genocide has left traces that inflect policies and discussions concerning race, religion, nationalism, and citizenship today. Attention to the history of Jews on the continent can serve as a timely warning not to homogenize conceptions of Europe on ethnic, racial, or religious grounds—a tendency that has understandably played an important role in postcolonial critique but is now more frequently associated with conservative (and increasingly liberal!) perspectives within Europe. While minority and postcolonial critique has had a tendency sharply to distinguish Jews from postcolonial subjects on the grounds of Jews' presumed "whiteness"—a tradition that harks back to founding texts by Césaire and Fanon and is based on a somewhat ahistorical understanding—the tradition uncovered here draws attention to possibilities for solidarity as well as distinction. Shared histories of racism, spatial segregation, genocide, diasporic displacement, cultural destruction, and—perhaps most important—savvy and creative resistance to hegemonic demands provide the grounds for new forms of collectivity that would not ignore equally powerful histories of division and difference.

Multidirectional Memory consists of four sections of two chapters each and addresses more than a half-century of cultural history in Europe, North America, the Caribbean, and North Africa. It begins with the observation that some of the earliest responses to the Nazi genocide placed it on a conceptual continuum with colonialism and antiblack racism. Part I, "Boomerang Effects: Bare Life, Trauma, and the Colonial Turn in Holocaust Studies," considers the figures through which such connections were made in two influential works from the beginning of the 1950s: Hannah Arendt's attempt to read the history of Nazi terror back through imperialism in *The Origins of Totalitarianism* (Chapter 2) and Aimé Césaire's understanding of Nazism as the return of the colonial repressed in his polemical pamphlet *Discourse on Colonialism* (Chapter 3). Arendt's notion of the "boomerang effect" and Césaire's "choc en retour" (translated as "boomerang effect," but more literally a backlash or reverse shock) both describe the unexpected debt of totalitarianism to colonialism, although the two writers approach these links from different directions and with significantly different political assumptions. Despite presciently drawing detailed connections between two now seemingly separate histories, Arendt proves unable to elude discourses of the human, the progressive, and the universal that remain complicit with the violence she is trying to explain. While Arendt remains at the limits of Eurocentrism, Césaire aims his polemic specifically against European self-understanding. Drawing on multiple intellectual and cultural traditions, Césaire uses the *choc en retour* to expose the multidirectional ripple effects of extreme violence. While focused especially on European disavowal of colonial atrocities, Césaire also exposes how an inability to come to terms with Nazism inflects late colonial discourse. Césaire's *Discourse*, along with his student Frantz Fanon's *Black Skin, White Masks*, helps us to forge a multidirectional trauma theory that accounts for the experience of colonialism and genocide, although investment in a certain version of Marxist theory and the exigencies of anticolonial struggle sometimes impair his attention to the specificity of the Nazi genocide.

Part II, "Migrations of Memory: Ruins, Ghettos, Diasporas," continues the consideration of the early postwar period and adds attention to the spaces and places of memory's movements. Two writers who successfully negotiate the multidirectional perspective opened up by Arendt and Césaire bookend this section: W. E. B. Du Bois and Caryl Phillips. In between, I discuss the more ambivalent case of André Schwarz-Bart. In Chapter 4, Du Bois's visit to the ruins of the Warsaw Ghetto in 1949, which he reflected on in a 1952 article, becomes the occasion for modeling multidirectional memory. Placing "The Negro and the Warsaw Ghetto" within the larger context of Du Bois's thinking about Jews, Nazism, race, and resistance, I demonstrate how, against the backdrop of the cold war and continued segregation in the United States, Du Bois rearticulates his concept of "double consciousness" to incorporate the experiences of other minority groups. In particular, his powerful response to the ruins of the ghetto and to Nathan Rapoport's much-maligned Ghetto Monument demonstrates the workings of a multidirectional memory able to hold together the disparate histories of blacks and Jews while simultaneously allowing for the rearticulation of their specificities. In Chapter 5, I continue the discussion of blacks and Jews through attention to two writers who also foreground ghettos, ruins, and other diasporic spaces as sites of multidirectional exchange. Here I pursue the anachronistic aesthetic projects of Schwarz-Bart and Phillips, which bring together that which is supposed to be kept apart. Although forms of anachronism constitute different types of "error" when perceived from a historicist perspective, they can also be powerfully subversive and demystifying in the ways that they expose the ideological assumptions of historicist categorization, as novels such as Schwarz-Bart's *A Woman Named Solitude* and Phillips's *Higher Ground* and *The Nature of Blood* demonstrate. While Schwarz-Bart struggles—and might ultimately be seen to fail—to find a literary form for the anachronistic juxtaposition of black and Jewish histories, Phillips employs fragmentation and intertextuality in order to develop an aesthetic premised on nonappropriative hospitality to histories of the other. Both writers, however, continue the attempt by Du Bois to think through colonialism's and genocide's disruptions of space and time, and, in different manners, they reflect on possibilities for resistance to the legacies of those disruptions.

The historical resistance to Nazi occupation and European colonialism lies at the heart of Part III, "Truth, Torture, Testimony: Holocaust Memory During the Algerian War," and Part IV, "October 17, 1961: A Site of Holocaust Memory?" Here I focus intensely on metropolitan anticolonial resistance during the late stages of the Algerian War of Independence. Part III explores how the resonance between the violence of decolonization and that of the Nazi genocide created a multidirectional network of memory that facilitated the emergence of survivor testimony as a powerful genre for exposing both forms of violence. At the very moment when the Israeli state was staging survivor testimony in the Eichmann trial, Jean Rouch and Edgar Morin set out to experiment with documentary form by producing what they called "cinéma vérité." Their documentary, *Chronicle of Summer*, the topic of Chapter 6, turns out to feature testimony by a Holocaust survivor at its center and juxtaposes that testimony with discussions of race, decolonization, and colonial war. Turning to contemporaneous discourses of the anticolonial movement in France, I demonstrate how the notion of "truth" that is central to cinéma vérité circulates in attempts to expose the violence of the late colonial state. In particular, controversies about torture, censorship, and the use of concentration camps in the fight against the Algerian independence movement lead to the importance of testimony as a mode of articulating the suppressed truth of colonialism.

26   *Introduction*

In the same year that the Eichmann trial and *Chronicle of a Summer* staged Holocaust testimony in public, Auschwitz survivor and memoirist Charlotte Delbo published her first book—a collection of open letters, surrounded by Delbo's editorial comments, on the Algerian War. Chapter 7 demonstrates how the same context of torture, censorship, and camps that elicits Rouch and Morin's film also prompts Delbo to reflect on the form of testimony and the shape of the public sphere. Much more explicitly than *Chronicle*, *Les belles lettres* is a political text; it takes part, materially and discursively, in a network of anticolonial activity. Harnessing memory of the Nazi occupation and genocide, Delbo's text offers possibilities for a critical, leftist politics of Holocaust memory that also possesses implications for a moment defined by "war on terror."

By the time *Les belles lettres* was published and *Chronicle of a Summer* opened in Paris in the fall of 1961, the country was facing another crisis pertaining to the war in Algeria. At the very moment when the war seemed headed for a certain end with the coming independence of Algeria, violence intensified in the metropole as well as in the colony. Ongoing violent confrontations between the French state, the Algerian independence group the Front de Libération Nationale (FLN), and the extreme right-wing Organisation Armée Secrète (OAS) culminated in a police massacre of dozens of unarmed, peacefully demonstrating Algerians in the streets of Paris during the evening of October 17. Part IV continues to explore the echoes that the Algerian War has cast around the globe and uncovers a multinational archive of texts that respond to the October 17, 1961 massacre and roundup by Maurice Papon's Paris police. Long absent from the dominant collective memory of France, October 17 has in recent decades become a significant site of mobilization for antiracist and migrant groups. Drawing on research into contemporaneous responses among the cohort of anticolonial activists discussed in the previous chapters as well as works produced long after the events, this section of the book argues that the October events constitute a significant turning point in French Holocaust memory and that a lasting multidirectional network connects the Nazi past to this episode of the Algerian War.

In Chapter 8, I focus in particular on contemporaneous responses in order to mount an argument about race, gender, and universalism. Considering both a little-known journalistic text by the French writer

Marguerite Duras and a recently rediscovered novel by the African American writer William Gardner Smith, I demonstrate how the French state's late colonial racialization of the war led to intensified connections with the experiences of Jews under Nazi occupation. I also show how these texts can help us rethink discussions of the universalization of the Holocaust by foregrounding complicity and revealing a multidirectional alternative beyond the universal/particular opposition—an opposition that nevertheless sneaks back into Smith's novel through a simplified gendering of memory. Chapter 9 tracks the return of attention to October 17 since the 1980s in order to argue for an ethics of multidirectional memory subtended by a fidelity to historical comparison. Here the key texts are a novel by the French detective fiction writer Didier Daeninckx, the Austrian filmmaker Michael Haneke's 2005 feature film *Caché*, and a novel for young adults by French-Algerian writer Leïla Sebbar. I also read the latter two works in relation to the 1997–98 trial of Papon for crimes against humanity during the Holocaust, which offers fascinating evidence of the current status of multidirectional memory and testimony and of the transformations under way due to generational shifts. As both the trial and the works of Sebbar and Haneke suggest, the figure of the child has taken center stage as a site of uneasy, multidirectional memory. This chapter reflects on the possible ethical and political significance of the child as a bearer of memory and postmemory in a moment of violent global transformation.[40]

As the scope and scale of *Multidirectional Memory* suggest, the book cannot possibly offer a comprehensive survey of all texts, films, or political movements that engage with both the Holocaust and European colonialism. But it does provide both in-depth analysis of many key texts from this not-yet-recognized, six-decade-old tradition and close consideration of moments of epochal change—such as the transitional early postwar years and the 1961 turning point when Holocaust memory increasingly entered the public sphere and many formerly colonized nations attained independence. I hope that other scholars will find it worthwhile to apply, adapt, or correct the approach undertaken here. Certainly, the methodology of the book could be directly applied to other obviously "multidirectional" works such as Michelle Cliff's *Abeng* (1984; Anne Frank and the Caribbean), Anita Desai's *Baumgartner's Bombay* (1989; the Holocaust and the colonization of India), Nancy Huston's *The Mark of the Angel* (1999; the Algerian War and the Holocaust), or W. G. Sebald's *Austerlitz* (2001; the Holocaust and Belgian colonialism). In addition, the writings of French–Jewish–North African scholars Hélène Cixous, Jacques Derrida, and Albert Memmi constitute a fertile terrain for further investigation. Perhaps more crucially, the concept of multidirectional memory might help scholars working on other historical and cultural traditions—histories and traditions that sometimes overlap explicitly with those discussed here and sometimes do not. Multidirectional legacies of violence haunt the histories of indigenous peoples on a global scale and cut across the former Yugoslavia and other parts of the former Soviet Bloc as well as Afghanistan, South Africa, Argentina, and other formerly colonized nations. Meanwhile, labor migrants and their descendants in Europe often find themselves confronted with the ghosts of the past at the same time that they experience the prejudices of the present.[41] Finally, there are the prospective multidirectional legacies of the American war in Iraq, a country scarred by colonialism, dictatorship, and genocide, and now by neoimperialism and civil war.

That unhappy current conjuncture shadows this book, but the book also directly confronts those shadows at a couple of key moments. Indeed, the Algerian War, which figures so prominently in these pages, has increasingly become a charged and highly politicized reference point at the turn of the new millennium, as Haneke's film *Caché* also attests. The Bush administration frequently references Algeria as an analogy for Iraq, and the Pentagon even hosted a screening of Gillo Pontecorvo's *The Battle of Algiers*, apparently in order to "benefit" from its insights into counterinsurgency.[42] Having considered the Algerian question throughout the second half of this book, I briefly turn to another multidirectional political hotspot in conclusion. Along with the Iraq War and the "war on terror," which, with their liberal use of torture and indefinite detention, have produced uncomfortable echoes of the Holocaust and colonial adventures past, the other dominant political site of multidirectional memory today is the ongoing Palestinian-Israeli crisis. In the Epilogue, "Multidirectional Memory in an Age of Occupations," I briefly consider the implications of my theory of collective memory for that intractable struggle as well as for the claims of indigenous peoples.

I use this short epilogue to make a few concluding points relevant to the book's exploration of multidirectional memories of genocide and colonialism. Through the example of the Israeli historian Benny Morris, I argue that invocations of the Holocaust in the context of the Israeli/Palestinian conflict are part of a larger multidirectional network that includes apocalyptic colonial fantasies of the dissolution of the "Western" self—fantasies that in Morris's case reference France's "loss" of Algeria and call upon the Conradian vision of savagery that plays a disruptive role in Arendt's account of imperialism and that Césaire acutely critiques. I further argue that despite the obvious ugliness of many of the invocations of the Holocaust in the context of contemporary Middle Eastern politics (and elsewhere!) and the temptation to declare a moratorium on such references, the theory and history of multidirectional memory suggests the need to confront a different possibility. While all intercultural memory does not foster cross-cultural understanding—as the case of Morris illustrates here—comparisons, analogies, and other multidirectional invocations are an inevitable part of the struggle for justice. Against the alternatives to comparison—an intense investment in the particularity of every case or the promulgation of absolutely neutral and universal principles—I offer the multidirectional option: an ethical vision based on commitment to uncovering historical relatedness and working through the partial overlaps and conflicting claims that constitute the archives of memory and the terrain of politics.

PART I

BOOMERANG EFFECTS

*Bare Life, Trauma, and the
Colonial Turn in Holocaust Studies*

2

At the Limits of Eurocentrism: Hannah Arendt's *The Origins of Totalitarianism*

"Atlantic Civilization": Conceptualizing Multidirectionality in the Early Postwar Period

In 1953, the French Communist painter André Fougeron produced a large canvas that makes visible the tensions of the postwar era. Although not himself a deportee, Fougeron had been active in the resistance during World War II and had produced journals and art denouncing the Nazi camps along with French collaboration; after the war, he contributed many canvases to the struggles of decolonization as well as the worker's movement.[1] Painted at a moment when France's war in Indochina was heading toward defeat and events in Algeria were beginning to heat up, Fougeron's *Atlantic Civilization* juxtaposes colonialism and Nazism in French space (see Figure 1). *Atlantic Civilization* represents a break with Fougeron's earlier attempts at developing a new Socialist realism and marks a turn toward the deployment of montage (a turn that was not welcomed by the Communist Party). In the center of the canvas, a uniformed German soldier with an SS insignia on his helmet aims his gun at an undefined target outside of the painting's frame while leaning over the hood of a large American automobile. Around the soldier and the car, in a cluttered nonperspectival space, we find a variety of figures and symbols of war, colonialism, the death penalty (a reference to the Rosenbergs), and the ills of an industrial society as well as scenes of a more everyday and jocular France, such as sweater-wearing poodles and a girlie magazine–reading man sitting with his legs propped up on a café table. As if presaging the next colonial war in Algeria that would start the following year, a pair of Arabs shrouded in black robes peak out from under a corrugated tin sheet in the bottom left-hand corner of the canvas while posters affixed on the side of a building celebrate the notorious "parachutistes coloniaux," who would also play a large and bloody role in Algeria. The overwhelming presence of the blue Cadillac in the center of this eclectic visual field, as well as the background scene of smoking chimneys, suggests that the central category of Fougeron's indictment is modernity itself, here rendered as a joint venture of French colonialism, American capitalism, and German bellicosity.

In its focus on modernity, *Atlantic Civilization* recalls Kristin Ross's reading of 1950s French culture in *Fast Cars, Clean Bodies* as constituted by the concurrence of Americanization and decolonization.[2] But Fougeron's painting—precisely because it is explicitly ideological—differs in two ways from most of the works considered by Ross. First of all, instead of displacing the anticolonial struggle through a domestic discourse of modern hygiene and technology, as do most of the texts and documents Ross analyzes, Fougeron highlights the overlap of the everyday with the punctuality of violent events. In creating such a montage, he uses an aesthetic form that will return in Algerian War–epoch works to be considered later, such as Rouch and Morin's *Chronicle of a Summer* and Delbo's *Les belles lettres*. Secondly, *Atlantic Civilization* demonstrates that the memory of German occupation, which Ross largely leaves out of her account, remains active in postwar discourses and in aesthetic and political projects. Colonial violence comes home, but under the sign of Nazism. Ross goes on to argue in *May '68 and Its Afterlives* that memory of the Algerian War underwrites the student and worker struggles of the late 1960s.[3] *Atlantic Civilization*, however, suggests the presence of a more multidirectional matrix of dissent in which memories of Nazism and genocide play a significant role along with those of colonialism and workers' struggles. Yet Fougeron leaves the precise nature of the links in that matrix unclear.

FIGURE 1   André Fougeron, *Atlantic Civilization* (1953). © 2008 Artists Rights Society (ARS), New York/ADAGP, Paris/Tate, London.

Fougeron's painting thus raises several questions pertinent to a theory of multidirectional memory. What kinds of aesthetic form are adequate to the task of representing and recalling history's overlapping forms of violence? Is the simple recollection of multiple histories indicative of the dynamic, productive interplay I have called multidirectional memory? Or do links such as that between an SS soldier and an American Cadillac only amount to an additive model in which histories are brought together without producing an interchange of memories and ideas? Opening up our powers of comparison requires a framework that takes the wayward currents of collective memory seriously but can also make judgments that distinguish between different articulations of relatedness. I argue that both individual and collective memory are always in some sense multidirectional. In "making the past present," recollections and representations of personal or political history inevitably mix multiple moments in time and multiple sites of remembrance; making the past present opens the doors of memory to intersecting pasts and undefined futures. Memory is thus structurally multidirectional, but each articulation of the past processes that multidirectionality differently. In other words, as soon as memory is articulated publicly, questions of representation, ethics, and politics arise. While Fougeron's painting invokes multiple historical legacies, it alone does not answer the questions that orient this section of the book: how to conceptualize and represent multidirectionality; and how to assess its ethical and political effects.

The dialectical relationship staged in Fougeron's painting between violence in the colonies and in the metropolis recalls two well-known texts from the same early postwar moment that I take up here in order to pursue the conceptualization of multidirectionality: Hannah Arendt's *The Origins of Totalitarianism* (1951) and Aimé Césaire's *Discourse on Colonialism* (1950/1955). Both Arendt and Césaire grasp a relationship between the two forms of colonial rule that Arendt distinguished as "continental" and "overseas" imperialisms. But their understanding of that relationship is significantly different. In his brilliantly provocative polemic, Césaire describes Nazism as "un choc en retour," which his translator later rendered as a "boomerang effect," but which we may want to preserve more literally as "reverse shock" or "backlash" so as to maintain the discourse of "shock." Arendt also considers the possibility of "boomerang effects" in *The Origins of Totalitarianism*, but her argument about causality in that unclassifiable scholarly work takes a different form than does Césaire's in his anticolonial pamphlet—a form at once more complex and yet more troubling.

With their references to "chocs en retour" and "boomerang effects," both Arendt and Césaire use metaphors of *directionality*. By charting what those metaphors make thinkable and where they break down, we can begin to imagine a specifically multidirectional approach. At stake in a comparison of Arendt's and Césaire's different articulations of historical relatedness are linked notions of uniqueness, universalism, and the human that continue to bedevil scholars of the legacies of violence. In exposing the limits of those notions as internal to the structures of violence they are meant to expose, I suggest that multidirectionality provides a conceptual logic beyond the unique and the universal and outside the problem of the human.

In the remainder of this chapter, I focus on Arendt's writings on totalitarianism and imperialism and then conclude with a short coda that also takes up the related and influential work of Giorgio Agamben on "bare life." I demonstrate that Arendt is ahead of her time in grasping the specificity of what would become known as the Holocaust as well as in linking the genocide to European colonialism, but that she simultaneously falls victim to tendencies within colonial discourse that she otherwise unveils. I argue, in particular, that Arendt's figuration of the colonized in Africa—derived in part from the cultural memory encoded in Joseph Conrad's novel *Heart of Darkness*—provides the grounds for her pathbreaking analysis of the Nazi camps, but in such a way that it confirms the racist suppositions of colonial logic. Arendt's still crucial consideration of the sources of Nazi genocide thus leaves us with a difficult question that gets to the heart of the contrast between competitive and multidirectional approaches to the past: How is it possible to remember the specificities of one history without silencing those of another? I continue to pursue this question in the following chapter in my discussion of Aimé Césaire. By reading closely Arendt's and Césaire's attempts to think colonialism and Nazism together, and by paying attention both to what they make possible and to where they reach their limits, I begin sketching this book's alternative model—a model that avoids the conceptual traps of uniqueness, universalism, and the human and reconfigures the conceptualization of violence, trauma, and memory around a multidirectional logic.

Blindness and Insight: Arendt and *The Origins of Totalitarianism*

Fougeron's *Atlantic Civilization* situates Nazi violence in a crowded constellation of the ills of modern capitalism—colonial war, environmental devastation, hunger, homelessness, rampant consumer culture, and alleged immorality. Arendt's nearly contemporaneous work on totalitarianism also deploys the constellation as a form for understanding the relation between the brutality of imperialism and the genocidal violence within Europe. While Arendt's approach brings significantly greater subtlety and complexity, not to mention scholarly weight, to such a project than does Fougeron's painting, her work also gets caught in its own ideological binds. *The Origins of Totalitarianism* demands a double reading, one that recognizes the unprecedented insights that Arendt brings to understanding modern history—insights that today's historians are only beginning to catch up to—while also revealing how those insights are interlaced with forms of blindness about race and colonialism that might be typical for the Europeans of the era in which she wrote, but no less crippling for their typicality. The ultimate stakes of reading Arendt involve unraveling this knot of blindness and insight and reconstructing a vision of history that can transcend the limits that define its initial articulation. Such a simultaneously deconstructive and reconstructive method assumes that Arendt's ideas are partially constrained by history and even biography, but also that their import remains urgent in a world still working through the aftermath of colonialism and genocide and indeed living through their new incarnations. Both as a historically situated example of multidirectional memory and as a theorization of historical comparison, Arendt's efforts at what she calls "comprehension" continue to speak to us today.

Arendt's ability to see what others could not see—and yet, at the same time, to remain blind to what was happening around her—no doubt derives in part from the very particular personal circumstances in which she undertook her study. When Arendt published *The Origins of Totalitarianism* in 1951 she had spent the previous eighteen years as a stateless person. Born in 1906 to a German-Jewish family, Arendt studied philosophy in Marburg with Heidegger and in Heidelberg with Jaspers. Beginning in the late 1920s and early 1930s she became increasingly involved with Jewish politics and Zionism, a movement toward which she maintained a complex and critical relationship throughout her life. Forced to flee Germany shortly after the National Socialist rise to power, she spent several years in Paris working for Jewish organizations such as Youth Aliyah, which helped young Jews emigrate to Palestine. After being detained in the French camp Gurs as an "enemy alien" in 1940 when war was declared between France and Germany, she escaped to Lisbon and made her way to New York in 1941 (the very trip that Walter Benjamin had failed to make the previous year). Arendt learned early on about the Nazi genocide, in the winter of 1942–43, and she quickly integrated it into her understanding of politics and history. Throughout the 1940s, while working on various versions of *The Origins of Totalitarianism*, she also wrote essays for Jewish journals such as *Aufbau*, *The Menorah Journal*, and *Jewish Social Studies*. Because of the unclassifiable nature of her writing, which mixes philosophy, political theory, social commentary, and history, and the unorthodox and often controversial tenor of her political positions, Arendt occupied an ambiguous position in the intellectual landscape during her lifetime—she was simultaneously marginal and central to major debates of the postwar years.[4] Since her death in 1975, however, her work has become increasingly important, if no less controversial, in scholarly circles.[5] From the vantage point of the present, it is possible to look back and see how the unusual mix of personal experience, collective history, and philosophical training that produced Arendt makes her work and life by no means representative, but perhaps revelatory or indicative of some of the major political and intellectual forces of the twentieth century.

As Arendt moves in *The Origins of Totalitarianism* from anti-Semitism, through the colonial encounter in Africa and the European refugee crisis after World War I, to the totalitarian camp system, she follows a trajectory that shuttles between European and non-European worlds. Yet she never quite achieves the "planetary" or transnational account of the "tensions of empire" in modernity called for by recent critics of postcolonial and global culture.[6] Because Africa remains an ahistorical backdrop against which European history plays out, Arendt does not make the transition that the Latin American philosopher Enrique Dussel calls for from a conception of European modernity as "an *independent*, autopoietic, self-referential system" to one in which it is "*part* of a world-system" (Dussel 4).[7] Dussel identifies how Eurocentrism has set inadvertent limits on modern and postmodern critiques of reason: "In general, no debate between rationalists and postmoderns overcomes the Eurocentric horizon. The crisis of modernity . . . refers to internal aspects of Europe. The peripheral world would appear to be a passive spectator of a thematic that does not touch it, because it is a 'barbarian,' a 'premodern,' or, simply, still in need of being 'modernized.' In other words, the Eurocentric view reflects on the problem of the crisis of modernity solely with the European–North American moments (or now even Japanese), but it minimizes the periphery" (17–18). Measured against Dussel's criteria, Arendt writes at the limit of Eurocentric models. Because she places events in Africa at the center of the making of modern politics, she avoids the danger of leaving the peripheral world "untouched" in her account. Like Conrad in *Heart of Darkness*, a text that figures centrally in *The Origins of Totalitarianism*,

Arendt exposes and strongly condemns European violence in the colonial encounter. Yet, also like Conrad, she reads that encounter only from one direction. Arendt's text is not simply like Conrad's, but draws heavily on the image of Africa it produces and circulates. Despite the attention Arendt draws to imperialism in the second section of *Origins*, she revives the colonialist cultural memory encoded in Conrad's novel and renders Africans "passive."[8] Her critique of modernity remains primarily internal to Europe because even as she tracks imperial expansion she is unable to render its victims as subjects.

One great irony of this inability to recognize the other is that Arendt was writing at one of the great moments of anticolonial agitation. At the same time Arendt was providing unprecedented insight into the singularity of totalitarianism and the Nazi genocide, anticolonial movements around the world and individual intellectuals such as Césaire and Du Bois were helping to bring the possibility of decolonization to the forefront of world history—and they were doing so in ways that also acknowledge Europe's recent Nazi past. Arendt's missed encounter with decolonization underlies *The Origins of Totalitarianism*'s story of blindness and insight. In fact, Arendt's *inability* to comprehend the subjects at Europe's periphery as bearers of history, memory, and culture is intrinsically related to—and even provides the conditions for—her *ability* to recognize Europe's internal others. The imagined savage without culture—the imagined barbarian—provides the metaphorical grounding for two of the central "characters" of Arendt's analysis: the naked human being deprived of culture, and the stateless concentration camp inmate stripped of the right to have rights.

Comprehension and the Constellation

In *The Origins of Totalitarianism*, Arendt sets out "to comprehend" one of the key political phenomena of the twentieth century by returning to its roots in the nineteenth.[9] Plans for the book took different forms as Arendt was writing it in the mid- to late-1940s, but in its final version it is divided into three semiautonomous sections, "Antisemitism," "Imperialism," and "Totalitarianism."[10] There are a number of puzzling features to Arendt's methodology and to the organization of the book. First, there is the fact that the phenomenon to be explained by the totality of the book, totalitarianism, is also one of the sections of the book. This would be less unexpected if the sections represented a clear narrative progression toward the apogee of totalitarianism, but in fact the connections between the sections are not explicit and the volume as a whole is characterized more by disjuncture than progression. In addition, Arendt's notion of totalitarianism differs from those more familiar accounts that posit it as a closed, totalizing system of control. Margaret Canovan, one of the best commentators on *Origins*, has succinctly summed up the distinctiveness of Arendt's theory: "Instead of referring to a political system of a deliberately structured kind, 'totalitarianism' in Arendt's sense means a chaotic, nonutilitarian, manically dynamic movement of destruction that assails all the features of human nature and the human world that makes politics possible."[11] This understanding of totalitarianism has two correlates that make it especially relevant for this book. First, it makes the Nazi genocide an extreme but exemplary instance of the larger phenomenon of totalitarianism because it consists of a "pure" form of the radically destructive attack on the human. Second, and seemingly paradoxically, it leads Arendt to situate the core of her argument not in the first section on anti-Semitism, but rather in the second section on imperialism. While the emergence of anti-Semitism in late nineteenth-century Europe explains why Jews became the targets of Nazi totalitarianism, Arendt argues that only the history of imperialism can explain the global and nonutilitarian dimensions of the genocidal dynamic of destruction (cf. Arendt, *Origins* xvi). With these two correlates of Arendt's theory of totalitarianism in mind, this chapter offers not a complete interpretation of *The Origins of Totalitarianism*, a task that far outstrips the scope of this book, but rather a focused reading of the relationship between the Holocaust and imperialism, with a particular emphasis on the way the concept of the assault on the human anchors and unsettles Arendt's analysis.[12]

In laying out a disjunctive constellation linking anti-Semitism, imperialism, and totalitarianism, Arendt sets herself a paradoxical task in *Origins*: to grapple with the unprecedented nature of the Nazi genocide of European Jews while simultaneously seeking the antecedent elements that help explain its possibility and marking the parallel phenomena that share its genus.[13] If the paradox of comprehending the incomprehensible has become one of the expected tropes in discussion of the Holocaust, this should not block from view the specificity with which Arendt approaches the question, nor should it obscure the relevant fact that it is often via the comprehension/incomprehension distinction that the Holocaust is articulated to—or, most often, disarticulated from—other histories of collective violence. Arendt's notion of comprehension is intended to finesse the paradoxical task of defining the novelty of the totalitarian catastrophe while at the same time locating it in some kind of historical framework: "Comprehension does not mean denying the outrageous, deducing the unprecedented from precedents, or explaining phenomena by such analogies and generalities that the impact of reality and the shock of experience are no longer felt. It means, rather, examining and bearing consciously the burden which our century has placed on us—neither denying its existence nor submitting meekly to its weight. Comprehension, in short, means the unpremeditated, attentive facing up to, and resisting of, reality—whatever it may be" (*Origins* viii). Arendt sets an exacting standard here for comparative approaches to history. She restricts usage of some of the most obvious conceptual tools of the comparatist (analogy, generalization, and deduction from precedent) while, conversely, reinforcing the need to feel history's "burden," its impact beyond its initial occurrence. Concurrently, she enjoins the thinker to take in the impact or shock of history while simultaneously resisting its force and, as she writes elsewhere, "destroying" it (qtd. in Bernstein 53). With these crosscutting demands in mind, Arendt's effort to "comprehend" totalitarianism in relation to imperialism and anti-Semitism in *Origins* can provide an opportunity both to reflect on the historical background against which the studies in the following chapters of this book emerge and also to consider the epistemological as well as political problems of writing comparative cultural and historical analysis. Facing up to and resisting reality: these are tasks both for a post-Holocaust and a postcolonial critique, and especially for a critique that seeks to transgress the discourses of separation and uniqueness that have taken hold in the wake of Arendt's writings.

In saying that Arendt's example can help us to avoid the discourses of separation, it is important to be clear, however, that Arendt by no means authorizes a reduction of disparate historical phenomena to versions of the same essence. To the contrary, in "A Reply to Eric Voegelin," a 1953 statement in which Arendt comes closest to laying out the methodology of *Origins*, she decries the "growing incapacity for making distinctions" that afflicts "the present state of the historical and political sciences."[14] But if she focuses on the distinctiveness of totalitarian domination, why would she construct a text structured by juxtaposition and implied linkage of disparate phenomena such as imperialism, Nazism, and Stalinism? The complexity of Arendt's project has always inspired misunderstanding. The political philosopher Voegelin read *Origins* as "a gradual revelation of the essence of totalitarianism from its inchoate forms in the eighteenth century to the fully developed" (qtd. in Arendt, *Essays* 405). Arendt refuses this account of her methodology as a narrativizing revelation because it seems to import a totalitarian essence into the past. Instead, she proposes an alternative model: "This essence, in my opinion, did not exist before it had come into being. I therefore talk only of 'elements,' which eventually crystallize into totalitarianism, some of which are traceable to the eighteenth century, some perhaps even farther back" (*Essays* 405). As has often been remarked, Arendt's metaphor of crystallizing elements provides a more trustworthy image of her approach to totalitarianism than the "origins" of the book's title. And yet Arendt's work continues to bear traces of the linear and progressive narrative of origins she disavows.

Arendt's methodology, as she lays it out in her response to Voegelin and practices it in *Origins*, cuts against the grain of traditional empirical history and makes productive alliances with memory, representation, and imagination.[15] Hence it is not accidental that Arendt's language in her response to Voegelin is close to that of Benjamin's "Theses on the Philosophy of History," in which he embraces the "constructive principle" of "materialistic historiography": "Thinking involves not only the flow of thoughts, but their arrest as well. Where thinking suddenly stops in a constellation [*Konstellation*] pregnant with tensions, it gives that constellation a shock, by which it crystallizes into a monad [*als Monade kristallisiert*]."[16] Famously dedicated to "blast[ing] open the continuum of history" through the rupture of the narrative of "the homogeneous course of history," Benjamin's theses draw on the powers of the memory of the oppressed, providing a method that contrasts sharply with Voegelin's idea of a "gradual revelation of essence." Benjamin's insight is that beneath the ideology of progress lies a particular conception of temporality—a "homogeneous, empty time" that serves as the backdrop for the idea of historical progression. In contrast to the homogeneous time of progress(ion), Benjamin's crystallized constellations provide an image of encounter in which different temporalities collide and in which movement and stasis are held in tension. Arendt's Benjaminian language thus suggests that instead of appearing as a three-part narrative, the structure of *Origins* (Antisemitism, Imperialism, Totalitarianism) offers a constellation in which synchronic and diachronic elements appear in tension, in patterns that are contingent but have taken on solidity in the course of history.

Nevertheless, Arendt's methodological commitment to the constellation increases the reader's sensitivity to the progressive narrative elements in *Origins*. As Seyla Benhabib has shown, there are ultimately two strands to Arendt's approach to the past: "one corresponding to the method of fragmentary historiography, and inspired by Walter Benjamin; the other, inspired by the phenomenology of Husserl and Heidegger, and according to which memory is the mimetic recollection of the lost origins of phenomena as contained in some fundamental human experience" (95). The persistence of this search for lost origins in Arendt's account of totalitarianism is the counterpart of a residual progressivism that haunts her text and her concept of the human.

"A New Kind of Human Beings"

Long before Arendt completed *The Origins of Totalitarianism*—and, indeed, at a moment when few in the world beyond the perpetrators themselves had grasped the scope of the genocide—she was already beginning to conceptualize fundamental features of her larger project of comprehending the political and moral questions of the twentieth century. In her dark and powerful 1943 essay, "We Refugees," originally published in *Menorah Journal*, we see an important step toward Arendt's yoking together of colonialism and genocide: an interrogation of the limits of the human. In "We Refugees," Arendt uses her own position as escapee from Hitler's Europe to reflect on the novelty of contemporary history and its implications for understanding the place of the Jews in it. Sounding themes that run through her writings of the 1940s, Arendt emphasizes the political significance of dislocation. As she concludes the essay and reflects on the meaning of the war raging around her, she places the experience of Jews at the center of history:

Those few refugees who insist upon telling the truth, even to the point of "indecency," get in exchange for their unpopularity one priceless advantage: history is no longer a closed book to them and politics is no longer the privilege of Gentiles. They know that the outlawing of the Jewish people in Europe has been followed closely by the outlawing of most European nations. Refugees driven from country to country represent the vanguard of their peoples—if they keep their identity. For the first time Jewish history is not separate but tied up with that of all other nations. The comity of European peoples went to pieces when, and because, it allowed its weakest member to be excluded and persecuted. (*Jew as Pariah* 66)

Locating her thought at the "vanguard" of history allows Arendt to draw large conclusions from supposedly marginal experiences. In this case, she understands the experience of radical marginalization itself—the "outlawing" of a human group—and the production of new categories of refugees that follows as a forerunner of the greater European crisis represented by the war. The point is not to uncover some essence of modernity or to argue for the inevitability of the history unfolding around her. Rather, the point is to search out what is new in the current crisis and then, through a method at once explosive in a Benjaminian sense and genealogical in a Nietzschean sense, to comprehend the elements that constitute the conditions of possibility of the crisis.

Already in "We Refugees," Arendt anticipates one of the sections of *Origins* that has proven the most fruitful to contemporary thinkers, her reflections on "the end of the rights of man." Considering the imperative to "forget" with which countries of haven address refugees, Arendt remarks, "In order to forget more efficiently we rather avoid any allusion to the concentration or internment camps we experienced in nearly all European countries. . . . Apparently nobody wants to know that contemporary history has created a new kind of human beings—the kind that are put in concentration camps by their foes and in internment camps by their friends" (*Jew as Pariah* 56). Although Arendt's writings on the camps are not usually considered as works of memory, she conceives the project that she outlines here and continues to develop in *Origins* as part of an anamnestic project dedicated to reclaiming contemporary history from instantaneous oblivion. Remembering the camps entails recognizing the novelty of the humanity produced there. This new kind of human is what, under Arendt's influence, the Italian philosopher Giorgio Agamben will later call "homo sacer" and "bare life."[17] Sacred or bare life is what has been radically excluded by the polis but is simultaneously still sufficiently included to be subject to murder: "*life that cannot be sacrificed and yet may be killed*" (Agamben, *Homo Sacer* 82). This inclusion of the excluded marks the realm of what Agamben, following Foucault, calls biopolitics, a politics that targets life itself and that Agamben sees coming to define the totality of contemporary politics.[18] For Agamben, as for Arendt, the Nazi concentration and extermination camps form the paradigm of biopolitics, but both thinkers, in different ways, see the biopolitical threat expanding well beyond that particular locus.[19]

As Arendt formulates the problem of biopolitics in 1943, the greatest danger to the "new kind of human beings" created in the camps is that all markers of culture and civilization have been stripped away from them, leaving them naked and radically vulnerable: "We expose ourselves to the fate of human beings who, unprotected by any specific law or political convention, are nothing but human beings. I can hardly imagine an attitude more dangerous, since we actually live in a world in which human beings as such have ceased to exist for quite a while" (*Jew as Pariah* 65). Human beings as such have ceased to exist because of the dense "artificial" networks of social, cultural, and political institutions that surround them under almost all circumstances. The loss of such a context is so dangerous because, as Arendt would go on to argue in *Origins*, it is only via constructed communal categories—especially citizenship in a sovereign state—that humans can attain the fundamental "right to bear rights." Without those categories, "the world found nothing sacred in the abstract nakedness of being human" (*Origins* 296, 99). In the section of *Origins* called "The Decline of the Nation-State and the End of the Rights of Man," Arendt notes how in the wake of World War I the phenomenon of statelessness that had seemed peripheral—"an unfortunate exception to an otherwise sane and normal rule," "peculiar to certain territories that deviated from the norm" (*Origins* 267–68, 276)—became definitive and marked a generalized crisis of the nation-state. In other words, the figure of the abstract, naked human is not simply an accidental effect of contingent crisis, but is revelatory of aporias in the structure of modern political organization. *Origins* thus confirms and develops the insights of "We Refugees," allowing us to see once again how Arendt connects the marginal and the central—and the Jewish vanguard to the comity of nations—as parts of a structured historical process.

The early essay "We Refugees" thus raises several issues crucial to the more fully developed project of *The Origins of Totalitarianism*. It suggests the methodological necessity of deploying a transnational lens, both to reveal that many quintessentially modern phenomena entail the transgression of national boundaries and to bring into focus the scale of the problems caused by the crisis of the nation-state. Realigning the methodological lens to bring into view the centrality of "marginal," transnational phenomena also allows insight into the importance of the categories of the "human" and the biopolitical for an understanding of extreme violence and genocide. As the work of Agamben testifies, it is at the margins of the polis that we find the determinant issues and figures of modernity such as bare life, sovereignty, the state of exception, and *homo sacer*. Yet, in the early essay, we are also left with a gnawing concern—In what time or place exactly *did* "human beings as such" exist? This question will come back to haunt *Origins* and reveal its imbrication in a colonialist vision of history.

Beyond Human Comprehension: Eurocentrism and the Discourse of Utility

Arendt's notion of comprehension bears a complex relationship to the category of the human, which is itself centrally at stake in her discussions of totalitarianism. Arendt distinguishes her own version of comprehension from the more common meaning of the term, which in a 1946 review essay she calls "human comprehension": "*Beyond the capacities of human comprehension* is the deformed wickedness of those who established such [monstrous] equality" as was found in the Nazi extermination camps (*Essays* 198; Arendt's emphasis). By "human comprehension," Arendt seems to mean the integration of events into the recognizably *utilitarian* framework of understanding that is "the very basis on which history is produced" (*Essays* 199). *Human* comprehension is inadequate because, for Arendt, totalitarianism entails precisely "the transformation of human nature itself," a transformation that cannot be subsumed under any utilitarian motivation and thus goes beyond any familiar notion of the human (*Origins* 458). Canovan summarizes Arendt's account of why the category of the human becomes inadequate in the face of totalitarian terror: "The totalitarian assault on human nature is an attempt to create something closer to nature than human beings ought to be, and to destroy the specifically human qualities that distinguish human beings from animals, namely their individuality and their capacity to initiate action and thought" (*Hannah Arendt* 25). While Arendt understands this destruction of individuality as pervasive in totalitarian societies, the camps and the genocide enacted in them represent an extreme point of the totalitarian assault. Despite the extremity of that assault, Arendt's notions of comprehension, the human, and totalitarianism also shape her understanding of nontotalitarian histories where the limits of the human are at stake—and, indeed, nontotalitarian histories (especially the history of imperialism) shape her conception of totalitarianism.

As becomes clear in her prescient 1950 essay "Social Science Techniques and the Study of Concentration Camps," Arendt's notions of the human and of comprehension—or of the destruction of the human and human comprehension—are crucial to her understanding of the relations between totalitarian genocide and its antecedents. Since the concentration camp system, which she sees as the defining and unprecedented moment of totalitarianism, is characterized by "an absence of . . . utilitarian criteria," then it cannot be equated with the "definite purpose" identifiable in other forms of terror. For Arendt,

The road to total domination leads through many intermediary stages which are relatively normal and quite comprehensible. It is far from unprecedented to wage aggressive war; massacres of enemy population or even of what one assumes to be a hostile people look like an everyday affair in the bloody record of history; extermination of natives in the process of colonization and the establishment of new settlements has happened in America, Australia, and Africa; slavery is one of the oldest institutions of mankind and forced-labor gangs, employed by the state for the performance of public works, were one of the mainstays of the Roman Empire. Even the claim to world rule . . . is no monopoly of totalitarian governments and can still be explained by a fantastically exaggerated lust for power. (*Essays* 233–34)

In contrast to these phenomena, Arendt writes, "The fate of European Jewry [and] the establishment of death factories . . . transcend anti-Semitic reasoning as well as the political, social, and economic motives behind the propaganda of anti-Semitic movements" (*Essays* 235). The attempt to understand the novelty of historical experience demands the kinds of unsentimental distinctions that Arendt makes here. In addition, the insight that extreme and unprecedented forms of violence can emerge from the normal and the everyday is both epistemologically productive and carries the critical corollary that the elements of totalitarianism might outlast the historical period of totalitarianism's eruption and lie dormant, waiting to be reactivated. Furthermore, the recognition that some forms of terror are familiar from history's bloody record need not minimize that terror. As Arendt concludes in this essay, "The point is that Hitler was not like Jenghiz Khan and not worse than some other great criminal but entirely different" (*Essays* 243). The insistence that historical difference does not necessarily entail moral distinction avoids slippage from a discourse of comparison to one of competition—a matter especially crucial when the discussion shifts from the evaluation of perpetrators to the recognition of the suffering of victims.

Nevertheless, the previous long passage also raises problems about how to think about victimization that return us to the question of human comprehension. What does it mean, for example, to relegate "extermination of natives" to the category of the "relatively normal and quite comprehensible"? On the one hand, Arendt's point is clear; she means to suggest, rightly or wrongly, that the process of colonization is an explainable, utilitarian pursuit that entails massacres and even genocide. This is not meant as a justification of colonization and its correlates, but is rather intended as a factual statement about what the pursuit of wealth and power entails. On the other hand, the absence of utility as one of the elements differentiating the Holocaust from other genocides and "exterminations" easily slides into less objective judgments that seem to grant "rationality" to some forms of killing.[20] The evaluation of colonialism as utilitarian also skirts essential conclusions of *Origins* itself.

Arendt's formulation in these early essays of the particularity of the Nazi genocide has become a standard feature of contemporary discourse on the uniqueness of the Holocaust. For example, Yehuda Bauer, one of the most important historians of the Shoah, cites the "nonpragmatic and irrational" ideology of National Socialist anti-Semitism as one of the things that led to "an unprecedented form of genocide."[21] Bauer's formulation seems to capture something important about the Holocaust—which one would never want to describe as "rational"—and yet it begs the question of who gets to decide on the definition of the pragmatic and rational. This conceptual uncertainty becomes especially significant when the question of comparison enters in. While the murder of Jews is considered irrational, Bauer consistently describes the murder of other groups as "pragmatic." While he insists (no doubt genuinely) that such distinctions are not meant to suggest a "gradation of suffering" (50), it is difficult to avoid reading the attribution of the pragmatic and rational as imbued with value. The problem is that using utility as a criterion raises the question of perspective. From what and from whose perspective is something utilitarian? For instance, Bauer writes that "in the Armenian genocide, arguably the closest parallel to the Holocaust, the motivation was political and chauvinistic, that is, it had a pragmatic basis. . . . The Armenians, an 'alien' nation, occupied stretches of Anatolia, the heartland of Turkey. They had to be done away with" (45). While there are obvious geographical, cultural, and political differences between Jews in Europe and Armenians in the Ottoman Empire, it is difficult to grasp how the elimination of one "alien" presence is more irrational than the other, or why motivation for the Holocaust could not be described as "political and chauvinistic." The definition of any act of extermination as pragmatic, and therefore rational, will always be ideological. Accepting claims that certain genocides or massacres are pragmatic often entails accepting the terms and worldview of the perpetrators—as Bauer does when he ventriloquizes the voice of the Turkish perpetrators ("They had to be done away with"). Bauer and others are willing to perform this act of definition for all genocides except for the Holocaust. The establishment of pragmatism and utility as standards of historical distinction in this instance presupposes European frameworks of evaluation—the Holocaust is unique based on modern European criteria of rationality. Seen from another perspective, such as that of the victims, however, the nonutilitarian basis of genocide is hardly relevant; ascribed motivation has no bearing on the results of genocidal procedures.[22] Even worse, the discourse of pragmatism reinforces and reproduces Orientalist and colonialist ideologies. As Chickasaw scholar Jodi Byrd writes in response to similar comments by Deborah Lipstadt differentiating the Holocaust from the genocide of indigenous peoples, "What happens to American Indians in such a competition for the 'true' genocide is that we become, yet again, the 'logical,' if tragic victims of modernization who stand in the way of progress."[23]

For Arendt, the question of utility is far more complicated than for Bauer and other contemporary proponents of uniqueness. She seems to waffle on the question of the utility of the camps. In *Origins*, she writes, "The uselessness of the camps, their cynically admitted anti-utility, is only apparent. In reality they are more essential to the preservation of the regime's power than any of its other institutions" (456). Far from being useless, the camps are a necessary component of the totalitarian regime's drive toward intensive total domination. Emphasizing how the question of utility is a question of perspective, Arendt actually takes on the voice of totalitarianism to make this point: "Common sense protests desperately that the masses are submissive and that all this gigantic apparatus of terror is therefore superfluous; if they were capable of telling the truth, the totalitarian rulers would reply: The apparatus seems superfluous to you only because it serves to make men superfluous" (*Origins* 457). Because Arendt self-consciously foregrounds her ventriloquism of the totalitarian rulers, her approach remains critical, whereas Bauer's risks sliding into the perspective of the perpetrators. Although Arendt insists elsewhere—and crucially—on the nonutilitarian values that drive totalitarianism, she also recognizes that the question of utility is a question of "common sense," or, in other words, of "human comprehension." Such a notion of sense and comprehension takes for granted the image of the human that totalitarianism (and, as we'll see in a moment, even imperialism) renders irrelevant. Only when pushed beyond the limits of common sense can a discourse of utility or of the human remain pertinent. But this is a difficult task to which even Arendt is not always equal.

The most striking difference between Arendt and most of those who locate the uniqueness of the Holocaust in its irrationality or nonutility is that Arendt locates the origins of nonutilitarian or, better, postutilitarian thinking in imperialism, and particularly in the "scramble for Africa." Arendt's account of the development of the Boers in the chapter of *Origins* on "Race and Bureaucracy" serves as a genealogy of the antagonism between utilitarian notions of rationality and the foundations of the racial state and identifies the most important links between colonialism and Nazi genocide. The Boers "were the first European group to become completely alienated from the pride which Western man felt in living in a world created and fabricated by himself" (*Origins* 194). Defined by "contempt for labor, hatred of territorial limitation, general rootlessness, and activistic faith in [their] own divine chosenness," the Boers proved themselves willing "to sacrifice productivity and profit to the phantom world of white gods ruling over black shadows." They thus stood in contrast to the British in South Africa, with their "simple utilitarian minds" (*Origins* 197). And indeed, in this "respect, the most important one, the Boers remained the undisputed masters of the country: whenever rational labor and production policies came into conflict with race considerations, the latter won" (*Origins* 204). As Canovan summarizes Arendt's argument in this section of *Origins*, "South Africa showed that it is possible for a modern society to be organised on quite uneconomic principles along racial lines. . . . [A]lthough in Arendt's account imperialism started from the subordination of politics to bourgeois economics, it culminated in the abandonment of economic imperatives, and the adoption instead of sheer violence by men who had discovered a new form of community, a chosen race" (*Hannah Arendt* 38–39). This dialectic of utility and nonutility, played out in the encounter between Europe and its others, gives the question of utility a different cast in Arendt's work than it takes on for many later Holocaust scholars, such as Bauer. For Bauer, the nonutility of the Holocaust is one of the key indices of its uniqueness and one of the factors that differentiates the murder of Jews from massacres of predominantly non-European peoples. As he writes, "It would be superfluous to analyze the motivation for the annihilation of the Caribs at the hands of the Spaniards, or the genocide of Mexican and Peruvian Indian peoples that followed— clearly the quest for gold, commerce, and natural riches was the central motive, and the conversion to Christianity an ideological 'superstructure'" (47). Bauer's mobilization of a logic of self-evidence (always a sure sign of ideology at work) is far from the insights of Arendt, for whom the very possibility of a "non-utilitarian" genocide emerges from European practices in non-European space. Consistent with Arendt's attempt in *Origins* to show the crystallization of elements that led to totalitarianism instead of charting a deterministic causality, the link between Nazism and imperialism in South Africa is "indirect." But the crucial idea that "societies can function according to principles other than economic" was an important lesson that

"South Africa's race society taught the mob" (*Origins* 206). By situating the emergence of a nonutilitarian dynamic of destruction in Europe's expansion beyond its borders, Arendt provides an opening for a non-Eurocentric Holocaust studies that would not take European categories of utility and humanity for granted. Rather, her example suggests the need to submit such categories to the dual historical test of imperialism and genocide. This insight applies equally to her own texts.

Before submitting Arendt's categories to the standards she establishes, let me sum up what we've learned so far about Arendt's understanding of comprehension and the human in the context of imperialism and genocide. Arendt's task is to explain a political movement that defies human comprehension by ceaselessly producing destruction. What Arendt calls human comprehension corresponds to events and actions derived from motives that are explainable with recourse to utilitarian reasoning. Historical events and political projects, like the Holocaust, that do not obey utilitarian logic are thus beyond human comprehension. Events beyond human comprehension are not mystical or sacred events, according to Arendt. Rather, phenomena beyond human comprehension require the form of paradoxical comprehension Arendt describes as facing up to and resisting reality. Such paradoxical comprehension thus involves breaking up phenomena and recomposing the fragments in the form of constellations. The fragmentary historiography of constellations does not mimic the linear causal thinking of utilitarian logic that lies behind humanly comprehensible actions. Rather, fragmentary historiography attempts to capture the ruptures in and with normality that characterize acts of extreme violence. Arendt uses this distinction between what is beyond and what is within human comprehension to distinguish between the Holocaust as the essence of totalitarianism and all other preceding forms of extreme violence and oppression. Yet, at the same time, she places this nonutilitarian genocide in a constellation that includes the emergence of a hierarchical "race society" in South Africa. Imperialism forms a condition of the Holocaust, even as Arendt fundamentally distinguishes the two phenomena.

While extreme events are beyond human (that is, ordinary) comprehension, they nevertheless (or, perhaps, consequentially) have as their stakes the definition of the limits of the human. For Arendt, extreme events are those that confront us with humanity in a pure form, "human beings as such." Mapping the contours of the human thus becomes one of the keys to understanding totalitarianism and the Holocaust. In Arendt's conception, human beings "as such" do not take part in a shared universal humanity, but instead represent an extreme point of isolation and vulnerability. The human being as such resides in the zone beyond human comprehension. The concentration camp inhabitant—especially the near-death, zombie-like figure who was known in the camps as the *Muselmann*—and the stateless refugee are figures of a new humanity; they are bare life that can be killed but not sacrificed. Understanding the fate of "abstract, naked" humanity requires a form of comprehension attuned to the ruptures in the human; the challenge of formulating a comprehension of the human beyond human comprehension motivates Arendt's project in *Origins*. But if the Holocaust victim epitomizes that challenge to understanding, what of the victim of colonial race society who represents the site at which, in Arendt's account, human action first exceeds human comprehension? How is it that this latter figure does not become the inspiration for the thinking of bare life in either Arendt or Agamben? In asking about the relationship between these two figures of victimization the point is not to work toward an equation of their experiences and the histories in which they find themselves, nor to play them off each other in a competition of victims, but to put pressure on the categories that Arendt uses to link and differentiate them. I argue that the figure of the colonized plays an essential role in the clarification of the Nazi genocide in *Origins*, but it is a role that seems to lie beyond even Arendt's radical form of comprehension.

The Colonial Encounter and the Trauma of Race

Arendt considers the formation of race society (that is, a society structured fundamentally by racial hierarchy) in the colonies a crucial step on the way to racial extermination within Europe. Yet the matter of race and racism in *Origins* and in commentaries on it by scholars as important as Canovan is complicated by the odd way Arendt describes race society's emergence out of the encounter between Europeans and Africans.[24] Arendt's depiction of the colonial encounter reproduces the central ambiguities that mark one of her key source texts in the chapter on "Race and Bureaucracy," Joseph Conrad's novella *Heart of Darkness*, which she describes as "the most illuminating work on actual race experience in Africa" (*Origins* 185n). Conrad's text illuminates for Arendt a vision of the colonial encounter as traumatic encounter. But if, in a postcolonial moment, we are not initially surprised by the notion that colonialism produces trauma, Arendt has something else in mind. The trauma is not on the side of the colonized, but of the colonizer:

> It is highly probable that the thinking in terms of race would have disappeared in due time together with other irresponsible opinions of the nineteenth century, if the "scramble for Africa" and the new era of imperialism had not exposed Western humanity to new and shocking experiences. . . . Race was the emergency explanation of human beings whom no European or civilized man could understand and whose humanity so frightened and humiliated the immigrants that they no longer cared to belong to the same human species. Race was the Boers' answer to the overwhelming monstrosity of Africa—a whole continent populated and overpopulated by savages—an explanation of the madness which grasped and illuminated them like "a flash of lightning in a serene sky: 'Exterminate all the brutes.'" (*Origins* 183–85)

On the one hand, Arendt's idiosyncratic manner of portraying the colonial encounter encourages rethinking of certain theories of modernity, such as Benjamin's, that place shock at the center of the modern experience.[25] Whereas, for Benjamin, shock describes an experience internal to European modernity, Arendt finds that definitively modern experience in the encounter with the periphery that produces the central modern category of "race" as an "emergency explanation" and provides the conditions of possibility for extermination and Holocaust. On the other hand, rather than fully exposing her theory to what is truly shocking and traumatic about the colonial encounter, Arendt's mode of narration consistently marginalizes the very colonial violence she recognizes, seems to reproduce the terms of colonial discourse ("monstrosity," "savages"), and reproduces a homogenized notion of Europeanness ("no European," and so forth). Despite her methodological interest in constellations, crystallizations, and the avoidance of linear narration, the unified point of view of the narration and the granting of narrative voice solely to the European perspective reduce the potential traumatic impact of the "massacres of enemy population" and "extermination of natives" that, to her credit, she so clearly sees.[26] Here, she doesn't follow through on Benjamin's insights in his "Theses on the Philosophy of History" about the co-constitutive encounter of "civilization" and "barbarism." Rather than understanding the categories civilization and barbarism as a constellation, Arendt turns them into a progressive narrative, despite her own suspicion of that form.

As the previous passage's closing citation of *Heart of Darkness* attests, Arendt's portrait of frightened and humiliated Europeans is distinctly Conradian, a line of influence that has particular implications for the link between comprehension and the human.[27] In a famous passage that Arendt quotes at length, Conrad's Marlow, who has been hired in the colonial metropolis to retrieve the ivory company's top agent in the colonies, describes his confrontation with Africans as he sets out on his steamer, heading through the jungle toward that agent, Kurtz. Arendt introduces this passage by remarking, "The world of native savages was a perfect setting for men who had escaped the reality of civilization. . . . [The Europeans] were confronted with human beings who, living without the future of a purpose and the past of an accomplishment, were as incomprehensible as the inmates of a madhouse" (*Origins* 190):

> The prehistoric man was cursing us, praying to us, welcoming us—who could tell? We were cut off from the comprehension of our surroundings; we glided past like phantoms, wondering and secretly appalled, as sane men would be before an enthusiastic outbreak in a madhouse. We could not understand because we were too far and could not remember, because we were travelling in the night of first ages, of those ages that are gone, leaving hardly a sign—and no memories.
>
> The earth seemed unearthly. We are accustomed to look upon the shackled form of a conquered monster, but there—there you could look at a thing monstrous and free. It was unearthly, and the men were—No, they were not inhuman. Well, you know, that was the worst of it—this suspicion of their not being inhuman. It would come slowly to one. They howled and leaped, and spun, and made horrid faces; but what thrilled you was just the thought of their humanity—like yours—the thought of your remote kinship with this wild and passionate uproar. (*Heart* 37)

Like Arendt's successor text, *Heart of Darkness* simultaneously confirms the humanity of Africans and removes them from present civilization and, implicitly, from past accomplishment and future world-making. While the depiction of this encounter calls into question the possibility of comprehension, memory, narrative, and self-orientation for Europeans, a progressive understanding of history that locates Africans and Europeans in different chronological frames continues to operate. The Europeans are baffled by what they find because it reminds them vaguely of what they left behind so long ago: "We could not understand because we were too far." While the first "we" is a disoriented, amnesiac subject, the second "we" returns as the modern subject, whose ignorance and inability to remember mark him precisely as modern, as capable of being "thrilled" and not simply overwhelmed. Despite the threat of uncanniness suggested by Africans' "remote kinship," Africa and Africans ultimately function as the sublime other that confirms the reason of European man—provided that he does not, like Kurtz, "go native" and regress to a precivilized state.[28]

The notion of the human does the most invidious work here. In both *The Origins of Totalitarianism* and *Heart of Darkness*, the notion of the human splits in the encounter between Europe and Africa: recognition of the monster as human institutes a narrative of "remote kinship" that draws Africans into the text only to leave them behind. Indeed, shortly after quoting Conrad, Arendt echoes him by portraying Africans in *Origins* as the past that Europeans have overcome:

What made them different from other human beings was not at all the color of their skin but the fact that they behaved like a part of nature, that they treated nature as their undisputed master, that they had not created a human world, a human reality, and that therefore nature had remained, in all its majesty, the only overwhelming reality—compared to which they appeared to be phantoms, unreal and ghostlike. They were, as it were, "natural" human beings who lacked the specifically human character, the specifically human reality, so that when European men massacred them they somehow were not aware that they had committed murder. (*Origins* 192)

The primary problem with this passage lies not in Arendt's final claim about the Europeans' lack of awareness of murder, which can be read as coming from the perspective of the colonizer and thus capturing something important about the conditions of possibility of genocide. The problem is the splitting in two of the human that emerges from Arendt's understanding of Africans as never having constructed "a human world." Like stateless refugees and concentration camp inmates slated for death, Africans are the included exclusion, they are bare life. Or, to put it another way, their inclusion within the realms of the human is precisely the source of their exclusion. But the "incomprehensibility" of Africa and Africans is of a different order from that of Europe and its refugees and camp victims. Although Arendt does not acknowledge it, her argument rests on a preexisting cultural difference that provides the distance necessary to protecting and preserving the European subject in the face of traumatic extremity. Deploying a Hegelian understanding of history as written practice, Arendt consistently represents Africa as "prehistoric" and Africans as "prehistoric man"—human, but not too human. Although the category of imperialism in *Origins* is not meant to be a cog in a narrative of the emergence of totalitarianism, but instead an element awaiting crystallization, the practice of imperialism nevertheless (according to Arendt) writes a history of progress: Europe brings history to naturally human Africa in the form of a recognizable and unnatural, if brutal and genocidal, human reality.[29]

One of the most consequential connections Arendt makes between imperialism and the Holocaust derives from this destabilization of the human—a connection that is thus partially troubled by its reliance on a colonialist version of encounter. The progressive, narrative dimension of Arendt's account of imperialism and the splitting of the human it produces also underlie her notion of totalitarianism and especially of the "new kind of human beings" produced in the Nazi camps. If imperialism entails the deadly encounter of "natural" human beings with civilization—an encounter that traumatizes but ultimately stabilizes the European subject—totalitarianism attempts to effect a regression to that natural state within European space. Such a coding of totalitarianism as regression (the mirror image of narrative progression) is reinforced when Arendt discusses the European pan-nationalist movements, whose racism she sees as the mediating link between overseas imperialism and Nazism, as expressions of "tribal nationalism" (*Origins* 227–43).[30] Such terminology reveals the metaphorical paths that Arendt's theory traverses: a primitivist conception of Africans is passed first to European colonists in Africa, then to continental imperialists in Europe, and finally to both the victims and the perpetrators in the totalitarian camps. In the "Totalitarianism" section of *Origins*, Arendt uses language that recalls Conrad's as well as her own discussion of the colonial encounter; she describes "the real horror [that] began . . . when the SS took over the administration of the camps":

The killing of man's individuality, of the uniqueness shaped in equal parts by nature, will, and destiny, which has become so self-evident a premise for all human relations that even identical twins inspire a certain uneasiness, creates a horror that vastly overshadows the outrage of the juridical-political person and the despair of the moral person. It is this horror that gives rise to the nihilistic generalizations which maintain plausibly enough that essentially all men are like beasts. Actually the experience of the concentration camps does show that human beings can be transformed into specimens of the human animal, and that man's "nature" is only "human" insofar as it opens up to man the possibility of becoming something highly unnatural, that is, a man. (*Origins* 454–55)

In understanding the camps as a site of the unmaking and remaking of the human, Arendt does not have in mind only the victims. As in the colonial encounter—where the traumatic shock of the confrontation impacts the colonizer—the horror of the camps rebounds in a boomerang effect on the very subjects who have constructed them. However, the difference between the two boomerang effects reiterates the splitting of the human. While in the colonial situation the spectacle of savagery disconcerts but ultimately confirms human (that is, European) possibility, here the uncanny (note the uneasiness inspired by twins) does not give way to the sublime reconstitution of the individualized modern subject. Arendt connects the killing of the prisoner's individuality with elimination of the killers' humanity: The "absolutely cold and systematic destruction of human bodies, calculated to destroy human dignity . . . turned [the camps] into 'drill grounds,' on which perfectly normal men were trained to be full-fledged members of the SS" (*Origins* 454). This passage not only anticipates later insights about the "ordinary men" engaged in the Nazi genocide (see esp. *Origins* 454n), but also sets the stage for one of Arendt's most original and chilling arguments about totalitarianism: "Men insofar as they are more than animal reaction and fulfillment of functions are entirely superfluous to totalitarian regimes. Totalitarianism strives not toward despotic rule over men, but toward a system in which men are superfluous" (*Origins* 457). Totalitarian functionalism—or "logicality," as Arendt calls it—leads to the attempt to produce a world bereft of superfluous humanity and, instead, fully consistent with the movement's "ideological supersense": "It is chiefly for the sake of this supersense, for the sake of complete consistency, that it is necessary for totalitarianism to destroy every trace of what we commonly call human dignity. For respect for human dignity implies the recognition of my fellow-men or our fellow-nations as subjects, as builders of worlds or cobuilders of a common world" (*Origins* 458).

For Arendt, the camps reveal in microcosm the narrative of man's emergence into humanity as a fragile victory over nature and the animal that can be reversed under the right (for example, totalitarian) circumstances. This formulation represents the aporia or undecidable impasse of Arendt's thought. Arendt hesitates between two understandings of the human: one in which the animal resides at the core of the human and one in which only the unnatural (the nonanimal) could ever constitute the human. These two versions of the human correspond, respectively, to the "lessons" of the "Imperialism" and "Totalitarianism" sections of *Origins*: in Africa, Europeans discover "the human animal," while in the camps of the twentieth century they discover how to produce the animalized human. If, as Canovan argues, Arendt's political vision is forged out of and in stark opposition to the experience of totalitarianism, this aporia cuts to the center of her thought. The properly human realm in which politics can be practiced is buffeted on either side by the forces of "nature." Politics is threatened as much by the "natural" nature of the non-European world as by the production of a second natural state by the crises of the modern European world. Such a vision ignores the constitutive role of the non-European in the making of modern Europe and the opportunities for a new constitution of the human that might arise from that space. At the very moment when anticolonial struggles are raising the possibility of a "third nature" that would remake the world beyond colonialism and without the fantasy of return to supposedly prelapsarian conditions, Arendt translates the conquering of the colonial world into that world's threat to the very constitution of the human.[31]

The relation between imperialism and totalitarianism in *Origins* is even more intimate than Arendt acknowledges. As the previous citations from Arendt make clear, the colonial difference—that is, the distinction between natural and unnatural humanity—figures the ultimate limit of the totalitarian barbarism of the camps: "the killing of man's individuality" and the refusal of recognition for "my fellow-men [and] our fellow-nations as . . . cobuilders of a common world." Arendt's description of the concentration camps relies on a distinction that she derives from the colonial encounter, but she cannot fully recognize that that encounter produces the very distinction she takes for granted there. That is, instead of understanding the traumatic nature of the physical and epistemic violence of colonialism as productive of the natural/unnatural humanity opposition, Arendt seems to hold that the Africans really are excluded from the project of building a common world (not essentially, perhaps, but historically and for the foreseeable future, nonetheless). The logic of her argument is that the Nazis turn their victims (and even their own adherents) into the deindividualized humans that Africans already are. This asymmetry leaves an unsettling mark on Arendt's account, despite the power and originality of the link she makes between the destruction wrought by the camps and that of imperialism. Arendt transforms the supposed absence of certain forms of life (European culture) into lack of all culture, all as a means of identifying what is lost under totalitarian conditions (the individualization of camp inmates and the SS).[32]

While it is of course troublesome that Arendt does not understand imperialism as producing Africans as bare life in the same way that the Nazis transformed the Jews into bare life, the problem potentially runs even deeper and has an impact on the category of comprehension. The splitting of the human in the colonial encounter is essential to Arendt's explanation of racism and the biopolitical world of the camps, a world in which a caesura is produced in the continuum of life between a "master race" and a category of "life unworthy of life" (or, in less extreme circumstances, between the citizen with rights and the refugee stripped of rights). The difficult problem to address is the degree to which Arendt's categorization of the Holocaust (and other aspects of totalitarianism) as beyond human comprehension depends on the assumption of a realm of humanity beyond human culture. In order to explain the reduction and splitting of the human that takes place in totalitarianism, Arendt has to posit such a split as already active in the colonial encounter. But her attempt to explain how that encounter produces the salience of race and the force of racism ends up requiring that racial difference preexist the encounter. She thus draws the very line within the human that she finds produced in the colonial encounter and camps. If we take seriously Arendt's own genealogy of the nonutilitarian in the formation of colonial race society, however, the source of incomprehension is brought closer to home, with unsettling results. It is not the confrontation with bare life that produces incomprehension, but the very norms of European culture and its conception of the modern subject out of which the paradoxes of the human emerge. Perhaps most provocative in this account is the possibility that the "shock" experienced by Europeans in Africa emerges from the very universalism and humanism of Enlightenment thought, which leads the colonizers to expect an encounter with sameness. It is from within the expectation of homogenous universality that difference becomes traumatic.[33] The category of race is more fundamental to Arendt's argument and historical account than she can admit; it is not simply an "emergency explanation," but a place where the emergency mingles with the norm.

Bare Life and the Boomerang Effect

In a series of recent books focusing on the biopolitics of "bare life," Giorgio Agamben has helped develop Arendt's accounts of imperialism and genocide. Unlike the discussion of Africa in *The Origins of Totalitarianism*, Agamben's investigations do not assume a preexistent realm of bare life or animality. In *State of Exception*, for instance, Agamben specifies that bare life is not "a natural biological given" but is "a product of the [biopolitical] machine."[34] Because he does not situate bare life in a preexisting state of nature, Agamben can develop insights into the proximity of bare life to European norms of sovereignty and personhood. Yet, Agamben's genealogical analysis of the growing indistinction of life and politics remains internal to Europe; he thus, symptomatically, never discusses Arendt's sections on the colonial encounter, which in my reading constitutes a key moment in the development of biopolitics (however ambivalently represented by Arendt). Agamben never offers an explanation of why biopolitics comes to triumph in modernity, a triumph that Arendt and more recent work in postcolonial studies suggest must have something to do with racial difference and a colonial encounter that radically transformed conceptions of the human. Agamben claims that "the camp—as the pure, absolute, and impossible biopolitical space (insofar as it is founded solely on the state of exception)—will appear as the hidden paradigm of the political space of modernity" (*Homo Sacer* 123). While provocative, this claim remains troubling both because it mobilizes an absolutist/purist logic and because of its inability to think the colonial encounter as a biopolitical event. As Arendt and Conrad demonstrate, sometimes against their own intentions, the colonial encounter is founded on a taken-for-granted state of exception in which there is no need for a "radical transformation of politics into the realm of bare life" (*Homo Sacer* 210), because contact with Africa already constitutes such a politics for Europeans. Agamben builds an artificial discursive wall around "the West" that prevents him both from seeing forces outside Europe as constitutive of modernity (as a range of minority and postcolonial thinkers have argued in recent decades) and from finding a way out of "the [biopolitical] machine" that is not apocalyptic. Agamben's "West" is a "pure, absolute . . . space" that cannot be productively transformed from within or without because its rise and fall are sealed off from a heterogeneous global history.

Insofar as she employs a Benjaminian methodology of constellation and crystallization, Arendt's *Origins* avoids both the absolutist nature of Agamben's argument and its extreme European exceptionalism—two methodological positions that thus appear as linked. Yet, she cannot fully account for the significance of the imperial encounter in her own reading of the camps. This failure manifests itself again when Arendt introduces the potentially fruitful concept of colonial "boomerang effects."[35] When, in the "Imperialism" section of *Origins* she explicitly addresses the connection between empire and Nazi genocide, she inadvertently reproduces the racial logic under analysis. She first suggests that, in comparison to the influence of the Boers' antiutilitarian thinking, their racism and anti-Semitism "influenced Nazism only in an indirect way" because it was "a matter of course and a natural consequence of the status quo in South Africa" (*Origins* 205–6). She then uses the figure of the boomerang to give form to that indirect influence:

There were, however, real and immediate boomerang effects of South Africa's race society on the behavior of European peoples: since cheap Indian and Chinese labor had been madly imported to South Africa whenever her interior supply was temporarily halted, a change of attitude toward colored people was felt immediately in Asia where, for the first time, people were treated in almost the same way as those African savages who had frightened the Europeans literally out of their wits. The difference was only that there could be no excuse and no humanly comprehensible reason for treating Indians and Chinese as though they were not human beings. In a certain sense, it is only here that the real crime began, because here everyone ought to have known what he was doing. . . . [S]ince the race principle supplanted the older notions of alien and strange peoples in Asia, it was a much more consciously applied weapon of domination and exploitation than in Africa. (*Origins* 206)

This passage condenses the possibilities and problems of Arendt's efforts to link imperialism and Nazi genocide. Arendt finds in the conscious taking up of race as a weapon the origins of the "real crime" of genocide, yet her explanation of the circuits of the race-concept's transnational migration itself reinscribes racialized valuations of humanness. Certain uses of race are "natural" and hence comprehensible, while others demand a genealogical explanation. Despite Arendt's care in differentiating her notion of "origins" from a progressive narrative, then, Africa serves as an unquestioned point of origin in her genealogy of totalitarianism. The passage demonstrates the terrible proximity of the category of "human comprehension" to the humanly incomprehensible and also shows Arendt as unable fully to attain her own notion of comprehension as that which goes beyond everyday comprehensibility. Only by excluding certain groups, such as Africans, from recognition as human can comprehension trace the origins of inhumanity: alleged African savagery is the necessary beginning for the boomerang movement from racism that is a "natural consequence" of the European presence in Africa, through unnatural and "no[t] humanly comprehensible" racism in Asia, to the "real crime" of genocide in Europe.

The boomerang effect in Arendt's own text is double. There is both sympathy and distancing in this figurative connection between colonialism and genocide. Colonial violence foreshadows totalitarianism at the same time that totalitarianism casts a shadow backward on the colonial archive. Affect flows in multiple directions, from Africa to Europe and from Europe to Africa, with stopovers in Asia, as colonialism, war, and genocide illuminate each other. However, the relation between these nodes is not symmetrical: the African is chronologically and conceptually prior to the stateless European, but that priority is closer to what Johannes Fabian describes as the "denial of co-evalness" than it is to recognition of the claims to justice of the colonized. Arendt's text thus raises a fundamental question of comparative history and multidirectional memory: Does the attempt to go beyond Europe in providing a global frame for European history risk displacing European responsibility? William Pietz's judgment is harsh: "It was Arendt's signal achievement to frame a set of historically grounded political concepts capable of locating the origin of 'totalitarianism' in general and modern European anti-Semitism in particular—and by implication, the responsibility for the Nazi holocaust—outside Europe, in the savage 'tribalism' of 'the Dark Continent'" (69). I find Pietz's critique of Arendt overly one-sided because it ignores the productive aspects of Arendt's linking of imperialism and Nazism, the aspects that provide a larger, European, and global explanatory frame for what is otherwise often reduced to an account of Germany's "special path [*Sonderweg*]." But I agree with Pietz that Arendt's text becomes contaminated by its own presuppositions about the nature of the human, Africa, and the colonial encounter.

The question then becomes: How can we describe a boomerang effect that doesn't silence one history of violence to convey another? The history of the word "boomerang" suggests that some of the tensions surrounding the comprehension of genocidal violence are already lodged deeply within the word. According to the *OED*, "boomerang" emerges in English in the late eighteenth and early nineteenth centuries as the "adoption or modification of the native name in a lang[uage] of the aborigines of N.S. Wales" for "an Australian missile weapon: a curved piece of hard wood from two to three feet long, with a sharp edge along the convexity of the curve. It is so made as to describe complex curves in its flight, and can be thrown so as to hit an object in a different direction from that of projection, or so as to return to or beyond the starting-point." One of the first mentions of the word, according to the *OED*, is "in a short vocabulary of the extinct language of George's River, Botany Bay, printed by Ridley."[36] The English word "boomerang" thus not only emerges out of a colonial encounter but also indexes a genocidal history in which languages, cultures, and people teeter—or are thought to teeter—on the edge of extinction. The taking up of the boomerang as a metaphor for historical transmission encodes the risks of the comparative imagination—as words are translated and transmitted violence is simultaneously carried forward and left behind. In the circular trajectory of the boomerang, certain histories risk falling into oblivion. Yet when we situate those histories on the arc of the boomerang we also gain the means to return to those silences and to return them to a multidirectional archive of collective memory. This risky notion of return also plays multiple roles in the writings of Aimé Césaire.

3

"Un Choc en Retour": Aimé Césaire's Discourses on Colonialism and Genocide

From *Riposte* to the *Choc en Retour*

In the summer of 1949, two years into France's colonial war in Vietnam, the C.G.T., the Communist-led union that represented French port and dockworkers, called on its members to refuse work on all boats headed for Indochina. Part of an effort by the French Communist Party (PCF) to harness antiwar emotions and put them into practice in concrete actions, the call was embraced first by dockworkers in Algeria in June and then later in Marseille and Dunkerque.[1] Along with demonstrations, strikes, and other forms of direct action, the Communists also employed cultural means in their struggle against the war. Among the documents testifying to the political conflicts of the era is a work by André Fougeron's artist-comrade Boris Taslitzky: the painting *Riposte* (1951).

Taslitzky's painting depicts a violent encounter between French police and dockworkers during one of the strikes protesting the war in Indochina and recalls two well-known nineteenth-century French paintings that also portray their contemporary history in dramatic form (see Figure 2). Assembled in front of a black ship that serves as a backdrop, the bodily mass of workers, policemen, and their dogs takes a pyramidal shape reminiscent of Géricault's *Raft of the Medusa* (1819), with corrugated tin sheets and cobblestones substituting for the raft. Like *Riposte*, Géricault's painting is also connected to colonial history. The *Medusa* was a French frigate that ran aground off the coast of Africa while carrying the new French governor of Senegal who was to take over from the British; more than a hundred died in the wreck, including both French and African crew members. At the top of the "Raft"-inspired pyramid of bodies, Taslitzky includes another reference to classical French painting. The tricolor flag of the Republic, put to new use as a weapon against the police by a muscular dockworker, recalls (and regenders) Delacroix's *Liberty Leading the People* (1830), in which the flag is held at an identical angle. (Like *Riposte* and the painting of Géricault, Delacroix's canvas also features a heap of bodies in the foreground.) *Riposte* thus reworks Géricault's depiction of a colonial catastrophe and Delacroix's depiction of the July revolution to situate the anticolonial and workers' movements within the *longue durée* of French political history.

Yet more is happening in Taslitzky's painting than first meets the eye. The workers' heroic "riposte," or response, takes on added—and provocative—resonance through allusion to the battle against fascism. In the bottom-center of the canvas, Taslitzky depicts one of the policemen locked in a chokehold by a brawny blond worker; this French policeman has the telltale moustache that identifies his face as that of Hitler. While the accusation that one's political opponents are "Nazis" has become a banal trope in the decades since Taslitzky's painting, such an allusion must have had special force in a country that only a few years earlier had been occupied by Hitler's forces. Indeed, the state seized the painting shortly after it was exhibited in 1951. Once we've noticed how Taslitzky recodes the present in terms of the recent fascist past, we also notice how other details are transformed—for instance, how a simple striped sailor's shirt turns into an emblem of a Nazi prisoner's garb. These subtle but effective details signal a reading of the "riposte" depicted in the painting as a *return* as well as a form of resistance. In the guise of this Hitlerian reference, fascism returns to France as a colonialist participant in the struggle over decolonization.

How can we read this striking visual reference to Nazism? To be sure, Taslitzky's biography makes this choice less surprising. The son of Russian Jewish exiles, Taslitzky took part in the resistance to the Nazi

FIGURE 2   Boris Taslitzky, *Riposte* (1951). © 2008 Artists Rights Society (ARS), New York/ADAGP, Paris/Tate, London.

occupation and was later deported to Buchenwald, where he drew a famous series of images of the camp on paper stolen from the SS. Meanwhile, his mother was murdered in Auschwitz after being arrested in the infamous Vel' d'Hiv roundup (an event whose remembrance during the latter stages of the Algerian War will play a significant role in Part IV of this book).[2] While *Riposte* cannot be said to invoke the specificities of the Holocaust, its invocation of Nazism may not represent a simple universalization or instrumentalization of evil, either. Certainly, the painting has a complex resonance in the French context. It suggests a double role for memory of the recent fascist past: the visual reference to Hitler and the camps not only assimilates colonialism to Nazism but also defines decolonization as an extension and continuation of the Franco-French civil war of collaboration and resistance. *Riposte* thus expresses a temporality reminiscent of Freud's writings on memory: it pulls the past into the present, while simultaneously reading the present as a continuation of a particular version of the past. Still, the meaning of that temporality and of the visual analogy between colonialism and fascism remains ambivalent.

Taslitzky's *Riposte*, painted in the same year that Arendt published *The Origins of Totalitarianism*, offers a visual variation on the boomerang effect she describes: if in Arendt's historico-theoretical work racial hierarchies produced in the colonies return to Europe as genocidal anti-Semitism, in Taslitzky's painting the figure of Hitler returns in the struggle over colonialism and decolonization. The inverse vectors of historical influence in these contemporaneous works suggest the potential for multidirectional understanding in this post-Holocaust, decolonizing moment. Yet our consideration of Arendt's writings has illustrated potential pitfalls in the attempt to conceptualize the "boomerang" linking imperialism and the Nazi genocide. What I have called Arendt's "expectation of homogenous universality" leaves her text stuck at the limits of Eurocentrism, unable to move "beyond human comprehension" and produce the multidirectional constellation between colonialism and totalitarianism she sets out to grasp. Attentiveness to the path of the boomerang suggests that Taslitzky's painting also reproduces the limits of the European imagination. Although the workers' strike certainly represents anticolonial activity on the part of the PCF, Taslitzky depicts the struggle as internal to Europe. In the battle between dockworkers and the police, he translates colonialism visually into class struggle and a matter of national history (as the references to Géricault and Delacroix confirm). The movement of the anticolonial "riposte" remains tied to the development of French history and firmly in the hands of French workers.

A year before Taslitzky painted *Riposte* and Arendt published *The Origins of Totalitarianism*, a work appeared that shares their interest in boomerang effects but was written from an explicitly anti-Eurocentric position. With its first edition published in 1950, Aimé Césaire's searing anticolonial tract *Discours sur le colonialisme* (*Discourse on Colonialism*) provides one of the earliest articulations of Nazi genocide in the context of the struggle for decolonization.[3] More effectively than Arendt or Taslitzky, Césaire reveals the metropolis as defined by and permeated with the violence of the colonial peripheries; in addition, the very force of his rhetoric serves to foreground the agency and subjectivity of the colonized within a French discursive sphere. In his *Discourse*, Césaire famously describes Nazi brutality as a "crime against the white man" that "applied to Europe colonialist procedures which until then had been reserved exclusively for the Arabs of Algeria, the 'coolies' of India, and the 'niggers' of Africa." Using a phrase close to Arendt's notion of the "boomerang effect"—and, indeed, rendered as "boomerang effect" by Césaire's English-language translator—Césaire describes the impact of this application of colonialist procedures as a *choc en retour* for European self-conceptions (*Discourse* 36).[4] Césaire's concept of *choc en retour* (reverse shock, backlash, boomerang effect) has contributed to an important tradition of "provincializing" European trauma and continues to inspire scholars in postcolonial studies. Although not without tensions and potential contradictions of its own, Césaire's prescient grasp of the "shock" of historical relatedness provides resources for a rethinking of trauma and civilizational discourses within the theory of multidirectional memory. It also helps us to map the contours of another contemporary scholarly tendency: scholars working in German and Holocaust studies who have sought to flesh out his insights about the *choc en retour* for a new account of genocide. Echoing Césaire's rhetoric, I label this recent tendency the "colonial *turn* in Holocaust studies."

Despite helping to advance the conceptualization of multidirectionality, Césaire's *Discourse* sometimes subordinates historical particularity to linear narratives of progress and regression that, like Arendt, he otherwise seeks to disrupt. As I demonstrate, Césaire often invokes "regression" to produce ironic rhetorical effects, but I also trace the subordination of particularity in part to the ambivalent role of Marxism within Césaire's work. While Communist internationalism can be a source of inspiration for grasping the interconnected, transnational, and frequently racialized dimensions of world history—as Taslitzky's and Fougeron's paintings and Du Bois's writings also illustrate—it sometimes has the tendency to subsume that multidirectionality within Eurocentric and economistic frames of reference. In articulating his own version of the boomerang effect, or *choc en retour*, Césaire bumps up against this paradox of twentieth-century Communist ideology and occasionally stumbles in his attempt to model the multidirectional cosmopolitanism toward which his work gestures. In addition, although Césaire offers an antidote to Arendt's Eurocentrism, he doesn't always attain her grasp of the particularity of different historical experiences—a shortcoming that we can already glimpse in his subsumption of the many victims of Nazism under the generic category "the white man." If Communist Party ideology constitutes a paradigm that both facilitates and ultimately stunts Césaire's historical vision, his *Lettre à Maurice Thorez* (1956), where he announces his break with the PCF, reveals Césaire once again attempting to further a multidirectional vision of cosmopolitanism.

Colonialism and Genocide in the Antillean Gaze

As much as Arendt—but in quite different ways—Césaire was the product of multiple historical and intellectual forces and his work is a matrix of insight tempered with blindness. Césaire, who died in 2008 at the age of ninety-four, was a cosmopolitan intellectual who worked in different intellectual and political fields and translated his minority status into an outpost for withering attacks on the alternatively genocidal and assimilationist forces of the center. Like Arendt, he was also a contradictory and controversial figure, at once the cocreator of negritude, one of the most well-known transnational, anticolonial intellectual and artistic movements, and an architect of Martinique's "departmentalization," which inadvertently led to its current neocolonial status as a marginalized department of France. Césaire's ambivalent relationship to Martinique as well as France, the Caribbean as well as Europe, Creole as well as European culture, has led many critics to speak of his life and work in terms of paradoxes.[5] Those paradoxes both provide the conditions of possibility for the multidirectional encounters Césaire stages and sometimes trouble the logic of those encounters.

When Césaire wrote *Discourse on Colonialism* in 1950, he was a young writer and politician who had emerged from World War II as a leading exponent of the emergent negritude movement, as the mayor of Fort-de-France, and as a French Communist Party member of the National Assembly. Césaire had returned to Martinique in 1939 after spending most of the 1930s in Paris, where he studied at two of France's most prestigious educational institutions, Lycée Louis-Le-Grand and the Ecole Normale Supérieure. He also took part in the cultural scene of the African diaspora and published the first version of his best-known poem, *Cahier d'un retour au pays natal* (*Notebook of a Return to the Native Land*). Although there is no evidence that they ever met in Paris, it is worth noting that Arendt and Césaire lived for six years in the same city, a city that for both of them was a stopping point on a more complicated itinerary. In staging an encounter between their texts, I find it worth keeping both this coincidence and this missed encounter in mind.

While Arendt was in Paris as a stateless refugee and Césaire as a subject of the French empire (although soon to be a citizen), they were both buffeted by some of the same political forces. The ship on which Césaire returned to Martinique was sunk on its way back to Europe by the Nazis, and the island itself was soon taken over by the Vichy rule of the notorious Admiral Robert and swamped by the grounding of thousands of racist French sailors. Although Césaire did not fight fascism as a solider, as did his student Frantz Fanon, his wartime experience included conflict with the Vichy government in Martinique and the production, together with his wife Suzanne Roussi Césaire and the philosopher René Ménil, of the surrealism-inflected literary journal *Tropiques*. Appearing between 1941 and 1945, *Tropiques* served, among other things, as a form of cultural resistance to Vichy rule in Martinique. Despite the indirect mode of its attack on the racist and nationalist Pétain regime, the provocative rhetoric of *Tropiques* led to confrontation between Césaire and his comrades and local Vichy powers and eventually to the effective censorship of the journal.[6] As Césaire's experiences already suggest, Martinique during the war experienced a very particular political and cultural *métissage*. The island's status as a site of intercultural exchange under extreme circumstances was also enhanced by the fact that it served as a temporary stopping point for French refugees fleeing the Nazis on their way to the United States, including Claude Lévi-Strauss and, most importantly, André Breton (who was initially held in the Lazaret concentration camp in Fort-de-France). Césaire's meeting with Breton at this time was of the greatest consequence for twentieth-century literary history insofar as it furthered the synthesis between surrealism and the Caribbean sensibility to which *Tropiques* was dedicated. As this short sketch suggests, the small island of Martinique was by no means "marginal" to the dramas of world history and culture in this era; rather, it offered the potential of a privileged perspective on the crosscutting events of war and colonialism, especially for an intellectual with a bifocal Caribbean/French outlook.[7]

Written out of this very particular historical and intellectual context, Césaire's *Discourse on Colonialism* is located at the intersection of discourses that coexist uneasily: anticolonialism, negritude, antifascism, surrealism, and Marxism. Césaire draws on these heterogeneous historical experiences and philosophical frameworks in order to bring together various forms of European violence, including colonialism and Nazi brutality, and to challenge the blind spots of European self-understanding.[8] As Georges Ngal has written, the *Discourse* designates Europe as "the accused" in its polemical indictment, but "Europe" in Césaire's text is "complex, plural, [and] constantly marked by the 'presence' of Hitlerism."[9] To paraphrase a Benjaminian language that is in fact close to Césaire's intent, the *Discourse* unveils the proximity of documents of civilization to practices of barbarism. He forces an encounter between center and periphery, past and present, culture and violence. His model for this encounter is a double one. That is, in terms of our focus here, the encounter he stages between genocide and colonialism ultimately serves to usher in another encounter: that of Europe with itself. The key to understanding that double encounter lies in the temporality Césaire assigns to it—that of the *choc en retour*. That temporality turns out itself to be double, announcing a disruption of progressive colonial discourses while simultaneously mimicking colonial models of regression and primitivism. This double temporality can also be found in different degrees and configurations in Arendt and in the writer who serves as a touchstone in these two chapters, Joseph Conrad. Yet even as the *Discourse* converges to a certain degree with *The Origins of Totalitarianism* and *Heart of Darkness*, it also diverges significantly: it refuses to naturalize colonialism or genocide in the figure of cultureless human beings; it recognizes the catalyzing role of Europe's disavowal of colonial violence; and it maps out the movement from colonialism to Nazism to decolonization as a multidirectional constellation in which each term modifies the others.

Césaire and the *Discourse on Colonialism*: Rethinking Return

Near the beginning of *Discourse on Colonialism*, Césaire builds up to his announcement of Nazism as a "choc en retour" with a paragraph-long sentence that details the brutal impact of colonialism:

First we must study how colonization works to *decivilize* the colonizer, to *brutalize* him in the true sense of the word, to degrade him, to awaken him to buried instincts, to covetousness, violence, race hatred, and moral relativism; and we must show that each time a head is cut off or an eye put out in Vietnam and in France they accept the fact, each time a little girl is raped and in France they accept the fact, each time a Madagascan is tortured and in France they accept the fact, civilization acquires another dead weight, a universal regression takes place, a gangrene sets in, a center of infection begins to spread; and at the end of all these treaties that have been violated, all these lies that have been propagated, all these punitive expeditions that have been tolerated, all these prisoners who have been tied up and "interrogated," all these patriots who have been tortured, at the end of all the racial pride that has been encouraged, all the boastfulness that has been displayed, there is the poison instilled [*il y a le poison instillé*] in the veins of Europe and, slowly but surely, the continent proceeds toward *savagery*. (*Discourse* 35–36; translation slightly modified)

In this passage, Césaire provides a powerful indictment of the brutality of colonialism and, with disturbing detail, foreshadows aspects of the discussion of torture that will rip France apart in the course of the Algerian War later in the 1950s, when "gangrene" will also be a central metaphor.[10] It is not only the content of Césaire's passage that speaks loudly; the argument of the passage emerges especially in its syntax. Césaire's masterful use of multiple forms of parallelism (that is, "each time . . . each time . . . "; "all these lies . . . all these prisoners . . . ") to expand his sentence to the breaking point serves to embody the global domain of imperial history in a multidirectional discourse. Moving from Vietnam to France to Madagascar and back to Europe in order to enumerate a series of colonial crimes produces a doubly performative effect. Not only does the passage weave together the metropolis and multiple colonial sites, but, by dramatically delaying the announcement of its ultimate message—"there is the poison instilled in the veins of Europe"—it also mimics the temporality of belated *return* that lies behind its account of intra-European violence. Through these syntactic effects, Césaire links two very different forms of brutality on both spatial and temporal planes: the repetitive and repulsive violence against the "other" and the cumulative self-destruction of the perpetrator.

In situating Nazism as the return of colonial violence, this passage also echoes some of the key terms of Conrad's *Heart of Darkness*, which we have seen replayed in *The Origins of Totalitarianism* as well.

Like *Heart of Darkness*, the *Discourse* tracks the "decivilization" of the colonizer and codes it as a "regression" defined by an infectious return to savagery and buried instincts. This echoing is both powerful and risky since, as Dominick LaCapra has noted in a discussion of attempts to develop explanatory models of Nazi violence, "the concept of a regression to barbarism rests on an indiscriminate and self-serving view of other societies to which modern, presumably advanced societies are compared."[11] LaCapra's insight helps to locate the ambivalence at the heart of Conrad's anticolonialism and Arendt's account of the trauma to Europeans of the colonial encounter, both of which seem to argue against empire primarily on the basis of its effect on Europeans and to situate the origins of its violence outside Europe. Why would Césaire echo such clearly colonial discourses?

Although Césaire's oeuvre flirts at various times with versions of "return" that appear close to primitivist regression, as many critics note, in the *Discourse* Césaire shows himself well aware of the provenance and implications of his terms.[12] Indeed, a pattern emerges whereby Césaire *anticipates* colonial discourse, using tropes in his own voice that *then* appear in citations from defenders of colonialism and European supremacy. While it is impossible to be sure of Césaire's intentions, of course, the highly parodic (and often darkly comic) style of the text suggests the value of an ironic reading of Césaire's citation of colonial clichés. The anticipatory nature of this mimicry of the colonial archive—Césaire's use of such clichés in his own voice *before* he cites them—suggests a second level of imitation with a performative impact: once again, Césaire's citation of tropes of return and regression reflexively works with a temporality that produces a readerly sense of return when those tropes reappear in their "original," colonialist context.

Césaire's sampling from the colonial archive constitutes a quantitatively large and rhetorically central portion of his text, as he allows a wide swath of the European (primarily French) intelligentsia to damn itself with its racist and genocidal "discourse on colonialism." Moving from classical humanist texts through science and literature, Césaire arrives finally at the "newspaper jargon" of critic Emile Faguet and the return of the rhetoric of regression. Césaire cites extensively from Faguet: "The barbarian is of the same race, after all, as the Roman and the Greek. He is a cousin. The yellow man, the black man, is not our cousin at all. Here there is a real difference, a real distance, and a very great one: an *ethnological* distance. *After all, civilization has never yet been made except by whites*. . . . If Europe becomes yellow, there will certainly be a regression, a new period of darkness and confusion, that is, another Middle Ages" (qtd. in *Discourse* 50; emphasis and ellipses in Césaire).[13] Not only has Césaire anticipated the discourse of regression in his passage on the decivilization of Europe, but he has also anticipated the admittedly conventional reference to the Middle Ages. A few pages earlier, he writes, "Think of it! Ninety thousand dead in Madagascar! Indochina trampled underfoot, crushed to bits, assassinated, tortures brought back from the depths of the Middle Ages!" (48).

The link between race and regression comes up yet once more as Césaire continues his citation of colonial discourses and leads us back to Nazism. Surveying the French paper of record *Le Monde*, Césaire finds the writer and critic Yves Florenne reflecting on one of the newspaper's readers. Florenne responds to a teacher, who has been "contemplating two young half-breed girls, her pupils, [with] *a sense of pride at the feeling that there is a growing measure of integration with our French family*," and he asks, "Would her response be the same if she saw, in reverse [*à l'inverse*], France being integrated into the black family (or the yellow or red, it makes no difference), that is to say, becoming diluted, disappearing?" (qtd. in *Discourse* 63; emphasis in Césaire). Césaire's commentary on this passage highlights its crude biological racism and asks how such thinking persists despite the defeat of Nazism: "In short, cross-breeding—that is the enemy. No more social crises! No more economic crises! All that is left are racial crises! . . . That is what the French bourgeoisie has come to, five years after the defeat of Hitler! And it is precisely in that that its historic punishment lies: to be condemned, returning to it [*y revenant*] as though driven by a vice, to chew over [*à remâcher*: ruminate over] Hitler's vomit" (63). In this series of linked passages, Césaire exposes the prevalence of fantasies of reversal, regression, and dissolution in a France marked simultaneously by an ongoing (but soon to be defeated) colonial project and amnesia about the significance of its recent occupation at the hands of a genocidal, racist regime. (To make clear the connection between these two historical experiences, Césaire once refers to colonialism as "the European *occupation*" of Africa and Asia, a phrase that, especially for a French-speaking audience of the time, can only echo the Nazi occupation [45; Césaire's emphasis].)

Unable to face up either to the blood on their own colonial hands or to draw lessons from their own recent victimization by fascism, the purveyors of colonial fantasies of regression posit a unidirectional view of history that points only backward. Césaire's re-citing of such fantasies and rhetoric, by contrast, seeks to create a multidirectional map of France's implication in world history. While the colonial apologists describe an apocalyptic return to the past, Césaire reveals that apocalyptic violence has already taken place: the past returns in the present and continues to haunt Europe in its abject rumination over the Hitlerian catastrophe. Anticipating, repeating, and twisting the terms of colonial rhetoric, Césaire's multidirectional discourse on colonialism suggests that the etiology of the intra-European trauma of Nazism lies not only in the empirical colonial encounters tracked by Arendt but also crucially in European *fantasies* about colonial peoples. At all levels of the text, from the word through the sentence to the discourse as a whole, Césaire weaves together the past and the present, fantasy and fact, and violence inside and outside Europe. Out of selective amnesia, ignorance, and unconscious investments, he seeks to create an active memory of both colonial atrocities and Nazi genocide. While Arendt theorizes the return of colonial racism in Nazi genocide and Taslitzky tracks the return of Hitler in decolonization struggles, Césaire combines these two temporalities in a multidirectional rhetorical constellation and extracts them from the Eurocentric frames that, despite everything, remain in Arendt and Taslitzky. Césaire shows both the return of colonialism in Nazism and the postwar forgetting of a very recent Nazism, a forgetting that facilitates the virulent racism of late colonialist discourse by Florenne and others. In other words, Césaire's partial focus on a specifically *post*-Nazi colonial discourse suggests that colonial discourse is not singular, but mutates historically. Not only has imperialist violence produced a "decivilization" of Europe; European fascism inflects and infects colonial discourse in the age of decolonization.

Disavowing Violence: The *Choc en Retour*

Césaire's notions of regression and return are not merely deployed for the purposes of parody, as we can see when we shift from an anthropological and cultural register to a psychoanalytic one. Reading Césaire's anticolonial text through a psychoanalytic lens is by no means anachronistic given Césaire's interest in a surrealism that helps him to "summon up . . . unconscious forces," as he explained to René Depestre.[14] Seen from this angle, Césaire makes several additional contributions to thinking through the multidirectional relation of extra- and intra-European violence. While the Freudian concept of "regression" is relevant insofar as it concerns the "reemergence of the past in the present," that concept remains close to the problems of Eurocentrism underscored by LaCapra with respect to the regression to barbarism.[15] Although this concept of regression is not entirely absent from the *Discourse*, emphasizing the degree to which Césaire links the decivilization of Europe to the question of knowledge opens up another, more productive path. Throughout the *Discourse*, "regression" signals knowledge denied, as evidenced, for example, by the repetitive invocation of "each time . . . in France they accept the fact" in the long passage cited above. "Acceptance" signals here a disinclination to take in the violence evoked. The text thus creates a constellation of "barbarism" and "civilized" denial that evokes Freud's notion of *disavowal* more strongly than the psychoanalytic sense of regression. Disavowal, as Laplanche and Pontalis clarify, "consists in the subject's refusing to recognise the reality of a traumatic perception" (118). As Freud makes clear in his essay "Fetishism," disavowal can be linked both to neuroses and psychoses.[16] While an absolute refusal to acknowledge a traumatic reality can lead to psychosis, other forms of defense against trauma can lead to more "ordinary" responses. Thus fetishism, for instance, involves a peculiar psychic state or "double attitude" in which the subject both knows and refuses knowledge of the traumatic truth: "When the fetish comes to life, so to speak, some process has been suddenly interrupted—it reminds one of the abrupt halt made by memory in traumatic amnesias. In the case of the fetish, too, interest is held up at a certain point—what is possibly the last impression received before the uncanny traumatic one is preserved as a fetish" ("Fetishism" 201). Although formulated at the level of the individual psyche, Freud's notion of disavowal links trauma, memory, and the question of knowledge in a way that is suggestive for analyzing the relation between colonial and metropolitan violence and the disavowal that Césaire links to the decivilization of Europe.

The suggestiveness of Freudian concepts for Césaire's project becomes more striking when we think through the return of colonial policy in Nazi genocide as a psychoanalytically inflected, traumatic temporality. Césaire's passage on the descent of Europe into "savagery [*l'ensauvagement*]" culminates in his first articulation of the *choc en retour*: "And then one fine day the bourgeois is awakened by a terrific boomerang effect [*un formidable choc en retour*]: the gestapos are busy, the prisons fill up, the torturers standing around the racks invent, refine, discuss.... Yes, it would be worthwhile to study clinically, in detail, the steps taken by Hitler and Hitlerism and to reveal to the very distinguished, very humanistic, very Christian bourgeois of the twentieth century that without his being aware of it, he has a Hitler inside him, that Hitler *inhabits* him, that Hitler is his *demon*" (*Discourse* 36). With his invocation of what the translator names a boomerang effect but which we prefer to preserve as *choc en retour*, Césaire renders Hitler uncanny—the strange and aberrant (genocidal violence) become all too familiar, while the familiar (European civilization) is estranged and shown to be corrupt at the core. In this passage, the *Discourse* moves closer to the temporality to which LaCapra opposes regression: the return of the repressed. In Freud, the defense mechanisms, including disavowal and repression, are always only partially successful and give way inevitably to various returns that represent displaced versions of what has been avoided. Indeed, in this passage Césaire echoes Freud's description of the return of repressed in *Beyond the Pleasure Principle*. Freud writes that "manifestations of a compulsion to repeat ... exhibit to a high degree an instinctual [*Triebhaft*] character and, when they act in opposition to the pleasure principle, give the appearance of some 'daemonic' force at work."[17] In LaCapra's nonorthodox extension of Freud, the notion of the return of the repressed proves useful for understanding the persistence of extreme violence in supposedly civilized societies. It avoids the colonial fantasies of regression and "is related to a very different understanding of temporality in which any features of society deemed desirable must be recurrently rewon, and less desirable ones pose a continual threat that reappears in different guises over time" (3n). Césaire gives historical specificity to LaCapra's general model and adds a significant component to attempts to understand Nazism and the inability of Europe to defeat it until unprecedented destruction had already been wrought: the "continual threat" that returns "in different guises" to a supposedly civilized Europe derives not simply from some unconscious psychic potential but from colonialism itself, a centuries-long project of violence that Europeans have considered with the double attitude of disavowal. Connecting Hitler to colonialism allows Césaire to unveil Hitler's function as a fetish in European discourse, as the psychic figure that "interrupts" understanding and enables "the abrupt halt made by memory in traumatic amnesias" ("Fetishism" 201).

In addition, invoking a temporality of return instead of one of regression avoids the positing of a normative progressive narrative. Such a narrative tends to keep Europe in place as the telos of civilization and to render genocidal policies in the colonies or at "home" as aberrations that do not ultimately impinge on underlying notions of progress. Although it is not clear whether Césaire would have known Benjamin's writings in 1950, it is striking that the phrase *choc en retour* appears in "Sur le concept d'histoire," the French version of Benjamin's "Theses on the Philosophy of History," in precisely the passage key to Arendt's methodology in *The Origins of Totalitarianism*. The *choc en retour* (*einen Chock* in German; "shock" in English) is the force that the "arrest" of thought produces and that leads to the crystallization of the constellation into a monad.[18] This shock is critical to materialist methodology, according to Benjamin, because it allows the critic to grasp time as dense with overlapping possibilities and dangers—an understanding of the present as, in the vocabulary developed here, the site of multidirectional memory. Benjamin argues that a progressive, historicist methodology has proven unable to account for the threat of fascism, and he traces that failure back to historicism's conception of "homogeneous, empty time." In contrast, the multidirectional temporality of Benjamin's crystallized monad provides a way of coming to terms with political extremity because it does not assume that "civilization" has left "barbarism" behind. We have seen how Arendt's account of Africa reproduces aspects of this progressive narrative despite her Benjamin-inspired attempts to employ a methodology of crystallization and constellation. In Césaire, the *choc en retour* works somewhat differently. Rather than constituting part of Césaire's methodological arsenal, as it is for Benjamin, the *choc en retour* is part of Césaire's *diagnosis* of Europe: the shock amounts to a sign of European traumatization. Because Europe has disavowed the violence it has perpetrated in the colonies, it remains unready to confront the return of genocidal violence to Europe—it remains without the sufficient *Angstbereitschaft* (preparedness for anxiety), as Freud called it, which might ward off or cushion the traumatic blow.[19]

Just as two forms of temporality coexist in Arendt's attempt to theorize totalitarianism—one tied to narrative and one to "fragmentary historiography"—so in Césaire's *Discourse* the ironically cited regression model is joined by a more disruptive, uncanny mode premised on traumatic return. In LaCapra's terms, the violence in the colonies returns "precisely as the repressed or as what *seemed* totally out of place and *unheimlich*" (39). Within this uncanny context, the notion that the Christian bourgeois has a Hitler inside him is not simply the banal universalization of Nazism that tends to exculpate the actual perpetrators for their deeds. Rather, Césaire refers to a very specific historical situation. He underlines the extent to which the European humanist subject has been constituted within conditions of violence to which he has not necessarily had direct and conscious access. Césaire was more poet than political thinker, and both poet and politician more than he was a historian. In other words, he doesn't provide a detailed historical explanation of how the uncanny transfer of violence takes place. Rather, his task is primarily critical. His concept of the *choc en retour* is meant to force an encounter between European and colonial histories in such a way that it becomes impossible for Europe to remain blind to its agency in the world. The first step in such a process will be a recognition of the blockages that mitigate against grasping the intertwinement of histories.[20]

Césaire's account of Europe's indirect access to a violence constitutive of its identity recalls the situation described by Fredric Jameson in "Modernism and Imperialism," in which the lifeworld of European subjects during the stage of high imperialism is made possible by relations of production in the colonies to which they remain blind: "A significant structural segment of the economic system as a whole is now located elsewhere, beyond the metropolis, outside of the daily life and existential experience of the home country." For Jameson, this produces a situation in which those subjects are marked by an "inability to grasp the way the system functions as a whole" and are thus unable to produce a cognitive map of their social situation (50–51). Césaire supplements this account, arguing that relations of violence underwrite—and even exceed—relations of exploitation. Just as the European subject is necessarily blind to the social production of his or her own well-being, a blindness that "no enlargement of personal experience . . . no intensity of self-examination" can overcome (Jameson 51), so that subject proves unable to recognize how the violence in the periphery necessary to secure that well-being will migrate to the metropolis and undermine metropolitan well-being. Here Césaire is once again partially in tune with Arendt, who considers imperialism a practice that, while initially undertaken for economic motives, will ultimately subordinate utilitarian reason to the demands of the racial community, thus contributing to the preconditions for genocidal violence.

In the course of probing the blindness of the metropolitan subject, Césaire highlights a temporal structure—the *choc en retour*—that is also present in Conrad's *Heart of Darkness*, if in somewhat attenuated form. Despite being written decades before the Nazis' "Final Solution," Conrad's novella may itself be one of the sources for the idea of "boomerang effects" and reverse shocks connecting imperialism and the Nazi genocide. Indeed, Césaire's *Discourse* ends on a particularly Conradian note. *Heart of Darkness*, which had been translated into French as *Le coeur des ténèbres* decades before Césaire wrote, concludes with an image connecting Europe to darkness.[21] In the final paragraph, after Marlow has finished recounting his tale of African adventure and return to Europe, the unnamed narrator himself returns to the text and looks out over the Thames: "The offing was barred by a black bank of clouds, and the tranquil waterway leading to the uttermost ends of the earth flowed sombre under an overcast sky—seemed to lead into the heart of an immense darkness."[22] Combining blockage (the offing barred) and access (the tranquil waterway), this final image holds together the key elements the novel contributes to a thinking of the boomerang effect relating metropole and colony. In *Discourse on Colonialism*, just before Césaire names the proletariat as the true subjects of history in the closing envoi (a point to which we will return), he writes that "unless it becomes the awakener of countries and civilizations . . . Europe will have deprived itself of its last chance and, with its own hands, drawn up over itself the pall of mortal darkness [*les mortelles ténèbres*]" (*Discourse* 77–78; *Discours* [1950] 61). In closing, Césaire scrambles the terms of Conrad's novel. Conrad assumes a deadly connection between center and periphery, yet situates the violence of that connection elsewhere, in the darkness at the end of the waterway, somewhere beyond the metropole. Césaire, by contrast, seeks a missing, nonviolent articulation between Europe and its colonies, but in the meantime locates the continuing potential for darkness in a reflexive verb and future perfect tense ("Europe . . . will have drawn up over itself [*se sera . . . de ses propres mains tiré*]"). The reflexivity and temporality of the verb hint strongly at Europe's likely self-infliction of further violence and yet refuse to naturalize Europe as inevitably following a particular course (as will the river Thames). A modicum of possibility remains, even for Europe.

Despite these significant differences, though, Conrad's text still provides suggestive hints at how the boomerang effect works and, thus, how we might think of the *choc en retour*. The end of *Heart of Darkness* not only details the "becoming savage" of the ivory agent Kurtz, a European cut off from "civilization" in the jungles of Africa (a significant component of Arendt's borrowing from it), but also tracks the transmission of that savagery back into the imperial metropolis (a significant component of Césaire's argument in the *Discourse*). In the novel's final pages, Marlow returns to the "sepulchral city" (70) from which he had set out on his adventure—recognizable as Brussels—and there encounters Kurtz's "Intended," his fiancée. As Marlow approaches the door, on his way to deliver Kurtz's last testament, he is haunted by a return of the "remarkable man," Kurtz (73):

I thought his memory was like the other memories of the dead that accumulate in every man's life—a vague impress on the brain of shadows that had fallen on it in their swift and final passage; but before the high and ponderous door, between the tall houses of a street as still and decorous as a well-kept alley in a cemetery, I had a vision of him on the stretcher, opening his mouth voraciously, as if to devour all the earth with all its mankind. He lived then before me; he lived as much as he had ever lived—a shadow insatiable of splendid appearances, of frightful realities; a shadow darker than the shadow of the night, and draped nobly in the folds of a gorgeous eloquence. The vision seemed to enter the house with me—the stretcher, the phantom-bearers, the wild crowd of obedient worshipers, the gloom of the forests, the glitter of the reach between the murky bends, the beat of the drum, regular and muffled like the beating of a heart—the heart of a conquering darkness. It was a moment of triumph for the wilderness, an invading and vengeful rush which, it seemed to me, I would have to keep back alone for the salvation of another soul [that is, that of the Intended]. (72)

Conrad portrays the interpenetration of colony and metropolis in this passage as a matter of both space and time. The temporal return of memory and the repetitive beating of the drum-cum-heart haunt Marlow at the same time that a space-invading vengeful appearance shadows him. Conrad makes the contamination of feminized domestic space allegorized here explicit soon after, when the return of Kurtz's ghostly presence is redoubled through the shadowing of the Intended by Kurtz's African lover: "I saw him clearly enough then. I shall see this eloquent phantom as long as I live, and I shall see her [the Intended], too, a tragic and familiar Shade, resembling in this gesture [of putting out her arms] another one [the African lover], tragic also, and bedecked with powerless charms, stretching bare brown arms over the glitter of the infernal stream, the stream of darkness" (75). In this world of phantoms and shades, Africans and Europeans find themselves part of a layered, multidimensional world of resemblances.

These final passages of the novel exhibit an extraordinary, but ambivalent, empathic reach, with Marlow, just as much as the two women he depicts and links, stretching out his arms to connect disparate geographies. The female body serves to bridge two tragic histories, that of the colony and metropole or of black and white women, but it simultaneously provides the vehicle for a discourse of shadowy, racial contamination. Whether Marlow, the novel's unnamed narrator, or even its author knows what is at stake, this conclusion maps out the logic of the boomerang effect. It demonstrates not simply the shadowing of the metropole by colonial violence, which Arendt too grasps, but also reveals the necessary blindness or silence that functions as the vector of transmission. Marlow understands his role as that of protector—he saves the feminized homeland from confrontation with the conquering darkness of Kurtz's exploits in Africa by shielding the homeland with a lie. Instead of revealing to the Intended Kurtz's actual last words—"The horror! The horror!"—he tells her, "The last word he pronounced was—your name" (Conrad 75). But it is precisely Marlow's lie, his inability to convey to the Intended and to the residents of the metropole the true "horror" of the colonial encounter, that will transmit that truth in an indirect manner, as Césaire would later recognize. The lie enables the boomerang effect or *choc en retour* by creating a screen behind which colonial violence can continue and thus become lethal in new ways, in new spaces—before ultimately returning "home."

While Césaire thus shares with Arendt and Conrad a certain notion of the boomerang effect or the shocking return of distant violence, important distinctions remain within that spatio-temporal trope. Both Arendt and Conrad premise the savagery in Europe on the savagery in Africa—yet the nature and source of "African" savagery remain ambiguous. Do they mean to identify the savagery of what the Europeans did to the Africans as the crucial element? Or is the savagery of Europe's African victims the source and content of what is transmitted back to the metropolis? While both Arendt and Conrad recognize the violence of colonialism—and are in fact two of its most compelling European narrators in the first half of the twentieth century—the logic of their accounts suggests that that violence has in some sense been provoked by the "worldlessness" or "culturelessness" of the victims. Like *Heart of Darkness* and *The Origins of Totalitarianism*, Césaire's *Discourse on Colonialism* radically puts into question European notions of the human. But, unlike the other two texts, the *Discourse* does not rest such questioning on the supposedly shocking experience of discovering "natural man." In a passage from the 1955 edition of the *Discourse* that echoes Arendt's account of the "killing of man's individuality" in the camps and resonates with the "horrors" of *Heart of Darkness*, Césaire links the animalization of Africans to that of Europeans in another articulation of *choc en retour*:

If I have recalled a few details of these hideous butcheries, it is by no means because I take a morbid delight in them, but because I think that these heads of men, these collections of ears, those burned houses . . . are not to be so easily disposed of. They prove that colonization, I repeat, dehumanizes even the most civilized man; that colonial activity, colonial enterprise, colonial conquest, which is based on contempt for the native and justified by that contempt, inevitably tends to change him who undertakes it; that the colonizer, who in order to ease his conscience gets into the habit of seeing the other man as *an animal* [*la bête*], accustoms himself to treating him like an animal, and tends objectively to transform *himself* into an animal. It is this result, this boomerang effect [*ce choc en retour*] of colonization, that I wanted to point out. (*Discourse* 41; *Discours* [1955] 16–17)

Césaire's account of the colonial reverse shock differs from Arendt's boomerang in not assuming a site of nature as lying at the origin of genocidal violence. Rather, Césaire describes a routinization of contempt that acts simultaneously in the external world and in the colonial subject. At stake here is not the animality of the other, but instead the habit-forming procedures of colonization that produce an unexpectedly traumatic backlash in the metropole.

It is true that a certain idealization of the precolonial can be found in Césaire's writings. For example, even in the *Discourse*, Césaire talks of the "natural *economies* that have been disrupted" by colonialism and the "communal societies . . . that were not only ante-capitalist . . . but also *anti-capitalist*" (*Discourse* 43–44). Yet Césaire's critique of colonialism does not rely on the positing of this prelapsarian vision, as Arendt's notion of the emergence of racial society in Africa does; the path of destruction clearly starts on the side of the Europeans regardless of how one characterizes the precolonial state of Africa or the Antilles. Arendt employs the notion of shock to describe cultured Europeans' response to their encounter with "worldless" Africans. In detailing Europeans' preexisting contempt and developing habits of perception, by contrast, Césaire situates the colonial encounter within a space predetermined by racial fantasies and ideologies.[23] The encounter itself still produces, as in Arendt, transformations in the colonizers that throw into question the limits of the human. Instead of mystifying the determining, driving force behind the encounter, Césaire draws attention to its basis in enterprise, conquest, and racial contempt.

To put the process described by Césaire in the previous long passage in the terms developed by Giorgio Agamben, colonialism blurs the distinction between the state of exception and the norm and thus collapses the opposition between "bare life" and political existence and between the animal and the human. Agamben shares with Césaire the desire not to "naturalize" the natural—not to render some humans fundamentally external to political existence, as Arendt seems to. Yet, besides leaving colonialism utterly outside his account, Agamben also depicts modernity as structurally defined by "the inclusion of bare life in the political realm," an inclusion he characterizes as "the original—if concealed—nucleus of sovereign power."[24] By locating an "original nucleus" in the structure of sovereignty itself, Agamben excludes colonialism (and all other historical sequences) from consideration not simply contingently but necessarily. Through the concept of the *choc en retour*, by contrast, Césaire recaptures the temporality of the event—here the event of violent colonial encounter. This temporality is not singular but rather ripples out from the encounter to produce and inflect other events—events such as the Nazi genocide, whose legacies in turn ripple back and inflect the death throes of colonialism.

Rethinking Trauma with Césaire and Fanon

Exploring the resonance of the *choc en retour* has taken us to the center of Césaire's contribution to the project of conceptualizing multidirectionality. The *Discourse*'s most significant legacy for that project lies in a new understanding of the two key terms that make up the *choc en retour*: that is, in Césaire's mobilization of discourses of shock and return to unsettle binary and linear conceptions of culture, violence, and history and to construct in their stead a model of relationality and ripple effects. Since the categories of "shock" and "return" are also central to the contemporary theorization of trauma, *Discourse* provides an occasion to engage with the multidirectional potential and Eurocentric pitfalls of trauma studies. The importance of rethinking trauma studies from a multidirectional perspective derives from several complementary issues: the centrality of traumatic histories to contemporary struggles over memory and identity (as evidenced by the example from Walter Benn Michaels that opens this book); the strong claims made by trauma theorists for the comparative dimensions of trauma and the empathetic possibilities of their own methodology; the close links between trauma theory and Holocaust studies; and the growing interest in trauma among postcolonial critics. Because trauma constitutes a seemingly ubiquitous modern phenomenon owned neither by a single discipline nor a single field, many scholars have sought in it a link between disparate histories and geo-cultural sites. Yet, at the same time, trauma often functions as the object of a competitive struggle, a form of cultural capital that bestows moral privileges.

Césaire's text helps us to elude the moralizing that often accompanies these discussions. It provides an unexpected perspective on two allegations that have been at the center of criticism of the trauma theory that has reemerged since the 1990s in the work of Cathy Caruth and her associates: that trauma theory elides distinctions between perpetrators and victims and that it remains trapped within a Eurocentric framework. Like *The Origins of Totalitarianism*, with its vivid depictions of the "shocking" encounter of Europeans with Africans, and *Discourse on Colonialism*, with its imagining of the *choc en retour*, Caruth's *Unclaimed Experience: Trauma, Narrative, and History* (1996), one of the ur-texts of contemporary thinking about trauma, also derives some of its central concepts from a scenario of perpetrator trauma.

When Caruth introduces her field-defining book, she begins with an analysis of Freud's reading of Tasso's *Jerusalem Delivered*; she focuses on the "parable" of Tancred and Clorinda that Freud discusses.[25] In this story from Tasso's epic, recounted by Freud in *Beyond the Pleasure Principle*, the "hero, Tancred, unwittingly kills his beloved Clorinda in a duel" and then, after her burial, "slashes with his sword a tall tree" from which "the voice of Clorinda, whose soul is imprisoned in the tree, is heard complaining that he has wounded his beloved again" (Freud, qtd. in Caruth, *Unclaimed Experience* 2). Caruth understands this odd story as emblematic of Freud's theory of trauma: "The actions of Tancred, wounding his beloved in a battle and then, unknowingly, seemingly by chance, wounding her again, evocatively represent in Freud's text the way that the experience of trauma repeats itself, exactly and unremittingly, through the unknowing acts of the survivor and against his very will" (2). For Caruth, however, the example of Tancred and Clorinda may even "excee[d] . . . the limits of Freud's conceptual or conscious theory of trauma" insofar as it draws our attention to "the moving and sorrowful *voice* that cries out, a voice that is paradoxically released *through the wound*." In other words, "Tancred does not only repeat his act but, in repeating it, he for the first time hears a voice that cries out to him to see what he has done" (*Unclaimed Experience* 2–3). The implications that Caruth draws from this story have marked many discussions of trauma in the years since: "Just as Tancred does not hear the voice of Clorinda until the second wounding, so trauma is not locatable in the simple violent or original event in an individual's past, but rather in the way that its very unassimilated nature—the way it was precisely *not known* in the first instance—returns to haunt the survivor later on" (4). In the wake of Caruth's book—and her equally influential edited collection *Trauma: Explorations in Memory* (1995)—a notion of trauma as an individual's repetitive, haunted, "unclaimed" experience of unknowable violence has found its way into scholarship across the humanities.

Yet, almost immediately, Caruth's theory of trauma and, especially, her discussion of Tancred and Clorinda generated controversy and strong opposition. In *Trauma: A Genealogy*, Ruth Leys provides an extended critique of Caruth's theory that culminates in a rereading of the Tancred and Clorinda parable.[26] Leys takes Caruth to task for representing perpetrators as victims of trauma in the Tasso discussion. While, in Caruth's reading, *Tancred* is the traumatized subject, Leys argues that in the story "it is not Tancred but *Clorinda* who is the indisputable victim of a wounding" (294).[27] This is far from Leys's only objection to Caruth's theory of trauma, but it leads to her most dramatic point and the argument that closes the main text of her book: "If, according to [Caruth's] analysis, the murdered Tancred can become the victim of the trauma and the voice of Clorinda testimony to *his* wound, then Caruth's logic would turn other perpetrators into victims too—for example, it would turn the executioners of Jews into victims and the 'cries' of the Jews into testimony to the trauma suffered by the Nazis" (297). Concerned especially with the power dynamics that pit colonizers against the colonized, postcolonial critics have vigorously seconded Leys's critique of the apparent collapse of distinction between perpetrators and victims. In a fascinating essay on African trauma novels, Amy Novak has even noted that the parable of Tancred and Clorinda has an unacknowledged colonial dimension: it concerns the slaying of an Ethiopian woman by a European crusader.[28]

We will return to the colonial question in Tancred and Clorinda below. But concerns about perpetration have not exhausted the debates concerning the postcolonial potential of trauma theory. Beyond Caruth's alleged elision of the specificity of subject positions and power differentials, some postcolonial critics have also added a further complaint: following feminist psychologist Laura Brown, they argue that the "event"- or "accident"-based model of trauma associated with Caruth assumes the circumstances of white, Western privilege and distracts from "insidious" forms of trauma that involve everyday, repeated forms of traumatizing violence, such as sexism, racism, and colonialism.[29] Such critics often supplement Brown's influential essay (collected, however, in Caruth's own volume *Trauma: Explorations in Memory* [1995]!) with discussion of the work of Césaire's one-time student Frantz Fanon. In Fanon critics find a theory of collective colonial trauma that offers an alternative to the individualizing, psychoanalytic model proffered by Caruth.[30]

Critics of trauma studies raise important issues and highlight the need for a more cosmopolitan and politically savvy trauma studies. But considering their objections in the context of Césaire's work provides a surprising rereading of both trauma studies and postcolonial approaches. Most significantly, Césaire, like Arendt, shows himself interested in the question of perpetrator trauma. However odd Caruth's decision to use Tasso's parable to open her book on trauma may be, the parable has implications that some of Caruth's critics have not yet acknowledged. Leys's and other critics' objections derive in part from a category error. Most crucially, Leys elides the category of "victim" with that of the traumatized subject. Similarly, Novak writes, "Tancred does not experience the trauma, Clorinda does" (32). However, while one speaks conventionally, as Leys does, of a "victim of trauma," such a formulation of victimization has a different ontological status from the distinction between perpetrators and victims with which it is often confused. Thus, on the one hand, we can conceive of a victim who has not been traumatized—either because the victimization did not produce the kind of disruption that trauma ought to signify in order to have conceptual purchase, or because the victim has been murdered, as in the case of Clorinda. The dead are not traumatized, they are dead; trauma implies some "other" mode of living on.[31] On the other hand, being traumatized does not necessarily imply victim status. As LaCapra has frequently pointed out, perpetrators of extreme violence can suffer from trauma—but this makes them no less guilty of their crimes and does not entail claims to victimization or even demands on our sympathy.[32] Indeed, much work on trauma from Freud on has taken up traumatized subjects who may (also) be perpetrators of extreme violence, especially soldiers. The categories of victim and perpetrator derive from either a legal or a moral discourse, but the concept of trauma emerges from a diagnostic realm that lies beyond guilt and innocence or good and evil. While everyday usage of these terms understandably lacks precision, scholarly approaches should carefully distinguish different discursive domains. Precisely because it has the potential to cloud ethical and political judgments, trauma should not be a category that confirms moral value—as Leys and Novak, but not Caruth, seem to imply.

Césaire's discourse on shock and return in a European framework builds on this insight about the possibility of perpetrator trauma to undermine Eurocentric knowledge claims. The disavowal of colonial violence Césaire tracks in *Discourse on Colonialism* produces a return shock that is no less traumatic for being locatable in a historical logic. The problem with Arendt's formulation, by contrast, is less that it sees a potential for shock and trauma on the side of the colonizers, but that it sometimes seems to locate the "cause" of that trauma in alleged characteristics of Africans and that it seems unable to imagine the concomitant traumatization (as opposed to murder) of the colonized. Despite her tracing of the boomerang effect of colonial racism, she doesn't attain a multidirectional understanding of the legacies of violence; the problem is not her conception of perpetrators as traumatized, but her inability to see colonialism's victims as subjects themselves capable of culture or susceptible to trauma. Césaire's focus on the shock of colonialism's return to the metropole attempts to bring together different scenes of violence and trauma without confusing perpetrators and victims.

Césaire also helps us to think through the second objection to Caruth's version of trauma theory—that its model of trauma remains tied to the expectations of a privileged Western worldview and ignores insidious, everyday forms of trauma. Traumatic violence in the *Discourse* appears in both eventlike and insidious modes and in the context of both perpetration and victimization; that is, I would describe what I have called the ripple effects of extreme violence and the *choc en retour* as a kind of ligament *between* these different understandings of trauma. Indeed, in Césaire, as Caruth predicts without explicitly demonstrating, trauma does function as "the very link between cultures."[33] However, this function confers no moral capital; nor does it serve as a universalist or humanist vision of harmony. To the contrary, the "link" trauma makes serves as a vector for the transmission of racial violence.

While drawing on psychoanalytic concepts, Césaire's text is not primarily psychological in orientation; it doesn't attempt to develop a full-blown theory of trauma. But the *Discourse* does suggest a multidirectional way of thinking about traumatic disruptions that Fanon seems to follow and build on in *Black Skin, White Masks*, a book published just two years later with an epigraph from his teacher Césaire's polemic. In "The Negro and Psychopathology," the influential and oft-cited chapter on colonial trauma from *Black Skin, White Masks,* Fanon moves back and forth between pathologies that affect blacks and those that affect whites in a racist society.[34] On the one hand, Fanon details the traumas that arise from the black child's confrontation with and internalization of a racist imaginary through education, popular culture, and contact with the dominant white society (cf. 145–50). On the other hand, Fanon proposes an account of the traumas of racial privilege. The Negro, writes Fanon, is "a phobogenic object, a stimulus to anxiety" (151). The racist imaginary not only wounds *blacks* psychically; according to Fanon, the phobogenic black man (and Fanon does refer specifically to the black *man*) creates traumatic phobias in *white men and women*. Drawing attention to both of these racialized poles, the long chapter begins by arguing that the psychic and social environment of the "man of color" is the "opposite" of that found in Europe, and he ends with a case study of a white French woman so terrorized by "the myth of the Negro" that she ends up institutionalized and unable "to resume a normal life in society" (143, 204, 209). But the trajectory of the chapter is by no means linear: as in much of Fanon's text, the movement of the argument is better described as multidirectional. That multidirectional movement back and forth between pathologies suffered by blacks and whites in racist, colonial society indicates that trauma in *Black Skin, White Masks* is fundamentally *relational*—psychopathologies affect both victims and perpetrators (and accomplices or beneficiaries) of racism, albeit in different ways. Fanon's emphasis on relationality does not relativize the moral or political meaning of racism or colonialism; rather, he suggests, as implicitly does Caruth, that questions of moral and political responsibility do not map onto psychic disorder in any clear way. Political context disrupts psychic order across the board. Colonial and race societies intensively police relations among social groups and seek to produce various kinds of segregation, of course. But Fanon's analysis reveals how, nevertheless, the traumas associated with racism create a psychically and socially relational intimacy across groups.

To this relational account of different traumas within racialized societies (which Fanon weaves together without explicit comment), Fanon adds another comparative dimension. Besides moving back and forth between "white" and "black" traumas, the chapter on "psychopathology" includes extensive discussion of anti-Semitism and traumas suffered by and associated with Jews.[35] If racism is traumatogenic, it is multidirectionally so. When Fanon published *Black Skin, White Masks* in 1952, World War II (which Fanon fought in) and the Nazi genocide were still recent events. With frequent reference to Sartre's *Anti-Semite and Jew* (*Réflexions sur la question juive*; 1948), Fanon carefully relates and distinguishes anti-Semitism and anti-Black racism, but the distinctions he makes are based not on difference between an event model and a model of everyday trauma, as postcolonial critics might lead one to believe. Rather, those distinctions turn on the different place occupied by the Jew and the "Negro" in the racist imaginary. If, Fanon writes, "to suffer from a phobia of Negroes is to be afraid of the biological" or sexual, to fear Jews is to possess a phobia about the "intellectual danger" that accompanies "civilization" (165). The intimacy of racism and anti-Semitism—and thus of blacks and Jews—supplements the account of white and black traumas in the chapter.

Yet Fanon's text proves ambivalent on the question of how to relate black and Jewish traumas. In so doing he seems to follow one of the odd, but easily overlooked dimensions of Césaire's famous formulation of Nazi genocide as colonialism come home: that "the white man" terrorized by Nazism is not precisely the same white man as the one responsible for colonialism. The *choc en retour*, in other words, claims many victims—such as Eastern Europe's Jews—who played no role whatsoever in the colonial project being replicated in the metropole. *Black Skin, Whites Masks* works similarly. While Fanon sometimes points to what Jews and blacks share, he also often "assimilates" Jews to "the white man." On the one hand, Fanon links blacks and Jews as "brother[s] in misery" (122) because of parallels between European racism and anti-Semitism. On the other hand, because of the primacy Fanon grants to the "racial epidermal schema" (112) in the constitution of the colonial subject, he ultimately separates the experience of blacks from that of Jews by virtue of Jews' allegedly greater ability to pass as white:

The Jew can be unknown in his Jewishness. He is not wholly what he is. . . . His actions, his behavior are the final determinant. He is a white man, and, apart from some rather debatable characteristics, he can sometimes go unnoticed. . . . Granted, the Jews are harassed—what am I thinking of? They are hunted down, exterminated, cremated. But these are little family quarrels. The Jew is disliked from the moment he is tracked down. But in my case everything takes on a new guise. I am given no chance. I am overdetermined from without. I am the slave not of the "idea" that others have of me but of my own appearance. (115–16)

Like Césaire, Fanon clearly employs an ironic rhetoric, here laced with litotes, which cannot be read literally. Nevertheless, even leaving aside the deliberate minimization of Nazi genocide as a "family quarrel," Fanon's passage ignores the contradictions and legacies of anti-Semitism that make it a very peculiar kind of family affair. On the one hand, seen from the present, Fanon's distinction between the central role that the visual plays in antiblack racism and the centrality of ideas and ideology in anti-Semitism seems like commonsense. On the other hand, this commonsense account amounts to a surprisingly unhistorical theory of Jewish visibility; it ignores the relative consistency of the image of the Jew over time, the frequent association of Jews with various "anomalous" physical traits, including blackness (as demonstrated, for example, in the work of Sander Gilman), and the—at the time Fanon and Césaire were writing—still recent production and mobilization of a visible, highly biologized, and even sexualized Jewish difference in the context of a genocidal project.[36] In addition, whether employed in the early 1950s by Césaire and Fanon or today in the works of some postcolonial critics, this simplified binary between blacks and white Jews risks homogenizing Europe and casting blacks definitively outside European space.

Césaire and Fanon each provide critical resources for a post-Holocaust, postcolonial theory of trauma. In linking colonialism to Nazism and racism to anti-Semitism they prove themselves far ahead of their time; they are also part of the countertradition that *Multidirectional Memory* seeks to recover. Yet their ambivalence about Jewish difference and about its relation to blackness also makes visible ambivalences that continue to haunt both postcolonial studies and trauma theory. Although I possess no evidence that Césaire and Fanon were readers of Tasso (although this is far from impossible), Freud's and Caruth's example of the Tancred and Clorinda parable may unwittingly provide a useful figuration of the possibilities and problems of thinking trauma multidirectionally. For Clorinda, as David Quint specifies in an extended literary and historical exploration of Tasso's sources for *Jerusalem Liberated*, "is a mass of overlapping and contradictory identities: a woman warrior, a white Ethiopian, a person of Christian birth and Muslim nurture" (244). The daughter of a black Ethiopian Christian mother, whose prayer to Saint George eventuated in the birth of a white child, Clorinda was raised by a Muslim eunuch and only baptized as a Christian after being mortally wounded by Tancred in the battle over Jerusalem. Besides drawing on and modifying literary sources such as *Orlando Furioso*, Tasso also wrote his epic in the context of the sixteenth-century rediscovery of Ethiopian Christianity, a rediscovery that brought into European consciousness a potential ally against the Muslim infidel and an ultimately troubling emblem of heresy because of the Ethiopians' divergent practices regarding baptism that separated them from Roman orthodoxy. In other words, Clorinda's "long-deferred baptism" after the battle "represents... the conversion not simply of a Muslim to the Christian faith, but of a schismatic Ethiopian to the Church of Rome.... The pagan foe Clorinda turns out to be a Christian heretic: the enemy without is really the enemy within" (Quint 245). Caruth, we recall, focuses especially on Tancred's response to Clorinda's unveiling and his double slaying of her as emblematic of trauma's repetitive haunting. In Quint's reading, "Tancred's reaction suggests the bad conscience of Tasso's epic, a chink in its ideological armor. For how can one both love and kill one's neighbor, especially when it transpires, in Clorinda's case, that the neighbor is a fellow, albeit a schismatic, Christian? The *Liberata* exalts a militant papacy whose universalism is an alibi for empire and whose spiritual power is a disguise for temporal violence" (246). Quint's reading confirms the postcolonial reading of Clorinda by Novak but also adds several additional pieces to the puzzle. Rather than contradicting Caruth's deployment of Tasso, however, I would argue that the imperial subtext of the parable can supplement her understanding of trauma as a link between cultures.

As a source text for contemporary theories of trauma in the wake of the Holocaust and colonialism, this complicated scenario has a series of implications. Tasso's parable figures the multidirectionality of identity, violence, and cultural memory. It stages the permeable relation, in cultural texts as well as in history, between enemies "inside" and "outside" of empire as well as between "perpetrators" and "victims" and "enemies" and "friends." It draws attention to the slippages between "black" and "white," but also indicates the power of those categories to shape and even produce racialized, traumatic histories. It locates race and cultural difference in relation to religious wars that cut across Christian, Muslim, and Jew, and it demonstrates the proximity of such racial and religious wars to the violence of imperial universalism. When read in relation to debates about colonialism, racism, genocide, and trauma, the story of Tancred and Clorinda becomes a parable of the need for a multidirectional trauma theory in the era of Holocaust and decolonization: a comparative theory that would track the interconnectedness of different perpetrators and different victims in overlapping, yet distinct, scenarios of extreme violence. With its notion of the *choc en retour*, Césaire's *Discourse on Colonialism*, as well as the further development advanced in Fanon's *Black Skin, White Masks*, provides some of the resources for such a theory, but it also remains caught in its own limiting universalist discourse: French Communist Party Marxism.

Between Marxism and Multidirectional Memory

Césaire's *Discourse on Colonialism* can be seen as a reflection on multiple encounters: the traumatic encounter between Europe and Africa; the traumatic intra-European encounter between fascism and its victims; a potential nonviolent encounter of cross-cultural contact hinted at in its critique of the "manner" in which the contact actually took place (45); and the aesthetic and intellectual encounter that all of Césaire's texts mobilize. In interrogating these encounters, Césaire is indebted not only to a surrealist aesthetic and to psychoanalytic conceptualizations but also, as his emphasis on enterprise and conquest makes clear, to a Marxism that he is simultaneously struggling against. As the paintings of Taslitzky and Fougeron also illustrate, Marxism provides one conceptual frame through which to stage the relatedness of history; it provides a universal narrative within which to situate seemingly disparate histories. Indeed, Césaire's famous argument that the uniqueness of the Nazi genocide lies only in its application to Europe of techniques invented in the colonies could have been influenced by two earlier Marxist thinkers: Rosa Luxemburg and the left-wing Hegelian Marxist Karl Korsch. Writing long before World War II, Luxemburg already recognized "that the secret underhand war of each capitalist nation against every other, on the backs of Asiatic and African peoples must sooner or later lead to a general reckoning, that the wind that was sown in Africa and Asia would return to Europe as a terrific storm."[37] In an obscure text on totalitarianism published in a 1942 issue of the Chicago-based "council communist" journal *New Essays*, Korsch updated Luxemburg and wrote in terms even closer to Césaire's: "The new techniques of imperialism which were invented almost simultaneously in the East and the West are utterly different from the methods applied by that old-style imperialism of the 19th century.... The difference does not consist, however, in an increase of violence; ruthless violence has been characteristic of every historical phase of capitalist colonization. The novelty of totalitarian politics in this respect is simply that the Nazis have extended to 'civilized' European peoples the methods hitherto reserved for the 'natives' or 'savages' living outside so-called civilization."[38] The proximity of Korsch's text to Césaire's can hardly be an accident.

Although Marxist theory seems mostly inessential and subordinate in Césaire's *Discourse*, it returns at key moments, especially in the final envoi. Césaire concludes the *Discourse* by denouncing "the mechanization of man," the capitalist "machine for crushing, for grinding, for degrading peoples," and by calling for "a policy of *nationalities*, a new policy founded on respect for peoples and cultures" (77). This agenda is recommended as the "last *chance*" for "the salvation of Europe," but one which can only be accomplished by "the Revolution—the one which, until such time as there is a classless society, will substitute for the narrow tyranny of a dehumanized bourgeoisie the preponderance of the only class that still has a universal mission, because it suffers in its flesh from all the wrongs of history, from all the universal wrongs: the proletariat" (78). As these concluding remarks illustrate, a tension characteristic of the Communist Party ideology of the moment runs through Césaire's perspective between the particularity of cultural difference (here, nationality) and the possibility of universality embodied in the proletariat and in the unfolding of colonial and capitalist expansion. In contrast to the direction the party would follow in subordinating the question of nationalities to the question of class, Césaire's work would continue to preserve this tension. His juxtaposition of Nazism and colonialism is based both on a universalizing historical perspective and on a grasp of how universalizing projects seek to eliminate particularity (that of Jews, that of colonized and indigenous peoples).

While Marxist dialectic can provide a logic for overcoming this tension, it can also just as easily be blamed for suppressing it. In October

1956, the year after the second edition of the *Discourse* was published and only a month after his lecture on "Culture et Colonisation" at the First International Congress of Negro Writers and Artists in Paris, Césaire broke definitively with the Communist Party in his famous *Lettre à Maurice Thorez* (*Letter to Maurice Thorez*). As James Arnold succinctly summarizes the issues, "Césaire eventually broke with the Communists for the same reason he joined them: having placed in the party his hopes for the economic and political liberation of blacks, and having found the party reluctant to move in these areas, Césaire could scarcely have taken a different course of action" (175). The problem is still that of the particular and the universal, but now Césaire has reversed his own conclusion in the *Discourse*. In his open letter to the French Communist Party leader he writes that "we are convinced that our questions, or, if you will, the colonial question, cannot be treated as a part of a larger ensemble.... [T]he struggle of colonized peoples against colonialism, the struggle of people of color against racism is much more complex—what am I saying?—of a completely different nature than the struggle of the French worker against French capitalism and cannot in any way be considered as a part, a fragment of that struggle" (8). However, while insisting on the colonial difference vis-à-vis the Marxist metanarrative, Césaire's emphasis on the "singularity" of the "'situation in the world'" of colonized peoples is not a narrow particularism.

Indeed, Césaire's articulation of his break with the party leads him to grant a greater degree of specificity to the issue of anti-Semitism than he does in the *Discourse*, where Nazi crimes are evoked at crucial moments but the specificity of Jewish suffering remains largely outside the text's purview. After summarizing the common indictments against the party—the crimes of Stalinism that had just been revealed by Khrushchev and, even more damningly, the French Communist Party's refusal to come to terms with those crimes—Césaire "add[s] a certain number of considerations pertaining to my identity as a man of color [*à ma qualité d'homme de couleur*]": "Putting it in a word: in light of the events (and reflection on the shameful practices of antisemitism that have taken place and, it seems, continue to take place in the countries that claim to represent socialism), I have come to the conviction that our paths and those of communism such as it is practiced do not merge purely and simply; that they cannot merge purely and simply" (7–8). Here, although Césaire has announced his intention to speak specifically as a man of color, it is in fact the reference to anti-Semitism that functions grammatically as the interruption of his commitment to actually existing socialism. Although the remainder of the letter will focus on the colonial question, anti-Semitism first names the problem of particularities that the party cannot subsume. Césaire goes on to indict Stalin's notion of "advanced" and "backwards" peoples, and he rails against the "inveterate assimilationism" of French party members, their "conviction—which they share with the European bourgeoisie—in the omnilateral superiority of the West; [and] their rarely avowed but real belief in civilization with a capital C; in progress with a capital P" (11). Ultimately, he calls for a "real Copernican revolution" (12) that would uproot the deeply implanted Eurocentric paternalism that maintains the colonized in a position of passivity or, as Arendt might say, "worldlessness."

The move from *Discourse on Colonialism* to *Letter to Maurice Thorez* is not a move from the universal to the particular. Rather, it marks a shift between versions of universalism—from one based on the subsumption of historical difference in a metanarrative of progress to a more properly multidirectional position. In other words, from a universalism in the *Discourse* that allows the articulation of genocide and colonialism but risks subordinating both to the master narrative of capital accumulation and proletarian revolution, Césaire shifts to a multidirectional universalism in the *Letter* that approaches contemporary notions of cosmopolitanism: "Provincialism? Not at all. I do not bury myself in a narrow particularism. But I also do not want to lose myself in a fleshless universalism [*un universalisme décharné*]. . . . My conception of the universal is that of a universal rich with all of the particulars, a deepening and coexistence of all the particulars" (*Lettre* 15). Dedicated as it is to the struggles of "black peoples" for "justice . . . culture . . . dignity and liberty" (16), the *Letter* nevertheless finds room in a parenthetical yet crucial place to invoke the sufferings of others. But although anti-Semitism occupies that important rhetorical position in Césaire's resignation from the French Communist Party, the Nazi genocide plays no role in this short text (nor is there any reason that it should). The case of the *Discourse* is the obverse: Nazi violence plays a critical rhetorical role in the critique of colonialism, but the specificity of the Shoah within Nazi policy is barely evoked. These inverse relations have something to do with the differences between the forms of universalism invoked in the respective texts. While the *Discourse* invokes a historical process as the basis of its universalist perspective (capitalist imperialism as a totalizing motor of history both outside and inside Europe; the proletariat as the privileged agent of change), the *Letter* invokes a cultural universalism (or cosmopolitanism) dedicated to recognizing the specificity of the claims and struggles of different oppressed groups. Although the *Letter* implies a way of bringing together colonialism and the Holocaust in a framework at once historically and culturally universal—that is, dedicated both to the fundamental unity of world history and to the specificities of the struggles and cultures within that framework—that project remains unfulfilled in Césaire's oeuvre.

There is, however, at least one additional sign that the events of the 1950s were leading Césaire in the direction of such a project. As evidence of the ongoing development of Césaire's thinking in the period between the 1950 edition of *Discourse* and the 1956 *Lettre*, we can also note that the only mention of Jews in the *Discourse* comes in the 1955 edition, where Césaire writes ironically of Roger Caillois. After citing various racist comments by the French ethnographer, Césaire remarks, "M. Caillois gives immediate proof of this superiority [of the West] by concluding that no one should be exterminated. With him the Negroes are sure that they will not be lynched; the Jews, that they will not feed new bonfires. There is just one thing: it is important for it to be clearly understood that the Negroes, Jews, and Australians owe this tolerance not to their respective merits, but to the magnanimity of M. Caillois" (72; *Discours* [1955] 57). Significantly, Jews appear here within a context that both marks genocide more explicitly than the 1950 edition did and immediately renders that perception comparative through the series "Negroes, Jews, and Australians" (that is, Aborigines). Although reference to Jews remains marginal to the *Discourse*, as opposed to references to Nazis, which are rhetorically central, we see in this added passage that a multidirectional framework can allow for specificity and comparison without necessarily lapsing into competition.

The Colonial Turn in Holocaust Studies

Whatever their shortcomings, Arendt and Césaire bring us to the brink of a multidirectional dialectic that holds together the universal and the particular and the objective and subjective sides of colonial and genocidal history. It has taken scholars half a century to catch up to these early insights. Until the very recent development I discuss below, scholars in Holocaust studies and German studies have remained too defensive about the uniqueness of the Shoah to venture into such comparative territory. By contrast, scholars of postcolonial studies occasionally acknowledge, but frequently marginalize the questions posed by an integration of the Holocaust and Nazi imperialism into their conceptual frameworks. A typical example can be found in Robert Young's important work on the challenges colonialism represents for European theories of history. Counterposing French poststructuralists to what he clearly understands as their competitors in the Frankfurt School, Young writes that "the French never regarded fascism as an aberration, concurring rather with Césaire and Fanon that it can be explained quite simply as European colonialism brought home to Europe by a country that had been deprived of its overseas empires after World War I."[39] Reducing fascism to something that can be "quite simply" explained threatens to normalize political extremity and does a great deal of conceptual violence to the difficult struggle to articulate the relatedness of colonial and genocidal histories. Although Young's clear reference is to a small group of intellectuals who have indeed contributed to this project of articulation, describing "the French" as a site of such straightforward knowledge flies in the face of decades of "French" disavowal both of the nation's implication in the Holocaust and in the bloody history of colonialism and decolonization. In addition, Young misses the way that multidirectional memory inflects the thinking of those who did critique humanism and "Western rationalism"—a critique that grew as much out of the memory of Nazism as out of the ongoing experience of decolonization.

Despite his somewhat facile references to fascism and the Holocaust, however, Young's interrogation of the colonial and postcolonial context of poststructuralist theory leads him to a question that has been essential to the project of this section of *Multidirectional Memory*: the question of humanism and the human. Given the ambivalences of humanism, its links to racist violence and its appropriation by anticolonial thinkers (and, we might add, post-Holocaust thinkers such as Primo Levi), Young asks "whether we should—and whether we can—differentiate between a humanism which harks back critically, or uncritically, to the mainstream of Enlightenment culture and Fanon's new 'new humanism' which attempts to reformulate it as a non-conflictual concept no longer defined against a sub-human other" (125). Young never provides an ultimate answer to this quandary, which remains as unsettled business despite his general embrace of antihumanist theory. This dilemma runs through the center of Arendt's writings on imperialism and genocide. Furthermore, as the work of Giorgio Agamben has demonstrated, the questions of the human and of "life itself" have today reached the center of politics. But, if Young tends to downplay the impact of the Holocaust on these questions, Agamben tends to leave out the question of colonialism altogether, even as he focuses on the concentration camp as the "nomos" of the modern. The works at issue in this section demand a thinking of the human that is simultaneously post-Holocaust and postcolonial, that grasps the politics of bare life in the complexity of its genealogy. Although the works of Arendt and Césaire do not avoid the paradoxes of humanism to which Young alludes, they do nevertheless contribute to such a genealogy of the politics of the human.

The historian Dirk Moses has asserted, "Arendt and Césaire did not have to infer the link between Nazism and imperialism. Hitler self-consciously placed his movement in the tradition of European imperialism" ("Empire, Colony, Genocide" 35). But how well do Césaire's *choc en retour* and Arendt's constellations and boomerang effects measure up against contemporary attempts to link imperialism and genocide? Because of both their strengths and their weaknesses, the theoretical insights of Arendt and Césaire, as well as Young and Agamben, deserve to be considered in historical detail. The exploration of historical causality is not the focus of my study. Yet, while I concern myself primarily with the modes of conceptualization and configurations of memory through which colonialism and the Holocaust have been brought together or kept apart, the question of contemporary historical accounts is nonetheless both crucial and enlightening. While still in a nascent state, the comparative study of genocide—and especially of genocide in colonial contexts and its relationship to the

Holocaust—is developing rapidly. Here I look briefly at some recent historical projects that explore the terrain opened up by Arendt, Césaire, and the others. My goal is not comprehensiveness, but a diagnosis of where things stand in contemporary scholarship.[40]

In *Absolute Destruction*, one of the most detailed contemporary studies exploring links between imperialism and genocide, historian Isabel V. Hull provides evidence that supports both Arendt and Césaire to a certain extent, while ultimately putting the emphasis on factors not central to their texts. Hull's study focuses on military culture and finds that genocidal killing can—and did—emerge out of the institutional structure of the German army. Thus, according to Hull, the genocide of the Herero and Nama in German Southwest Africa was less the product of racist or imperialist ideology than the playing out of a dynamic internal to the army that was given free reign in an area of the world from which Europe considered itself "insulated."[41] While this view tends to support aspects of Arendt's argument—like Arendt, Hull argues that racism was more the product of imperialism than its driving force (330)—Hull differs from Arendt in locating the origins of the "boomerang" not in colonial space, but in preexisting European practices: "The point . . . is not that Europeans learned beastliness from their imperial encounters but that they could try out abroad the techniques, assumptions, doctrines, and scripts they carried with them, in an atmosphere relatively unlimited by law and conducive to the application of more force when the first allotment failed to achieve the goal. The Germans at least learned nothing from colonial warfare that did not confirm their prejudices about the correct way to fight wars. Imperialism strengthened the military template" (333). In privileging the military template over ideologies of race and empire as the source of genocide, Hull understands herself as providing the missing link in Arendt's argument about how imperialism fed into the Nazi "Final Solution."[42] Besides adding the previously underexplored dimension of military organization to the discussion, her argument also has the advantage of locating one of the key elements of genocide deep within European society broadly understood. Like Césaire, she locates the possibility of extreme violence in the normal practices of the modern world, in her case in bureaucratic, organizational structures. This "return" to Europe allows her to expose the fantasy of European insulation from the world and to avoid the Conrad-derived problem we have identified with *The Origins of Totalitarianism*: the conceptual slippage from Africa as the site of racialized violence to Africa as the origin of racial thinking and extreme violence. Yet, in so thoroughly shifting the matrix away from the colonies, Hull risks once again writing Africa and imperialism out of world history in general and out of its crucial role in the unfolding of modern European history in particular. Most crucially, she seems to downplay both the ideological work necessary to create Africa as a site of exception ("unlimited by law" and suited to radical experimentation) and the force of that experience in preparing Europeans for genocide on European soil. It may well be true, as Hull argues, that ideological factors were more determinate in Nazi genocide than in Imperial Germany's "final solutions," but, as the writings of Césaire suggest (and those of Du Bois will also argue), the racist articulation of the global color line precedes both and helped prepare the ground for slaughter.[43]

Hull's stress on the transmission of military techniques from Europe to Africa should be complemented by the work of scholars such as Jürgen Zimmerer on the transmission of colonial policies from Africa back to Europe. In a series of recent studies, Zimmerer has begun to chart the circulation of ideas about race and space that infuse genocidal policies both within and outside Europe. If Hull emphasizes the "rationality of extreme actions" internal to military culture, Zimmerer identifies the roots of genocide in an imperial legacy, what the historian of Nazi genocide Christian Gerlach has called the "biologization of the social": "This biological interpretation of world history—the conviction that a Volk needs to secure space in order to survive—is one of the fundamental parallels between colonialism and Nazi expansion policy."[44] In drawing attention to such parallels, Zimmerer begins to provide a historical explanation for Du Bois's juxtaposition of the Warsaw Ghetto and Jim Crow America and Schwarz-Bart's juxtaposition of Warsaw and the Caribbean as differently organized sites of spatial racialization (or racial spatialization). Zimmerer goes beyond noting parallels between colonialism and Nazism and has begun to chart the material and discursive means of transmission that link them. He draws attention to the role of firsthand experience, institutional memory, and collective imagination in that process of transmission, and concludes:

The German population's awareness of colonial history . . . was much stronger than is generally presumed. Sites for the dissemination of this knowledge included colonial clubs, geographical societies, political parties as well as popular novels and magazines, and university lectures. Consequently, ordinary citizens would have had some contact with notions such as the "racial society," "mixed marriage," "expulsion and resettlement to special reserves," "a declining and ailing race" or "uneducated natives," even if they only came across them in reports by the various missionary societies. Attending to the colonial dimension in German history for an understanding of Nazi politics enables the recognition of various types of precursors and models. Some practices that, from a narrow Eurocentric perspective, seem unprecedented prove, on closer inspection, to be radicalized versions of forms found in earlier colonial times.[45]

At stake in drawing parallels and establishing lines of transmission is not only a rethinking of the Eurocentric conception of the Holocaust's uniqueness but also an explanation of how "ordinary Germans" became genocidal killers. In a phrase that confirms our reading of the crucial role played in transmission by the disavowal of colonial violence we have found documented in the texts of Conrad and Césaire, Zimmerer proposes that, among other factors, "the positive reading of European colonialism . . . contributed to concealing the criminal character of the German occupation from contemporary witnesses" ("Spirit of Colonialism" 219). More work needs to be done in establishing the "thickness" of the modes of transmission so that they become more than striking parallels and individual cases of influence.[46] Zimmerer also finesses to a certain degree the question of the Holocaust's relationship to overall Nazi colonialism. Just as Nazi genocidal actions reach well beyond the Jews, the genocide of Jews, as Zimmerer recognizes, extends well beyond the colonization of the east. The colonial paradigm possesses less explanatory force when considering the deportation of Jews from Western or Southern Europe than when Nazi policy in Poland and the Soviet Union are at issue. When it comes to the Holocaust, race and space do not align themselves perfectly, since the first "race" scheduled for extermination was not found uniquely in the spaces slated for the most extreme form of colonization. As Du Bois and Caryl Phillips will teach us, our maps of race and space need to draw attention to asymmetries as well as parallels.

However open to revision Hull's and Zimmerer's different conclusions might be as the study of colonialism and genocide continues to develop, they complement each other and help us sharpen a conceptual point about the logic of the boomerang effect—a point that both Arendt and Césaire at their best also recognized. The search for the "origins" of Nazi genocide (or any other example of extreme violence) has at least two risks: it can lead to the erasure of the specificity of the event, which collapses back into its antecedents once its "true" origins have been located; or it can lead into conceptual dead ends that reimport the categories of racist and primitivist anthropologies, as if the origins must be as shocking as the deeds those origins seek to explain. As we seek to move from a Eurocentric notion of the Holocaust's uniqueness to a decolonized "double consciousness" (Du Bois) of the Holocaust's relation to other histories of violence, we need to beware of such forms of unidirectional thinking. Rather, the focus on constellations of causality and the *choc en retour* suggests that a better way to think about historical causality—as about the dynamic of memory—will be in terms of a multidirectional transmission of ideas and practices. In proposing a colonial "turn" in Holocaust studies we need to take the questions of "turns" and "returns" quite seriously.

Besides encouraging attention to the directions and locations of causality and provoking a rethinking of the Holocaust's place in world history, a focus on the re-turns of extreme violence should also turn against received notions of colonialism. Much of the historical work on colonialism and genocide remains wedded to a chronological model and indebted to narrative structures of knowledge. For good historical reasons, work such as that of Hull and Zimmerer has thus concerned itself with the movements from Europe to the colonies or from colonialism to Nazi genocide and asked about the lines of transmission and influence that link those sites and histories to each other. But if we take Benjamin's model of the constellation seriously, as well as the models of boomerang effect and *choc en retour*, we need to be open to thinking about how the Nazi genocide turns around our understanding of what came before it. The intertwined character of colony and metropole has been one of the fundamental insights of recent colonial/postcolonial studies. Yet that insight has generally not led to a consideration of how National Socialism and the Nazi genocide might illuminate what Ann Laura Stoler and Frederick Cooper call "the tensions of empire." The rhetoric of turning and returning embodied in notions of boomerang effects and the *choc en retour* points to the need to go beyond linear models relating the Holocaust and colonialism. It suggests that the time of historical influence consists not only of mechanical, transitive causality but also of repetitions, reverse shocks, and returns of the repressed. But "turns" also take place in space and suggest the need to consider the spatial coimplication of colonialism, racism, and genocide.

The early postwar period proves of particular interest in charting the emergence and transformation of multidirectional memories of colonialism and genocide because in this period the key terms that we use today to think about these events (the Holocaust, imperialism, decolonization) had not yet solidified into their familiar forms. The first decade after the end of World War II thus appears as a moment of transition and a laboratory for thinking about the relationship between different legacies of violence. The results of that thinking may be surprising and even disturbing, but they deserve to be uncovered both because they continue to mark our thinking in ways we might not recognize and because they offer us conceptualizations that we have forgotten but remain worth pursuing. The works of Arendt and Césaire, as well as those of the French Communist painters, possess a special temporal status as "residual/emergent" documents both "ahead" of their time and "behind" certain developments that have taken place since. By virtue of their own complex temporal structure, these works draw our attention to the turns and returns of colonial discourse and practice. A dialectical encounter between Arendt and Césaire demonstrates how intersecting memories of colonialism, slavery, and genocide lead to unprecedented insights in their work but also sometimes cloud the clarity of their vision. The multidirectional dialectic of colonialism and fascism in their texts remains incomplete, but an archaeology of the comparative imagination shows how a dialogical view of history has also shaped the work and actions of many other important intellectual and political figures of the twentieth and twenty-first centuries. In the following section we pursue three writers—Du Bois, Schwarz-Bart, and Phillips—who produce multidirectional approaches to the legacies of colonialism and Nazi genocide. The juxtapositions they track are simultaneously spatial, involving ghettos, ruins, and diasporas, and temporal, involving the memory, persistence, and return of racial violence over many centuries.

PART II

MIGRATIONS OF MEMORY

Ruins, Ghettos, Diasporas

4

W. E. B. Du Bois in Warsaw: Holocaust Memory and the Color Line

1949

In 1949, the African American scholar and activist W. E. B. Du Bois traveled to Poland, where he witnessed firsthand the rubble left behind by the Nazi occupation and war. Observing the remains of the Warsaw ghetto, site of the heroic and desperate 1943 revolt of Jews condemned to die in the Treblinka death camp, Du Bois reflected on matters of race, identity, and resistance. He later wrote in "The Negro and the Warsaw Ghetto," an essay published in 1952 in the magazine *Jewish Life*, that this visit led him to reassess and revisit his declaration of 1900 that "the problem of the twentieth century is the problem of the colour line."[1] In the *Jewish Life* article, Du Bois recounts earlier visits to Poland in the late nineteenth century and prewar twentieth century and discusses how they helped him to "become aware of the Jewish problem of the modern world" (14). Turning to his most recent visit to Warsaw, Du Bois then remarks on the novelty of the Nazi assault, the complete destruction it left in its wake, and the efforts of the Polish people to reconstruct their city. He focuses particularly on the fate of the Jews of the ghetto and mentions visiting the recently unveiled Warsaw Ghetto Monument.

Although relatively unknown and quite brief, "The Negro and the

Warsaw Ghetto" deserves close attention here for several reasons. First, it supplements the discussion we have started with Arendt and Césaire about the relationship between the Holocaust and the discourses of race and resistance that were circulating in proximity to the cold war and anticolonial movements. While Arendt and Césaire take us to the brink of a workable notion of multidirectionality, they don't always elude the pitfalls of the universal/particular dichotomy; Arendt leaves us stranded at the limits of Eurocentrism, while Césaire's anti-Eurocentric antidote sometimes hesitates about the specificity of Jewish particularity. In contrast, Du Bois can serve as a model of multidirectional memory because of the way his writings on Jews, race, and genocide hold together commonality and difference in a revised version of double consciousness. In addition, the insights Du Bois derives from the ruinous geography of the Warsaw Ghetto about the links between spatial organization and racial violence echo throughout the alternative, multidirectional tradition.

The years in which Du Bois visited and wrote about Warsaw remain underexamined in Holocaust studies, but they have left their mark both on Holocaust memory and on interdisciplinary cultural studies. I have in mind not only Arendt and Césaire but also the German-Jewish philosopher Theodor W. Adorno, who contributed one of the first reflections on the cultural impact of the Holocaust in the same year that Du Bois visited Warsaw. While Adorno's "Cultural Criticism and Society," written in 1949 and published in 1951, consists primarily of a Marxist critique of the concept of culture, that essay is probably as well known today for one particular phrase in its surprising final paragraph as it is for the concerns that occupy the vast majority of Adorno's text. In concluding his discussion of cultural criticism Adorno inaugurated what has become a long-standing discourse on the relationship between Nazi terror and aesthetic representation. Adorno's claim that "to write poetry after Auschwitz is barbaric" continues to be quoted and misquoted long after his death in 1969.[2] Over the years, Adorno's reflections on Auschwitz have come to stand for much more than a judgment on poetry and instead have been taken to suggest the impact of extreme, socially sanctioned violence on culture in its broad, anthropological sense. Both Adorno's 1949 dictum and Du Bois's equally famous assertion about the color line testify to the effects of such quintessentially modern experiences as genocide, slavery, and colonialism on conceptions of history, culture, and community. Adorno and Du Bois each link a conceptual problem (how to think about aesthetics or history) with a material reality defined and divided by categories of "race" (Auschwitz, the color line). With their rhetoric of "after Auschwitz" and the twentieth-century color line, both writers further link the problem of racial division to spatial and temporal caesurae.

While I have considered the writings of Adorno on Auschwitz elsewhere, here I focus on how Du Bois's less well known visit to Warsaw reveals a dynamic intertwining of histories and memories that has methodological implications for Holocaust studies, postcolonial studies, and African American studies.[3] Du Bois's encounter with the remains of the Warsaw Ghetto in 1949 confirms the need for a comparative approach to the multidirectionality of collective memory that considers questions of politics, aesthetics, and the public sphere in a nonreductive, transnational framework. Du Bois's post-Holocaust reinvocation of the color line—a line that can be understood as at once material and conceptual—takes on further significance in the light of the discourses that have come to define the place of the Holocaust in contemporary scholarship. All disciplinary and interdisciplinary formations necessarily draw lines that both differentiate their field of inquiry from other fields and delineate territories within their field, but not all lines are equal. At present, scholars of the Holocaust tend to fall into two dominant positions, which, in an effort to bring together questions of epistemology and questions of representation, I have elsewhere termed realist and antirealist. On the one hand, there exists a well-known antirealist discourse that draws an infrangible line between the Holocaust and all other events. Filmmaker and writer Claude Lanzmann illustrates this position in his response to the 1978 *Holocaust* television series: "The Holocaust is unique first of all in that it erects around itself, in a circle of flames, a limit which cannot be breached because a certain absolute is intransmissable: to claim to do so is to make oneself guilty of the most serious sort of transgression."[4] On the other hand, another strain of scholarship on the Holocaust insists on erasing all lines of discontinuity between the genocide and other histories. In his realist study of "moral life" in the concentration camps, for example, Tzvetan Todorov "affirm[s] the continuity between everyday experience and that of the camps."[5] Ultimately, these starkly opposed visions mirror each other since each is necessarily predicated on what it excludes—whether evidence of the Holocaust's comparability to other events or of its specificity. Because Du Bois's essay on the Warsaw Ghetto avoids the binary opposition between absolute discontinuity and complete continuity that characterizes much discourse on the Holocaust and its relation to other histories, it helps point the way toward new, multidirectional approaches to genocide, racism, and collective memory. My analysis of "The Negro and the Warsaw Ghetto" suggests that a modified notion of Du Boisian "double consciousness" may supply a methodological innovation crucial to helping Holocaust scholars move beyond the realist/antirealist deadlock and cultural theorists move beyond competitive models of memory.[6]

Du Bois's response to the catastrophe of Nazi genocide also suggests the possibility that other interdisciplinary projects that have had little to say about the Holocaust, such as postcolonial studies and cultural studies, may benefit from an encounter with discussions in Holocaust studies. The image of Du Bois in Warsaw focuses questions about the politics of memory and the production of discourses on the past, and it provides a point of intersection from which to remap the seemingly divergent genealogies of Holocaust memory and the global color line. While both Holocaust memory and the color line may seem today like stable, quasi-natural objects, our consideration of the context of the late 1940s and early 1950s reveals the instability and nonobviousness of their significance. At the same time that Du Bois was revising his notion of double consciousness in the face of the ruins of Warsaw, Hannah Arendt was forging a constellation connecting imperialism and totalitarianism, Aimé Césaire was reading the Nazi genocide in the light of colonial violence, and the French Communist painters André Fougeron and Boris Taslitzky were imagining a haunted postwar France marked by the encounter of fascism and colonialism. Du Bois's writings on the Holocaust, Jews, and Nazism both confirm the general climate of the period and offer new insights.[7] The cases of Césaire and Arendt have illustrated the difficulty of holding together in memory and historical understanding a sense of the specificity of the Holocaust and colonialism and an account of more general processes of modern Europe's racialized violence. In rethinking the color line from the ruins of Warsaw, Du Bois provides both an example and a method for conceptualizing memory beyond the logic of competition.

The lesson of Du Bois in Warsaw is in the end equally crucial for Holocaust studies, postcolonial studies, and ethnic studies in general: the varieties of racial terror that have marked and marred the twentieth century—in everyday as well as extreme forms—leave their tracks on all forms of knowledge. While my discussions of Arendt and Césaire have demonstrated the importance of temporality for the conceptualization of the colonial encounter and its uncanny return to Europe, here I argue that space is also determinant: Du Bois's article on Warsaw reveals how racial thinking as well as racial violence emerge simultaneously with the production of "biopolitical" space. Just as the previous discussion highlighted the importance (and difficulties) of reconceptualizing narrative so as to avoid the progressive temporality upon which colonialism feeds, analysis inspired by Du Bois suggests that both disciplinary and social space must be the locus of resistance to racial discourses and practices. In order to understand the extent of racism's relevance to the disciplinary and interdisciplinary production of knowledge, we as critics need first to map the conceptual and material lines of demarcation that hold together as well as divide different histories.[8] Seeking points of contact between apparently separate histories, I foreground the unevenness of historical processes and the multidirectionality of memory in moments of cultural translation, even as I begin from the assumption that such processes and memories are—at some fundamental level—deeply implicated in each other. To render intelligible Du Bois's transnational encounter with Warsaw and his article in *Jewish Life* necessitates working out of multiple histories; to render it significant for contemporary concerns necessitates also working against the grain of those histories.

The Climate of Memory

In the year 1949 Du Bois addressed international Peace Congresses in New York, Paris, and Moscow and voiced his opposition to the cold war.[9] In September of that year, while on the way back from Moscow he also made his third trip to Poland. The first had come during his time of study in Wilhelmine Germany in 1893; the second had been during an extended visit to Nazi Germany in 1936. As Du Bois wrote in "The Negro and the Warsaw Ghetto," his 1952 *Jewish Life* essay, these visits had a profound effect on his thinking of the problem of the color line:

> The result of these three visits, and particularly of my view of the Warsaw ghetto, was not so much clearer understanding of the Jewish problem in the world as it was a real and more complete understanding of the Negro problem. In the first place, the problem of slavery, emancipation, and caste in the United States was no longer in my mind a separate and unique thing as I had so long conceived it. It was not even solely a matter of color and physical and racial characteristics, which was particularly a hard thing for me to learn, since for a lifetime the color line had been a real and efficient cause of misery. . . . [T]he race problem in which I was interested cut across lines of color and physique and belief and status and was a matter of cultural patterns, perverted teaching and human hate and prejudice, which reached all sorts of people and caused endless evil to all men. (15)

In this passage, we see the same proximity of problems of conceptualization to the material conditions of racism that is found in the more famous prophecy of the problem of the twentieth century. Here, however, Du Bois displaces the clear-cut distinctions that previously isolated the "problem of the twentieth century" in the fact of the "color line," and instead shifts to a discourse that questions such isolation at both the conceptual and material levels. Du Bois registers this shift in the Negro problem at two levels: both as a phenomenon "conceived" "in [his] mind" and as an element of the "real." The displacement of the problematic of race and the transgression of the color line that Du Bois contemplates after his 1949 visit to Poland by no means entail the abandonment of his insight about the twentieth century. Rather, it points to the ongoing need to return and revise that line of thought and to appreciate its historicity—a revisionary task already in process in Du Bois's repeated rearticulations of "the problem of the twentieth century." If the situation of black Americans is now, for Du Bois, no longer conceived of as "separate and unique," the color line has not ceased to register its effects; it remains the "real and efficient cause" and condition of African American life. In this new conception the "race problem" cuts across a variety of lines of social demarcation, but precisely this transversal conceptual movement demonstrates how those lines remain in force as efficient, local causes. The color line lives on, as does the specificity of African American life, but the lines that connect the African diaspora from within and those that differentiate it from European American life without exist in a new relation to other histories of racism and violence.

In order to understand the specific qualities of those relations between black and Jewish histories and their effects on conceptualizing race and culture, we need to address the question of why Du Bois was so powerfully moved by the spectacle of postwar Warsaw and what in particular might have catalyzed this process of theoretical revision. First, we need to take account of the historical dynamics shaping the appearance of Du Bois's article. The period surrounding Du Bois's trip to Warsaw in 1949 and the eventual publication of the article in 1952 comprised the height of cold war hysteria and of Du Bois's persecution by the United States government—he was indicted in 1951 as an "unregistered foreign agent." Although not yet a party member, Du Bois was, in fact, closely aligned to communism at the time and *Jewish Life* was a Communist Party journal. While it is necessary to approach critically the Stalinism of intellectual and activist figures like Du Bois and the editors of *Jewish Life*—especially in considering a moment when anti-Semitic repression was reaching new heights in the Soviet Union—temporarily bracketing our post–cold war sensibilities can also produce unexpected insight into issues of history and memory.[10] The cold war produced a very particular context for discussions of racism and the Holocaust in the United States. Mainstream organizations of both African Americans and Jewish Americans attempted to tailor their concerns to the cold war anti-Communist consensus. For African Americans, this meant an evisceration of a previously prominent internationalism. According to Penny Von Eschen's study of African American responses to the global dimensions of the color line, "By 1950 there was a fundamental transformation of anticolonial discourse and a dramatic narrowing of coverage of Africa and the Caribbean in the black American press. Headlines concerning anticolonial movements, labor strikes, and the changing role of American corporations had disappeared. The greatly reduced volume of discussion of colonialism and Africa mirrored U.S. security concerns that British or French colonial excesses might open the door in Africa to the more dangerous Communists."[11] While the mainstream black press generally decontextualized and de-historicized the international scale of the problems of race, color, and empire in this era, some marginalized intellectuals on the left, such as Du Bois, continued to put forth radical critiques that linked global and local contexts of racism.

At the same time, and contrary to current practices, most Jewish American organizations were reluctant to draw public attention to the Nazi destruction of European Jewry. Although a variety of factors were at play in this decision, the desire of most American Jews of the time to integrate into mainstream American society led to tacit or overt support for a foreign policy that downplayed past German crimes in favor of an alliance against Soviet "totalitarianism." Contrary to her intentions, Arendt's conceptualization of totalitarianism was used as part of this project. The conjunction of a communal desire to assimilate with a broader national shift in geopolitical alliance meant that in the late 1940s and early 1950s the American Left became the dominant purveyor of what we would now call Holocaust memory. We have already seen in our discussion of Fougeron, Taslitzky, and Césaire how the French Communist Party fostered continued discussion of Nazism in the context of postwar France's colonial wars, but in the United States, at least, the party went even further in recognizing the specificities of Nazi oppression of Jews. According to Peter Novick, "One of the most striking features of Communist and pro-Communist rhetoric in the late forties and fifties—and particularly of the Jewish Communists and pro-Communists from whom the mainstream Jewish organizations were desperately trying to dissociate themselves—was the frequency with which that rhetoric invoked the Holocaust."[12]

Given these political splits within the cold war discourses of African Americans and Jewish Americans, the existence of Du Bois's article is both anomalous and easily locatable. During this era, the pages of the Communist *Jewish Life* were filled with references both to the Holocaust and to local and global racial politics. The magazine was supportive of Du Bois during his cold war troubles, as it was of other black leftist initiatives such as the *We Charge Genocide* campaign.[13] Although it is difficult to grasp today, despite our several significant examples, communism provided one of the discursive spheres, both in the United States and elsewhere, in which the articulation of genocide and colonialism could first be attempted—and this long before the intellectual vogue for either Holocaust or postcolonial studies. To put it in other terms, a notion of the specificity of Nazi genocide emerged against a background of relative silence and universalizing condemnations of atrocity precisely through its articulation in the kind of comparative framework that would later be stigmatized as relativizing the uniqueness of the Holocaust. That this emergence of Jewish specificity happened within a universalist movement that was simultaneously persecuting Soviet Jews is not only a cruel historical irony but another indication of the irreducible complexity of collective memory.

Besides noting this larger historical context, it is also important to consider the specificity of Du Bois's address in "The Negro and the Warsaw Ghetto." While shaped by the cold war context, Du Bois's article might furthermore be seen as a strategic intervention within the Left, since it is clearly intended for a Jewish Left audience. The article was indeed first presented as a talk at the *Jewish Life* "Tribute to the Warsaw Ghetto Fighters" on April 15, 1952 (Du Bois, "Warsaw Ghetto" 14). Du Bois's political solidarity with Jewish suffering in World War II was not always automatically given. In response to a 1944 campaign by the American Jewish Committee (AJC), which wanted to present a Declaration of Human Rights to address the fate of Jews and others in Europe, Du Bois responded sharply. In answer to a letter of appeal from the AJC's president Joseph Proskauer, Du Bois wrote:

Under paragraph five you appeal for sympathy for persons driven from the land of their birth; but how about American Negroes, Africans and Indians who have not been driven from the land of their birth, but nevertheless are deprived of their rights? Under paragraph six you want redress for those who wander the earth but how about those who do not wander and are not allowed to travel and nevertheless are deprived of their fundamental human rights?

In other words, this is a very easily understood declaration of Jewish rights but it has apparently no thought of the rights of Negroes, Indians and South Sea Islanders. Why then call it the Declaration of Human Rights?[14]

Du Bois's response remains relevant today insofar as it anticipates concerns with the contemporary status of depoliticized "humanitarianism."[15] In this letter, as in his *Jewish Life* article, Du Bois places emphasis on differentiating black (and other) politics from a falsely universalist human rights discourse and from the history of European Jews. In a classic example of ideology critique, Du Bois reveals the specific interests behind the universal claim, and he invokes instead a differentiated field of potential rights.

Yet Du Bois's debunking of the universal and insistence on specificity are enunciated against a background of shared concerns.

Long before the Holocaust or even the Nazi period, Du Bois reports that he had already recognized certain commonalities between the experiences of African Americans and those of Jews and other minorities in the United States and in Europe. Referring in *Dusk of Dawn* to the "continuing and recurrent horror" of lynching during his college days at the end of the nineteenth century, Du Bois writes, "Each death was a scar upon my soul, and led me on to conceive the plight of other minority groups." Along with mention of the lynching of Italians in New Orleans and anti-Chinese riots in the West, he also reports that "echoes of Jewish segregation and pogroms in Russia came through the magazines."[16] Such echoes of Jewish history also appear in *The Souls of Black Folk* when, for example, the protagonist of the short story "Of the Coming of John" compares himself to Esther, the Jewish queen who risks her life to save her people: "Here is my duty to Altamaha [his hometown] plain before me; perhaps they'll let me help settle the Negro problems there,—perhaps they won't. 'I will go in to the King, which is not according to the law; and if I perish, I perish.'"[17] John's identification as a Jew in the interests of addressing the Negro problem—a not unheard of trope in African diaspora political rhetoric—finds its equivalent in a story Du Bois tells in the *Jewish Life* article and elsewhere, a story that might be seen as allegorizing his position of enunciation in "The Negro and the Warsaw Ghetto."

During his first trip to Europe in the 1890s, Du Bois writes:

I was travelling from Budapest through Hungary to a small town in Galicia, where I planned to spend the night. The cabman looked at me and asked if I wanted to stop "unter die Juden." I was a little puzzled, but told him "Yes." So we went to a little Jewish hotel on a small, out of the way street. There I realized another problem of race or religion, I did not know which, which had to do with the treatment and segregation of large numbers of human beings. I went on to Krakow, becoming more and more aware of two problems of human groups [that is, Jews and Poles], and then came back to the university, not a little puzzled as to my own race problem and its place in the world. ("Warsaw Ghetto" 14)

As he enters the site of Central and Eastern European Jewish life and the pages of *Jewish Life*, Du Bois passes into a "Jew," and it is from this geographical and discursive position among the Jews that Du Bois articulates his response to Nazi terror and the Warsaw Ghetto. But the anecdote also suggests that such a position can only be the product of necessary misunderstanding. This passage stages a series of misapprehensions: from the cabman's misreading of Du Bois's ethnicity, through Du Bois's own inability to place the Jewish question on his conceptual map of human communities, to the way those two confusions displace Du Bois from his customary self-conception. In this passage, as throughout the article, "separate and unique" racial, ethnic, or religious group identities are revealed as all but category errors, even as they are also revealed as "a real and efficient cause of misery" (to reprise the language cited earlier). Here, however, Du Bois goes further in suggesting that puzzlement might be an appropriate rhetorical and political strategy for the apprehension of the simultaneously global and local dimensions of intersecting histories. The anecdote thus serves both as a warning against the perils of transcultural and transnational encounters and a defense of the idea that only by passing through such perilous encounters can the traveler gain insight into the world. It is perhaps especially significant that Du Bois stages himself in this article precisely as a traveler, since mere months before the appearance of this article he had been denied a passport to attend another peace conference in Brazil because of his allegiance to communism.[18]

We can already see that "The Negro and the Warsaw Ghetto" is a multidimensional performance that walks a line between and across a series of overlapping spaces: that of cold war America, that of the Left and, in particular, the Jewish Left, and that of African American and African diaspora experience in an era of segregation at home and decolonization abroad. Du Bois acknowledges the heterogeneity of those spaces, yet he also cautions against discourses of "uniqueness" and "separation." If, as David Levering Lewis has suggested, "the signature of Du Boisian racial discourse" is that "seemingly unconnected turning points in history [are] tied together didactically," this article avoids the two most obvious pitfalls of that method: equation and separation (*Biography of a Race* 129). Rather, in essaying to create a map contoured by relationships of heterogeneity, Du Bois removes Holocaust memory (and African American life) from the respective risks of stultification and banalization attendant upon hyperbolic discourses of uniqueness or similarity.

The Space of Destruction and the Rebuilding of Memory

The overlapping spaces alluded to above only tell half the story, however. Until we acknowledge the specificity of Warsaw in 1949, the full implications of Du Bois's article for understanding racism and genocide and for renewing Holocaust studies and postcolonial studies remain partially obscured. While the cold war and Du Bois's potential political strategies play an important role in shaping the discourse of "The Negro and the Warsaw Ghetto," the text and the particular history it recounts cannot be reduced to its historical context or to an instrumental understanding of Du Bois's intentions. Two fundamental features of Du Bois's experience need to be taken into account that exceed the determinations of the cold war moment: the landscape he encountered and the aesthetic form of Nathan Rapoport's Warsaw Ghetto Monument. The situation in Warsaw in 1949 brought home to Du Bois the extent to which Nazi violence, and in particular the genocide and the *Vernichtungskrieg* (war of annihilation) in the East, constituted a particularly radical and perhaps new instance of global racial terror:

> I have seen something of human upheaval in this world: the scream and shots of a race riot in Atlanta; the marching of the Ku Klux Klan; the threat of courts and police; the neglect and destruction of human habitation; but nothing in my wildest imagination was equal to what I saw in Warsaw in 1949. I would have said before seeing it that it was impossible for a civilized nation with deep religious convictions and outstanding religious institutions; with literature and art; to treat fellow human beings as Warsaw had been treated. There had been complete, planned and utter destruction. Some streets had been so obliterated that only by using photographs of the past could they tell where the street was. And no one mentioned the total of the dead, the sum of destruction, the story of crippled and insane, the widows and orphans. ("Warsaw Ghetto" 14–15)

When Du Bois visited Warsaw, the city was in the middle of a massive project of reconstruction. Upon liberation from the Nazis on January 17, 1945, "the city area was covered with a mass of rubble estimated at 20 million cubic metres" (see Figure 3).[19] Two-thirds of the population had been killed (including hundreds of thousands of Jews from the Ghetto) and the city was 85 percent devastated (*Warsaw* n.p.). At the time of Du Bois's visit

FIGURE 3 Photograph by Israel Gutman of the ruins of the Warsaw Ghetto in July 1945. Courtesy of the United States Holocaust Memorial Museum Photo Archives.

parts of the city had already been reconstructed, but vast areas remained in rubble, in particular on the site of the former Ghetto (as 1948 photographs of the newly unveiled Ghetto Monument illustrate).

Du Bois's reaction registers several different disturbances. For instance, he clearly appears shocked at the conjunction of civilization and barbarism now revealed as definitive of a certain moment of German history. As various commentators have remarked, Du Bois had a particular affinity for German culture. In Russell Berman's convincing interpretation of *The Souls of Black Folk*, Du Bois was able to imagine the notoriously racist Wagner and his opera *Lohengrin* "standing in as sites of a life without prejudice" at a moment when racial violence and segregation were at a peak in the United States.[20] Even while condemning pre-Holocaust Nazi oppression of Jews, Du Bois asserts that during his German visit of 1936 he "cannot record a single instance" of "personal insult or discrimination," something that "would have been impossible . . . in any part of the United States" (*Du Bois: A Reader* 734). Thus, the intersection of the material evidence of later Nazi atrocities with an appreciation of German high culture probably had a particularly powerful effect on Du Bois. His mention of literature and art in this context also brings him close to Adorno's dictum on poetry after Auschwitz.

But the landscape itself registers the greatest impact in this passage. Above all, the sight of Warsaw as a postapocalyptic null point calls for a rethinking of the social geography of race. Du Bois, as he makes clear, is no stranger to racial violence. And indeed, in an earlier postwar moment before his visit to Warsaw, Du Bois was more likely to equate Nazi and colonial violence. For instance, in *The World and Africa* (1947), Du Bois writes, "There was no Nazi atrocity—concentration camps, wholesale maiming and murder, defilement of women or ghastly blasphemy of childhood—which the Christian civilization of Europe had not long been practicing against colored folk in all parts of the world in the name of and for the defense of a Superior Race born to rule the world."[21] In contrast to this earlier view of commensuration, however, the analogies Du Bois makes with American racism in the previous passage from "The Negro and the Warsaw Ghetto" are offered only to mark their difference from postwar Warsaw. They suggest a landscape of enforced and policed segregation, while the site in front of him seems to call for a different analysis and mapping. On the one hand, Warsaw has experienced the erasure of all lines of social differentiation. By the end of the war, the "obliteration" is so complete that only "photographs of the past" can orient the process of rebuilding. On the other hand, such absolute destruction could only result from a racist vision of absolute segregation different from, but related to, that which lies behind the racist violence that Du Bois mentions and with which he is already amply familiar in the United States. This situation of absolute erasure predicated on absolute separation contextualizes the "Negro problem"—not in the sense that Warsaw somehow belittles or trumps American racism with the invocation of a "greater" violence, but rather insofar as it reveals the more subtle and insidious operation of the color line in the very different political geography of Jim Crow America.

Together with his writings on the color line in *The Souls of Black Folk* and beyond, Du Bois's reflections on the landscape of Warsaw provide a complex portrait of how race and space are produced simultaneously: it is not only "color" that matters, the Warsaw article makes clear, but also especially the "line" that articulates and produces spatial differences together with racial ones. In Du Bois's careful articulation of relation and difference, Warsaw and Jim Crow lie at separate points along what Giorgio Agamben, following Foucault, calls a "biological continuum."[22] In a suggestive discussion of the ethical and philosophical implications of Auschwitz, Agamben helps locate the key to understanding the kind of violence and destruction Du Bois witnessed both in Europe and in the United States. Agamben notes that the Nazis seemed to combine two forms of power—sovereign and biopolitical—that Foucault had theorized as distinct: "In Hitler's Germany, an unprecedented absolutization of the biopower to *make live* intersects with an equally absolute generalization of the sovereign power to *make die*, such that biopolitics coincides immediately with thanatopolitics" (83). In a 1976 course at the Collège de France discussed by Agamben, Foucault identified racism as "precisely what allows biopower to mark caesuras in the biological continuum of the human species, thus reintroducing a principle of war into the system of 'making live'" (Agamben 84). In this account, racism represents the ability to rewrite the political domain of "the people" as the biological space of a population and then to "mark caesuras" in that space in order to differentiate and isolate various (and variously valued) populations. As both postwar Warsaw and Jim Crow America make clear, the concept of a biopolitical *space* is not a metaphor but the goal of a political project. In Warsaw, Du Bois confronts the result of Nazi plans to create "a *volkloser Raum*, a space empty of people" in Central Europe (Agamben 85). This empty space, which Agamben calls "an absolute biopolitical space" (86), is the extreme result of the production of a racial geography. Rethinking the color line from the ruins of Warsaw means grasping legalized segregation as part of a shared logic of biopower (a shared logic that Agamben himself does not pursue historically). Not simply confined to their own "ghettos," blacks and Jews are linked by virtue of the very caesura that divides them along the biological continuum. Du Bois's unpacking of the intimate links between race and space proves more able than Césaire or Arendt to mark distinctions within Europe and America, while simultaneously bearing witness to the shared biopolitical logic that cuts across dominant and colonized societies.

Du Bois's discourse, however, does not consist only of this mapping of the biopolitical space of violence and destruction, but attempts also to locate the place of a counterdiscourse. Just as Du Bois's entry into the Left public sphere of *Jewish Life* allows the articulation of a strategic relationship between black and Jewish histories, his engagement with the aftermath of Nazi genocide reveals another form of relatedness in the efforts to resist total destruction. Again, the conceptual and the material are closely aligned, as the respective reconstructions of discursive and urban space come together in an act of resistance against terror. After noting the city's obliteration, Du Bois remarks on the process of reconstruction that had begun immediately following the war:

The astonishing thing, of course, was the way that in the midst of all these memories of war and destruction, the people were rebuilding the city with an enthusiasm that was simply unbelievable. A city and a nation was [*sic*] literally rising from the dead. Then, one afternoon, I was taken out to the former ghetto. I knew all too little of its story although I had visited ghettos in parts of Europe, particularly in Frankfort [*sic*], Germany. Here there was not much to see. There was complete and total waste, and a monument. And the monument brought back again the problem of race and religion, which so long had been my own particular and separate problem. Gradually, from looking and reading, I rebuilt the story of this extraordinary resistance to oppression and wrong in a day of complete frustration, with enemies on every side: a resistance which involved death and destruction for hundreds and hundreds of human beings; a deliberate sacrifice in life for a great ideal in the face of the fact that the sacrifice might be completely in vain. ("Warsaw Ghetto" 15)

If, in contemplating the city, Du Bois opens this passage with an unpromising Christian discourse of resurrection in which the city "literally ris[es] from the dead," the next lines change direction once again. The temporal marker "Then" denotes a new moment in the discourse and introduces a somewhat different model of resistance to destruction: that of the futile but heroic Warsaw ghetto uprising. The ambivalences and shifts of this discourse draw attention to what is not quite spoken but haunts the passage: the landscape of Warsaw, even in destruction, is not *one*. The site of the Jewish ghetto does not rise as the rest of the city does—indeed there is "not much to see" there—because there is no "people," no "city and nation" to revive it. While destruction tends literally toward a leveling of the landscape, Du Bois silently reinscribes a difference within the forms of extreme violence. In the place of the political terms that are relevant to the reconstruction of the postwar Polish polis, on the site of genocide remain only the ruins of memory: "waste, and a monument."

Indeed it is Nathan Rapoport's monument whose agency is highlighted in this passage and which "brought back" the key Du Boisian problem of race—here linked with the related problem of religion and with the article's persistent questioning of notions of separateness and uniqueness. Nathan Rapoport's famous monument had been unveiled the previous year amidst the rubble of Nazi destruction on April 19, 1948—the fifth anniversary of the beginning of the ghetto uprising. Considering that the Nazis had destroyed 782 of the city's 987 historical monuments (Muszynski and Krajewska, *Warsaw* n.p.), Rapoport's monument must be imagined as significant, not just as a memorial to the fate of Polish Jews but as a symbol of Warsaw's rebirth. Yet, if the memorial to the ghetto is linked to the city as a whole, it also stands apart from it and, as Du Bois recognizes, carries its own story. While the Polish nation "ris[es] from the dead," Du Bois himself must "rebuil[d]" the ghetto narrative "from looking and reading." Why does Du Bois bother to distinguish between the immediacy of the heroic Socialist resurrection of Poland and the highly mediated and ambivalent heroism of the ghetto? Again, while tactical political matters related to the specificity of Du Bois's address to the Jewish

Left may be at stake, a more interesting explanation can also be found in the monument itself.

Rapoport's monument, I would argue, spoke so directly to Du Bois because its form is itself Du Boisian: it is a monument of and to a kind of double consciousness. Rapoport, a Polish Jewish sculptor, had spent time in the Soviet Union during the war as a refugee from the Nazis. His work is marked both by Socialist realism and by Jewish motifs, as well as by other currents in classical and modern art to which he had been exposed during study and travel in France and Italy.[23] The Warsaw Ghetto Monument presents these different currents in the form of a stark opposition between the heroism and suffering of the Jews. The monument is double-sided: it consists of a wall of blocklike granite with a statue of bronze figures emerging from one side of the wall and a stone bas-relief carved out of the other side. The bronze figures represent the ghetto fighters, whose resistance and sacrifice Du Bois notes, while the bas-relief depicts a train of huddled figures herded toward their death by barely visible Nazi soldiers. As James Young notes in *The Texture of Memory*, the monument brings together "the broadest of cultural archetypes—the lumbering mytho-proletarian figures of the Stalinist era and the typological image of Jews in exile" (155). On the one hand, the monument fixes these two forms in a doubled portrait of Jewishness that—despite details such as guns, a grenade, and Nazi helmets and bayonets—tends toward the timeless in its classical portraits. On the other hand, Young points out, there is also a "movement between sides" in which "the ancient type seems to pass *into* the shaded wall only to emerge triumphantly out of the other side into the western light: one type is literally recessive, the other emergent" (174). The ambiguities and oppositions of this double-sided, multiply significant form recall Du Bois's own theory of double consciousness and his commitment to a progressive, universalist historical narrative, as they speak to the polarized cold war political context in which Du Bois found himself in the late 1940s.

Rapoport's monument has been the subject of controversy within Holocaust studies, receiving criticism in particular for its universalizing, Socialist dimension from those who seek to maintain Jewish particularity within Holocaust memory. In his landmark *Against the Apocalypse: Responses to Catastrophe in Modern Jewish Culture*, David Roskies provides a powerfully pessimistic assessment of Rapoport's work. Reading the monument as a capitulation to a Stalinist aesthetic that compromises the Jewish tradition of response to catastrophe, Roskies asserts, "When mourning goes public in a public idiom, the price for accessibility can be very high indeed." He takes Rapoport to task for "separat[ing] and dichotomiz[ing] the knowledge of apocalypse and the statement of group survival" (301–2). Roskies does capture an important risk of Holocaust representation in general and an important feature of Rapoport's monument in particular. But Du Bois's remarks on the monument and the apparently active role that it and the spectacle of Warsaw played in his thinking lead me to dispute Roskies's pessimism, if certainly from a different perspective. While Roskies favors a "synthesis" that would bring together "old and new artistic forms to create a new archetype of destruction" over the "dichotomized" form of Rapoport's monument (302), it may be the very split within the monument that opens it up to nonappropriative readings of the sort practiced by Du Bois. Not simply an ossifying dichotomy, the double-sided form of the monument serves as an occasion for the articulation of multidirectional memory.

The response of Du Bois demonstrates another possibility for the reception of Holocaust memory beyond the universalist, de-Judaizing camp and the autonomous Jewish tradition propounded with such eloquence by Roskies. At least in Du Bois's contemporary reading, Rapoport's monument is situated at neither of these poles. Rather, that reading combines a recognition of the specificity of the Jewish catastrophe—signaled by the break in his discourse on the rebuilding of the city that introduces the monument—and a broad understanding of how that history forms part of a larger path of destruction premised on an unusually virulent biopolitical vision of racial segregation. For all of its Stalinist triumphalism, the memorial does also suggestively embody the double vision necessary for understanding the Nazi genocide beyond competitive models that would seek to displace its memory or enshrine it in a quasi-sacred uniqueness. The dual structure of Rapoport's monument bears comparison to the antiphonal structure of *The Souls of Black Folk* and to the exploration therein of the "two-ness" of African American culture. Double consciousness in that text refers to the fact that minorities are both "gifted with second-sight" by virtue of their inside/outside position vis-à-vis dominant culture and are plagued with a lack of "true self-consciousness" because they are "always looking at [their selves] through the eyes of others" (*Souls* 10–11). The simultaneity of estrangement and insight that Du Bois locates in the black experience of modernity certainly finds its analog in twentieth-century Jewish history and its articulation in Rapoport's monument.

In suggesting that the form of Du Bois's imaginings of black culture parallels the form in which Rapoport articulated Jewish history, I am not suggesting that Du Bois equates the experiences of slavery and colonialism with those of genocide. It is precisely the question of form to which I want to draw attention. The doubleness inherent in the transmutation of exile into resistance that characterizes the Warsaw memorial also characterizes the ultimate expression of African American culture's "two-ness" in *Souls*: the Sorrow Songs. In concluding his book, Du Bois turns to "these songs [that] are the articulate message of the slave to the world" (156), and that message turns out to parallel the monument's: "Through all the sorrow of the Sorrow Songs there breathes a hope—a faith in the ultimate justice of things. The minor cadences of despair change often to triumph and calm confidence. Sometimes it is faith in life, sometimes a faith in death, sometimes assurance of boundless justice in some fair world beyond. But whichever it is, the meaning is always clear: that sometime, somewhere, men will judge men by their souls and not by their skins" (162). In fact, however, Rapoport's monument is similar less to the Sorrow Songs themselves than to Du Bois's interpretation of them, for both Rapoport and Du Bois are trying to find forms to express a postemancipation context of extreme suffering twinned with hope for a different future.

If, as both Young and Roskies suggest, the monument seems to put forth a narrative in which the particularity of Jewish alienation and exile is transcended in the universality of socialist resistance and insight, it also resists that narrative by freezing the two sculptures in what Walter Benjamin might have described as a tense constellation of dual claims. While Communist ideology was open to the articulation of Holocaust memory in the immediate postwar period, the particular form Rapoport gave it might be seen also as subversive to the Stalinist context through its smuggling in of Jewish particularity, even if only on the backside of the monument. Du Bois's concept of double consciousness and his response to the monument in his 1952 article serve as a further reminder that both sides of the oppositions between the particular and the universal, exile and resistance, need to be understood as relational terms. Not only are the two sides ineluctably related to each other, but both Du Bois and Rapoport suggest in their different media that, on the one hand, experiences of particular suffering can be brought into dialogue with each other and that, on the other hand, emblems of universality need to be understood within specific historical and political contexts.[24] As a framework for thinking about the Nazi genocide, this relational view contrasts with the dominant understandings of the Holocaust both in the academy and in popular culture. It neither sacrifices the specificity of the Holocaust to a generic notion of modernity as catastrophe nor does it isolate the genocide of the Jews as an unrecuperable "excess" beyond history and representation.

When seen in the context of his many writings on racism, anti-Semitism, and Nazism, Du Bois's short article can be seen as bringing to fruition the cosmopolitanism with flesh that Césaire would call for a few years later in his *Lettre à Maurice Thorez*. Through allusion to Rapoport's Warsaw Ghetto Monument, Du Bois suggests a model of resistance to racial terror premised on double consciousness. But double consciousness does not remain what it was in his earlier writings. The "unique" bifocal relationship of double consciousness that Du Bois charts in *The Souls of Black Folk* between African American subjects and dominant culture gets refigured in "The Negro and the Warsaw Ghetto" as a more general *form* for the expression of particular relationships between minority and majority culture and between victimization and survival. Double consciousness is no longer simply a condition of African American life or, for that matter, of Jewish life in Europe. Rather, it is a conceptual, discursive, and aesthetic structure through which the conditions of minority life are given shape in order to ground acts of resistance to the biopolitical order. Displacing the color line and the problem of race entails conceptual work as well as political engagement. That remains true today.

Problems of the Twenty-First Century

The encounter of W. E. B. Du Bois with the ruins of the Warsaw Ghetto serves as a model of memory's multidirectionality. Du Bois's article is at once a reflection on the process of memorialization he observed during his visit to the devastated site of one of the Holocaust's most tragic sequences and a generous act of memory in its own right that cuts across ethnic boundaries. Du Bois defies the logic of scarcity that defines so much thinking about collective memory and group identity, especially when the memories and identities involved are those of blacks and Jews. He demonstrates how the other's history and memory can serve as a source of renewal and reconfiguration for the self—granted one is willing to give up exclusive claims to ultimate victimization and ownership over suffering. In the "second-sight" of Du Bois, the ruins of the ghetto become a common property, a public resource for reflection on the lines of race, culture, and religion that divide groups from each other even as they create new possibilities for alliance.

The problem of the twenty-first century may not be the problem of the color line.[25] And yet all those concerned with the legacies of violence that marred the twentieth century and have carried over into the twenty-first would do well to reflect on the variety of lines that demarcate contemporary societies. Considering race and violence in a comparative framework allows those interested in the Holocaust to benefit from a relaxation of the border patrol that too often surrounds and isolates discussion of the Shoah in antirealist discourses. Without collapsing the Nazi genocide into the banal litany of modern catastrophes that realist approaches sometimes court, a modified form of Du Boisian double consciousness allows a more subtle, multidirectional approach to the dialectic of the universal and the particular.

Such an opening up of Holocaust studies can also lead to a productive dialogue with those interested in colonial and postcolonial issues—especially if the latter are also willing to engage in self-reflection on the assumptions about memory and identity that often underlie their work. If developments within Holocaust studies have contributed to the Holocaust's marginalization in other fields, that is by no means an adequate explanation for the extent to which one of the most important events of the twentieth century has *not* played a role in the elaboration of a politically and historically sensitive cultural theory. Cultural studies in general and postcolonial studies in particular have tended to avoid questions of extreme violence of the kind that Du Bois reflected on after his visit to Warsaw and focus instead on everyday forms of violence, power, and knowledge. Meanwhile, the trauma studies tendency within literary theory has not for the most part developed a vocabulary for bringing its sophisticated exploration of psychic extremity together with the kinds of mundane political and material circumstances that my archaeology of Du Bois's visit demonstrates are unavoidable in assessing the meaning of traumatic histories (although, as my discussion of trauma theory in the previous chapters suggests, these questions are very much on the agenda). The coexistence of multiple tendencies within disciplinary and interdisciplinary fields is, of course, not only unavoidable but also welcome as the source of further innovations. Yet without crossing conceptual, geographical, and material borders in pursuit of shared problems, how would we ever find W. E. B. Du Bois in Warsaw?

Du Bois's visit to Warsaw took place under very precise, overdetermined circumstances, but the text he wrote in order to reflect on and draw conclusions from that experience may still serve as a paradigmatic example of the kind of transnational encounter that interdisciplinary studies at their best should pursue. Neither free from the tactics of political calculation nor simply dogmatic propaganda, "The Negro and the Warsaw Ghetto" traces a limit experience—that is, it directs us toward the border regions of thought and history. In this text's work of multidirectional memory, multiple categories and experiences collide and coexist: histories of slavery, colonialism, and genocide; the politics of the cold war; extreme and everyday forms of violence; the marginal cultural identities of European Jews and American blacks; the aesthetics of exile and resistance. Setting all of these factors into play against the backdrop of Warsaw in ruins, Du Bois becomes, like Walter Benjamin's Angel of History, an observer of the catastrophe of modern history.[26] Yet, unlike the Angel, Du Bois also faces forward and attempts to wrest a place from which to speak and act from the sedimented layers of history and memory. In the words of the last subtitle of the article, he seeks a "path to the future."

The path that Du Bois began to chart in "The Negro and the Warsaw Ghetto" would not remain his alone. The French Jewish novelist André Schwarz-Bart would pick up on the ruinous landscape of the Warsaw Ghetto as the basis for his own multidirectional moves in *La Mulâtresse Solitude*, an African Caribbean novel that also prompts a rereading of Schwarz-Bart's Holocaust classic, *Le dernier des justes*. A generation later, the space of the ghetto and the uncanny geographies of diaspora would similarly subtend the writing of Du Bois and Schwarz-Bart's Caribbean heir, Caryl Phillips. Following an extended discussion of the way that black and Jewish histories intersect in the literary memory work of Schwarz-Bart and Phillips, the following two sections illustrate how the lessons of Du Bois's visit could also resonate powerfully in a rather different context—that of France during and after the Algerian War of Independence. Here also acts of multidirectional memory serve as the grounds for resistance to a situation of routinized racial violence. Deploying the materials of memory with equal care, metropolitan opponents of the colonial war—some of them Holocaust survivors—and an international set of writers, activists, and artists (including the African American novelist William Gardner Smith) juxtaposed the German occupation and genocide of World War II with the practices of torture, censorship, and racialization deployed by the French state in its effort to maintain and manage its most prized colonial possession. Such juxtaposition both provided a platform for anticolonial resistance and contributed to a greater consciousness of the specificity of the Holocaust in the French public sphere. Like Du Bois, these activists demonstrate that the transnational circulation of memories cannot be contained by a zero-sum logic.

5

Anachronistic Aesthetics: André Schwarz-Bart and Caryl Phillips on the Ruins of Memory

In the concluding lines of André Schwarz-Bart's novel *A Woman Named Solitude* (*La Mulâtresse Solitude*, 1972), the narrator recalls the "humiliated ruins of the Warsaw Ghetto" while describing the site of a failed Caribbean slave revolt.[1] Schwarz-Bart, who died on September 30, 2006, was a French Jew of Polish origin who lost his family in the Nazi genocide and who remains best known for his novel of Holocaust and Jewish history, *The Last of the Just* (*Le Dernier des Justes*, 1959). After the surprising success of that prize-winning novel, Schwarz-Bart, in collaboration with his Guadeloupean wife Simone Schwarz-Bart, set out on an ambitious, multivolume project to write a comparative fictional history of blacks and Jews in diaspora. Only sections of that project in multidirectional memory have ever been published—besides *A Woman Named Solitude* there is the coauthored *Un plat de porc aux bananes vertes*, which is dedicated to Elie Wiesel and Aimé Césaire (1967)—but enough of it exists to allow us to continue to address fundamental questions pertaining to the literatures of genocide, slavery, and colonialism that we have begun in previous chapters: What does it mean to bring histories into contact at the site of a ruin? Indeed, what does it mean to write and remember from the site of a ruin? These questions, which are crucial for the study of multidirectional memory as well as both Holocaust and postcolonial literatures, can be addressed by considering the writings of Schwarz-Bart alongside those of the contemporary Caribbean-British novelist and travel writer Caryl Phillips.[2]

André Schwarz-Bart was not the first writer to link black and Jewish histories through the ruinous geography of the Warsaw Ghetto.[3] Warsaw in ruins also provided the occasion for W. E. B. Du Bois to meditate on what blacks and Jews share, as well as what divides their historical experiences in Europe and America. Like Du Bois, Schwarz-Bart and Phillips also draw particular attention to the spatial dynamics and outcomes of racialization through their writing of ghettos and ruins. The desire to develop aesthetic and discursive strategies adequate to linking different minority histories characterizes the work of these writers as much as that of Du Bois, but in place of the figures deployed by Du Bois, such as double consciousness and the biological continuum, new forms emerge from the work of the two novelists. Furthermore, while, in "The Negro and the Warsaw Ghetto," Du Bois conceptualizes such linkages by writing in a relatively direct mode that mixes the genres of travel report and political journalism, Schwarz-Bart's and Phillips's juxtapositions of black and Jewish histories are self-conscious acts of the imagination that work through deliberate anachronism. In addition, the work of Schwarz-Bart and Phillips focuses our attention on yet another condition of multidirectional memory in the postwar period: the migration during and after decolonization of former colonial subjects to the erstwhile imperial metropolis, a migration that marks the lives and work of both of these writers. The experience of and confrontation with postcolonial migrations also raise for Schwarz-Bart and Phillips the question of diaspora—a perennial site of geographical and conceptual contact for two perennially displaced peoples.

Bringing together Schwarz-Bart and Phillips, I continue this book's methodology of putting into question taken-for-granted assumptions about which fields and authors belong together and which do not. Against restrictive conceptions that keep the histories and aftermaths of the Holocaust and European colonialism separate from each other, I pursue the power of anachronism, which brings together that which is supposed to be kept apart. Anachronism, as Vico suggested, can derive from one of at least four forms of error: "The first error regards as *uneventful* periods which were actually full of events.... Conversely, a second error regards as *eventful* those periods which were actually uneventful. . . . A third error *unites* periods which should be separated. . . . Conversely, a fourth error *divides* periods which should be united."⁴ Although these forms of anachronism constitute different types of "error" when perceived from a historicist perspective, they can also serve as powerfully subversive and demystifying means of exposing the ideological assumptions of historicist categorization, as the writers under investigation here demonstrate. Different forms of anachronism play key roles in the literary experiments of Schwarz-Bart and Phillips.

Schwarz-Bart struggles to find a literary form for the anachronistic juxtaposition of black and Jewish histories in order to develop an aesthetic premised on hospitality to histories of the other. While he explicitly attempts to forge an aesthetic of multidirectional memory in *A Woman Named Solitude*, a reading attuned to postcolonial thematics such as migration can illuminate the composition of Schwarz-Bart's canonical Holocaust novel *The Last of the Just* as well. If Schwarz-Bart might ultimately be seen to fail in this attempt to create a multidirectional black-Jewish epic, the fault lies less in his anachronistic desire to move between different histories than in the particular way he writes trauma. In assessing Schwarz-Bart's success and failure, Dominick LaCapra's distinction between structural and historical trauma becomes an important lever helping us to distinguish between different modes of writing in the aftermath of the Holocaust and colonialism.⁵

Phillips may be Schwarz-Bart's most interesting heir, as his staging of black-Jewish relatedness in works such as the travel report *The European Tribe* (1987) and the novels *Higher Ground* (1989) and *The Nature of Blood* (1997) demonstrates. If memory works according to a multidirectional logic, questions remain about what narrative forms correspond to and express the work of intercultural remembrance and what the effects of those narrative forms are. Mobilizing intertextuality and the fragmentation of narration, Phillips's writings do not establish an equation between black and Jewish history, or even strictly parallel histories, as can be found in Schwarz-Bart, but rather highlight both similar structural problems within those histories and missed encounters between them. Through his particular juxtaposition of blacks and Jews in a transnational narrative frame, Phillips alludes to Schwarz-Bart's oeuvre in order to decompose it; he thus produces a fractured form of relatedness characteristic of the Holocaust's multidirectional legacies in a globalized, yet unevenly developed age.

The Memory of Slavery and *The Last of the Just*

Schwarz-Bart's work of anachronism can be glimpsed through a comparison of the openings and closings of his two single-authored works, *The Last of the Just* and *A Woman Named Solitude*; such a comparison highlights the sites where the novels most explicitly seek to establish their relationship to the historical imagination, a relationship that Schwarz-Bart explicitly thematizes in two important and little-known texts from 1967: an interview on "Jewishness and Negritude" and a programmatic essay, "Pourquoi j'ai écrit *La Mulâtresse Solitude*." Moving between these varied fictional and nonfictional texts, I seek to destabilize Jewish identity and experience as the presumed grounds of Schwarz-Bart's literary project. Yet, while I argue that Schwarz-Bart's project is grounded instead in an openness to cultural and historical difference, I also suggest that it ultimately reinstates the same mythic structure that underlies the discourse of uniqueness.

In *The Last of the Just*, Schwarz-Bart's first novel, the narrative follows the fortunes of the fictional Levy family across a millennium of Jewish history from twelfth-century England to the Nazi camps. As he unfolds this epic history, Schwarz-Bart also draws on and reshapes the Jewish legend of the thirty-six just men. In this legend, from which Schwarz-Bart significantly deviates, there "are thirty-six Zaddikim, or just men, on whom—though they are unknown or hidden—rests the fate of the world."[6] In the legend, these thirty-six just men exist at any given time; in the novel, they are not unknown or hidden and instead succeed each other generationally as part of the same family. As D. Mesher clarifies in a useful overview, *The Last of the Just* has a complicated relationship to history and cultural tradition: "The novel is a blend of one part history (the fate of the Jews in Europe from the Middle Ages onward), one part folklore (the Jewish legend of the thirty-six secret saints), and one part fiction (the involvement of a single family in many of the major events of Jewish history in Europe for almost a millennium)."[7]

Problems of chronology and anachronism inevitably accompany such a historical montage and are partly to blame for what Francine Kaufmann has called "l'affaire Schwarz-Bart," the controversy that was generated after the appearance of *The Last of the Just* in 1959. In that controversy, Schwarz-Bart, a working-class autodidact, was accused not only of plagiarism (examples of which proved to be quite minor), but also of betraying Jewish history and culture and of misdating and misnaming certain references throughout the text.[8] Despite these accusations, *The Last of the Just* was an enormously popular and critical success; shortly after being published in the fall of 1959 it won the Prix Goncourt, the most prestigious French literary prize, and became a best seller. Nevertheless, impassioned debate has always accompanied the novel's multilevel depiction of Jewish history and, especially, its relation to Christianity, a Christianity that seems to be radically indicted in this depiction at the same time that its notion of redemptive suffering is mobilized.

While "l'affaire Schwarz-Bart" illuminates significant issues pertaining to understandings of the Holocaust and the depiction of genocide (issues whose significance has changed in the forty years since publication, of course), my reading seeks to move beyond the controversy and even the text itself into a para- and intertextual space of multidirectional memory. Such a reading may not completely transform understandings of *The Last of the Just*, but it will help to explain the turn Schwarz-Bart takes toward the history and culture of the African diaspora. I locate that turn in a different source than do most critics. In one of her only references to Schwarz-Bart's interest in the African diaspora, Kaufmann writes, for example, that "only a Jew is in a position to feel completely the absoluteness of Jewish abandonment," and that "through his experience the Jew is in a position to understand the suffering of other men, to recognize not the identity but the contiguity of limit-experiences" (120). Kaufmann's notion of contiguity is important—and is closely linked to the multiple encounters that underlie many of my examples—but her explanation of historical empathy is too one-directional, as is her notion of Jewish experience. It is not simply that Schwarz-Bart's experience as the son of Holocaust victims opens him to the suffering of others—although this is certainly true—but also that a recognition of the other's suffering opens up a new way of thinking about his own historical location. Although much of the controversy surrounding the novel involves the dominant diachronic structure of the text (its movement across a millennium of history and legend), little-known comments by Schwarz-Bart suggest that the novel's investment in history is in part the product of an implicit spatial relationship—the presence in 1950s Paris of migrants from the Caribbean.

Already in its opening sentences *The Last of the Just* articulates the ruling conceit that has continued to generate critical response. As this opening makes clear, Schwarz-Bart is interested in a deep history of the Holocaust: "Our eyes register the light of dead stars. A biography of my friend Ernie could easily be set in the second quarter of the twentieth century, but the true history of Ernie Levy begins much earlier, toward the year 1000 of our era, in the old Anglican city of York. More precisely, on March 11, 1185."[9] These lines move in two directions simultaneously: while the narrator returns to the past in the interests of portraying a "true history," the past reappears in the present as a kind of celestial afterlife. Such a double movement may characterize all acts of historicization, yet here it creates an ambiguity in the novel that remains difficult to clarify. First and most obviously, as many contemporary readers suspected and some reacted strongly against, the novel serves as an uncompromising condemnation that locates genocide in the *longue durée* of Christian anti-Semitism. In so doing, it proposes a historicization of the Holocaust that shares the form of historical explanation ("true history"), but which few historians would today accept; although Christian anti-Semitism is seen as among the conditions of possibility for Nazi policy, Nazi anti-Semitism is now generally understood as a form of racism quite distinct from traditional anti-Judaism.[10] But this teleological writing of history, which draws a straight line from 1185 to 1945, coexists with another, less linear form of time. Regardless of its status as historical explanation, the novel's opening also suggests that it has an unavoidable stake in a kind of ghostly anachronism: the fact that "our eyes register the light of dead stars" complicates the search for origins that the novel seems so invested in and reveals the irony in the precision with which the narrator claims to locate the beginnings of Ernie Levy's story. That is, if the very conditions of seeing and understanding are themselves subject to a form of anachronism—the nonsynchronicity between the source of light and our registration of it—then the very possibility of grasping historical particularity would seem to be put in question.

Anachronistic Aesthetics   141

The problem of historical particularity in the novel is one of the conundrums that critics have always noted. The key question tends to take a form such as this: In *The Last of the Just*, is Auschwitz part of the continuity of Jewish history or a novum that extinguishes it? As Lawrence Langer has commented, "The dispute over whether [the Holocaust] represents a singular atrocity unparalleled in previous history or 'merely' an extreme and more thorough example of the periodic assaults and pogroms which the Jewish people have suffered throughout time will probably never be settled."[11] The conundrum, already present from the first page of the novel, is further intensified by its ending. After traveling some eight hundred years in time and witnessing the martyrdom of various Jewish individuals and communities, we arrive at, and even in, the gas chambers of the Holocaust. Ernie Levy, the "last of the just men" of Schwarz-Bart's rewriting of Jewish legend, volunteers to be sent to his death in order to be with his beloved Golda, first by entering the transit camp Drancy, then by volunteering for a convoy to Auschwitz, and finally by requesting to join those being sent to the gas chambers. Within that rarely represented space of the gas chambers, Schwarz-Bart famously entangles the Jewish prayer for the dead, the mourner's Kaddish, with the names of the well-known Nazi concentration and extermination camps: "And praised. *Auschwitz.* Be. *Maidanek.* The Lord. *Treblinka* [. . .] And praised . . . " (*Last of the Just* 374). While the novel's opening unsettles the chronology of Jewish history, its ending raises the question of Jewish cultural continuity: there is no sure way of saying whether in these penultimate lines "the horror of the concentration camp is enveloped by a spiritual transcendence" or whether, to the contrary, that horror "muffle[s] the paean to God with the terror-stricken echoes of unredeemable suffering" (Langer 263). Although the novel has seemed to be building toward precisely this latter vision of the unredeemable, its very last lines, just after the fractured prayer, suggest a form of persistence, if not exactly transcendence. The unnamed first-person narrator of the opening paragraph returns with an ambiguous assessment. Sensing that Ernie Levy remains alive somewhere, the narrator stands "in the street trembling in despair, rooted to the spot, a drop of pity fell from above upon my face. But there was no breeze in the air, no cloud in the sky. . . . There was only a presence" (*Last of the Just* 374). Invoking presence in the face of annihilation and juxtaposing prayer with sites of death, Schwarz-Bart's first novel refuses to resolve the dilemmas of chronology and tradition provoked by a millennium of Jewish history; the ambivalence of the opening, in which a strong drive toward historical continuity coexists with a ghostly discontinuity, remains.

Because, in *The Last of the Just*, this problem of continuity seems located so squarely within Jewish history and culture it comes as a surprise when, in an interview published in an American Zionist journal at the time of the appearance of *Un plat de porc* in 1967, Schwarz-Bart locates this double form of temporality outside a uniquely Jewish context. Responding to interviewer Michel Salomon's suggestion that Schwarz-Bart might "baffle [his] readers" by following his Holocaust novel with a series of works "dealing with the condition of the Negro," Schwartz-Bart replies, "There is no division here between an older inspiration and one that has succeeded it, since the idea and the basic decision to write this book [*Un plat de porc*] date from long before the completion of *The Last of the Just*: the decision was made in 1955, and *The Last of the Just* was finished in 1959."[12] According to Francine Kaufmann's reconstruction of the genesis of *The Last of the Just*, 1955 was also a particularly significant moment in the drafting of that first novel. In that year, Schwarz-Bart completed a first version of the novel, set during the war in France. The author was unhappy with it, however; as Kaufmann recounts, "The characters singularly lack density because they float free, cut off from their roots. The present remains opaque without the revelatory echo of the past" (19). In versions drafted after 1955, Schwarz-Bart begins to broaden the time frame of the novel significantly. The second version, a section of which was published at the end of 1956, reaches back to the early nineteenth century, while the final version, completed in 1958 and 1959, extends several hundred years into the past (Kaufmann 19–21). Beyond their common date—1955—what is the link between the conception of a literary cycle treating African diaspora history and the reconceptualization of *The Last of the Just*? Further comments by Schwarz-Bart suggest that his ability to add the density of historical echo to *The Last of the Just* derives from a surprising source.

In retrospect, at least, Schwartz-Bart blurs the question of the "origins" of his two novels: the later novel on "the Negro condition" is not a break with the Jewish history of the earlier novel, but neither is it a simple extension or development of it. Rather, the works seem to mutually influence each other and to emerge together, if also nonsynchronously (there were eight years between the publications of the two novels). Like so many of the examples I consider in this book, this textual encounter is accompanied by a biographical encounter, and the ricochets between text, life, and diverse histories suggest the presence of multidirectional memory. Schwarz-Bart ascribes the mutual influence of his novels of black and Jewish history to a particular relationship to the past that he discovered among West Indians in Paris during the 1950s:

> One can readily understand what was for me the most moving aspect of this world that I was able to encounter among people living in Paris, in the Latin Quarter—the element of slavery in their background. They would talk about this element in their history, they would relive it, one might say, in much the same way that we Jews, more than twenty years later, still relive the Holocaust and will go on doing so for a long time to come. To some extent their tragedy reflects the history of our own. We Jews are reliving something that is still of the present era; but now I was seeing for the first time individuals who were living in another era, one of which they had not yet rid themselves, a historical epoch which existed in the present for them and which, for the first time, I was led to compare with the Jewish experience.

In this passage the grounds for comparing Jewish and black histories—and, more personally, the means for Schwarz-Bart to break out of the "solitude of Jewish destiny" within which he previously had felt "sealed"—lie in the shared sense of "reliving" historical tragedy (Salomon 4). As recounted in 1967, the encounter with a Caribbean temporality seems not only to look ahead to Schwarz-Bart's novels of the African diaspora but also to look back to the temporal form of *The Last of the Just*; for it is not so much Jews in this passage as the descendants of slaves who live anachronistically, as if in the light of dead stars.[13] The paradox of "a historical epoch which existed in the present" describes well Schwarz-Bart's use of Jewish legend and chronicle as a means of accessing the trauma of genocide. Previous to his encounter with another diaspora, Schwarz-Bart felt that "our recent tragedy isolated us [Jews], not only with respect to the rest of humanity, but with respect to the past and to the future" (Salomon 4). The combination of distance and presence he locates in black history, however, seems to open up a space for the anachronistic aesthetic of *The Last of the Just* by allowing the Holocaust, an event that he understands as "still of the present era," to resonate with histories beyond it. According to Schwarz-Bart's comments, and the textual evidence of his oeuvre, the memory of slavery unlocks Jewish memory (and futurity) and makes possible an aesthetic project of multidirectional remembrance.

The multidirectionality of *The Last of the Just*, suggested by Schwarz-Bart's comments in the interview, may even inhere in the very legend that inspired the novel, although it is not at all clear that he would have known this. In an essay written in the wake of Schwarz-Bart's book, Gershom Scholem, the renowned scholar of Jewish mysticism, traces the convoluted origins of the legend of the thirty-six hidden just men. His inability definitively to locate a single source for the various components of the legend suggests that Schwarz-Bart's novel emerges directly out of the terrain of multidirectional memory. According to Scholem, its key source may even involve an example of Jewish-Islamic syncretism: "For the present we cannot determine whether this conception [of the hidden just men] originated in a Jewish tradition which had already taken on new form when it penetrated Islamic circles or whether the metamorphosis occurred in Islam and then the tradition returned to Judaism in this new form at an as yet undetermined time" (Scholem 254). Although asserted cautiously and tentatively, Scholem's archaeology of the legend illustrates how difficult it is to preserve cultural traditions from the relays of multidirectional memory.

Writing Ruins: *A Woman Named Solitude*

In *The Last of the Just* the contact between black and Jewish histories remains virtual and is primarily perceptible through genetic criticism, paratextual materials such as Schwarz-Bart's interview with Michel Salomon, and the intertextual sources of the legend of the just. In *A Woman Named Solitude*, by contrast, that contact is ultimately made explicit in its concluding juxtaposition of Poland and Guadeloupe. From the beginning, Schwarz-Bart's third novel adopts the anachronistic style of his first and mixes historical chronicle and mythical elements. Its opening combines a fairy-tale framework with secular-Christian European chronology and geography, although there is nothing in the novel's discourse of history that hints at the juxtaposition with which the novel will conclude:

> Once upon a time, on a strange planet, there was a little black girl by the name of Bayangumay. She had made her appearance on earth about 1755 in a calm and intricate estuary landscape, where the clear water of a river, the green water of an ocean, and the black water of a delta channel mingled—and where, so it is said, the soul was still immortal. But the inhabitants of this region had no Olympus, no Valhalla or heavenly Jerusalem. They were not inclined to lose themselves in the clouds, for they were too much attached to their cows, their salt meadows, and most of all to their rice paddies, which were known and prized throughout West Africa. (3)

The point of view in this passage is dialogical; the passage simultaneously addresses a European audience for whom Bayangumay lives both on "a strange planet" and in "West Africa" and invokes local forms of knowledge (about rice and other aspects of everyday life). While, as Bella Brodzki argues, the coming of European slave traders may already be foreshadowed here, the more gentle tone of this opening, in comparison to *The Last of the Just*, in which a Jewish community commits ritual suicide (*Kiddush haShem*) on the first page, suggests an initially different relationship to history; unlike the Jews of Europe, the inhabitants of this particular estuary have not yet been inserted into the violence of European history.[14] We are far here from the Conradian tradition of European depictions of Africa that makes its way so crucially and with such damaging results into Arendt's writings on imperialism. If a split of worldviews is implied between European assumptions and African concerns, the fairy-tale tone and bucolic landscape suggest a peaceful coexistence of cultural temporalities—like the "mingling" of the waters of the estuary—rather than a clash of civilizations. Additionally, in contrast to those members of the African diaspora whom Schwarz-Bart encounters in the 1950s, these fictional African villagers are also not "living in another era"; within their deliberately idealized perspective anachronism is not even possible since there don't yet appear to be historical periods that could be collapsed or opposed to each other. Nevertheless, from the implicit perspective of the nonnative reader, the combination of the "ordinal function" of dating ("about 1755") with the mythic time of the extrahistorical ("Once upon a time") echoes the opening of the earlier novel.[15]

By the end of *A Woman Named Solitude*, in any case, such mingling of times and cultures has given way to the conjuring of ghosts, and contact between the European and the non-European has become a matter of catastrophe and displacement. The descendants of that idealized African landscape have become diasporic subjects, still tilling the land, but under significantly different conditions. Captured, deported, and raped during the Middle Passage, Bayangumay gives birth to a daughter, "la mulâtresse Solitude," a legendary figure in Guadeloupe's history. Solitude is later executed for her role in a slave rebellion the day after giving birth to a child destined to live as someone's property. In the novel's brief epilogue, the narrator breaks the historical frame of the novel and imagines that a tourist will one day come to visit the plantation where Solitude and other rebels fought against their enslavement—a site that was dynamited in desperation by the rebellion's leader:

If the traveler insists, he will be permitted to visit the remains of the old Danglemont plantation. The guard will wave his hand, and as though by magic a tattered black field worker will appear. He will greet the lover of old stones with a vaguely incredulous look, and they will start off.... [T]hey will stroll this way and that and ultimately come to a remnant of knee-high wall and a mound of earth intermingled with bone splinters.... Conscious of a faint taste of ashes, the visitor will take a few steps at random, tracing wider and wider circles around the site of the mansion. His foot will collide with one of the building stones, concealed by dead leaves, which were dispersed by the explosion and then over the years buried, dug up, covered over, and dug up again by the innocent hoes of the field workers. If he is in the mood to salute a memory, his imagination will people the environing space, and human figures will rise up around him, just as the phantoms that wander about the humiliated ruins of the Warsaw ghetto are said to rise up before the eyes of other travelers. (149–50)

In these concluding sentences of the novel Schwarz-Bart mobilizes multiple forms of anachronism and *anatopism* (or, spatial misplacement). As in the novel's opening paragraphs, the mythical mingles with the mundane. But in the place of the fairy-tale "once upon a time," new, more gothic temporalities emerge. Like the fragments of bone, time is literally splintered. While the novel proper moves continuously from Africa to Guadeloupe and from the mid-eighteenth century to the beginning of the nineteenth, the epilogue jumps to the contemporary moment of the novel's enunciation and to a hypothetical, layered European/Caribbean space. Both the presumably European traveler and the West Indian guide appear equally displaced spatially and temporally—the former because of his perplexing love of "old stones," the latter because of his magical emergence and tattered appearance. As ruin, the site of the plantation is itself disjoined from the present, half-buried by nearly two centuries of "innocent" activities but still testifying to a traumatic past.

When, in the very final line, the narrative invokes the ruins of the Warsaw Ghetto, it conjures up multiple associations.[16] As Brodzki has suggested about this passage, reference to the Ghetto implies a "double legacy" of "destruction" and "heroic resistance," because of the well-known history of the Ghetto Uprising (225)—a suggestion that would apply equally to Du Bois's article on Warsaw. This double sense of terror and resistance describes well the tenor of Schwarz-Bart's novel, even if this final passage, with its emphasis on humiliation and ghosts, seems less affirmative than Brodzki implies. Why, though, does Schwarz-Bart evoke this double legacy through an anachronistic and anatopic analogy? That is, what does the fact of anachronism add to the story that the novel has already told about slavery and resistance? While Du Bois links Warsaw Ghetto and the color line (both in the United States and globally) in order to make a point about the relationship between race and space as well as resistance and terror, Schwarz-Bart's anachronisms throw the very grounds of historicization into question. Schwarz-Bart most obviously commits Vico's third error; he links two periods and places—the early nineteenth-century Caribbean and mid-twentieth-century Central Europe—that are not traditionally viewed in tandem. This "error" might be understood, however, as functioning to expose how Vico's first form of anachronism has distorted understandings of Caribbean history. While Nathan Rapoport's monument rose on the site of the Ghetto a few short years after the liberation of Poland from Nazi occupation, Brodzki remarks that the slave revolt that the novel recounts "has never been memorialized" (225).[17] That is, appeal to the well-known event of the Warsaw Ghetto Uprising helps make a point about the mistaken rendering of the Caribbean as an "uneventful" site outside of the dominant narrative of world history. Schwarz-Bart performs an archaeological unearthing of events that have been anachronistically obscured by layers of forgetfulness.

Even more radically, Schwarz-Bart's gesture may challenge the very terms through which his analogy could be termed anachronistic; it may suggest precisely that the two periods juxtaposed do belong together in a new narration of history that begins with the specters of those who have been silenced. Not only is the memory of the Holocaust brought to bear on a "forgotten" piece of world history, but that fragment of the Caribbean past unexpectedly recontextualizes the Nazi genocide. In placing the two histories side by side, the novel does not so much normalize or relativize the "uniqueness" of the Holocaust, but renders it as part of a parallel series of singular events. The parallel invocation of ruins and the specters that haunt them bespeaks a temporality not easily recuperable by historicist renderings.

The Problem of Form: Between Absence and Loss

A little-known and untranslated commentary in which Schwarz-Bart describes his literary-historical project suggests the possibilities and problems of such a new narrative, founded as it is on parallel, ruinous histories.[18] In "Pourquoi j'ai écrit *La Mulâtresse Solitude*," published in 1967 at the time of the release of his previous novel, *Un plat de porc aux bananes verts* (coauthored with his wife Simone), Schwarz-Bart provides a tortured account of his attempt to write a history with a "global dimension [*la dimension planétaire*]" (8). This relatively short text provides one of the most searching attempts to articulate—or as Ronnie Scharfman writes, to "relate," in both its narrative and connective senses (255)—the histories of colonialism, the Holocaust, and their aftermaths. In this context, I want to focus on two aspects of the text—the first Schwarz-Bart had published since *The Last of the Just*—that are relevant to my larger argument: Schwarz-Bart's description of his identification with West Indians and the program he articulates for a literary joining of seemingly disparate histories.

After mentioning his long-standing admiration for West Indians, whom he describes as possessing the very desirable "qualities that I do not possess," Schwarz-Bart identifies the word "Slavery" as the ultimate source of his fraternal feelings. In glossing the significance of that word, which figures also in the contemporaneous interview discussed above, Schwarz-Bart outlines a complicated sense of black-Jewish relations:

Certainly, this word affected me as a Jewish man, member of a community that had just experienced the price of human life. And yet, as strange as it might seem to you, the word touched me above all as a Jewish child, as the far-flung descendant of a people born in slavery and who emerged out of it three thousand years ago. I remember that in 1941, on the first night of Passover, the honor of posing the ritual question to the head of the family came to me: "Ma nishtana halaila haze nicol ha lelot?" which means "How is this night different from all other nights?" And I remember the response that my father gave me in Hebrew: "My child, it was during a night like this one that our ancestors came out of Egypt, where they had been held as slaves." And I believe that it is that Jewish child whose fathers were slaves under Pharaoh, before becoming so again under Hitler, who was taken by a definitive, fraternal love for West Indians. (8)

In an attempt to explain the relationship between his novels on the Jewish and African diasporas, Schwarz-Bart both evokes and displaces the significance of the Nazi genocide. Through the figure of the remembered Passover seder, this passage returns to the year in which Nazi policy entered its genocidal phase (although this could not have been known at the time by the victims), but it does so in order to evoke a much older—indeed mythic—history. This passage takes the intertwining of identities and histories that we have already begun to explore in relationship to *The Last of the Just* and *A Woman Named Solitude* even further. It implies that Schwarz-Bart's identification with West Indians—an identification that allowed him to escape the isolation produced by the Nazi genocide—is itself underwritten by the imaginary (which is not to say, unreal) quality of Jewish identity: its foundation, enacted in the Passover seder, on what Michael Walzer has called "vicarious experience," an anachronistic identification with unknown and unknowable ancestors.[19] The anachronistic linkage of "slaves under Pharaoh" and "slaves under Hitler" authorizes the anachronistic linkage of black and Jewish former slaves in the present. Paradoxically, it is by virtue of its nonhistorical nature that the power of the imagination to bridge the rupture, or "déchirement" (8), internal to each culture—whether it be slavery or genocide—becomes a resource for multidirectional relation, that is, for narrative and linkage.

Despite the "definitive, fraternal love" Schwarz-Bart evinces for West Indians, the identificatory links he describes do not translate easily into literature; the problem of form remains critical. The difficulty of the task of finding an adequate literary form for expressing black-Jewish relatedness is indicated both by the intricacies of the program Schwarz-

Bart articulates in "Pourquoi j'ai écrit *La Mulâtresse Solitude*" and by his ultimate inability or lack of desire to fulfill that program. In contrast to Du Bois's text, which solves the problem of form by implicitly reworking the theory of double consciousness so that it might capture comparative dimensions of minority life, the form suggested by Schwarz-Bart's text is less symmetrical and binary. Schwarz-Bart describes his project, humorously, as an "accordion," because its projected size continually expanded and contracted. Not only was the ultimate form of the *Mulâtresse Solitude* cycle in question, but so too were the sections focused on Jewish history. While *The Last of the Just* had been published eight years earlier, the completion of another novel, already underway, which would treat the concentrationary universe more directly, remained "more than improbable." Nevertheless, Schwarz-Bart continues:

> The ideal ensemble would present itself in the form of a triptych. The first panel would consist of *The Last of the Just*. The central panel would consist of the M[ulâtresse] S[olitude] cycle, of which each volume is conceived as its own entity, as an original and autonomous work—in the sense that one can compare the ensemble to a necklace of seven stones each of which would have a different form, color, and luster. . . . Finally, the third element of the triptych, which would be a counterpart to *The Last of the Just*, would obviously be this concentrationary novel which I am not sure it is reasonable to evoke already. (8)

Fascinating about the program outlined by Schwarz-Bart is not only its ultimate nonfulfillment (after *Solitude* he never published another novel), but also the excess of figures through which he evokes it. Each of the figures—accordion, triptych, necklace—represents an attempt to give form to the literary-historical problem. It is precisely in the inverse proportion between the excess of figuration and the paucity of results that a very particular "solution" emerges. Rather than simply reading Schwarz-Bart's unfulfilled program as a failure, we can understand it as testifying to a deficit in the available frameworks and conditions of possibility for the telling of such stories. The recourse to anachronism, imagination, and figuration suggests that, for Schwarz-Bart, the story of black-Jewish relatedness cannot be written in a realist, historicist mode—even one that takes into account the doubleness of minority consciousness. Nor, however, was he ultimately able to find a realizable alternative. What the histories of the African diaspora in the Caribbean and the Jewish diaspora in Europe share is not any "positive" experience, but rather the negativity of rupture and the necessity of imaginative work that spans that abyss: as the epilogue to *A Woman Named Solitude* makes clear, the ghosts that haunt the plantation and the ghetto mark an unrecuperable loss that can be "filled" or "peopled [*emplira*]" (*Solitude* 150/140) only by the imagination of those who come after.

Yet, in order for that imagination to respond adequately to the challenges of loss, it must be able to differentiate that which has been lost from that which was never present in the first place, that which is constitutively absent. The distinction between loss and absence, usefully linked by LaCapra to historical and structural trauma, respectively, helps to clarify where Schwarz-Bart's project breaks down. Historical trauma is "related to particular events that do indeed involve losses," while structural trauma "is related to (even correlated with) transhistorical absence (absence of/ at the origin) and appears in different ways in all societies and all lives." Examples of historical trauma include slavery, the Holocaust, and war; examples of structural trauma tend to be more speculative and include "separation from the (m)other, the passage from nature to culture, . . . the entry into language" (LaCapra 76–77, 80–81). As LaCapra remarks, it is not surprising that these two forms of trauma would overlap in certain contexts, especially posttraumatic ones; however, blurring the distinction between absence and loss can have debilitating intellectual and political consequences. On the one hand, deflecting historical losses into structural absence can lead to melancholia or despair about possibilities for moving beyond the past or confronting the problems of the present. Reducing structural trauma to a historical event, on the other hand, can reinforce myths of omnipotence and lead to dangerous attempts at totalizing political solutions.

Despite his obvious sympathies for history's victims, Schwarz-Bart seems to transfer historical losses into a de-historicized realm. Part of the impasse that characterizes his work may derive from what Sidra Ezrahi diagnoses as his commitment to a static vision of history characterized by "the eternal recurrence of human suffering"—a vision, in other words, that transforms historical losses into transhistorical absence. Despite the multiple levels of temporality explored in his books, Schwarz-Bart's protagonists—both Jewish and black—seem "destined from birth to martyrdom by an inexorable historical process that ordains that certain groups be lambs and others butchers" (Ezrahi 136–37). Even as he multiplies the figures for relating black and Jewish histories, Schwarz-Bart returns again and again to the same fundamental scenario of violence; in LaCapra's terms, he remains within the spell of trauma, acting out victimization instead of working it through. Elevating the shared black-Jewish relationship to the negativity of rupture from a contingent historical relationship to a transcendent, extrahistorical inevitability, Schwarz-Bart blurs the distinction between loss and absence. The dependence of that historical vision on a binary understanding of victims and perpetrators suggests that in order to break the hold of inevitability a more complex account of victimization will be necessary. Ironically, even as Schwarz-Bart's oeuvre disrupts the sacralized uniqueness of the Holocaust through its commitment to comparison, it does so by employing the same mythic elements that uniqueness discourse uses to canonize the historical event as a "founding trauma" (LaCapra 81).

LaCapra's distinctions between absence and loss and historical and structural trauma allow us to ask what it means to write ruins. The problem in Schwarz-Bart's work is not a fixation on ruins as such; after all, the histories of the Jewish and African diasporas are littered with destruction and victimization. It is both logical and a social fact that members of those diasporas see each other through the prism of extreme violence—a form of mutual recognition that has led both to periods of solidarity and incidents of antagonism of the sort that can only emerge from those who perceive themselves as "almost the same."[20] Rather, the problem lies in the conception of the ruin mobilized by the work. Instead of understanding ruins as a sign of history and change, Schwarz-Bart writes ruins as humiliation and absence—as the absence of power signified by failed and desperate revolt.[21] There are then two versions of anachronism in Schwarz-Bart's work. While the first is a force of rehistoricization that cuts through the calcified distinctions of period and identity in order to create new ways of seeing history as a dynamic force field of intersecting stories, the other is a force of de-historicization that removes those intersecting stories from any relationship to power and thus from any possibility of change. If Schwarz-Bart's oeuvre remains something of an anomaly in the canon of Holocaust literature, the oscillation we find in it between re- and de-historicization, and between structural and historical trauma, carries implications for all attempts to write ruins and articulate multidirectional memories.

Mediated Identifications: *The European Tribe*

Through his fiction Caryl Phillips also seeks to "people" history's abysses through risky acts of imagination, and he does so through an anachronistic aesthetics. In many ways his biographical itinerary and literary oeuvre complement those of Schwarz-Bart. I can think of no other two authors whose projects turn so definitively on interrogating the links between European Jewish and African, African diaspora, and Caribbean history. Nevertheless, their writings emerge from very different historical locations. Schwarz-Bart wrote at a transitional moment (1959–72) when the struggles of decolonization were transforming into the problems of postcolonial politics and when Holocaust memory was beginning to take its more familiar contemporary form separate from the generalized category of "Nazi atrocities." His writings are marked both by a desire to find a complex, multidimensional form for the articulation of historical relationship and by a strong pull to reduce that form to a de-historicized victim/perpetrator binary marked by oppressive violence and heroic, if tragic, resistance. Phillips writes from a world thoroughly transformed by postcolonial migrations and saturated with consciousness of the genocidal past, present, and perhaps future of Europe (and the rest of the world).[22] While the memory of the Warsaw Ghetto also marks his novels and nonfiction prose, and serves as a site for exploring the intersections of black and Jewish history, the lessons he draws from the past are more ambiguous than those espoused by Schwarz-Bart. In Phillips's oeuvre, the frontier between victim and victimizer is never as clear as it is in Schwarz-Bart. Scrambling the forms of historical comparison he finds in Schwarz-Bart, Phillips's narratives situate blacks and Jews not only outside or at the margins of Europe but also inside, at the center.

Fifteen years after Schwarz-Bart conjured the ruins of the ghetto from a site of Caribbean trauma, and thirty-five years after Du Bois found himself compelled to rethink his understanding of the color line, Phillips also wrote about visiting Warsaw. In his 1987 travel report *The European Tribe*, he tells of a yearlong journey through the Europe of the mid-1980s that included a stop in Poland. Phillips writes from a different Europe than the one Schwarz-Bart abandoned for Guadeloupe, yet his sense of both the racist legacies of the past and the foreboding of the racial and ethnic violence of the near future seems to echo the French writer's insights. Beyond the prescient sense of latent violence that Phillips had in the 1980s, what accounts for the particular interest in the Holocaust that runs through his work?

The European Tribe provides various keys to understanding Phillips's investment in the Holocaust. At the most explicit level, a chapter on "Anne Frank's Amsterdam" brings together black and Jewish experience through a model of identification. Here Phillips describes the inspiration for his first fictional work:

> I was about fifteen when Amsterdam first began to fascinate me. There was a programme on television, part of the *World at War* series, which dealt with the Nazi occupation of Holland and the subsequent rounding up of the Jews. . . . One thing I could not understand about the programme was why, when instructed to wear the yellow Star of David on their clothes, the Jews complied. They looked just like any other white people to me, so who would know that they were different? As the programme progressed my sense of bemused fascination disappeared and was supplanted by my first mature feelings of outrage and fear. These yellow stars were marking them out for Bergen-Belsen and Auschwitz. I watched the library footage of the camps and realized both the enormity of the crime that was being perpetrated, and the precariousness of my own position in Europe. The many adolescent thoughts that worried my head can be reduced to one line: "If white people could do that to white people, then what the hell would they do to me?"[23]

The passage is dense with multiple acts of looking that indicate different levels of narration and focalization: the narrator looks back at his teenage self as that younger self watches a television film constructed out of diverse sources of archival footage. This staging of race and visuality moves beyond the face-to-face encounter famously depicted by Fanon in *Black Skin, White Masks*—"Look, a Negro!"—into a world characterized by multiple layers of mediation: the fifteen-year-old migrant child in England does not directly *face* the racist gaze but *looks on* as the flow of a television program concatenates archival imagery with postwar narration. In order to comprehend the complexity of this viewing scene, it is important to remember the likely sources of such imagery: both footage taken on liberation by Allied soldiers and earlier images produced by the Nazis themselves. While the latter footage might be more or less assimilable to the racist gaze of which Fanon speaks, the Allied footage represents a different type of problem involving even the sympathetic depiction of abject victimization. In both cases, however, the perspective of the camera misrecognizes its objects, indeed precisely turns human subjects into objects, albeit in different ways. What is most significant for the moment, though, is the representation of the viewer's relationship to these images of extreme racialization: it is simultaneously decentered and decontextualized, not only by the overlap of nonsynchronous perspectives staged in the film, but, more importantly, by the fact that the viewer is a black child from the former colonies in a post-Imperial metropolis. In this passage, we receive something like a "reverse shot" of the story Schwarz-Bart tells of the impact Caribbean migrants had on his understanding of diaspora and Jewish history.

Yet, if Schwarz-Bart's encounter produced a shock of knowledge, it is precisely the film's lack of sense for the young Phillips—its depiction of victimization at the limits of understanding and its mobilization of contradictory perspectives—that proves productive, that produces a writing subject. (Here Phillips may be closer to Du Bois, who is initially baffled by his encounter with the ruins of Warsaw.) Musing on the film leads the young Phillips to produce his first fictional work: a short story about a young Dutch boy in occupied Amsterdam who resists wearing the yellow star. Ultimately, during "resettlement" to the east, the boy escapes from the cattlecar and is saved when "the sunlight shining on his yellow star . . . attracts a kindly farmer's attention" (67). Phillips later writes of this story, "The Dutch boy was, of course, me."[24] In Phillips's telling, his first significant exposure to the Holocaust—an exposure importantly mediated by televisual images—takes place on the cusp between "adolescent thoughts" and his "first mature feelings." Through a process of identification, the history of the Holocaust helps to form Phillips as an adult subject and as a writer. At this moment of his youth, Phillips's relationship to Jewish history carries the hallmarks of what Diana Fuss, following Freud, has called the "obviousness" of identification, its "predicat[ion] on a logic of metaphoric exchange".[25] "The Dutch boy was, of course, me." Such a logic, while understandable from the perspective of a fifteen-year-old boy, might be considered to carry the danger of appropriation, the full-scale metaphoric substitution of one identity or history for another.

But *The European Tribe*, like *Higher Ground* and *The Nature of Blood*, the novels that emerged out of it, demonstrates a more complex logic, one that also reminds us that, for Freud, identification is much more ambivalent and indirect than the simple process of metaphoric substitution. In fact, the identificatory processes at work in both the travel book and the novels are metonymic rather than metaphoric. This more complex notion of identification is captured in Eve Sedgwick's assertion that "the paths of allo-identification are likely to be strange and recalcitrant": "To identify *as* must always include multiple processes of identification *with*."[26] The paths and multiple processes in Sedgwick's formulation correspond to the metonymic displacements that underwrite Phillips's approach to the otherness of Jewish history and the Holocaust. Tracing those paths of displacement reveals the stakes of identification in these texts. Metonymic identification is both enabled and made necessary by the deficit of representations of black suffering in the England of Phillips's youth. As he also writes in *The European Tribe*, "The bloody excesses of colonialism, the pillage and rape of modern Africa, the transportation of 11 million black people to the Americas, and their subsequent bondage were not on the curriculum, and certainly not on the television screen. As a result I vicariously channeled a part of my hurt and frustration through the Jewish experience" (54). At stake, in other words, is less the will to take the place of the other than the desire to map out the uncanny geographies of diasporic life; Phillips's diasporic subject shares spaces and histories with *various* others without developing a sense of being at home in that terrain. In Phillips's work, metonymic identification helps to capture the contingent contiguities of diasporic experience, its necessarily multiple locations and syncretic cultures.[27] Phillips's childhood vicarious experience—clearly related to that of Schwarz-Bart's prototypical Jewish child—represents an alternative to notions of competitive memory: the other's history does not screen out one's own past, but rather serves as a screen for multidirectional projections in which solidarity and self-construction merge.

Not only is Phillips's interest in the Nazi genocide revealed in *The European Tribe*, but so too is an ongoing fascination with the figure of Othello and the history of Venice. Following this route returns us to the

Holocaust, but in a more roundabout way. Phillips's visit to Venice forms something of a turning point in his travel book: "I saw only one other black man in Venice. He looked nothing like Othello. . . . How did Othello live in this astonishing city? Sixteenth-century Venetian society both enslaved the black and ridiculed the Jew" (45). While Phillips is clearly interested in the common experience of racism suffered by blacks and Jews in Europe, this chapter is nonetheless called "A Black European Success." Despite the obvious irony, that title does tell us something about what is important for Phillips: not simply the existence of a hatred that can turn genocidal but also the productive presence of racial others in the midst of Europe. Venice is a significant choice, not only because of the two relevant Shakespearean figures it conjures up—Othello and Shylock—but also because of its place in the world economy of its day. Indeed, for the sociologist Giovanni Arrighi, the Venetian city-state stands as "the prototype of the leading capitalist state of every subsequent age."[28] Othello's presence in the early modern Italian city thus represents an historical mirror for Phillips's own condition as a "black European success" who now lives in two of late modernity's global cities, New York and London.

But Venice also has further significance, since it was the location of the first Jewish ghetto; indeed, Venice is where the word "ghetto" originated. In the twentieth century, the concept of the ghetto has provided one of the most salient links in the identificatory chain connecting blacks and Jews, as we have already seen with respect to Schwarz-Bart and Du Bois. This lexical connection also leads Phillips to explore those other ghettos, the ghettos established by the Nazis as part of the genocidal destruction of the Jews of Europe. The associations fostered by *The European Tribe* are not simply grounded in a metaphoric identification of racism against Jews with racism against blacks, although this link is not excluded. Nor are many of the historical associations of a sort that would be accepted by the discipline of history. Rather, this travel book leads us to identify a metonymic chain of multiple identifications that works through more accidental associations of history, geography, and literary reference; as in Schwarz-Bart, but in even more thoroughgoing fashion, anachronism is at work. Shifting from a metaphoric to a metonymic conception of identification helps to bring the mediated nature of Phillips's historical references to the fore: the Holocaust arrives via a television documentary; Venice is as much a literary space (Shakespeare's Venice) as it is a geographical place.

The notions of anomalous success and of the singularity of the black man in exile—which serve to link Othello and Phillips to each other—seem to risk taking part in "the displacement of the collective diasporic subject" that Khachig Tölölyan diagnoses in some strands of the contemporary celebration of diaspora (29). While some version of this individualism does characterize much of Phillips's work—both the fiction and the nonfiction—the discourse of exceptionalism coexists with recognition of the force of collective experiences. Othello is, after all, not only a personally successful military leader employed by a world power but also a former slave. This simultaneity of individual success, fear of co-optation by the imperial center, and an unerasable legacy of collective suffering provides an allegory for Phillips's own journeys through contemporary Europe and constitutes an engagement with the very tensions that constitute contemporary diaspora discourses.

Phillips's more recent fictional work continues to chart this new imaginative terrain. As the references to school curricula, canonical literature, and television programming in *The European Tribe* indicate, the project of diasporic mapping undertaken by Phillips involves an engagement with and appropriation of multiple forms of narrative and textuality. Such acts of engagement and appropriation, however, are not meant to render history or identity as entities that can be "owned," either by individuals or groups. Indeed, as Timothy Bewes has argued, Phillips's novels constitute radical acts of de-propriation, in which characters are rendered "incapable of speaking 'authentically,' on their own account or in their own voices" (43). As Bewes demonstrates with respect to the novels *Cambridge* and *Crossing the River*, Phillips consistently deploys clichés and "ventriloquism" instead of individualized, "realist" voices in order to enact "the systematic evacuation of every discursive position that might claim freedom from implication in colonialism" (46). While Bewes correctly stresses the complicity in colonialism that marks much of Phillips's work, Phillips's intertextual, anachronistic aesthetic also produces a larger conception of complicity, connects colonialism to other histories, and thus sets the stage for the articulation of multidirectional memory. Multidirectional exchange takes place beyond the forms of cultural ownership that motivate competitive struggles over the past.

Missed Encounters: *Higher Ground*

In *The European Tribe*, Phillips narrates his coming to writing as an effect of his specular identification with Jewish history and, in particular, Jewish suffering under the Nazis; in *Higher Ground* (1989), his first novel after the publication of *The European Tribe*, and in *The Nature of Blood* (1997), Phillips returns to related terrain in order to fracture further such identification. Phillips's "Jewish" novels have received mixed reviews, with detractors asserting (as in the title of one review) that "black is not Jewish" and proponents lauding Phillips's "attempt to mix different cultures and traditions into a diverse whole."[29] In contrast to these positions, Phillips's project is not to establish an equation between black and Jewish history, but rather to highlight both similar structural problems within those histories and missed encounters between them. Despite moving toward a more fractured form of relatedness, however, the fictional texts still maintain the sense of urgency that lies behind black-Jewish identification in the earlier travel report.

Higher Ground consists of three disconnected, novella-like parts. The first is narrated from the perspective of an African man who works in a slave fort as a go-between and translator. The second is made up of letters from Rudi Williams, an African American man discovering the philosophy of Black Power while imprisoned during the late 1960s for having stolen forty dollars during an armed robbery. The novel concludes with the story of Irene, a Polish Jewish refugee in England, who seems to have lost her family in the Holocaust and who struggles with madness and depression. *Higher Ground*'s three separated stories bleed into each other and suggest a desire for contact across identities and histories. Most relevant here, Rudi deploys Nazi- and Holocaust-inflected figures in an attempt to make sense of his situation, while Irene yearns for a connection with Louis, a sympathetic but distant Caribbean immigrant. Yet, despite the different desires for contact evinced by these characters, the novel ultimately stages a series of missed encounters. Although Bénédicte Ledent has shown that common themes and problems cut across the three sections of the novel (54–79), what unity the novel has derives primarily from what is absent, both within and between the sections.

The first section, "Heartland," set during the slave trade, establishes the theme of the missed encounter. The narrator, an African collaborator with the British, seeks to carve out a zone of normality within a situation of radical extremity and violence. After falling in love with a village girl who has been abused by the governor's deputy, the narrator smuggles the girl (as he calls her) into the fort and attempts to lead a "domestic" life within this site of inhumanity. His plans are doubly foiled, first when one of the soldiers discovers the presence of the girl and takes advantage of her and the narrator's vulnerability; second, when the soldier betrays them and lands them in the slave hold. Shipped to America, the narrator ends up as one of "the prime nigger heathens" on the auction block, "resigned to the permanence of [his] separation" from the girl. In the last lines of the section, he recognizes that his "present has finally fractured; the past has fled over the horizon and out of sight."[30] Like the figures that people Schwarz-Bart's novels, the narrator finds himself displaced and fractured by history. Unlike them, however, Phillips's protagonist is neither innocent victim, nor heroic resistor, nor martyr. Hence, I disagree with Bryan Cheyette's assertion, in an otherwise excellent essay on Phillips, that the "construction of an endless victimization of both the Jewish and black minorities" characterizes Phillips's oeuvre (60). Rather, those minorities tend to occupy an in-between space characterized by complicity and moral ambiguity.

The narrator's missed encounter with his beloved—inevitable given his misrecognition of his place in history—finds its echo in the succeeding sections. Rudi, the letter-writing protagonist of part two, "The Cargo Rap," is no collaborator with oppression, but he similarly misconceives his place in history. To be sure, as a working-class African American man, he is certainly a victim of the same system of racialization that in an earlier phase claimed the life of the narrator of "Heartland." Yet his attempts to carve out a place for himself in history—attempts made from the none-too-spacious confines of a maximum-security prison cell—leave him even more imprisoned. In letters to his family and the few strangers who take up his cause, Rudi frequently figures himself in the place of Holocaust victims. In a letter to the president of his "Defense Committee," Rudi introduces himself as serving "one to life in a concentration camp of their [the state's] own choice" (92). In prison, which Rudi refers to on several occasions as "Belsen" (69, 84, 145), he suffers tortures that, he suspects, compare well with those inflicted in Nazi Germany (72).

Rudi's references to the Holocaust ultimately serve neither the interests of history nor those of his own liberation. Although Rudi uses the "opportunity" of prison to read important works of black, anticolonial, and leftist resistance, all of which he recommends to his family in self-righteous and didactic terms, he ultimately succumbs to madness and despair. His last letter, written to his mother after she has already died, demonstrates that overidentification with victims of the Holocaust is premised on an anachronistic reading of African American history. Here, as in his opening letter, Rudi imagines himself a slave, but while the opening letter uses the language of slavery metaphorically, in his confused state the metaphor is literalized: "Dear Moma, / The overseer has a horse named 'Ginger.' The plantation is wide and stretches beyond the horizon.... The master is cruel, but nobody 'knows' him better than his slaves. There is strength in this" (172). Besides importing a sly reference to Hegel, Rudi's final letter demonstrates a complex, but ultimately self-defeating logic of identification; his identification with Jewish victims is premised on a prefigurative identification with slaves that founds his identity in the first place. While, as Schwarz-Bart's work suggests, such identifications can provide sources of selfhood that allow for survival and resistance, they can also lead into polarized and static discourses when all distance collapses between past and present. Such discourses replay narratives of trauma so insistently that they become structural features in the present instead of historical legacies that are susceptible to working through. If, then, "Rudi's recurrent references to Nazism ... reinforce his dehumanization by echoing the holocaust horrors that suffuse the last story" in the novel, as Ledent has argued (65), this is so in a different sense than intended. Phillips's point is that part of the horror lies in the very "recurrent references"—not because Rudi is doing violence to Jewish history in loosely appropriating it to his own situation, but rather because he is doing violence to himself by trapping himself in a rhetoric of absolute victimization that ultimately eliminates all agency.

In "Higher Ground," the third part of the novel, the Jewish immigrant through whom the story is focalized also remains trapped in the past, but for quite different reasons. In contrast to Rudi, who contributes to his own entrapment through overidentification with African American as well as European Jewish history, "Irene" is overwhelmed by the split that marks her life, a split that inheres in her very name, or what she calls "the Irene-Irina-Irene-Irina-Irene-Irina-Irene problem" (183). Sent from Poland to England on a *Kindertransport*—a transport of Jewish children away from the Nazi threat—the young Irina soon becomes Irene, "for English people were too lazy to bend their mouths or twist their tongues into unfamiliar shapes" (183). Phillips highlights the ensuing split by referring to his protagonist as Irina during flashbacks and as Irene for the period after her move to England. Separated from her family, who could only have been murdered at the hands of the Nazis, and assimilable into English society only at the cost of losing part of her identity, Irene is trapped into an unhappy marriage and then suffers a breakdown that sends her to a psychiatric hospital for ten years. The present of the novel finds her living in a rooming house and working in a library, but falling back into madness and about to be sent back to the hospital. Her persistent foreignness seems to draw her close to Louis, a brand-new West Indian migrant suffering in the alien English landscape. The logic of the story seems to be leading toward contact and bonding across black and Jewish differences—a supposition reinforced by the novel's use of colonial discourse to describe Irene's condition, as Ledent has shown (68). But once again the novel turns away from such a redemptive possibility; black and Jewish histories do not actually intersect, but approach each other and then veer away asymptotically. Although drawn to Irene, Louis has already decided to return home to the Caribbean: "She touched him, but he knew that he must steel himself and step out into the crisp, sweatless, fresh, cold, white, snowy night. . . . Then at dawn he would return to the men's hostel and take his bag and his leave. It was probable that this woman would extend and demand a severe loyalty that he could never reciprocate. Not now. Sorry" (216). Louis refuses—or at least defers indefinitely—Irene's offer of contact and solidarity and leaves Irene "for ever lost without the sustaining love," waiting for the nurse to take her back to captivity in the hospital (218).

Although thematically unified in its exploration of forms of imprisonment, displacement, and racialized violence, *Higher Ground* refuses redemptive closure and easy analogy across histories and identities. Even as it encourages readers to search for links between the stories, the novel also keeps them distinct from each other, as is especially clear in the missed encounter between Irene and Louis. In the final story, differences of gender, social status (refugee versus migrant), ethnicity, and nationality overrule the commonalities that nonetheless draw the two characters together. Victimization proves not to be the best grounds for solidarity since processes of victimization take multiple, contradictory forms and erode the bases of selfhood necessary for relationship with others (as illustrated by Rudi's descent into fantasy and Irene's madness). In addition, as the case of the narrator of "Heartland" demonstrates, possessing the status of the victim does not grant immunity from complicity or prevent the occupation of other subject positions, such as collaborator. While in Schwarz-Bart's novels victimization becomes a quasi-metaphysical category capable of uniting people across centuries and continents, in *Higher Ground* the position of victims is revealed as unstable and shifting, and therefore not susceptible to the construction of facile linkages.[31]

Intertexuality and Stratified Minoritization:
The Nature of Blood

When, several years later, Phillips takes up many of the same issues explored in *Higher Ground*, his exploration of the intertwining of different historical traumas even more clearly resonates with and ultimately diverges from the work of Schwarz-Bart. In *The Nature of Blood* (1997), Phillips refashions the materials of *The European Tribe* and *Higher Ground*, as well as many other texts, into a fictional narrative that spans four hundred years and links Nazi Germany, fifteenth- and sixteenth-century Italy, and contemporary Israel. The novel focuses primarily on Eva Stern, a young German Jewish woman who survives the death camps before succumbing, like Irene, to madness after the war and a tragic end in England. The novel additionally presents us with Eva's uncle Stephan, a doctor who leaves Europe before the war and is part of the Jewish underground in Palestine; he also shows up many years later in Israel. Such a story would already be relatively surprising coming from an Afro-Caribbean/British writer whose first several novels deal primarily with the history of the black Atlantic world. But *The Nature of Blood* goes further in its exploration of history and identity. Interwoven with the story of the Sterns is a chronicle-like account of a fifteenth-century Venetian ritual murder case and a first-person narrative by none other than Othello. All of this is recounted in a fragmented text characterized by rapid shifts in perspective, a dense intertextual fabric, and alternation between carefully constructed historical milieus and deliberate anachronism.

Working from the same chain of associations that stands behind the interlocking histories of blacks and Jews in *The European Tribe*, *The Nature of Blood* extends the earlier book's exploration of diasporic identity. What is most striking about the novel is the narrative form that exploration takes. The novel employs more than a dozen different narrative voices and shifts perspective several dozen times. It also mobilizes a markedly interdisciplinary set of cognitive genres, from the clinical diagnosis of Eva's doctor in England through interpolated dictionary definitions to the disturbingly blasé historical voice of the chronicle-like ritual murder case. Characterized by discontinuity between multiple forms of knowledge and multiple forms of violence, *The Nature of Blood* testifies to the existence of new possibilities for thinking the relatedness of the unrelatable.

How can we make sense of the juxtaposition of histories in *The Nature of Blood*? Like *The European Tribe*, with its staging of two different forms of identification, the novel also contains two different logics of comparison. On the one hand, the title, *The Nature of Blood*, gestures at a commonality that links the different stories as essentially the same. A transhistorical racist imaginary obsessed with purity of blood seems to unite the various Jewish and black victims across time. This sense of commonality is reinforced by certain textual echoes that link the stories to each other—as when the Jews of fifteenth-century Portobuffole recite the same prayer while being burned at the stake as the Jews who arrive at a Nazi camp (155, 164), or when Eva's suicide echoes Othello's. Were this logic to dominate, the novel would risk reproducing the racist discourse that it obviously seeks to contest. But ultimately—and whether intentionally or not—the differences between the stories overwhelm the apparent similitude suggested by the title. The novel's primary focus is not the simple binary between perpetrators and victims of racist violence. Instead, the novel emerges as an exploration of ambivalent modes of belonging and exclusion in which accidental contiguity plays a greater role than correspondence of historical essences.

The first word of *The Nature of Blood* is "between" (just like the main text of Du Bois's *The Souls of Black Folk*, incidentally), and indeed the novel begins in the interstices, in a liminal zone between geographies and histories. The opening scene takes place between the end of World War II and the beginning of a new era. It is set on the still-contested island of Cyprus, between Europe, Africa, and the Middle East, in camps established by the British for refugees refused entrance into Palestine. Stephan, the doctor, is talking to a young camp survivor named Moshe:

Between us a small fire sputtered. . . . The new kindling snapped, and the flames rose higher and illuminated the boy's face. He spoke quietly.
 "Tell me, what will be the name of the country?"
 "Our country," I said. "The country will belong to you too."
 The boy looked down at the sand, then scratched a short nervous line with his big toe.
 "Tell me, what will be the name of our country?"
 I paused for a moment, in the hope that he might relax. And then I whispered, as though confessing something to him.
 "Israel. Our country will be called Israel."[32]

In this scene, Phillips describes the moment of transition when a collective "we" is being formed, a new nation imagined and named from a nonnational space. The narrative begins between the waning days of one colonial regime and the establishment of a new state that will be perceived as independence and homecoming by some and as recolonization, catastrophe, and displacement by others.

While the novel quickly leaves behind twentieth-century Cyprus, the tensions of place and time evoked by this opening persist. Indeed we return to Cyprus in the second half of the novel when Othello sails there in order to counter the Ottoman Empire's threat to Venice. It becomes clear at this point that, as in *The European Tribe*, Othello's position in the novel is double. He has certainly been marked out as "alien" in Venice and has suffered because of it, but he is also portrayed as driven by a will to assimilate and a willingness to be exploited in the fight against other, more "dangerous," outsiders. Upon arrival in Cyprus, Othello finds that the Ottoman fleet has drowned in a storm, allowing Othello to reflect on his situation there: "This island of Cyprus, to which fate had deposited me safe in both body and mind, would serve as the school in which I might further study the manners of Venice, before eventually returning to the city to embark upon my new life. However, my first action as both General and Governor was to order that revels should commence within the hour to celebrate both the drowning of the heretical Turk and the happy and fortuitous marriage of their commanding officer to fair Desdemona" (166). The conjunction of death and marriage does not seem to bother Othello or distract him from his revels. By suggesting that the consolidation of Othello's identity as "black European success" takes place through possession of a "fair" prize, through the mimicry of normative manners, and through the fatal disappearance of another "foreign" group, Phillips initiates a critique of minority consciousness under diasporic conditions.[33] Phillips's work does not simply celebrate diasporic consciousness. Rather, the contingent association of the two Cypruses allows Phillips to probe the formal problems of the diasporic subject who is ambiguously situated between home and exile. The historical palimpsest of Cyprus provides an imaginative space for rethinking the ways that binary relationships—such as self/other and victim/perpetrator—can transform into more complicated configurations such that new figures come into view: the other of the other, the victim of the victim.

Phillips clearly shares Schwarz-Bart's desire to explore forms of comparison and cross-cultural relatedness, yet the figures each writer imagines differ greatly from each other. Seen from the historically later perspective of Phillips's texts, Schwarz-Bart's attempts to elude the static binaries that separate the histories of different ethnic groups are now revealed as nevertheless reproducing such binary forms as resistance/oppression, victim/victimizer. The mythic character Solitude and the blacks and Jews of Schwarz-Bart's texts more generally represent figures of pure victimization and of heroic, if suicidal, resistance to overwhelming power. In its foundation in such binaries, Schwarz-Bart's work can be seen to take part in what Susan Koshy has described as "the racial politics of the sixties." Although her focus is on struggles within the United States and makes no mention of Jews, her analysis also describes more global shifts in the conceptualization of race and ethnicity and can help illuminate the contrast between Schwarz-Bart and Phillips. In the 1960s, a construct of "*parallel minoritization* . . . challenged white supremacy by positing the opposition between white and nonwhite positionality and strategically deferred theorizing the relationship between racial minorities outside this framework."

By the 1980s and 1990s, however, an emphasis on *"stratified minoritization"* had emerged in the wake of the breakdown of the *"coalitional rationality* that grounded the strategic alliances of people of color in the 1960s."[34] In *Solitude* and elsewhere, Schwarz-Bart employs parallel minoritization as a form of coalitional rationality, yet at the same time the strain of maintaining parallelism shows in the multiplication of anachronistic, nonparallel figures used to describe his project. Phillips, by contrast, writes from a situation in which contradictions within and between minority groups have produced a more obviously stratified map of minoritization.

The figures of Othello and Stephan in *The Nature of Blood* trouble the narrative of minority resistance that underlies the texts and binary structures of Schwarz-Bart via the invocation of Solitude and the martyrs of the Warsaw Ghetto uprising. As Othello's speech on Cyprus has already indicated, Phillips's Othello is at best an ambivalent model of minority subjectivity. Unlike the abject and silent Solitude, who, despite her hybrid status as "mulâtresse," is depicted as completely external to power, Othello becomes a model of the minority subject who has migrated into the spaces of power: "I had moved from the edge of the world to the centre. From the dark margins to a place where even the weakest rays of the evening sun were caught and thrown back in a blaze of glory. I . . . had been summoned . . . to stand at the very centre of empire" (107). This movement to the center of empire might be said to presage the kinds of postcolonial migrations that brought West Indians like Phillips to the metropolis. Less literally, it charts a more general movement whereby the formerly colonized and enslaved emerge into a stratified space of overlapping complicity and resistance—a space that would encompass both the assimilated "model minority" and the elite of the newly postcolonial states.

Phillips's critique of diaspora does not imply, however, that an acceptable alternative to it exists. As for Stephan and the refugees of the Holocaust, Cyprus serves Othello as a way station, a point between a condition of exile and a wished-for home. In both cases, though, this inbetween state will prove terminal. Not in the sense that the characters will stay on Cyprus (Stephan will not), but rather in the sense that their ends will prove as dissatisfactory as the other points of their journeys. Stephan returns at the very end of the novel in contemporary Israel, lonely and haunted by the absence of his murdered nieces and the family he abandoned for Palestine. The society in which he lives is portrayed in turn as haunted and divided by race. The novel makes no direct reference to the plight of Palestinians, but their presence shadows the text from the opening page and Phillips has raised the issue in other places. Instead, the novel ends with the encounter between an aged Stephan and a much younger Ethiopian Jewish woman. The complete lack of understanding between them and the dire poverty and hopelessness of the Ethiopians conjure up a multiply stratified society far from the Promised Land evoked by Stephan on Cyprus. Returning "home" is no solution in the worlds Phillips creates and about which he reports (this is demonstrated especially by a more recent hybrid-genre work, *The Atlantic Sound*).

Othello's end, by contrast, is so well known that Phillips does not even need to narrate it. Rather, Othello's suicide is displaced onto Eva, the survivor of Nazi camps, who loses her grasp on reality when her immediate family disappears in the Shoah. Other than its end, Eva's story is quite unlike Othello's, but, like Othello, Eva is more a product of the literary imagination than she is an historical figure. Although a greater portion of the novel is narrated in Eva's voice than any other, her depiction is still ultimately indirect. The Holocaust sections are, for example, scattered with intertextual borrowings from accounts of Holocaust survivors, such as Primo Levi and Elie Wiesel, and from other Jewish writers, such as Cynthia Ozick. The indirection of the novel's account of the genocide becomes even more marked as Phillips nears the center of the disaster. When Eva enters the cattlecar that will transport her to the death camps, the narrative switches from first to third person and then back (155, 163). As the train approaches and then enters the camps, the narrative starts to fragment into a collection of dispersed voices:

The boxcar was near the locomotive, so Eva was able to listen to the engine die. Silence. The world remained silent. And then, some hours later, a roar and a shudder, and once again the locomotive tugged against the weight of the train. . . . A long-drawn-out whistle. Then a loud crash and a judder. The darkness began to echo with barked orders. Then the doors to the boxcars roll open. . . . Already, a loudspeaker is blasting instructions to remove all clothing. Remove artificial limbs and eyeglasses. Tie your shoes together. Surrender any undeclared valuables and claim a receipt. Children go with the women. Where are we? The thin and the handicapped, this way, please. All gold rings, fountain pens, and chains. Roll up. Where is God? Where is your God? . . . A uniformed adolescent kicks an old man. Then he laughs. The old man stops and stares. I am your father. He reloads his weapon. I am your father. Each time he fires the young man laughs louder. (161–62)

In this passage we see the dark inversion of the scene of identification in *The European Tribe*. Here, mediation and intertextuality do not create possibilities for identity formation and solidarity, but instead index dehumanization. The references, for example, to the Yiddish title of Wiesel's memoir (*Un di Velt Hot Geshvign*; "The world remained silent") and to the archetypical questioning of God and the father/son conflicts that mark that memoir do not so much call upon authoritative survivor testimony as stage the collapse of all (patriarchal) authority in the face of an inhuman, genocidal machine. The narrative's dispersed voices correspond to the disembodied voice of the loudspeaker and its command to disassemble an already artificial body. There is, of course, an implicit and perhaps appropriate modesty in Phillips's approach. He does not attempt to portray realistically a scene he can never know; thus, the ultimate site of horror, the gas chamber, is portrayed in a distanced and a-subjective third-person voice ("The process of gassing takes place in the following manner" [176]).[35] Most crucially, Phillips's generalized intertextual approach to history accomplishes two things at the level of form: it evokes a form of narration that refuses to gloss over the disruption it portrays, and it opens itself to the global circulation of memories beyond competition and identitarian conflict.

The novel's indirect, intertextual technique is not simply a matter of playful postmodern pastiche. Rather, this indirect mode gestures toward another crucial feature of the diasporic condition shared by blacks and Jews: at the limit, diaspora frustrates all forms of metaphoric identification because it is rooted in, or—better—uprooted by, traumatic history.[36] While, as Cathy Caruth suggests, trauma may provide "the very link between cultures," that link is premised on an initial violence that installs loss at the origin of diaspora.[37] Loss—which LaCapra helpfully distinguishes from absence—is related to the specificities of historical trauma. Any metaphoric identification with specific losses will always perform a kind of violence. But Phillips's strategy is to juxtapose particular losses—such as those of Eva and Othello or those of Jews of the fifteenth and twentieth centuries—through indirect invocation. This indirect, metonymic form of reference to unrepresentable extreme violence not only is a mark of the contingencies of diasporic geographies but also signals the disruptions of traumatic history. That history in its "presence" is significantly "lost" and definitively unrecoverable, but its effects register nonetheless.[38]

The disruptions of traumatic history indexed by *The Nature of Blood* become particularly clear through comparison with what may be the novel's most significant unremarked intertext: Schwarz-Bart's *The Last of the Just*. Like Phillips's work, Schwarz-Bart's links the medieval and modern persecution of Jews. Yet, despite the multidirectional sources that spurred Schwarz-Bart's composition, *The Last of the Just* presents that link as a thousand-year genealogical "biography" of the Levy family that unfolds in a continuous chronicle of pogroms, persecutions, and auto-da-fes. Such a continuous narrative form cannot fully acknowledge the traumatic losses that call it into being—it risks becoming a version of what Eric Santner has called "narrative fetishism," as, in fact, the more disjunctive narrative of *A Woman Named Solitude* also suggests.[39] Acknowledging the force and form of discontinuity, Phillips deconstructs—takes apart and reconfigures—Schwarz-Bart's first novel, maintaining the contact between different histories of persecution without rendering them as pieces of a totalizable collective biography. This resistance to narrative fetishism also helps explain the foregrounding in *Higher Ground* of missed encounters, one of the forms in which trauma "appears," according to Lacanian psychoanalytic accounts.

While in *The Last of the Just* Schwarz-Bart draws on the unfolding temporality of the chronicle (even if he later complicates this temporality briefly in the epilogue to *A Woman Named Solitude*), Phillips can be located within the multitemporal space of an "anthological" aesthetic, to draw on terms developed by Rebecca Walkowitz. Walkowitz situates Phillips's oeuvre within an emergent category of self-consciously global works that she names "comparison literature." As she notes, Phillips is suspicious of claims to uniqueness, yet he remains "engaged with debates about *historical* distinctiveness, such as whether the Holocaust can be usefully compared to other examples of racism and genocide" (537). Engaged in this dialectic between distinctiveness and comparison, Phillips turns especially to the form of the anthology: "Phillips's novels and nonfiction works are like anthologies in that they sample and collate stories of racism, slavery, European anti-Semitism, and recent violence against immigrants. But unlike other anthologies, which create a single series, Phillips's books tend to promote various microseries within them. In addition to collating the lives of several migrants, his books also represent the life of any single migrant, including their author, as yet another collated account" (539). The infinite regression of the microseries—the fact that each element of the series is itself defined by another series ad infinitum—distinguishes Phillips's aesthetic of anthological collation from the parallel series found in the invocations of the Warsaw Ghetto in *A Woman Named Solitude* and even in Du Bois's "The Negro and the Warsaw Ghetto."

While Phillips's work bears comparison to the considerations of the minority condition carried on by Du Bois and Schwarz-Bart in previous decades, the condition Phillips describes—as well as the means he uses to describe it—exceeds the tropes and forms that they employ. As the hold of a single normative cultural center declines, forms such as double consciousness and parallel minoritization are also thrown into increasing confusion. Phillips writes from a contemporary moment in which the means of communication and transport have been globalized well beyond what could have been imagined in the 1950s, 1960s, and 1970s, when Schwarz-Bart was writing, not to mention at the turn of the century when Du Bois first formulated his notion of double consciousness. New forms of cultural and economic exchange multiply the possibilities for identification with the histories of others. Yet the multiplicity of those very same means of communication also ensures that the paths of identification will be difficult to stabilize or limit to binary forms of substitution.

The different ruinous histories narrated by Du Bois, Schwarz-Bart, and Phillips—histories involving genocide, slavery, everyday racism, and state power—resist conflation. Even when such histories are brought together in the space of one text, their juxtaposition can serve more to bring differences into relief than to melt them into banal equation. Questioning the rhetoric of uniqueness and the separate spheres of post-Holocaust and postcolonial literary studies in the name of multidirectional memory should lead not to a smoothing over of contradiction but to a heightening of the perception of the contradictory terrain on which memories intersect and collide. Each of the authors and texts considered here struggles against the limits of his/their own era and the possibilities that era offered for thinking comparatively about historical trauma and its legacies. The conceptual and formal innovations of Du Bois, Schwarz-Bart, and Phillips bear witness to the difficult task of breaking out of taken-for-granted frameworks of historical and cultural understanding. Wandering anachronistically through the ruins and traumas of modernity, they force readers to confront the legacies of violence that persist beyond the places and times of textbook history and television documentary.

In making a transition from Du Bois, Schwarz-Bart, and Phillips to the next two sections, *Multidirectional Memory* takes a significant turn. I now move from the focus on the early postwar period that dominated much of the discussion thus far to a concentrated look at the moment around 1961 when movements of decolonization were at their peak and Holocaust memory began to emerge in its more familiar, contemporary form thanks to the Eichmann trial in Jerusalem. I also expand the focus on the black-Jewish relation—one of the most well-known sites of multidirectional memory in the twentieth-century—to include consideration of the Algerian War of Independence, which turns out to be an equally dense site of intercultural exchange and sometimes even builds on the tropes of black-Jewish commonality, as well. For French intellectuals and activists, but also for a broader international set of participants and observers, the Algerian War brought together issues of extreme violence, racial stigmatization, and political and ethical claims that almost immediately were understood to call upon the still recent legacies of World War II, Nazi occupation, and the Holocaust. The link between the wars—between the suffering they produced and the resistance they elicited—has proven enduring, as the final chapter of this book demonstrates. In addition, in the post–9/11 world, the Algeria/Holocaust connection has been supplemented by a set of associations linking those earlier forms of violence to emergent practices in the "global war on terror" and the Iraq War. The multidirectional links connecting Auschwitz and Algeria turn out to be a perfect staging ground for arguments about the politics and ethics of memory in an age of globalization.

PART III

TRUTH, TORTURE, TESTIMONY

Holocaust Memory During the Algerian War

6

The Work of Testimony in the Age of Decolonization: *Chronicle of a Summer* and the Emergence of the Holocaust Survivor

1961

Intellectuals such as Césaire, Arendt, and Du Bois and writers such as Schwarz-Bart and Phillips have long wrestled with the question of how to conceive of Nazi ideology and practice in a larger European and global frame. Against the backdrop of the global *longue durée* of Europe's colonial project in Africa, the Americas, and elsewhere, as well as more national issues such as American segregation, most of these figures engaged the proximate events of the Holocaust at a moment when no singular concept existed to describe the destruction of European Jewry. Although the results vary considerably, all of those discussed in the previous four chapters attempted to cut a multidirectional path through questions of race, space, narrative, and violence.

By the late 1950s and early 1960s two significant changes had taken place: on the one hand, it had become increasingly clear that colonialism as it existed in the late nineteenth and early twentieth centuries was nearing its end due to worldwide anticolonial movements and the formation of newly independent nations; on the other hand, a more differentiated approach to World War II was emerging in which the previously marginalized massacre of Jews would assume a central place in narratives of the century and in the consciousness of broad reaches of the public in Europe, the United States, and Israel. The cultural producers and activists whose work makes up the focus of the two following sections created films, documentary and journalistic texts, and literary works in a context defined by one of the most violent anticolonial struggles—the Algerian War of Independence—and one of the most vexed experiences of Nazi occupation. Not all of the figures discussed here are French, but we will nevertheless see once again how the very particular crosscutting histories of modern France captured on canvas by painters such as Taslitzky and Fougeron have made that nation into a kind of laboratory for the activation and exploration of multidirectional memory. In the French laboratory of remembrance, one particular year holds a disproportionate importance: 1961.

The year 1961 is generally considered a turning point in the history of Holocaust memory; it is also a key moment in the history of decolonization. In the spring and summer of 1961 the trial of Adolf Eichmann took place in Jerusalem. Anchored by the dramatic testimony of 111 survivors, the Eichmann trial brought the Nazi genocide of European Jews into the public sphere for the first time as a discrete event on an international scale. The trial was explicitly designed, in the words of Israeli Prime Minister David Ben-Gurion, to present "the Holocaust that the Nazis wreaked on the Jewish people . . . [as] a unique episode that has no equal . . . [and] as the only crime that has no parallel in human history."[1] Ben-Gurion's strategy was largely successful. According to the Israeli journalist and historian Tom Segev, "The Eichmann trial marked the beginning of a dramatic shift in the way Israelis related to the Holocaust" (361). The impact of the trial was by no means limited to Israel, however. In his history of Holocaust memory in the United States, Peter Novick has demonstrated that "the Eichmann trial, along with the controversies over [Hannah] Arendt's book [*Eichmann in Jerusalem*] and [Rolf] Hochhuth's play [*The Deputy*], effectively broke fifteen years of near silence on the Holocaust in American public discourse. As part of this process, there emerged in American culture a distinct thing called 'the Holocaust'—an event in its own right, not simply a subdivision of general Nazi barbarism."[2] Arendt herself claims that at least in the short run "there is no doubt that the Eichmann trial had its most far-reaching consequences in Germany," where it stimulated for the first time a series of arrests and trials of perpetrators of mass murder against the Jews.[3] Annette Wieviorka's analysis of the memory of the Shoah in France cites the trial as the moment at which previously private individual and family memories of the genocide came to "penetrate the social field."[4] By almost all accounts, the effects of bringing Eichmann to justice in Jerusalem have been long-lasting and widespread.

What is specific to the Eichmann trial and the Arendt controversy it unleashed is not the unprecedented nature of the questions they raised—many had already been posed—but rather their linkage of several different realms in one dramatic context.[5] First, the trial and Arendt's report have been a lasting touchstone for thinking about questions of responsibility, justice, and the nature of genocidal perpetration; since Arendt's report on the "banality of evil," Eichmann himself has come to represent the peculiar bureaucratic nature of the Nazi persecution of the Jews. Second, because of the prosecution's decision to present eyewitness testimony by dozens of survivors of the Nazi terror—a decision that had less to do with matters of evidence than with the state's pedagogical aims—the trial also helped create a new public identity: the Holocaust survivor. Third, as the metamorphosis in the status of the victim already suggests and as Arendt pointedly complained, the Eichmann trial contributed to an understanding of trials in general as forms of publicity or performance that exceed the restricted demands of justice. Fourth, tied to the trial's performance of survivor identity was a narrative of Jewish suffering, also controversially contested by Arendt, in which the Holocaust appeared simultaneously as part of a long history of anti-Semitism and as unique in modern history. Finally, in a move with a long-lasting impact on Middle Eastern politics as well as global memory, that narrative of Jewish suffering was in turn linked to a particular Israeli worldview that emphasized Zionist resistance as well as Arab collaboration with the Nazis. All of these matters—of responsibility and perpetration, performance and narrative, Jewish victimhood and Zionist resistance—combine to make the Eichmann trial and *Eichmann in Jerusalem* key sites of collective memory of the Nazi genocide.

While the trial established a powerful narrative of the Holocaust's uniqueness, framed that narrative within Zionist ideology, and provided a deeply moving affective glue for that ideology through the use of survivor testimony, in other parts of the world Holocaust testimony was emerging at the very same moment with a radically different political resonance. In this chapter and the next, I decenter the Eichmann trial's canonical position and provide an alternative account of the emergence of testimony in which Holocaust memory does not serve to consolidate an exclusivist national identity premised on a unique suffering. Rather, in this renarration of the turning point of 1961, the Jewish experience of World War II emerges as part of a multidirectional network connecting it to movements of decolonization.

The broadcast of parts of the Eichmann trial in the United States and Europe via videotape has led Jeffrey Shandler, the leading scholar of the representation of the Holocaust on television, to see the trial as an anticipation of the "cinéma vérité of due process" marked by the advent thirty years later of cable television's Court TV.[6] Although Shandler makes no mention of it, 1961 was also the year in which a film explicitly described itself as a work of cinéma vérité for the first time, a film that, moreover, features the testimony of a Holocaust survivor at its very center. In the same year that the Eichmann trial definitively changed Holocaust memory, Jean Rouch and Edgar Morin's film *Chronique d'un été* (*Chronicle of a Summer*) appeared in France. While absent from scholarship on memory of the Nazi genocide for more than forty years, *Chronicle of a Summer*'s almost forgotten scene of Holocaust testimony suggests the need to look beyond the Eichmann trial for other instances of Holocaust remembrance in the public sphere at this key moment of Holocaust memory's transformation.[7] The pursuit of such instances in the second half of *Multidirectional Memory* has the power to alter substantially understanding of the evolution of the Holocaust's meanings; revealing unexpected moments of multidirectional memory contributes to an archaeology of nondominant forces at work during the very consolidation of the Holocaust's significance as a unique event. Even if evidence of these forces was not ultimately preserved in dominant archives, their recovery has considerable implications for the theorization of collective memory beyond a competitive, zero-sum logic. The juxtaposition in *Chronicle of a Summer* of the memory of the Nazi genocide and the history of decolonization provides an opportunity to rethink the "unique" place that the Holocaust has come to hold in discourses on extreme violence.

Highlighting the various kinds of personal and political encounters staged in a key sequence from the middle of the ninety-minute film reveals the stakes of *Chronicle of a Summer*'s aesthetic of juxtaposition: an exploration of the encounter between the traumas of genocide and colonialism.[8] The film's juxtaposition of the Shoah and decolonization suggests that narratives of Holocaust memory that focus primarily on the memorial agency of the Eichmann trial may be incomplete. Europe's contemporaneous experience of the limits of its colonial project—here represented especially by the Algerian revolution and the independence of African nations—also served to catalyze Holocaust memory, while that memory in turn expressed a displaced recognition of the violence of the late colonial state. Although a certain political ambivalence attends this multidirectional mobilization of different histories in the film, *Chronicle*'s vision of overlapping and mutually reinforcing memories resonated with its historical moment. Indeed, the charged context of Fifth Republic France also produced more militant versions of memory politics, some of which build on or radicalize *Chronicle*'s challenges to the limits of the public sphere and its creation of alternative forms of testimony and publicity.

Recognizing the multidirectionality of memory encourages us to pay close attention to the circulation of historical memories in encounters whose meanings are complex and overdetermined, instead of proceeding from the assumption that the presence of one history in collective memory entails the erasure or dilution of all others. The purpose of this chapter is both to continue thinking the Holocaust beyond the uniqueness paradigm and to begin drawing attention to the very particular, multidirectional forms of overlap in memory and discourse between the Holocaust and the French-Algerian War—forms of overlap that will remain our focus throughout the remainder of the book. If, as I argue here, the Eichmann trial was not the only significant force that propelled the Holocaust into the public sphere, but did indeed set the stage for the discourse of uniqueness, returning to a moment before the trial's impact was felt can contribute to breaking apart the ossified positions in the memory wars.

Traumatic Encounters

Chronicle of a Summer provides an opportunity to reopen the historicization of Holocaust memory at the very moment of the Eichmann trial. Despite being ignored by Holocaust scholars, Rouch and Morin's film was quickly recognized as a landmark in nonfiction filmmaking. In this experiment, Rouch, known especially for his dozens of ethnographic films about Africa, turns his gaze to the metropolis. Accompanied by the sociologist Morin and a team of young coworkers, Rouch sends interviewers into the streets of Paris in the summer of 1960 in order to ask passersby if they are content with their lives. These street scenes are mixed with interviews of individuals and couples in domestic spaces as well as with staged encounters between groups and documentation of the conditions of French workers. Noted for its early use of self-reflexivity, the film also includes a scene in which the participants and interviewees are asked to comment on an almost complete version of the film. Additionally, Rouch and Morin themselves are frequently present on screen—from the opening scene in which the filmmakers discuss their vision of the film to the final, retrospective dialogue set in the African section of Paris's Musée de l'Homme.

Although it is difficult in an era of the webcam, "reality" television, and indeed Court TV to grasp *Chronicle of a Summer*'s novelty, Rouch and Morin's film was, in the early 1960s, a radical aesthetic and sociological experiment that had a profound impact on the French New Wave and whose most important elements still resonate today. The film is significant for at least four reasons: its place in film history, its relationship to the political history of France, its contribution to French intellectual history, and its status as a source for charting a history of memory. *Chronicle*'s film-historical significance lies in its reinvention of a genre: it draws on previous documentary experiments by Robert Flaherty and Dziga Vertov (from whose concept of *Kino-pravda* the term *cinéma vérité* derives), but moves beyond them because of the way it incorporates emergent technological innovations in camera and sound technology. In terms of political history, the film makes reference to the contemporaneous decolonization of the Congo as well as the ongoing Algerian War—Morin even claims that it was the only film of its time to question the war.[9] Intellectually, it both derives from and contributes to the thinking of everyday life, a category that was being theorized at the time by Henri Lefebvre and Morin himself. Finally, Rouch and Morin's film includes a curious and overlooked contribution to considerations of Holocaust memory.

In *Chronicle*, these four modes of history—film, politics, ideas, and memory—intersect and come into dialogue with each other through the reinvention of the genre of cinéma vérité. It should be noted that Rouch and Morin themselves do not present a unified vision of what cinéma vérité is or does.[10] While, in Morin's words, its purpose is to document "the authenticity of life as it is lived" (Morin 229) at a particular moment and in a particular place (for example, Paris, summer 1960), Rouch possesses what we might today call a "performative" understanding of the genre. *Cinéma vérité*, he has remarked, "does not mean the cinema of truth, but the truth of cinema" (*Ciné-ethnography* 167). That is, Rouch recognizes the camera as a "stimulant" (100) that "stages . . . reality" (185) by intervening into and shaping the very environment that it records. While the deliberate and provocative staging of scenes would seem to prevent them from authentically capturing "life as it is lived," the *form* of cinéma vérité does respond, although not univocally, to the historical imperatives of its moment.

That *Chronicle of a Summer* will contribute to a rethinking of Holocaust memory and its relationship to decolonization is not immediately obvious in its opening scenes. The film begins with exterior shots of Paris and its suburbs, while Rouch's voice is heard introducing the project of cinéma vérité: "This film was not played by actors, but lived by men and women who have given a few moments of their lives to a new experiment in *cinéma vérité*" (*Ciné-ethnography* 274).[11] A scene follows in which Morin, Rouch, and a young woman named Marceline sit around after dinner and Morin explains to Marceline the nature of their project: "What Rouch and I want to do is a film on the following idea: How do you live? How do you live? We start with you, and then we're going to ask other people" (275). In this scene and over the course of the next forty minutes in which *Chronicle* explores the contours of Parisian everyday life, the trauma of the Nazi genocide seems far away. In the streets Marceline and Nadine approach strangers and ask them if they are happy; in a series of cramped apartments, various couples detail their daily joys and trials;

a worker, Angelo, and a young African student, Landry, converse about racism, class conflict, and consumer society on the staircase of an apartment building; and Marceline's boyfriend, Jean-Pierre, an angst-ridden philosophy student, recounts his feelings of bitterness and impotence.

In these scenes, however, the traumas of World War II lie just below the surface. The husband in one of the couples interviewed about their living conditions, for example, turns out to have been a deportee, although this is only divulged in the published version of the script. More dramatically, when Jean-Pierre complains of feeling personally and politically "fucked over" and "impotent," Marceline takes responsibility for Jean-Pierre's political defeatism, admitting that "it's partly through me that you . . . knew all those people who were ready to cry after their political experiences. . . . Me too, in fact." As Marceline somberly continues that "in spite of everything" she thought it was possible to make Jean-Pierre happy, the camera pans down from her face to her arm and reveals the tattoo that marks her as a survivor of Auschwitz (303–5). Although Morin claims in the following scene that the film "up to here has been enclosed in a relatively personal and individual universe" (305), the still unspoken memory of the Nazi period and the concentrationary universe emerges in the scene with Jean-Pierre as a force that cuts across public and private realms, across political crises and everyday intimacies.[12]

When the Nazi genocide finally emerges as an explicit theme after the conversation with Jean-Pierre, it does so in the context of discussions about contemporary racism and the struggles for decolonization in Algeria and the Congo.[13] The content of these discussions and the film techniques that render them reveal both a movement from private to public and a sense that these realms are inextricably implicated in each other because of the traumatic effects of political violence. On the one hand, the mise-en-scène of the sequence echoes Morin's claim that the film moves from the personal to the public, as the scene with a couple in a cramped apartment gives way to a group scene in a dining room, then to a group scene in a roof-terrace restaurant (first shot in the direction of the street below), and finally to a pair of travelling shots in the streets of the city. On the other hand, the personal dimension clearly persists throughout the film and the public dimension seems always to haunt it.

Throughout the sequence, the filmmakers employ a series of close-ups of the participants speaking and listening to each other, and alternate those with occasional medium shots that display the participants as a group or look over the shoulder of one of the participants, creating a subjective point of view. The effect of these relatively tight and often subjective shots is to establish an intimacy between viewers and participants that grounds the illusion of capturing everyday life in a relatively unmediated fashion. Yet, through its very staging, the film reveals this everyday life as shot through with politics and violence. First, Rouch and Morin film their friends in an after-dinner discussion of the Algerian War, a scene that testifies to the ambivalence among the French about the war, and their somewhat distanced response to it (even in a left-wing intellectual milieu such as this one). If, in the previous scene with Jean-Pierre and Marceline, an everyday affair is ruptured by memory of extreme violence, in the discussion of the Algerian War, state violence is revealed as having become quotidian, "a sort of mutual habit," complains a young Régis Debray. Following Debray's exhortation that "You've got to wager . . . that men can finally put an end to this war," sound effects of machine gun fire are heard and a series of newspaper headlines are displayed, first concerning the war and then events in the newly independent Congo (306–7).[14] The montage of newspaper headlines and gunfire, rare nondiegetic elements resonant of fictional film techniques for the creation of dramatic tension, reinforces the sense that 1960 is a moment in which everyday life and the punctuality of political events are intersecting, even despite public indifference.

In the following scene, we observe how through the provocation of the filmmakers Marceline's identity as an Auschwitz survivor enters the film explicitly during a discussion of contemporary racism and anticolonial solidarity among Africans. The setting of this scene—the "Totem" restaurant at the Musée de l'Homme—takes on added significance when we realize that the museum had functioned as one of the initial organizational sites for the Resistance during the German occupation and houses the ethnographic artifacts collected during Marcel Griaule's famous Mission Dakar-Djibouti.[15] Oddly, though, the scene begins with a mild expression of racism on the part of Marceline: "Personally," she claims, "I would never marry a black" (307). A brief discussion of racial stereotypes follows before Morin interrupts with a question about responses

184   TRUTH, TORTURE, TESTIMONY

to the events in the Congo, where the Lumumba government was struggling against Belgian military forces. Landry, a student from the Ivory Coast, explains the solidarity of Africans from different nations with all anticolonial struggles and Marceline, perhaps trying to save face after her embarrassing revelations, expresses understanding for Landry's position based on her own experiences: "I understand that very well, because while the example is not completely, completely a good one . . . but if there is a manifestation of anti-Semitism in any country in the world . . . well, then I'm involved . . . I can't allow it . . . [. . .] it's all the same, for me" (310; first four ellipses in the original). The willingness of Marceline to proceed so quickly to an analogy between anti-Semitism and colonialism reveals the presence of a historical sensibility at odds with the discourse of uniqueness that would become dominant, but was only just emerging at this moment. The rooftop discussion of different forms of prejudice also hints at an emergent discourse of race during the late stages of the Algerian War (see Figure 4).

Prompted perhaps by Marceline's analogy between Jewish solidarity in the face of anti-Semitism and Africans' solidarity in the face of colonialism, Rouch asks the African students Landry and Raymond if they know what Marceline's tattoo is. They don't. A few moments of embarrassment mixed with joking about the possible sources of the tattoo ensue—an affectation? a telephone number?—and then, after the camera has zoomed in on her arm and receded, Marceline explains, "Well, it's not my telephone number . . . uh . . . I was deported to a concentration camp during the war because I'm Jewish, and this is a serial number that they gave me in that camp" (311). A quick pan reveals that the usually voluble Landry has been silenced. Raymond knows something about the camps, having seen a film about them, probably Alain Resnais's 1955 *Night and Fog*. This scene, an exemplary instance of Rouch's notion of cinéma vérité as provocation, produces discomfort in the viewers as in the participants (even Rouch was later embarrassed about his demeanor here). In the course of a brief scene, an odd displacement has taken place from actuality—signaled by the newspaper headlines and the discussion of ongoing events—to memory—registered by the inscription of a tattoo and the invocation of a historical film. Furthermore, a disturbing hierarchy of knowledge has been established in which the white French figures are put

The Work of Testimony in the Age of Decolonization 185

FIGURE 4 Marceline, Rouch, and Landry discuss racism and anti-Semitism in the rooftop restaurant of the Musée de l'Homme. Jean Rouch and Edgar Morin, *Chronique d'un été* (1961). Author's collection.

in the place of those who know, while Landry and Raymond are relegated to the status of those who do not and Marceline comes to embody history. Given the relatively low level of knowledge about the specificities of the Nazi genocide in 1960, the establishment of such a hierarchy is particularly dubious.

As that scene ends, we cut to a sequence that follows Marceline through the Place de la Concorde and into the empty markets of Les Halles as she recounts her story of deportation and return: how she was deported with her father, was beaten in front of him by an SS man the one time they were reunited in the camps, and then returned home without him to the remnants of her family (see Figure 5). Once again, mise-en-scène is significant and contributes to a layering of past and present, everyday and extreme: the now innocent looking Place de la Concorde triggers a memory of Marceline's arrest, while the architecture of Les Halles

FIGURE 5 Marceline recounts the story of her deportation while walking through the Place de la Concorde. Jean Rouch and Edgar Morin, *Chronique d'un été* (1961). Author's collection.

echoes that of the train station to which she would have returned and thus seems to prompt the content of her testimony. The confusion of past and present, here and there, is further reinforced through Marceline's mode of address: "And then here I am now, Place de la Concorde . . . I came back, you stayed. [*She sighs.*] We'd been there six months before I saw you" (312). Speaking directly to her dead father, Marceline creates a ghostly space in which places (the camps, Paris) and times (the war, the postwar) intersect with little transition. If the remainder of the film shifts toward more mundane themes (such as love affairs and vacations), and Marceline herself plays a less central role, her dramatic testimony continues to mark viewers' memories (as comments by critics and participants in the film demonstrate).

Marceline's narrative is brief and cryptic, and yet, viewed from the present, resolutely familiar. Its story of deportation and return to a shattered family echoes numerous other camp memoirs, most closely the third volume of Charlotte Delbo's trilogy, *Auschwitz and After*, in which Delbo creates a collection of short narratives by survivors focused on the difficulty of reintegration into postwar social and family conditions.[16] But if the elements of Marceline's story sound familiar now, that is because of the many texts that have been published, like Delbo's, or rediscovered, like Primo Levi's, since the early 1960s. At the time, the stories of Jewish victims of Nazism were only beginning to be recognized. Elie Wiesel's *Night* (*La nuit*) and André Schwarz-Bart's *The Last of the Just* (*Le dernier des justes*), two key texts of what would become Holocaust literature, were published in the two years preceding the filming of *Chronicle*, yet these texts can only retrospectively be seen as forming part of an autonomous discourse. And indeed Schwarz-Bart's own accounts of his writing emphasize how significantly decolonization contributed to his oeuvre.

The sequence of scenes that runs from the confrontation of Marceline and Jean-Pierre through the dinner discussion of the war and the rooftop dialogue to Marceline's testimony constitutes a series of encounters of different types. Each of the first three scenes stages an encounter between individuals around difficult personal and political issues, while the fourth depicts an encounter between past and present in the form of the reemergence of traumatic memories. Furthermore, both between and within scenes, the filmmakers deliberately force encounters between different histories, between public and private spaces, and between everyday practices and traumatic violence. This technique of productive encounter recalls Rouch's surrealist heritage—which, like Aimé Césaire, he imbibed during his youth in 1930s Paris—and especially James Clifford's notion of "ethnographic surrealism," which is meant to capture the creative energy and methodological innovation of that era. For Clifford, "ethnographic surrealist practice . . . attacks the familiar, provoking the irruption of otherness—the unexpected" (145).[17] Referring to anthropology's tendency to produce encounters "in which distinct cultural realities are cut from their contexts and forced into jarring proximity," Clifford suggests that "the surrealist moment in ethnography is that moment in which the possibility of comparison exists in unmediated tension with sheer incongruity" (146).[18] Surrealists intend their practice of juxtaposition to provoke access to levels of reality beyond the everyday and the conscious.

In *Chronicle of a Summer*, the ethnographic surrealist method of encounter reveals the presence in 1960s Paris of two further forms of encounter: the traumatic encounter with memory of genocide and the unsettling encounter with colonial legacies. Both of these encounters continue to echo to this day and shape contemporary French culture in unexpected ways. The "jarring proximity" of these two forms of encounter—which in these scenes from *Chronicle* seems to exceed the filmmakers' intentional manipulation—produces ambivalence and discomfort, but it also reveals the political unconscious of the moment: the inscription of an as-yet-unacknowledged memory in urban space and the hierarchies of race and nation that continue to haunt even progressive milieus in the metropolis. While for many today this proximity produces an effect of "sheer incongruity," the juxtaposition of legacies of the Nazi genocide and colonialism has its historical logic. In order to understand the significance of the inclusion of these scenes in *Chronicle* it is necessary to reestablish the context of their emergence. Within this context, the curious displacement enacted in the film from anticolonial actuality to the memory of genocide also takes on further dimensions.

Cinéma Vérité and the Emergence of the Survivor

The scenes following Marceline into the streets of Paris link the reinvention of cinéma vérité to the emergence of a new public form of Holocaust memory. If the film's sequencing of this act of testimony implies that it has been included as a kind of remediation for the "ignorance" of Landry and Raymond, its conditions of possibility are more complex. Rather, these new forms of film and public memory take shape at the intersection of technology, aesthetics, and the conjunctural politics of decolonization. In these scenes, and unlike in *kinopravda* or even *Night and Fog*, the documentary mentioned in *Chronicle*, film and firsthand testimony work together dramatically.[19]

The technology that enables cinéma vérité also seems to elicit the form of testimony, a genre in its own right that has only grown in importance since the early 1960s. The light and mobile Éclair 16 mm camera, developed during shooting with Rouch's feedback, and the portable Nagra tape recorder that Rouch and Morin employ facilitate the capturing of synchronous image and sound without relying on a large crew.[20] Technology allows the filmmakers simultaneously to be intrusive and to remain aloof; intimacy and distance combine to set the stage for an unprecedented articulation of personal experience in a public medium. We see this combination especially in the shots of Marceline as she crosses the public space of the Place de la Concorde and enters the markets of Les Halles, all the while withdrawn into a traumatized, trancelike reminiscence, which is captured by the portable sound equipment. Although her words are ultimately intended for the public, they are articulated "as if" privately, with even the crew unable to hear her as she speaks. Anticipating the invention of Holocaust video testimony, which would only begin to be archived starting in the 1970s, cinéma vérité deploys the latest technology and documents the emergence of the Holocaust survivor. Like the video archive, Rouch's cinéma vérité displays an embodied, speaking subject.[21] As Michel Marie has suggested, cinéma vérité and the related "direct cinema" movement possess "an aesthetic based on a return to the primordial function of spoken language."[22] Much of the power of both video testimony and cinéma vérité derives from their apparently phonocentric deployment of a self-present body.

The direct synchronized sound deployed in cinéma vérité and the extreme close-ups made possible by the new camera technology certainly encourage understanding of the embodied subject, in this case Marceline, as a carrier of authenticity. Yet, while the scenes with Marceline are quite moving—and quite unprecedented—they cannot simply be considered "authentic"; rather, they unsettle notions of authenticity that have since come to adhere to the very powerful genre of audiovisual testimony. An unquestioned association of testimony with authenticity emerges even in a sophisticated scholar of Holocaust representation like Lawrence Langer, who asserts that such testimonies bypass "the mediation of a *text*" and reach us "in their raw frankness" via "the immediacy and intimacy of . . . interviews."[23] Such claims, already dubious in the case of video testimony, are even more mystificatory when we examine *Chronicle*, despite their echo of Morin's conception of cinéma vérité. Far from being an unmediated example of sound and image, Marceline's testimony emerges through the very mediation of film. Cinema is present in this scene not only in the form of sophisticated editing decisions, the visible and invisible sound and camera equipment, and the crew who, off screen, ride alongside and then ahead of Marceline in a car (see Rouch 153).[24] Cinema also circulates here as what Marceline herself later called "cinematographic fantasies." "Certain lines from *Hiroshima, mon amour* came to me" during the filming, she writes, and indeed Marceline's scenes in the Place de la Concorde and Les Halles visually echo the nighttime meanderings of Emmanuelle Riva in Resnais and Duras's 1959 film (qtd. in Rouch 341). The very choice of the Concorde as a location was determined, Morin reports, by the expected presence there of a crew shooting a film on the German occupation, which—had it still been there—would have offered signs in German and extras wearing Wehrmacht uniforms (Morin 240). Marceline's trancelike testimony is actually a kind of "ciné-transe" in Rouch's sense—an event of mutual possession mediated by the presence of the camera (Rouch 99–100).[25] As Marceline writes in her contribution to the published version of the script, "I put myself in the situation, I dramatized myself, I chose a character that I then interpreted within the limits of the film, a character who is both an aspect of the reality of Marceline and also a dramatized character created by Marceline" (qtd. in Rouch 341). The mixture of fantasy, staging, and technologically mediated access to reality in these scenes constitutes an unusual context for thinking about the emergence of testimony, but one which is not without some suggestive ties to more canonical works of Holocaust representation. For instance, with its mixture of staging and testimony, *Chronicle* begins to look like an unacknowledged predecessor of Claude Lanzmann's opus *Shoah*, a film based entirely on testimony, but which Lanzmann understands less as a documentary than as a form of performative reenactment.[26]

While Marceline's testimony would not have been possible without the technology and aesthetic ideology of cinéma vérité, both the act of testimony by a Holocaust survivor and the genre of cinéma vérité need to be historicized.[27] First of all, reference to Marceline as a Holocaust survivor is somewhat anachronistic—not only because the word "Holocaust" was not used in French until much later, but also because the concept of the "survivor" was only then in the process of emergence. The years of *Chronicle*'s filming and release, 1960–61, are crucial moments in the history of Holocaust memory; it is at this time that a notion of the specific nature of the extermination of European Jews emerges. Eichmann's abduction by Israeli agents in 1960 already raised many legal and moral questions that were hotly debated in the lead up to the trial, but it was ultimately the decision on the part of prosecutor Gideon Hausner to call 111 witness to testify in the 1961 trial that has had the longest-term effect on the shape of Holocaust memory (see Segev; Novick; Wieviorka; Shandler). In the words of French historian Annette Wieviorka, "The Eichmann trial marks a turning point.... The memory of the genocide becomes constitutive of a certain Jewish identity at the same time that it claims a presence in the public sphere" (81). In addition, Wieviorka goes on to argue, it is through the agency of the trial that "the survivor" becomes a social identity: "Before the Eichmann trial, the survivor maintains her identity by and in intimate associations, an associative life closed in on itself.... The Eichmann trial changes the situation. At the heart of survivor identity, a new function [emerges], that of the carrier of history" (117–18).[28]

If the public discourse of the Holocaust's uniqueness dates to the early 1960s and is closely tied to the survivor as bearer of history, as Wieviorka and others argue, then *Chronicle of a Summer* has provocative implications for that discourse. The technology that makes Marceline's testimony possible is precisely a technology of reproducibility, a set of synchronized recording devices that facilitate the passage of intimacy into publicity. Furthermore, the very "staginess" of these scenes, the difficulty of assessing their degree of spontaneity or scriptedness, mirrors that of the Eichmann trial itself. Like Marceline's testimony (by her own account) and Rouch and Morin's film as a whole, the trial was deliberately staged; it took place not in a courtroom, but in Jerusalem's Beit Ha'am, "a large public theater and community center" that had been "remodeled to provide hundreds of print and broadcast journalists with work space and telecommunications services" (Shandler 90). Since the Israeli government had set as its goal the creation of a new narrative of the Holocaust and not simply the rendering of justice, the trial became, in Shandler's words, "a kind of hyperhistory," a "self-conscious performance of the past as 'historical'" (104). The trial thus shares with the film both a self-conscious aesthetic strategy and the use of the latest technology as vehicles for the dissemination of its truths. While, in the case of the trial, this mix ultimately contributes to the worldwide propagation of a discourse of uniqueness, the evidence of the film suggests other possible routes that might have been taken.

Truth and Decolonization

How can we situate *Chronicle* and Marceline's testimony in relation to the epochal change ushered in by the 1961 trial? It is not only their relationship but also their lack of relationship that proves instructive for thinking about transformations in Holocaust memory. Obviously, while the lead up to the trial could well have influenced Rouch and Morin's decision to place a survivor at the center of their film, the dramatic testimonies that constituted a large part of the trial and changed the contours of Holocaust memory could not have been influential since the scenes with Marceline were filmed in August 1960 and most of the editing of the film had been completed by the time the trial commenced. (In addition, I have not found reference to the Eichmann trial in any of Rouch and Morin's writings about the film.) While the evidence of this one film cannot be said to change the dominant narrative of Holocaust memory and the role played within it by the critical Eichmann trial, the unprecedented scene of Marceline's testimony together with other evidence that we will discuss in subsequent chapters does suggest that we need to think more about the social context in which public memory of the genocide and the figure of the survivor emerged together.

The context established by the film suggests that an important role can be ascribed, especially in France, to the contemporaneous history of decolonization, which was bringing questions of everyday and extreme forms of state violence and racism into the public sphere. While Nazism and colonialism had been linked as early as 1950 by Césaire, *Chronicle* explicitly addresses the Holocaust in its particularity in a way that Césaire did not initially intend to do. It is in the context of discussions of race and colonialism that Rouch and Morin choose to highlight Marceline's mark as a survivor and then to capture her on film in an act of testimony. I would go farther and claim that the very concept of *vérité*, or truth, however contested, that buttresses the genre of cinéma vérité takes some of its force from the struggles against colonialism that were at their height when Rouch and Morin first conceptualized the genre in the years 1959–62. The key elements of the war and the anticolonial movement relevant here are torture, censorship, and testimony.

Throughout the war, and despite controversy, France used torture as an ordinary measure in its war against the Algerians. Almost immediately, intellectuals took up torture as a defining struggle of the era of decolonization; as Morin himself wrote in a July 9, 1959, article in *France-Observateur*, "The new *cogito* of the left can only be the unconditional and universal refusal of torture."[29] The practice of torture also evoked memories of the German occupation of France, both among members of the leftist resistance and even among some state officials. For example, in submitting his resignation in 1957, the secretary general of the police in Algiers, Paul Teitgen, a former deportee, wrote that he recognized in Algeria "profound traces . . . of the torture that fourteen years ago I personally suffered in the basements of the Gestapo in Nancy."[30] When, in the mid-1960s, the Austrian Holocaust survivor Jean Améry came to write his well-known essay "Torture" about his experiences at the hands of the Nazis, he made reference to contemporary practices in Vietnam as well as to the "numerous" books on torture in Algeria that appeared in France "around 1960."[31] The frequency of such analogies and links between past and current histories received further impetus from the presence of at least one million Algerians in concentration camps (*en camp de concentration*) in Algeria in 1959 and thousands in administrative detention in the metropole (Stora 34). Such extreme procedures were immediately experienced by camp survivors, including Charlotte Delbo, as unwelcome echoes of the past (cf. *Les belles lettres* 65–66).[32]

But it is not only the fact of Nazi-like tactics deployed by a nation recently victimized by fascism that constitutes the context of *Chronicle of a Summer*. The discourse of truth and the practice of testimony deployed in the film might also be understood to derive their inspiration from the extensive, if inconsistent, censorship undertaken by the state. After 1958, and the suppression of Henri Alleg's famous exposé of torture, *The Question*, 14 percent of all books on the war were censored, as well as hundreds of periodicals. Censorship reached its height in 1960 and 1961, precisely the years of the production of Rouch and Morin's film (Stora 25–28). The undeclared status of the war, and the consequent inability to name the enemy (was he Algerian, French, Muslim?), along with the open secret of torture, heightened the effect of censorship and produced the felt need among some French citizens for what historian Benjamin Stora has called "a truth cure" (53)—the need to expose, to the extent possible, that which has been suppressed. Although much was known at the time—or available to be known by those who were interested—the aura of suppression would continue for decades after the war's end; indeed, it was only in September 1999 that the French Assembly voted that the "events" in Algeria be officially known as a war.[33]

This context of secrets and suppression entailed that, at least in the metropolis, a discourse of "truth" was circulating in proximity to anticolonial struggles at the moment when Rouch and Morin were creating the new cinéma vérité. Most obviously, several journals of the French anticolonial movement deployed the concept of "truth" as definitional in their titles. There was *Vérité-Liberté*, which began publication in May 1960 and was edited by the historian Pierre Vidal-Naquet, among others, and there were, in addition, *Vérités Anticolonialistes* and *La Vérité des Travailleurs*, a Communist newspaper whose February 1961 headline reads, "All Our Forces for the Algerian Revolution."[34] In 1958 Sartre's radical comrade Francis Jeanson had founded the journal *Vérités Pour* in order to unify various clandestine resistance groups; the arrest and trial of members of Jeanson's network of support for the Algerian Front de Libération Nationale (FLN) bracketed the primary filming of *Chronicle of a Summer* in 1960 and led to the drafting of the famous "Manifesto of the 121," written by Maurice Blanchot and others in September of that year in favor of the right not to serve in the army.[35]

The link between cinéma vérité, the Algerian War, and memory of the Nazi genocide is further supported by the fact that not only truth but also its articulation, specifically through the act of testimony, was central to resistance to the Algerian War. Anticolonial activists attempted to circumvent state censorship through the publication of banned articles and books in journals such as *Témoignages et Documents* (Testimonies and documents), also edited by Vidal-Naquet before a split in 1960 led him to found *Vérité-Liberté*.[36] Indeed, for people like Vidal-Naquet and André Mandouze, an associate of Fanon in North Africa, the acts of testimony and resistance bridged the eras of the two wars.[37] During World War II Mandouze was one of the founders of Témoignage chrétien (Christian Witness), a group that helped save Jewish children and whose magazine was active in resistance to the Algerian War. Years later Mandouze titled the first volume of his memoirs *D'une résistance à l'autre* (From one resistance to another), and thus testified to the persistence of the link between fascist and colonial violence in at least a certain segment of French collective memory.[38] Vidal-Naquet, a French Jew whose parents had been deported and murdered by the Nazis, retrospectively observed, "I personally entered the fight against the Algerian war and specifically against torture . . . with a constant point of reference: the obsessive memory of our national injustices—particularly the Dreyfus Affair—and of the Nazi crimes of torture and extermination."[39] In his memoirs, Vidal-Naquet specifies that the motivation was even more personal: "My father Lucien had been tortured by the Gestapo in Marseilles in May 1944. The idea that these same techniques were—after Indochina, Madagascar, Tunisia, and Morocco—used in Algeria by the French police and military, horrified me" (*Mémoires* 2.32). Indeed, although he later would regret some of his most explicit comparisons between World War II and the Algerian War, Vidal-Naquet wrote in the very first editorial of *Vérité-Liberté* in May 1960 that "nobody can claim today that the Nazi years are completely behind us" (Vidal-Naquet, *Face* 83; cf. *Mémoires* 2.91, 107).

My argument is that Marceline's testimony was made possible by and became meaningful in a discursive context in which the association of torture, truth, testimony, and resistance underwrote a link between the Algerian War and Nazi atrocities. The emergence of the survivor from silence and the private sphere of intimate associations—indeed the emergence of that very private sphere—into a public space of articulation parallels the process of the Eichmann trial, but derives its impetus at least in part from the intense, ongoing struggles of decolonization, which were forcing a new recognition of racialized state violence, at least among a small cadre of French leftist intellectuals and activists. Those struggles to bring the truth of colonial violence into the public sphere were, however, confronted with two difficulties. In the summer of 1960, as in the years immediately preceding and following it, the recognition of state violence was, unsurprisingly, being actively resisted by none other than the ideological and repressive apparatuses of that very state. But in addition, and perhaps more significantly, the great majority of the French public demonstrated an indifference to the truths that could be known despite the censorship, a censorship that was in fact applied inconsistently. In the words of Stora, "*Society knows*, but contents itself to share the secret of an undeclared war" (73). The preservation of this secret demands an active work of forgetting and exclusion that "disappears" the violence of the state and the nationalist insurgency. Just at the moment that memory of the Nazi genocide is, according to Wieviorka, emerging out of the intimate sphere, contemporary consciousness of the Algeria War is, according to Stora, already relegating collective history to oblivion. With no special funeral orations, tombstones, or monuments marking the return of dead French soldiers from the war, "the relationship to death, exclusively private, is excluded from public life" (Stora 73).

Given a situation in which the memory of one series of events begins to emerge just as another series enters into a long process of forgetting, it is tempting to assign a relationship of causality between remembrance and oblivion. In that reading, which is not uncommon, the growing obsession with the Holocaust serves as a screen memory that blocks access to the more recent and more troubling complicity with colonial violence.[40] In the long run this may well capture a partial truth for the situation in France—as in other locations, such as the United States, where unpleasant memories of slavery and the genocide of indigenous peoples remain muted in comparison to a large-scale fascination with the events of the Shoah and World War II. But the evidence provided by a contextual reading of *Chronicle of a Summer* suggests a more complex memory dynamic. It is important to note, for example, that even as the new social identity of the survivor arises in France, the general climate remains hostile to a full reckoning with the past. According to Henry Rousso, the early 1960s represent the heart of that stage of the "Vichy syndrome"—France's initial repression of and later obsession with its World War II past—during which French complicity and collaboration with Germany and its "Final Solution" were largely ignored in favor of the myth of a unified resistance to Nazism. Yet even in those years the Algerian War did spark a politicized memory work, especially among former members of the resistance who identified themselves with a Dreyfusard inheritance.[41] In other words, even if the majority of the French public remained uninterested in remembering or knowing crimes committed in the name of France, those who did speak out about Algeria were all the more likely to foster a work of memory and testimony that drew on and helped create memory of the genocide.

The transitional and conflicted context of France in the late 1950s and early 1960s ensures that collective memories of genocide and colonialism had not settled into stable forms but remained in dynamic tension.[42] *Chronicle of a Summer* bears this out. On the one hand, a displacement does take place in the film from the immediate and pressing question of colonialism and decolonization to that of the temporally removed Holocaust. On the other hand, this displacement takes place in a political context in which discourse on contemporary events was significantly restrained. Instead of identifying this displacement only as a struggle between memories, it represents an instance of multidirectional memory: a process in which transfers take place between events that have come to seem separate from each other. Thus, it is not only the case that the actuality of decolonization struggles helps produce a context in which memory of the Shoah can be articulated. It may also be true that the articulation of that memory serves as an allegory for that which cannot be publicly spoken or that which the public does not want to hear. In the film, traumatic memory of the genocide is staged as moving from the implicit to the explicit and from the private to the public sphere. Given the enormous state censorship and repression that targeted opposition to the Algerian War—hence the need for journals such as those mentioned above—Marceline's testimony may carry an added symbolic burden: she speaks as a victim whose experiences can finally be narrated and who thus stands in allegorically for those victims whose experiences cannot yet be spoken and recognized.

The fact that Marceline's memory does not emerge "naturally"— that it derives from overlapping forces of technology, imagination, and politics and is situated in a context seemingly far removed from the Nazi genocide—ought to provoke further reflection on the history of Holocaust memory. The interarticulation of Holocaust memory and anticolonial history suggests that attempts to separate the legacies of the Holocaust from those of other histories of violence are not only morally suspect but also miss the productive dynamic that occurs in the acts of juxtaposition, comparison, and analogy. *Chronicle of a Summer* carries a trace of memory that does not fit into the dominant understanding of the Nazi genocide as "a unique episode that has no equal," as a crime with "no parallel," to reprise Ben-Gurion's language. Rather, at the very moment that such an understanding is emerging into international public consciousness, *Chronicle* bears witness to an alternative vision—a vision in which the specificity of the Nazi genocide is marked not in opposition to colonial violence but through an encounter with it.

However rooted *Chronicle* was in the very particular national and transnational circumstances of France in the early 1960s, its vision is not unique, as the example of Du Bois and others demonstrates. Other works emerge out of or confront the same context of the Algerian War—works by an international group of writers, scholars, and filmmakers who also experiment with the form of testimony and the creation of new public spheres and who sometimes even seem to take direct inspiration from Rouch and Morin's film.

7

The Counterpublic Witness: Charlotte Delbo's *Les belles lettres*

Nineteen sixty-one, the year of *Chronicle of a Summer*'s release, was a year in which *Les Temps modernes* published excerpts from Primo Levi and Frantz Fanon in their May issue and later juxtaposed accounts of the Eichmann trial and the October 17 massacre of Algerians in Paris.[1] Nineteen sixty-one also marks the year of Charlotte Delbo's first book publication. In the last couple of decades, Delbo has been justly hailed as one of the most articulate memoirists of the Nazi camps, primarily on the strength of her trilogy *Auschwitz et après* (*Auschwitz and After*) and her posthumous *La mémoire et les jours* (*Days and Memory*). Delbo's newfound reputation derives from the at-once emotionally searing and formally challenging quality of her work; in an effort to capture the extremity and long-term traumatic impact of the Nazi camps she experiments with documentary form.[2] Critical appreciation of Delbo, a non-Jewish survivor who was part of the Communist French resistance and who maintained contacts with the intellectual Left in France after the war, has not yet, however, led to a rediscovery of her works that do not focus on Auschwitz.

Although Delbo had written *Aucun de nous ne reviendra* (*None of Us Will Return*), the first volume of her Auschwitz trilogy, soon after her return from the camps, it took her years to decide to publish it. Appearing in 1965, that volume turns out not to be her initial book publication. Four years earlier, in 1961, Delbo published her first experiment in documentary form, the ironically titled *Les belles lettres*—not a Holocaust memoir, but a collection of letters pertaining to the Algerian War.[3] These letters, generally selected by Delbo from well-known French newspapers and magazines, such as *Le Monde*, but occasionally from overtly political sources, such as *Les Temps modernes*, *France-Observateur*, and *Vérité-Liberté*, provide a more or less chronological capsule history of some of the most important controversies surrounding the war during the period between late 1959 and early 1961. In between the letters, which are reprinted in standard typeface, Delbo inserts her own brief and often cutting commentary in bold type. Delbo's comments and her selection of letters locate her within the heterogeneous leftist metropolitan resistance, which, as the war dragged into its seventh year, was becoming increasingly radicalized. The formal innovation and provocative content of *Les belles lettres*, which has been almost completely ignored in the recent wave of Delbo criticism (including my own previous work), suggest the need to reread the emergence of Delbo's powerful oeuvre in light of an as-yet-unremarked political and historical context. While there is no reason to doubt Delbo's claim that she let her Auschwitz memoir sit for twenty years in order to see if it would stand "the test of time," the evidence of the social and political context of her publishing history suggests a supplementary reason why she finally began to publish: the urgency of the charged political climate of the 1960s, with its anticolonial struggles that tore at the fabric of postwar Europe.[4]

Reading Delbo in this context has significant historical and theoretical implications. First, such a reading contributes to the new understanding I have been developing here of the emergence of Holocaust memory and the unfolding of decolonization as overlapping and not separate processes. Although scholars of both Holocaust memory and decolonization recognize the early 1960s as a historically salient moment, no one has yet attempted to consider this moment's status as a nodal point of intersecting histories or to speculate about how such intersections might inflect narratives of the era. Many historians of the Nazi genocide trace the emergence of Holocaust memory into the public sphere to the affective power of the 1961 Eichmann trial in Jerusalem. Because, like *Chronicle of a Summer* and in the very same year, *Les belles lettres* mobilizes memory of the Nazi camps alongside a recognition of the violence of colonialism and harnesses those two histories of violence together in an experimental testimonial and documentary form, Delbo's text confirms the need to look beyond Eichmann to explain the emergence of public Holocaust memory and testimony. In comparison to *Chronicle*, the references in *Les belles lettres* may look less like contemporary Holocaust memory, which puts much greater emphasis on Jewish specificity than does Delbo. But the text offers glimpses into how such specificity emerged and together with Rouch and Morin's film suggests that that emergence took place through dialogue with—instead of opposition to—proximate histories of violence, including the violence of colonialism and decolonization.

For the same reasons, Delbo's text also offers new insights into the history of metropolitan anticolonial resistance. While public and scholarly attention to the legacies of Vichy and the Nazi genocide in France has, since the end of the 1960s, significantly outstripped attention to France's colonial wars, recent attempts to redress the balance risk segregating events that many contemporaries, including Delbo, experienced as deeply linked. Kristin Ross's valuable rewriting of French postwar history and culture represents a telling example. In two sharply argued books Ross has sought to revise understandings of postwar France by placing the French-Algerian War at the center of the era: in *Fast Cars, Clean Bodies* Ross demonstrates how the mainstream refusal to acknowledge the war as it was being waged manifested itself in displaced form in a range of modernizing discourses, from domestic hygiene to high structuralism; while in *May '68 and Its Afterlives* she finds the origins of the student-worker revolt of the late 1960s in memories of colonial violence and activists' resistance to it.[5] Ross's work makes significant inroads into the postcolonial amnesia that continues to afflict France more than forty years after Algerian independence, but it simultaneously reproduces other forms of forgetting. In particular, Ross has little to say about how the phantom presence of Algeria she uncovers intersects with the legacies of Nazi occupation and genocide, Vichy collaboration, and antifascist resistance that also shape the postwar era. In this silence, she follows most scholars of World War II and its aftermath, who have also generally ignored the overlapping legacies of genocide and colonialism.

Les belles lettres exposes the limits of both the conventional narrative of Holocaust memory and Ross's revisionist account of postwar history by drawing attention to the multiple forms of cross-referencing between decolonization and Nazi genocide that characterize the 1950s and 1960s in France and elsewhere. In this chapter, I continue to focus specifically on the politics of multidirectional memory, a politics that I now suggest demands a rethinking of the categories of the public sphere and testimony. A significant problem with the "competitive memory" model is that it assumes that both the arena of competition, the public sphere, and the subjects of the competition are given in advance. The model of "multidirectional memory," by contrast, supposes that the overlap and interference of memories help constitute the public sphere as well as the various individual and collective subjects that articulate themselves in it.

If neither the space nor the subject of public discourse is given in advance, then the testimonial articulation of memory becomes a site of potential political engagement; it creates subjects and helps shape what counts as the terrain of politics. Most studies of Holocaust testimony have relied on a notion of testimony premised on the psychoanalytic dialogue. This framework, articulated most influentially by Shoshana Felman and Dori Laub, has proven useful for understanding the anguish of survivors of various traumatic histories and for foregrounding the role of the listener in helping authorize testimony.[6] Yet, when testimony leaves the intimate sphere and becomes public by entering into the media, the legal system, and other social spaces, the psychoanalytic conception of dialogue proves inadequate to comprehending testimony's circulation and potential political impact. In order to describe the political work of witness and memory in *Les belles lettres* I develop an alternative notion of "counterpublic testimony" by drawing on Michael Warner's theory of publics and counterpublics. I locate that work of memory not only in the *content* of the memories at stake in Delbo's text—powerful as that content is—but especially in the text's self-reflexive epistolary *form*. Precisely the form of Delbo's work matters here because it is via formal experiment that Delbo makes claims on the construction of a new public sphere. In other words, Delbo's work helps us to see that testimony and memory do not simply move from private to public at a particular historical moment, as is assumed in standard histories of Holocaust representation; rather, their public articulation and address help redefine what counts as public and therefore what terrain exists for political struggle. That terrain is contoured not only by the institutions of the state and media, *Les belles lettres* illustrates, but also by the nature of individual and collective memory and by the aesthetic innovation memory can inspire.

Along with other anticolonial intellectuals and activists, Delbo clearly saw the need to inject post–World War II France with a "truth cure"—a cure that would take the form, as it would for Rouch and Morin, of an experimental documentary oeuvre bringing together the truths of decolonization and Nazi genocide. Through its unusual form, *Les belles lettres* makes claims on public space and bears a lesson about the politics of testimony and memory: it suggests not only that memory, truth, and testimony are central to postwar political movements and processes of decolonization, but also that memory in the form of letters (understood broadly) can take part in the necessary task of re-forming what counts as public and, therefore, what is politically thinkable. The issues raised by *Les belles lettres* are not without implications for the present. The very echoes of the Nazi past that motivated French intellectuals and activists during the Algerian War are there to be heard in our own moment, an issue I return to in the coda of this chapter and again in the following section. If we want to think about and intervene in contemporary politics we ignore the truths of memory at our own peril.

Between the Everyday and the Extreme (Again)

With its focus on the daily, weekly, and monthly press, Delbo's aesthetic project in *Les belles lettres* is marked, in part, by intense engagement with the everyday, an engagement that reflects something of the intellectual and cultural tenor of the times. In such a context, it seems by no means unimportant that starting in 1960, after finishing a thirteen-year stint with the United Nations in Geneva, Israel, and Greece, Delbo also worked at the Centre National de la Recherche Scientifique (CNRS) as an assistant to the key Marxist theorist of everyday life, Henri Lefebvre. Although Delbo's association with Lefebvre is often noted, no one has yet attempted to make sense of that connection; nor has there been any substantial analysis of Delbo's non-Auschwitz works from that period.[7] But besides being a topic of interest to the Parisian intelligentsia, the interrogation of everyday life was also a pressing question for survivors of the Nazi camps, who sometimes found themselves compelled to read their experiences in light of current events in the decolonizing world. This connection between the everyday, decolonization, and Holocaust memory shows up especially in the writings of Delbo.

At the heart of Delbo's Auschwitz memoirs is the problem of how to calibrate the extremity of the camp situation with the everydayness of the postwar world. Thinking seriously about the social and political context of 1960s France, as well as Delbo's personal association with the foremost theorist of the everyday, suggests that her post-Holocaust aesthetics were forged in a crucible of postwar history sometimes only tangentially related to the historical fact of the Nazi genocide. Although her most powerful works recount the experience of the Nazi camps, Delbo does not hesitate to juxtapose (without equating) Nazi crimes with those of colonialism and neocolonialism. Indeed, this juxtaposition bookends her oeuvre and can be found both in her very first publication, *Les belles lettres*, and at the end of her last, *Days and Memory*. Additionally, in *Useless Knowledge* (1970), the second volume of her Auschwitz trilogy, a narrative of the execution of four resistors who denounced the German occupation is followed immediately by an extract from a newspaper article that tells of the execution of an Algerian in 1960.[8] While, according to Lawrence Langer, sections of *Useless Knowledge* were written soon after the war in 1946–47, it is clear from this passage that the volume's composition bears the traces of multiple histories ("Introduction" x). Algeria continues to echo through Delbo's later writings, long after the war itself has ended—a testimony, as Ross would rightly insist, to the war's formative influence on the intellectual and political culture of the 1960s and beyond. In the last volume of her trilogy, *Auschwitz and After*, published in 1971, Delbo relates the stories of numerous survivors of the Nazi camps by juxtaposing narratives in diverse voices. Presented with little or no authorial comment, these narratives offer no singular master discourse on what it means to survive Auschwitz (in fact, quite the opposite seems to be the point), but with few exceptions all of the narratives reflect on the difficulty of return from the camps and on the problems of reintegrating into the everyday life of postwar France. One survivor, Gaby, reports, "We don't have television. One sees too many horrors. We used to have it, but when it broke down Jean didn't have it fixed. It was during the Algerian War. Uniforms, soldiers, machine guns . . . " (*Auschwitz* 330). In Delbo's rendering of Gaby's testimony, memory of Auschwitz merges with the wars of decolonization to disrupt the fabric of the everyday. For camp survivors the very mechanisms of modernization and Americanization—read by Ross as the agents of forgetting in decolonizing France—break down in a surplus of painful memories.

Delbo, in contrast to Gaby, discovers and defines her project in that breakdown of the everyday catalyzed by the intersection of camp memory and the wars of decolonization. A note appended to one of the final sections of *Days and Memory* (1985), Delbo's last, posthumously published work, reinforces how insistently events of the early 1960s related to the Algerian War of Independence weighed on and, indeed, stimulated Delbo's writing. For Delbo, the disruption of war attains the very material of writing—language itself. Here, at the end of her last work, she reproduces a dialogue between her narrative persona and a half-Jewish German woman in Ravensbruck late in the war. The woman, Hannelore, recounts her strong desire to leave Germany once the war is over, the country having been rendered unlivable to her by virtue of the "stinking abcesses" of mass graves and camps that cover "the whole face of Germany."[9] Back in Paris after the war, Delbo runs into Hannelore, who reaffirms her plans to leave Germany, even though her Jewish mother and non-Jewish father have reconciled. For Hannelore, such a familial reconciliation cannot so easily be translated into a larger national project for Germans in general: "You cannot erase history. The day will come when they will have to answer their children's questions" (116). Delbo neither affirms nor contradicts Hannelore's last judgment, but rather appends an italicized response in which, retrospectively, she generalizes (without universalizing) the problem of coming to terms with state-sponsored crimes:

Torture in Algeria.
Men have made of my tongue the language of torturers.
Villages burned by napalm in Indochina.
Algerians hunted through the streets by the Paris police one day in October of 1961.
Algerians whose bodies were fished out of the Seine.
How often I have thought of you, Hannelore. (117)[10]

Unlike Hannelore, who is on her way to the United States when we leave her, Delbo never chooses exile as a response to the political shame she clearly feels—perhaps because she is more circumspect about the kind of alternative the United States represents. Instead she chooses an aesthetic solution—one that is also political: she chooses to document the crimes of state and to do so not as a historian or journalist, but as a writer who produces truth through the crafting of testimony. This project continues through her many books that remember Auschwitz, but it begins with Algeria and in 1961.[11]

Letters Against the Republic

Les belles lettres is at once intensely localized in space and time—collecting letters from Paris-based newspapers during a twelve-month period—and interested precisely in the flow of information across boundaries of space and time through media and memory. Delbo's text maps a network of testimonial and documentary writings that make up the archive of truth production wielded against the state as part of the anticolonial struggle in the metropolis. It appeared in Les Editions de Minuit's "Collection Documents," alongside works that brought the French-Algerian War "home," such as Henri Alleg's *La Question* (1958), Pierre Vidal-Naquet's *L'affaire Audin* (1958), and Francis Jeanson's *Notre Guerre* (1960), not to mention Nazi camp memoirs such as Micheline Maurel's *Un camp très ordinaire* (1957). Les Editions de Minuit was itself, as the back cover of Delbo's book proudly attests, originally conceived as a resistant publishing house and had been founded clandestinely by Jean Bruller (Vercors) and Pierre de Lescure in 1942.[12]

Taking its place in this highly politicized public space, *Les belles lettres* is both a work of documentary and a self-reflective interrogation of the act of representation in exceptional situations. While the writing in *Les belles letters* lacks the poetic form and startling, traumatic imagery of many of Delbo's writings on Auschwitz, it does inaugurate the public revaluation of the word as documentary intervention and "truth cure" that persists throughout her oeuvre. In engaging with the French-Algerian War, Delbo's text shows itself conscious that it must also engage with the institutions that frame discourse and the forms of publicity. The text begins with a brief prefatory note, printed in italics across from the copyright information:

The art of letter writing [*L'art épistolaire*], which flourished in the 17th and 18th centuries and fell into decadence during the 19th, practically died out in the 20th century. In our days, marquises and Portuguese nuns do what everyone does: they telephone.

It was sufficient that Power take History backward for the genre to become once again in fashion. Of the influence of institutions on literary history . . . (7)

In Delbo's ironic literary history, the genre of epistolary literature waxes and wanes in the face of extrinsic developments, be they technological invention or acts of state. After having fallen out of favor over the course of a century and half, epistolary literature returns to haunt the regressive, barbaric practices of the current regime. Of course, history doesn't actually move backward and the literary modes of the eighteenth century are unlikely to return untouched as the fashions of today. The impetus for letters and the form to which Delbo submits them are rather different.

Although it consists primarily of letters, *Les belles lettres* is not simply an epistolary work but an attempt to amplify and give form to the remainders of public space. "Il n'y a pas de vie politique," Delbo remarks: when democracy retracts under the conditions of war and counterinsurgency, and protests, strikes, and voting lose their efficacy—an efficacy they still had "in the years that preceded the war of 1939"—resistance takes the form of what once seemed the most intimate of arts (9). Under the new conditions of censorship and intimidation of dissidents, intimacy exposed has the potential to gain in political resonance. Drawing attention to the crimes of the state by republishing letters both from mainstream journals and resistance publications, Delbo's text gives new meaning to the notion of "belles lettres": the torture, murder, censorship, and mistreatment recounted by French and Algerian resistors, intellectuals, and camp internees—as well as international observers like Graham Greene—are by no means pretty, but the use to which those figures put the written word becomes, in Delbo's recirculation, a reinvention of literature for an age of extremity.

The unfamiliar, mixed genre of *Les belles lettres*—in this case, halfway between a nonfictional epistolary novel and a commonplace book of quotations—is also one of the most remarked-upon characteristics of Delbo's writings on Auschwitz, and it has been linked to her questioning of community and social norms in the wake of genocide.[13] Such questioning is, unsurprisingly, at the center of *Les belles lettres*, which bears witness, above all, to a breakdown in consensus that left France in a state of virtual (or actual) civil war. Delbo's first text suggests that her mixing of genres not only expresses a questioning of community but also derives from the "multidirectionality" of memory—in this case, the manner in which postwar France is buffeted simultaneously by the nonidentical, yet overlapping and equally conflictual legacies of the Nazi occupation and the unraveling project of colonialism. Indeed, *Les belles lettres* illustrates how these legacies are understood through each other and how tensions around social cohesion in France constitute one of the sites of transfer between the memory of World War II and genocide, on the one hand, and the process of decolonization, on the other.

Surveying the legacies of Nazi occupation in France, Belgium, and the Netherlands, historian Pieter Lagrou concludes that while "the First World War had homogenized European societies through the horrors of mechanized warfare and mass death," "the Second World War shattered these solidarities" because of its highly differentiated impact on an array of religious, ethnic, ideological, and national social groups.[14] That shattered solidarity produced in turn a fragmented postwar memory politics in societies, like France, that had suffered under—but also collaborated with—Nazi occupation. During the French-Algerian War in particular, which entailed its own community-fragmenting effects, the impact of memory of the past on present experience was unpredictable and multidirectional. In a study of the political views of French deportees, Olivier Lalieu demonstrates that no consensus existed among the major associations or *amicales* of survivor and resistance groups about what kind of stand to take in relationship to Algeria's decolonization. Some groups, such as the Amicale de Dachau, remained predominantly silent about the camps and torture employed by the French army during the Algerian conflict, even as some of their individual members did speak out. Others, such as the Communist-influenced Amicale d'Auschwitz, which consisted of many members of Delbo's own convoy of deportees, pursued a more militant line of opposition to war, torture, and domestic repression.[15]

As the historical accounts of Lagrou and Lalieu suggest, there is no direct line from victimization and resistance under one set of circumstances to solidarity and opposition under another. Yet, in bearing witness to the multilayered memories and ideologies that constitute its context, *Les belles lettres* not only questions dominant visions of community and cohesion but also suggests the contours of what, following Michael Warner, I will later call a *counterpublic*. The formation of this counterpublic takes different routes, but I concentrate especially on what the text reveals in its many references to genocide, World War II, and resistance to the Nazi occupation. These references do not form a homogenous whole, but constitute two axes, each consisting of two alternate articulations: victimization and resistance during World War II are mapped onto victimization and resistance during the French-Algerian War, sometimes under the category of similarity and sometimes under that of difference.

The two issues agitating France while Delbo was documenting public discourse on the Algerian conflict were the forms of resistance taken by some opponents of the colonial war—the refusal to serve in the army and active support for the FLN—and the state's persecution of such resistance through criminalization, censorship, and torture. These two issues converged in the case of the Francis Jeanson network, to which I will return in my discussion of the "Manifesto of the 121." For now, let's note how the question of resistance formed a link between different eras and different wars. Delbo cites a Catholic soldier, Jean Le Meur, who refused to take part in "pacification" actions in Algeria and was eventually sentenced to two years in prison. Le Meur declared himself not a pacifist, but a principled objector to the war: "I would make war against the Nazis without displeasure. But against them [that is, Algerians], no" (*Belles lettres* 14). Le Meur's differentiation between past and present is based, as Delbo's selection indicates, on continuity, that is, on memory of the lessons of the Nuremberg trials. He writes that even if "one is in an office . . . one is an organ of the repressive machine, in solidarity with the whole organism—and responsible. What I believe I have discovered is precisely the permanence of individual responsibility in a system that claims wrongly to abolish it" (12).[16] Le Meur's image of the bureaucratic machine would, within a few years, become one of the dominant metaphors for understanding (and, in less ethical hands, obscuring) responsibility during the Holocaust, as the "desk murderer" Adolf Eichmann became a common reference point.

Le Meur's simultaneous attempts to link and to differentiate the two wars characterize many of the invocations of the Nazi period in *Les belles lettres*. Francis Jeanson himself, in an open letter to Jean-Paul Sartre published in *Les Temps modernes* and reproduced by Delbo, at once invokes the UN convention on genocide, evokes the two million Algerians in French concentration camps, and rhetorically plays on the absence of gas chambers and crematoria: "Must we console ourselves by holding on to the fact that in these camps there are neither gas chambers nor crematoria?" (27). In her own voice, Delbo also uses irony and the rhetorical question to invoke similarity in the face of distinction:

That the French authorities could open camps in Algeria already shows their scorn for public opinion. But Algeria, that's far away. That they can open camps even in France shows that their scorn was well founded. Deportees can tell you how heartbreaking the indifference of German civilians was when they passed in front of them in their striped uniforms, walking in rows while going to work outside the camp. . . . There are Algerians in camps in France, camps surrounded by barbed wire, camps surmounted by watchtowers where guards armed with machineguns keep watch. . . . Of course, it's not Auschwitz. But isn't it enough that innocents (a priori, people not condemned are innocent) are in camps for our conscience to revolt? (65–66)

Les belles lettres contains plenty of letters that describe in graphic terms the horrors of colonial war—for example, Djamila Boupacha's letter in *Le Monde*, which provides an account of how in French custody "torture with electricity alternated with cigarette burns, punches, and 'waterboarding' [*le supplice de la baignoire*]" (56). But the book's focus—as the previous passage makes clear—lies rather in the conditions of visibility in which the state performs its dirty work. As Delbo indicates here, this was also a theme of her experience of Nazi oppression. In the poem "Auschwitz," from the first volume of her memoirs, for example, she writes, "This city we were passing through / was a strange city. / . . . None of the inhabitants of this city / had a face / and in order to hide this / all turned away as we passed" (*Auschwitz* 87). It is the structure of these conditions of visibility— the intimacy between the "concentrationary universe" and the everyday world, the refusal of the public to look through the barbed-wire fence—as much as it is the content of the horrors beyond those fences that produces the leap of memory from French camps to Auschwitz, even in the face of historical distance.

Memory is often castigated, especially by historians, for being homogenizing, instrumentalizing, and mystifying. These selections from Le Meur, Jeanson, and Delbo—as well as others in *Les belles lettres* that bring together National Socialism and the French colonial state—demonstrate the presence of a differentiated collective memory capable of holding together similarity and difference and of mobilizing remembrance in the service of political responsibility without relativizing or negating historical specificity. Kristin Ross has shown how the French colonial system in the late years of the war strove to "modernize" torture by turning it into a form of "clean" mass production that recalled factory work and everyday life in the metropolis and could yet escape the notice of metropolitan subjects: "Torture in the Algerian War strove to 'leave no traces'—which is to say, to immobilize time, or to function as an ahistorical structural system."[17] Despite the will of the state, however, traces were uncovered, even in the face of massive censorship and repression. How was this possible? The memory work of *Les belles lettres* suggests that listening to the echoes of the past in the present helps save the past from premature burial and the present from instant oblivion. Delbo excavates "the profound traces" of the past recognized, for example, by police Secretary General Paul Teitgen, who was reminded in camps in Algeria of the "cruelties and tortures that I personally suffered fourteen years ago in the basements of the Gestapo in Nancy" (80–81). If, as Nietzsche once remarked, pain is the best aid to memory, it is also true that memory can represent a nonfetishistic form of work that turns back on pain, recognizes its claims, and seeks to transform the social and political conditions that continue to produce it. Resistance to French prosecution of the Algerian war sought to transform the cruelties of the present by working with and through the cruelties of the past.

From the Ethics of Testimony to the Counterpublic Witness

Delbo's text documents challenges to the state's hegemony in controlling meaning in part by collecting traces of memory that transgress historical boundaries. But the content of the text does not necessarily clarify the form of Delbo's act of collection. Derived predominantly from well-known sources and divulging no state secrets, *Les belles lettres* differs from clandestine journals, such as *Témoignages et Documents*, that published censored reports—although state censorship is one of its most evident themes. Unlike those journals, Delbo's text does not contribute new information to the anticolonial struggle, but rather reproduces letters that had already entered the public. Why does she *recirculate* memories of genocide and colonialism in this particular form? Rather than breaking through censorship by challenging the state directly on its own terrain, *Les belles lettres* constitutes a reflection on the genres of dissent that ultimately seeks to shift the terrain of debate. With its framing in terms of literary history and its frequent reference to and citation of writers, actors, academics, and other intellectuals, the text implicitly puts forward its own form as one answer to the needs of the day. What is that form?

Far from rendering her work too "belle lettristic" and hence apolitical, the citational, intertextual nature of Delbo's text—its reliance on previously published work by other writers for the core of its content—illustrates precisely its orientation toward a *public*. As Michael Warner has compellingly argued, "*A public is a social space created by the reflexive circulation of discourse.*"[18] That is, for Warner, "a public is understood to be an ongoing space of encounter for discourse"; it "exists only by virtue of address" and the "degree of attention, however notional," granted by a text's addressees (62, 61). The key term here is "circulation," which carries two important implications. First, Warner distinguishes circulation from conversation: the circulation of texts implies that the importance of a text or discursive event extends beyond the "dyadic speaker-hearer or author-reader relation" of private discourse and comprehends an audience of onlookers, strangers, and passive interlocutors. Such is the space of the public: "a multigeneric lifeworld organized not just by a relational axis of utterance and response, but by potentially infinite axes of citation and characterization" (63). Besides this multidimensional space of address, circulation also implies a new form of temporality; specifically, the temporality of circulation is "punctual" and involves "distinct moments and rhythms, from which distance in time can be measured" (66). The letters published in daily newspapers and weekly magazines that Delbo cites are perfect examples of the punctual and multigeneric circulation of discourse Warner describes as constitutive of the public.[19] In recirculating such letters, Delbo both continues the work of making publics and reflexively demonstrates an awareness of the political stakes of publicity.

While the letter in its purest form is not a public genre—it involves precisely the dyadic relationship of author/reader that renders it private—a letter published in a newspaper or magazine already supposes a dual, public address. With few exceptions, the authors of the letters collected by Delbo intend their texts as "open letters," letters addressed both to a particular addressee ("Monsieur le président," "Cher J.-J. S.-S." [Jean-Jacques Servan-Schreiber, the editor of *L'Express*]) and to a concerned public. Even those letters that were originally intended for a more intimate audience—such as the two that close the volume—have already been rendered public by recirculation in magazines. In collecting and reproducing these letters, Delbo reflexively seeks to produce a new public, one situated at the axes of multiple discourses about Algeria. By drawing attention to the "punctual rhythm of circulation," Delbo saves the letters from the isolation and forgetting of the editorial page of newspapers that would otherwise mark their fate and instead brings them into "a sphere of activity": "Publics have an ongoing life: one doesn't publish to them once and for all. . . . It's the way texts circulate, and become the basis for further representations, that convinces us that publics have activity and duration" (Warner 68). By reanimating the otherwise dead letters of the journalistic archive, Delbo contributes to the formation of an emergent genre closely tied to action: testimony.

Paying attention to the particular *public* form testimony takes in Delbo's work can lead to a rethinking of the contemporary theory of testimony. In recent years, the genre of testimony has received extensive discussion and theorization in academic discourse, especially in the field of Holocaust studies. Shoshana Felman and Dori Laub's volume *Testimony: Crises of Witnessing in Literature, Psychoanalysis, and History* has helped raise the level of theoretical sophistication by foregrounding the performative dimension of testimony. For Felman and Laub, giving testimony does not simply involve a legalistic witness meant to establish preexisting objective truths about an event. Read through literary and psychoanalytic theory, testimony becomes instead a signal instance of "how art inscribes (artistically bears witness to) *what we do not yet know of our lived historical relation to events of our times*" (xx). Testimony, in other words, enables and produces a new understanding of, or at least approach to, what has remained unconscious and unarticulable. Felman and Laub focus in particular on the links between testimony and trauma. Their claim, adopted from Elie Wiesel, "that our era can precisely be defined as the age of testimony" (5), relies heavily on the experience of the Nazi genocide, but opens itself to other crises. For Felman and Laub, the essence of the experience of the Holocaust, and by extension trauma more generally, is the "collapse of witnessing": "Not only, in effect, did the Nazis try to exterminate the physical witnesses of their crime; but the inherently incomprehensible *and* deceptive psychological structure of the event precluded its own witnessing, even by its very victims" (80). Because the "historical imperative to bear witness could essentially *not be met during the actual occurrence*" (84) due to the lack of "an other to which one could say 'Thou'" (82), the goal of testimony becomes "helping to create, after the fact, the missing Holocaust witness" (85). This performative dimension of testimony involves two figures: the traumatized victim, who is not yet in possession of her own experience, and the listener to whom the testimony is addressed, who "comes to be a participant and a co-owner of the traumatic event" (57). As in psychoanalysis, "*it takes two to witness the unconscious*" (15).

Felman and Laub's theory of testimony bears an interesting relationship to Warner's account of the formation of publics and counterpublics. Both theories recognize the performative dimension of discourse and the way performativity derives partially from the power of address: discourse has the ability to bring into being that which it simply seems to talk about and those to whom it seems to speak. But Felman and Laub's account of testimony inscribes itself, via the psychoanalytic model of therapy, in precisely the scenario of conversation that Warner uses as a foil to public discourse. Drawing attention to the effects of trauma on the possibilities of address and witness, Felman and Laub's theory offers a useful reminder about the kinds of scenarios that can impinge on and limit capacities for taking part in performative, world-making activity. The creation of an intimate addressable other may be a precondition for public poetics à la Warner. But Warner's theory of publics and counterpublics may prove more useful for addressing the fact of testimony's circulation beyond the dyadic relationship of the psychoanalytic dialogue.[20] And indeed, much of what receives discussion in study of testimony involves public discourse and not conversation. This is true of Felman and Laub's book as well, which, although it draws on psychoanalytic theory and practice (Laub is a practicing analyst who works with traumatized people), takes most of its examples from the world of public discourse, including literary works, films, and video testimonies. In fact, while the Fortunoff Video Archive for Holocaust Testimonies at Yale, which serves as the backdrop and partial inspiration for Felman and Laub's book, models its practice on the intimate encounters of a therapeutic situation, the use of a camera recording testimonies produces the doubled address that also defines the public dimensions of Delbo's recirculated letters.

In reflexively citing letters from the press, *Les belles lettres* shifts readers' attention from the dyadic aspects of letter writing toward the open address of public forms of circulation. This transformation not only makes the text part of the construction of a public or counterpublic but also teaches us something about testimony, something identified through the contrast between Felman and Laub and Warner. Whatever the untranscendable necessity of the witness/addressee relationship, as highlighted by Felman and Laub, public testimony (as opposed to therapy) possesses a wider, more amorphous address that includes strangers and undefined potential addressees. In "going public," as both Holocaust testimony and testimony to colonial crimes did around 1961, testimony ultimately becomes part of the historical record and larger democratic debates, as it also potentially enters the field of legal justice. But, Delbo's text indicates, given the constricted space of the official public during the French-Algerian War, questions of history and legality were secondary to the battle over the very contours of public space. Delbo's desire to recirculate testimony derives from recognition that the politics of testimony involves the creation of a public; the importance of testimony's public face lies in the possibilities for action that are created by circulation.[21]

The French state was quite aware of the power of public circulation and used all means at its disposal to limit the "address, temporality, mise-en-scène, [and] citational field" of resistant discourses (Warner 82). The famous "Déclaration sur le droit à l'insoummision," in September 1960, which serves as one of the foci of the texts collected in *Les belles lettres*, illustrates exactly what is at stake. The "Manifesto of the 121," as it is also known, was occasioned by the arrest and trial of members of Francis Jeanson's network of support for the FLN and for young Frenchmen refusing to serve in the army. Signed initially by 121 intellectuals and artists, with more adding their names soon after, the manifesto "recognizes and judges as justified the refusal to take up arms against the Algerian people" and the desire to lend material support "to the aid and protection of Algerians oppressed in the name of the French people"; it declares "the cause of the Algerian people, which contributes in a decisive fashion to the destruction of the colonial system, the cause of all free men." While the focus is decidedly on contemporary events, the manifesto sets them against a relevant historical background and uses the same structure of rhetorical questioning we saw in other such articulations: "Is it necessary to recall that, fifteen years after the destruction of the Hitlerian order, French militarism, by virtue of the demands of such a war, has managed to restore the practice of torture and to make it once again a European institution?"[22] The force of the manifesto's challenge to state legitimacy can be measured by the extremes to which the state went to prevent its circulation—and even to limit the public presence of those associated with it. Not only was the manifesto banned from publication, but all signers were banned from appearing on television and radio, and academics, such as Pierre Vidal-Naquet, were suspended from their positions.[23]

Such state tactics went to absurd lengths and ultimately produced a greater unity among opponents than did the actions of Jeanson's network itself. In recirculating texts that challenge state-sponsored terror, Delbo directly (but with light irony) sets herself against a moment defined by a constricted public sphere, one in which "composing radio and television programs has become a delicate task. Songwriters will have to submit their texts ten days before broadcast. It will be necessary to guard against citing either the names or the works of writers, musicians, and composers who have 'signed,' as it will be to re-watch films before broadcasting them to be sure that no banned actor appears so much as in silhouette" (127). The notion of a "ban on representation"—familiar in discourse on Auschwitz from the writings of Adorno as well as Delbo's own self-reflexive memoirs—here emerges from the state and sets into motion a dialectic of repression and resistance whereby even a discursive "silhouette" become a threat to state legitimacy.[24] Delbo documents the many people inside and outside France who voice their opposition to this censorship (regardless of their position on the question of draft evasion), putting particular emphasis on composers, actors, students, and writers—including Aldous Huxley, Pulitzer Prize laureates, and Danish and Finnish intellectuals (128–31). Delbo's "citational field" models a global reading public and draws attention to the multifaceted address that defines even the most straightforward forms of documentation and testimony.

Delbo's public is called into being at the site of memories that link current and past struggles and sufferings. At the same time, Delbo also deliberately transgresses the national space of the public. Much French discourse around the war is oriented internally toward Franco-French conflicts, conflicts that are themselves something of a replay of the resistance/collaboration binary of the occupation years. Delbo, by contrast, includes a certain number of Algerian voices and provides a discursive stage for those resistance forces committed not just to peaceful negotiations but also to active support for the FLN. In addition, she concludes her text with a subtle but significant move toward a transcultural and multilingual address. Most of the letters Delbo includes are texts written by intellectuals and originally meant for public circulation, even if they bear a more individual primary address. Yet she concludes by stating that the subject of her book is not simply a "dispute among intellectuals and ministers [*une querelle d'intellectuels et de ministres*]. Its subject is rather liberty. More than 14,000 men are currently being detained in France as political prisoners. They also receive letters" (148). She then includes a June 1960 letter from an Algerian woman in Paris to her husband, who is being interned in the Fresnes prison camp.

"Mon Ahmed chéri," begins Yamina's letter, "Today it is two years since they came to get you. And it is two years that I am as if dead" (148–49). Written in an informal and sometimes ungrammatical style, Yamina's letter mixes accounts of everyday occurrences, worries over her husband's health (beware of the dentist, she warns, "he's a butcher"), reports of other arrests, and fears about racism in the streets. It ends on a note of resistance and longing: "We listened to the 'Voix des Arabes' on M's radio; you can imagine what that did for us. My poor Ahmed, if only you could have heard how they spoke of the resistance [*maquis*] and all. Your brother and the children join me in embracing you strongly and hope that you will be out soon. Inch' Allah" (150). Yamina's letter contains various echoes of the Nazi period. Her (or possibly a translator's?) use of "maquis" inevitably refers back to the internal French resistance that fought the Nazi occupation, and her fear of the camp dentist, whether intentionally or not, echoes well-known stories of the expropriation of tooth fillings from Jewish prisoners and other barbaric medical practices in the Nazi camps. Most striking, the letter, with its intimate mode of address and its mix of references to everyday and exceptional occurrences, also foreshadows Delbo's own writings on the memory of Auschwitz. The opening lines in particular—"Today it is two years since they came to get you. And it is two years that I am as if dead"—will, for readers of Delbo, immediately recall the striking lines of the testimony attributed to "Mado" in *The Measure of Our Days* (the third part of *Auschwitz and After*, published in 1971): "Time doesn't pass over me, over us. It doesn't erase anything, doesn't undo it. I'm not alive. I died in Auschwitz but no one knows it" (*Auschwitz* 267). There are obvious and significant historical and discursive differences between Yamina's letter and Mado's monologue—including the position of the speaker, the medium of the text, and the nature of the conflict about which each reports. What is relevant here, however, is the link between voice, testimony, and public intimacy that forms a bridge between the projects of *Les belles lettres* and *Auschwitz and After*.

The final two letters of Delbo's first published text bring "foreign" voices into French space—voices that, like those of the survivors who populate *The Measure of Our Days*, are revealed to be already inside and intimate with the space of the nation even as they remain dissonant with respect to dominant discourses. Those voices can be disturbing, even to other victims. Recall, for instance, the testimony of Gaby, who shuts out the media in order to avoid the connections television inevitably makes for her between the Algerian conflict and her own camp experience (*Auschwitz* 330). Yamina, however, finds resistance in the ability of voices to pierce through the protections of the public sphere: she mentions listening to "La Voix des Arabes," a radio station created under Nasser in Cairo that broadcast daily reports on the Algerian revolution. And her testimony ends in Arabic, with a fragile expression of hope for the future, a hope that is immediately picked up and further ironized in the final letter, from Bousetta Hamou. Before being guillotined in the Santé prison in December 1960, Hamou wrote the following letter to his wife (soon reprinted in *Afrique-Action*): "Ma chère femme, I will soon be dead because independence doesn't come for free. General de Gaulle is executing me like a criminal, so I die *Chahid* [je meurs *Chahid*]. You can be proud of me and say around you: Long live the ALN! Long live Algeria!" (*Belles lettres* 151). Delbo again underlines connections between contemporary events and those of the occupation. She introduces Hamou's letter by remarking, "How many have mounted the scaffold, in the courtyard of the Santé, in the courtyard of Montluc, how many Frenchmen during the 1940s, how many Algerians since 1954" (151). Delbo will return to such a link a few years later when she includes the reference mentioned above to a similar execution from 1960 in *Useless Knowledge* (*Auschwitz* 132–33). But what is most striking about this final letter is the difference it insinuates via the additional insertion of Arabic: "je meurs *Chahid*." *Chahid* means martyr, but it shares a root with the word for witness: hence, "I die a martyr, but also a witness."[25]

Delbo's first text works toward the production of the witness, but in doing so it anticipates later insights common to her own texts and to scholarship on testimony: the witness to extreme, political violence is always to some extent a foreigner, one who disturbs the status quo, who speaks another language. In *The Measure of Our Days*, Mado will translate this problem of the foreignness of testimony into an irresolvable paradox: "The very fact that we're here to speak denies what we have to say" (*Auschwitz* 257). Yet in Delbo's Auschwitz trilogy, as in *Les belles lettres*, the witness's testimony to her or his own foreignness serves as a form of public pedagogy in the struggle against forgetting, even as it marks psychic and physical losses that cannot be transcended. As Felman writes in a discussion of the pedagogical use of witness accounts, "In the age of testimony, and in view of contemporary history, I want my students to be able to receive information that is *dissonant*, and not just *congruent*, with everything that they have learned beforehand" (Felman and Laub 53). The effectivity of dissonant pedagogy builds on the ethical, face-to-face encounter that Holocaust studies has heretofore used to model testimony, but the reception of dissonant information ultimately rests on forms of public circulation that assume and create multiple, open-ended forms of address.

In transgressing the homogenized national space of the public in the interests of a dissonant pedagogy, Delbo's text becomes the bearer of what

Warner would call a "counterpublic" address. Counterpublics constitute themselves as do other publics—"by projecting the space of discursive circulation among strangers as a social entity" (Warner 87)—but they also recognize that that very space of circulation, with its rules and conventions, can itself be a tool of exclusion and domination. For instance, the rules of politeness that define public space may facilitate certain kinds of rational exchange, but they also limit what counts as rationality and preempt certain embodied forms of discourse, such as expressions of dissident sexuality or, more immediately relevant here, the exposure of torture and state-sponsored crimes. While the dominant public sphere of "rational-critical dialogue" assumes a shared, transparent language of debate, counterpublic discourse, like *Les belles lettres*, draws on foreign idioms—and idioms of foreignness—to mark its distance from the dominant. A counterpublic need not start out as a subaltern group; rather, it sets itself against the dominant by producing and circulating a stigmatized identity through forms that challenge the supposed neutrality and transparency of the "general public." Counterpublic discourse entails "risked estrangement," the entry into "spaces of circulation in which it is hoped that the poesis of scene making will be transformative" (Warner 88). In the articulation of counterpublic discourse, both dominant public space and stigmatized identities undergo transformation.

By bringing embodied truth into contact and conflict with a certain formation of the bourgeois public sphere, *Les belles lettres* both anticipates the power of the genre of testimony, which was recognized concurrently during the Eichmann trial, and seeks to model forms of address alternative to the channels favored by the state. In this experimental modeling, it even exceeds Rouch and Morin's experiment in cinéma vérité, which also recognizes the power of testimony but takes a less antagonistic position vis-à-vis state power. *Les belles lettres* serves as the call for a counterpublic that would remake the space of the public in light of the resistance, trauma, and state criminality that define its contemporary moment and remembered past. Along with other works in Les Editions de Minuit's "Collection Documents," Delbo's text pushes at the limits of public resistance; it seeks to work not underground, like Jeanson's network or the publishers of censored documents, but at the level at which notions of the public are constructed and contested. Instead of moving below the surface of the public, Delbo's counterpublic testimony excavates multidirectional memories of genocidal and colonial violence and reveals them as already present but subject to ongoing forgetting. In the multidirectional process of excavation, Delbo (and others whose texts she cites) transforms what it means to be the survivor of a traumatic history as well as an engaged citizen in the present.

Between Algeria and Abu Ghraib

How ought one to live in a society that practices torture shamelessly and systematically? Delbo helps us to confront this very timely and urgent ethical question.[26] While it is self-evident that multiple forms of opposition to torture and state-sponsored oppression are necessary, I have focused on how memory puts the past into circulation, opening up possibilities for unexpected acts of solidarity. By virtue of its circulation, memory in the form of testimony can help build counterpublic spheres dedicated not only to exposing the dirty secrets of the state but to refiguring what counts as a collective—a crucial aspect of the politics of memory.[27]

The multidirectional echo of memories *Les belles lettres* embodies has not dissipated in the forty years since Algeria achieved independence. Today, once again, it is necessary to ask, with Delbo, "But isn't it enough that innocents (a priori, people not condemned are innocent) are in camps for our conscience to revolt?" And to listen to testimonies like those of Djamila Boupacha: "After four or five days I was transferred to Hussein-Dey. That way, they told me, I would learn about the 'second degree.' I learned what that meant: torture with electricity, first of all; since the electrodes placed on my breasts didn't hold, they taped them to my skin with scotch tape; they burned me in the same way on the legs, the groin, the sex, on the face" (qtd. in *Belles lettres* 56). Remembering (with) Delbo means hearing the echoes that Delbo records, responding to the "profound traces" of the past that some members of her generation experienced. These are also our echoes, our traces:

When I was in Room #1 they told me to lay down on my stomach and they were jumping from the bed onto my back and my legs. And the other two were spitting on me and calling me names, and they held my hands and legs. . . . One of the police was pissing on me and laughing at me. . . . And then they put the loudspeaker inside the room and they closed the door and he was yelling in the microphone. Then they broke the glowing finger and spread it on me until I was glowing and they were laughing. They took me into the room and they signaled me to get on to the floor. And one of the police put part of his stick that he always carried inside my ass and I felt it going inside me about 2 centimeters, approximately.[28]

This testimony is taken from an anonymous prisoner held by the U.S. Army at Abu Ghraib prison in Iraq in 2003. I cite here from *Torture and Truth*, Mark Danner's compilation of his own journalistic writings on war and torture in Iraq, published together with relevant documents, pictures, and official reports.

Is Danner's collection a latter-day version of *Les belles lettres*? Despite the parallels between some of the accounts contained in the two texts—the invasive, world-destroying sexualized violence described above, for instance—there are, of course, significant textual and historical differences. Yet it is likely that *Torture and Truth*, like *Les belles lettres*, will not stop the war and will soon be relegated to the same oblivion that Delbo's first book—and, to a lesser though still significant degree, the horrors it documents—occupied for several decades. What Danner documents is well known and widely available on the Internet and in other books and magazines. The same was more or less true in Delbo's time, despite the state's active censorship and the comparatively underdeveloped state of the media. As Danner writes, "Like other scandals that have erupted during the Iraq war and the war on terror, [Abu Ghraib] is not about revelation or disclosure but about the failure, once wrongdoing is disclosed, of politicians, officials, the press, and, ultimately, citizens to act. The scandal is not about uncovering what is hidden, it is about seeing what is already there—and acting on it. It is not about information; it is about politics."[29] The difference between the contexts of *Les belles lettres* and *Torture and Truth*—that is, between war in Algeria and Iraq—is a political difference. Not information is lacking, but collective organization—the type of organization that *Les belles lettres* cites, recirculates, and seeks to model through its collective, epistolary form, its counterpublic testimony.

If testimony and documentation are to have a politics, they must be oriented toward the creation of publics, toward circulation and not just exposure. What is perhaps most difficult to find today is the attention Warner deems necessary to the creation of a public: the encounter with torture has been fleeting, a flickering image on the screen of public attention.[30] Whatever the marginality of the French Left in its struggle against the late colonial state, the force it did possess derived from the collective memories that haunted it. Those memories of war and genocide helped forge a counterpublic that, if nothing else, established a legacy for the politics of the future. To be sure, collective memory is not simply an archive awaiting political instrumentalization; the haunting of the past cannot be harnessed in the present without unforeseen effects. And yet *Les belles lettres* teaches us that the work of memory not only preserves the past but can slow down the vanishing of the political present.

Delbo and other French leftists of the 1960s drew on the resources of memory and their encounters with extreme, political violence to construct a radical counterpublic sphere. But it is also necessary to acknowledge that that counterpublic sphere did not succeed in radically transforming the conditions of national publicity, even though it did succeed in scaring the state into ever-more extreme forms of repression and even though Algeria did achieve independence in 1962. Indeed, it has taken almost forty years for France to begin to come to terms with torture, the war, and the larger context of colonialism. As recently as 1979, public opinion polls showed only 59 percent of French citizens believing that torture had been practiced in the Algerian War. By 1992, 94 percent had come to recognize at least that truth of the era, but it wasn't until the late 1990s and early twenty-first century that a significant public discussion emerged and began to cast doubt on the larger myth of France's "civilizing mission" in its overseas possessions—even if disturbing signs indicate that the myth strongly persists.[31] In the following section, I consider the significance of the sometimes slow-moving nature of dominant collective memory by arguing that a politics of memory based on the punctual temporality of public circulation needs to be complemented by an ethics of memory attuned to the problem of duration and to that which remains hidden in the past.

As it turns out, one of the catalysts of the new critical memory work in France was the 1997–98 trial of Maurice Papon, the police prefect who (almost unbelievably) was not only responsible for atrocities during World War II but also served as a prefect in Algeria during the French-Algerian War and ordered deadly actions in Paris during the October 17, 1961, demonstrations against French repression of Algerians.[32] However extraordinary his trajectory (particularly for a book such as this one!), Papon was not an anomaly; as Jim House and Neil MacMaster have argued, Papon's "career and core ideological beliefs were representative of a whole generation of government ministers, senior civil servants, army commanders, prefects, and politicians that sought to resolve the Algerian War through deepening repression rather than political negotiation." Although House and MacMaster do not emphasize this, their description of this grouping also echoes disturbingly with contemporary American politics. While today Islamic extremism serves as the occasion and target of a revived American imperialism, for Papon and his generation cold war anticommunism and the threat of third world "revolutionary war" provided their impetus: "The perceived deadly and terminal nature of this [third world, revolutionary] challenge to the West ... legitimated an abandonment of the normal rules of domestic and international law: higher values could only be saved, in the desperation of the final hour, by recourse to exceptional forms of counter-violence." As is true again today with respect to approaches to Islamism, a "key element in the elaboration of state terror in both Algeria and metropolitan France derived from the refusal of the French government to recognize Algerian nationalist fighters as legitimate combatants."[33] Papon's illuminating career provides fertile ground for multidirectional links that not only move backward from 1961 to World War II but also forward to the contemporary "war on terror." As the Papon case makes clear, history is an echo chamber; an ethics of memory establishes fidelity to the echoes.

PART IV

OCTOBER 17, 1961

A Site of Holocaust Memory?

8

A Tale of Three Ghettos: Race, Gender, and "Universality" After October 17, 1961

On the evening of October 17, 1961, tens of thousands of Algerian demonstrators converged on central Paris, and they were soon met with "the bloodiest act of state repression of street protest in Western Europe in modern history."[1] The Algerian Front de Libération Nationale (FLN) had called the demonstration as a show of strength and as a protest against a curfew ordered by Maurice Papon, the Paris police prefect who many years later would be revealed as having collaborated in the Nazi genocide. Although the demonstrators were peaceful, and included women and children in their ranks, the police response was brutal. By the end of the evening more than eleven thousand would be arrested and up to two hundred murdered; the bodies of many victims were dumped in the Seine. Despite the scale of the demonstration and the extremity of the police response, the events of October 1961 quickly disappeared from public recollection, as many scholars have demonstrated. Marginalized by much of the French Left, ignored and later instrumentalized by the emergent Algerian nation, and buried in silence by the families most intimately affected, the massacre of October 17, 1961 went "underground" for two decades before reemerging into public light in the 1980s and especially the 1990s and early twenty-first century. In *Paris 1961: Algerians, State Terror, and Memory*, Jim House and Neil MacMaster provide detailed and compelling reasons for the collective forgetting of the October 17 massacre. Seeking to render "the reactions to 17 October . . . more 'readable,' and their scale and nature relatively predictable," House and MacMaster situate the events in relation to a preceding colonial history, tensions on the French Left around the question of colonialism, and postcolonial dynamics in France and Algeria (184). They emphasize especially how in the immediate aftermath of the event the French Left "deferred" and "displaced" the specificity of colonial and racist power relations in favor of a broad antifascist coalition.[2]

Rather than understanding the displacements and deferrals tracked by House and MacMaster as signs of silencing or competition, such displacements and deferrals might rather be seen as fundamental to the work of memory; in certain circumstances, they might even constitute ethical acts that enable memories to unfold, albeit in an uneven, nonsynchronous temporality. While acknowledging the many forces that have contributed to the marginalization of October 17, I seek to shift the scholarly emphasis to an exploration of the multidirectional links that have nevertheless provided a context for the articulation of collective remembrance—for its expression and its role as a connective tissue between seemingly disparate histories. By paying particular attention to the massacre's connections to the Nazi genocide, as well as to more recent returns of extreme, racially inflected violence, one can see that the Holocaust has played a crucial role in the response to the 1961 events *from the very start.*

The practice of torture and the use of detention camps by France in its war against the Algerian independence movement provided triggers that stimulated remembrance of the Nazi occupation and genocide and inspired new forms of testimony and witnessing. The events of October 17, 1961, add further vexed issues to the multidirectional networks linking past and present: in particular, the question of "race" and the problems of recognition that attend it. As a reading of contemporaneous anticolonial discourse in France demonstrates, the massacre and roundup of Algerians in Paris—as well as the repressive curfew that prompted the FLN demonstration in the first place—sparked insight into new processes of racialization that accompanied decolonization. Yet it did so by recalling anti-Semitic persecution during the Nazi occupation. The inherent instability of "race" comes into especially clear focus when tracked in the changing contexts of post–World War II France. As my selective exploration of the almost half-century-old archive of the memory and representation of October 17, 1961 demonstrates, the October events have long functioned as a relay articulating anti-Semitic racialization during World War II, colonial and postcolonial racism, the violence of decolonization, and the problems of twentieth- and twenty-first-century multicultural societies faced with new forms of globalization and imperialism.

By shifting from a competitive memory model to a multidirectional model, one can see that what is happening around 1961 is neither a simple forgetting nor the erasure of one set of memories by another. Rather, we find the production of a new memory of the Holocaust and the establishment of links between the Holocaust and anti-Algerian violence that, in turn, will later help to produce new memory of October 17. The theory of multidirectional memory allows us to see that deferral and displacement are among the means through which publics come to terms with troubling histories and begin to integrate them into collective memories. The Holocaust and October 17 have served as vehicles of remembrance for each other: the racist repression of the early 1960s served as a means to continue the very incomplete coming to terms with Nazi genocide then in its early stages in France and elsewhere, while in the 1980s, 1990s, and early twenty-first century, a more established Holocaust memory archive has come to serve as a source for the articulation (the expression and cross-cultural linking) of memory of the October events. Nor do these two events interact in an isolated way: collective memory is truly multidirectional (not simply bidirectional). Other experiences and events that contribute gravity to the following discussion include American antiblack racism and the contemporary "war on terror."

Such linkages between the Holocaust and other forms of racism and violence have led many scholars to talk about the "universalization" of the Holocaust, a process that some scholars deplore and others celebrate. In this context, universalization signifies the unmooring of the Holocaust from its historical specificity and its circulation instead as an abstract code for Evil and thus as the model for a potential antiracist and human rights politics. Consideration of the memory of October 17, 1961 has the potential to stimulate an alternative account that highlights the *multidirectional* circulation of Holocaust memory instead of its abstract universalization. Through an emphasis on multidirectionality, an alternative ethics and politics of memory also emerges. Political journalism in the immediate wake of the events by intellectuals such as Marguerite Duras, Claude Bourdet, and Henri Kréa brings questions of race into focus and illuminates how the conjunction of the Holocaust and decolonization could produce forms of comparison that don't necessarily result in a universalizing commensuration of the different histories; rather, the texts specify these histories through distinctions of temporality and affective impact. The expatriate African American writer William Gardner Smith's novel *The Stone Face* (1963) adds a focus on complicity and gender to the question of race. Smith draws on the matter of racism to stretch the analogy between different histories, as did Du Bois in the early 1950s and as did the political journalists of Smith's own time. As he stretches this analogy, he also grows conscious of how complicity emerges as an unavoidable complication that unsettles the opposition between the universal and the particular. While Smith's insights into complicity help us think through moral responsibility, he also simultaneously employs a gendered logic of memory and activism that sacrifices the anamnestic links of solidarity to the urgent temporality of politics.

Smith's novel—as well as the Austrian director Michael Haneke's film *Caché*—suggests that memory of October 17 is strikingly transnational.[3] While the simultaneous shaping influence of French and Algerian forces on the remembrance of the events is a frequent and important topic of investigation in recent discussions of October 17, critics have given the more broadly international and multidirectional dimensions of memory less attention.[4] But if scholarship on October 17 has not yet moved beyond the national frames of France and Algeria, recent years have seen an increasing focus on the globalization of Holocaust memory—a phenomenon that the transnational flows circulating around October 17, 1961 make visible. The most important work on Holocaust memory's global reach suggests that the very uniqueness ascribed to the Nazi genocide has also contributed to the universalization of its significance—an argument I set out to contest in the conclusion of this chapter by way of a sympathetic engagement with two important sociological accounts of the globalization of Holocaust memory. Both the immediate and the deferred response to the police massacre of October 17, 1961 provide evidence for an ethical vision based not on universalization but on multidirectional interactions between the Holocaust, decolonization, and other instances of modern state-sponsored violence. Far from emphasizing what the sociologists Daniel Levy and Natan Sznaider call "the abstract nature of 'good and evil' that symbolizes the Holocaust," the transnational and multidirectional responses to the massacre foreground historical asymmetry, troubling embodiment, and unacknowledged complicity.[5]

Between History and Memory: October 17, 1961

To understand how and why October 17 became a site of multidirectional memory, it is important to understand the context of the event and its aftermath. In late 1961 it was clear that Algeria was headed for independence, but in the closing months of the year both the FLN and the French state sought to secure the strongest possible negotiating positions and were escalating violence both in Algeria and within the hexagon of mainland France. Meanwhile, a group of extreme-right-wing French generals formed a terrorist group, the *Organisation Armée Secrète* (OAS), which killed thousands while fighting to maintain *l'Algérie française* (French Algeria). In addition, as part of the continuing practice of torture and detention, the French employed groups of Algerian collaborators, known as *harkis*, who were especially feared for their brutality. In response to such tactics, the FLN assassinated dozens of French police officers—although they had declared a stoppage of the killings prior to October 17. In early October, in an attempt to disable FLN organizing in France, Parisian police prefect Maurice Papon put into place a curfew for Algerian workers. Because a curfew directed against a particular group violated the universalist tenets of French law, Papon instead "issued a communiqué which 'advised [Algerians] most urgently . . . to abstain from movement at night,' although in reality the police treated the order as mandatory and a means for further harassment" (House and MacMaster 100; my interpolation). The curfew created hardships for individual workers and disrupted FLN activities and fund-raising. Hoping to overturn the curfew order and demonstrate the scale of their support in France, the FLN called for a massive demonstration of men, women, and children in the streets of central Paris on October 17. Explicit instructions from the FLN insisted that this would be a peaceful demonstration on the part of Algerians, although leaders were also aware that previous such events had ended in police violence (such as a smaller scale massacre on July 14, 1953). Indeed, everyday life was already dangerous for Algerian workers in the metropole due to arbitrary roundups and violent repression by the police and *harkis*. On the evening of October 17, and with no provocation, Parisian police immediately attacked the demonstrators who were gathering at various points across the city. By the next day more than eleven thousand demonstrators had been arrested and taken to detention centers at the outskirts of Paris (from which many would be deported back to Algeria and held in camps there), and untold numbers had been shot, beaten to death, or drowned in the Seine. French officials initially lied and said that only two Algerians had died, but later studies have argued that the numbers were between thirty-nine and more than two hundred, although it is unlikely that historians will ever arrive at consensus.[6]

In the initial days and weeks after the massacre, both the mainstream and radical press covered the events and their aftermath in reports to which we will return.[7] But a police and governmental cover-up—including a refusal to open a serious investigation into the killings—as well as the rapid pace of events at the end of the war and the French public's general disinclination to concern itself with the fate of its Algerian-Muslim neighbors meant that within months October 17 had begun to sink into oblivion, at least at the level of public discourse. Despite initial attention in the press and the organizing of a number of smaller-scale demonstrations by Algerian and French groups, the events of October 17 are generally thought to have "disappeared" from collective memory for approximately two decades. When, on February 8, 1962, nine leftist French protestors were killed by the police at the Charonne metro station during a Communist-sponsored antifascist rally, the massacre of Algerians seemed definitively lost to French awareness. In House and MacMaster's account, "A 'dominant' memory on the left would henceforth largely obscure 17 October 1961. Charonne, rather than 17 October, came to symbolize police violence during the Algerian War, a point that the far left would remind the PCF of during and after May '68. Charonne and 17 October have often been parallel and competing memories, constituting one key strand of the politics of memory of 17 October" (*Paris 1961* 256). Despite such "competition," recent years have seen a proliferation of publicly articulated memories and representations of the massacre. The "return" of October 17 after a twenty-year period of "underground" existence has taken place in a context of ethnic and racial tension and vigorous debate over the status of history and memory in democratic societies—a context directly linked to the period of the Algerian War of Independence and yet simultaneously quite distant from it.[8]

While October 17 has become a legitimate topic of historical research in recent years, that legitimacy owes its emergence to forces outside the discipline of history. The two earliest sources of the event's return were social movements and works of the imagination. Starting in the late 1970s and picking up steam in the 1980s, migrant groups—and especially youth groups—began to reclaim the memory of the massacre as part of an effort to establish their voices within the mainstream. Organizations such as Sans Frontières and SOS Racisme reached back to the anticolonial struggle for independence in order to fight a different battle in the postcolonial moment against racism in the metropole. Interestingly, as House and MacMaster demonstrate, "these descendants of Algerians often came across 17 October via the resilient counter-memories of French former anti-colonial activists rather than memory transmission within their own Algerian families" (*Paris 1961* 19).[9] Thus, the return of October 17 owes its existence in part to the very same multidirectional dynamic that defined the early responses of those anticolonial activists in the first place. Meanwhile, in 1984, Didier Daeninckx published his first detective novel, *Meurtres pour mémoire*, a work that linked memory of Vichy with October 17 and became a significant spur to historical memory. A year later Nacer Kettane's novel *Le sourire de Brahim* appeared, with its dedication foregrounding the duty to memory—"A mes parents pour que jamais la mémoire ne devienne souvenir"—and its opening chapter "Octobre à Paris" recalling the militant film by Jacques Panijel and the Comité Audin made in the immediate aftermath of the massacre.[10] It was only in the wake of these "popular" social and literary events that work of historical recovery began to take place. While Michel Levine's *Les rattonades d'octobre: Un meurtre collectif à Paris en 1961* appeared in 1985, it received very little attention, and serious historical research and debate began especially with the publication in 1991 of Jean-Luc Einaudi's *La bataille de Paris*.[11] It is important to remark, however, that Einaudi is not an academic historian, a fact that reemphasizes the degree to which October 17 has, until very recently, remained outside the provinces of mainstream, disciplinary history. The thirtieth anniversary of the massacre in 1991 also marked a threshold in commemoration after which October 17 entered definitively, if unevenly, into the French public sphere—although almost entirely due to the pressures of civil society and the representational powers of literature and film.

It would take several more years for even the most minimal official recognition to take place, recognition that was spurred especially by the 1997–98 trial of Maurice Papon. Papon had been the prefect responsible for police repression in the late stages of the Algerian War and on the night of October 17, but he had been brought to trial for other crimes: his responsibility for deportations of Jews during his time as prefect under Vichy, a responsibility unknown during the initial responses to the 1961 massacre. It took sixteen years from the initial 1981 revelation of Papon's role during World War II until the trial actually took place—a period that corresponds precisely with the rise to greater prominence of October 17 memory. Despite the primary focus of the trial on Vichy and the Holocaust, what came to be described as a "trial within the trial" took place after Einaudi testified about the massacre of Algerians as part of the phase of the trial dedicated to laying out the itinerary of Papon's career. Papon himself then ensured that the October events would receive even further attention when he filed suit against Einaudi for defamation. Not only did Papon lose that case (as well as being convicted for crimes against humanity during the Vichy period), but, in its decision, the court gave for the first time official credence to the assertion that the police response to the Algerian demonstration constituted a "massacre," and the case also contributed to the gradual opening of previously inaccessible governmental and police archives. This legal decision was also translated back into the field of memory when, in 2001, Parisian mayor Bertrand Delanoë dedicated a commemorative plaque on the Pont Saint-Michel, close to where many Algerians were drowned on October 17 and only a few meters from the police prefecture.[12]

Revelations of Papon's "hidden" past became known in the early 1980s, putting an end to his career—which had continued brilliantly up to that point despite the many known bloody episodes such as October

17 and Charonne. Through these new revelations he became a material embodiment of the links between the Holocaust and the violence of colonialism and decolonization. As Joshua Cole suggests, "For twenty years, from 1981 until the 40th anniversary of the events in October 2001, this conjunction [of Vichy and Algeria] was the engine that drove widespread public discussion of 17 October 1961 in France."[13] Since the Papon trial this link is often observed and has indeed become an unavoidable part of the discussion of October 17, but thus far little has been done to consider its significance. Many commentators, moreover, go on to discount its importance, often on the grounds that the histories of Vichy and decolonization have little in common. Alluding to the current acceptance of complicity in Vichy and ongoing denial of the crimes of colonialism, as well as the shaping influence of Algerian politics in the 1980s and 1990s on October 17 memory, Cole comments, "The two controversies seem to be linked in so many ways by their common themes: repressed memory, official complicity with atrocity, and the impression—however mistaken—of a public taboo being broken. Nevertheless, the connection and the presumed parallels between the two affairs misleads [sic] as much as it [sic] illuminates" (32). Cole and other commentators are correct that the events and contexts of Vichy and decolonization, as well as their memory, do not fully correspond to each other, although House and MacMaster have now shown significant continuities in tactics and personnel between those different contexts (cf. esp. House and MacMaster 34–35). Despite Cole's objections, however, the fact remains that such parallels have been asserted continuously *since the very moment of the events*—and it is this fact, a fact about the multidirectionality of memory, that must be taken into account and given its due.[14]

Other historians share and generalize Cole's suspicion about the historical validity of memory. In a 2006 interview, Pierre Nora, best known for his work on the massive *lieux de mémoire* project, attempts to subsume memory under history's "authority of reconciliation." Disciplinary history, according to Nora, is best situated to help society overcome the intolerable "conflictual incompatibility of memories" in a multicultural public sphere.[15] But the history and aftermath of October 17, 1961 demonstrate that conflict and reconciliation are not necessarily opposed terms. The dynamics of collective memory differ from the reason of history, with memory offering its own versions of recognition and reconciliation. As the case of Delbo's *Les belles lettres* demonstrated, the intersection of Holocaust memory and anticolonial politics produced a particular milieu in which recognition of a current crisis and a dark past emerged together. The response to October 17 illustrates that process of recognition as well, but in addition it points to the way that memory can take on a particularly ethical charge by highlighting unfinished business and actively deferring reconciliation. Indeed, in instances of actual conflict, especially around the definitions of national and group identity, recognition may only be possible when reconciliation is deferred. The belatedness of October 17's return—as well as the belated recognition of racial anti-Semitism that accompanied initial responses to October 17 and the belated trial of French complicity via Papon in the later 1990s—are signs not only of a failure of memory but of the constitutive force that displacement plays in the formation of collective memory. Belatedness tells us that an ethics of memory is at work and not just the force of repression. Because of endemic crises in the definition of French identity—crises that are not identical "then" and "now"—October 17 remains a site of conflict over recognition but also the source of a potential future reconciliation.

"Doesn't That Remind You of Something?": Racialization and the Response to October 17

On November 9, 1961, the novelist Marguerite Duras published an article called "Les deux ghettos" (The two ghettos) in the newsweekly *France-Observateur*.[16] Duras, who was born and grew up in Indochina, was well known at the time for her screenplay for Alain Resnais's 1959 film *Hiroshima, Mon Amour*, a film that uses a love story to juxtapose memories of life under Nazi occupation in France with memories of the bombing of Hiroshima. "Les deux ghettos" also uses an aesthetic of juxtaposition: taking the form of two interconnected interviews, it brings together memory of the Holocaust and recent developments in the ongoing struggle between France and the FLN. Summarizing *France-Observateur*'s contents on its front page, the magazine's editors explicitly link Duras's article to the events of October 17, 1961. They describe Duras's method by comparing it to the magazine's own attempts to get to the bottom of the police massacre: "Marguerite Duras also asked questions, first to two Algerian workers and then to a survivor of the Warsaw ghetto. The questions are identical, the answers are eloquent. The time of the ghettos, which we thought had disappeared, has it returned?" This note is accompanied by a pair of photographs juxtaposing an Algerian man, bundled into a winter coat and rubbing his hands for warmth, and a Jewish ghetto inmate, her face in shadow and a yellow star marking her fate (see Figure 6). Alongside the article itself another photograph shows the deplorable conditions of the Nanterre *bidonville* or shantytown—a scene that, without the dark-skinned girl in the right foreground of the picture, could easily be mistaken for a Nazi ghetto. Like Du Bois, but to different effect, Duras's article draws on a persistent analogy that links Jews with other racialized groups through the figure of the ghetto's segregated social space.

Perhaps equally striking with respect to the archive under construction in this book, Duras's interview format seems inspired, at least in part, by *Chronicle of a Summer*, which had just opened in Paris and had been reviewed in *France-Observateur* two weeks earlier. While *Chronicle* received only a mixed review—it was termed a "demi-réussite"—the reviewer describes the film in terms that echo in Duras's article as well as other articles that appear around the same time: *Chronicle* is a "film of testimonials [*film à témoignages*], that is, a film in which human beings who are not, to be sure, actors playing a role, but actually existing individuals, are invited to speak of themselves or to let themselves be filmed in their everyday life."[17] Not only does Duras, like the film, juxtapose the effects of colonial and genocidal policies through a comparative approach to everyday life drawing on personal testimonials, but she even asks the same kinds of questions that characterize Rouch and Morin's film: Duras's "Do you still have an easy, simple, idea of happiness?" echoes the film's "Are you happy, sir?" Duras's interviews also mirror the gendered nature of the setup in *Chronicle*—with the colonized represented once again by men ("X." and "Z.") and the Holocaust survivor a woman (moreover, one whose identification as "M" seems to echo the name of Marceline).

While the title and formal structure of the article seem to assert an equation between the experiences of Algerians and Jews, that structure also foregrounds differences. The editors assert that Duras's "questions are identical," but this is not entirely true. Of course, there are a few minor

FIGURE 6   The November 9, 1961, cover of *France-Observateur* featuring Marguerite Duras's "Les deux ghettos." Author's collection.

variations in the questions, and Duras includes some references to historical specificities—for example, when she asks the Algerians about "Les Grandes-Carrières, La Seine?" thus alluding to the commissariat where many Algerians were tortured and the river into which many bodies were thrown. But more subtle is the shift in tenses between the two sets of questions. This shift draws attention to the differences of temporality that distinguish the two experiences above and beyond important differences in the types of victimization suffered by Jews under the Nazis and Algerians under the French. While the questions Duras addresses to the Algerians are always in the present tense, those to the Warsaw survivor are always in the past tense. Thus, she asks the Algerians, "Do you still have an easy, simple idea of happiness?" and she asks the Warsaw survivor, "Did you still have an easy, simple idea of happiness?" This temporal asymmetry, illustrative of the never strictly parallel intersection of Holocaust memory and the actuality of decolonization in all of the cases in this book, complements an explicit discussion of comparison. Duras asks the Algerians, "Do you believe that your condition resembles that of anyone else?" She asks M., "Did you believe your condition resembles that of anyone else?" (9–10). Here the tense shift is slightly jarring, and it is not clear whether Duras is actually asking the survivor if this was her belief while in the ghetto or in retrospect. While the tense implies the contemporaneous belief, the answer treats the question as addressing the present: "None," replies the survivor:

> But if I were asked if the existence of the ghetto is possible, I think it is still possible. I believe there are still "objective" conditions that can take that form. The Algerian history is horrific, but it hasn't taken that particular form. I think that if there is an exaggeration on the part of the French police with respect to Algerians, that exaggeration is common to all the police of countries that are menaced with or in the middle of losing their colonies. I learned yesterday that a lot of Algerians were drowned in the Seine. There is nothing surprising in that for me. I take that as practically a natural fact. Politically, nothing can enthuse me and nothing can surprise me anymore. (10)

This complex response echoes and inverts that of the Algerian "X.": "Me, I think of the Hindus before the arrival of national independence, before even Gandhi. Some comrades say that we are like the Jews under the German occupation. They say: 'This recalls Eichmann's coup [*le coup de Eich-*

mann]. All that's lacking is the crematorium and the gas chamber'" (9). While X. asserts a historical analogy between Algerians and Jews, he does so in a displaced way, attributing the analogy to others and not to his own opinions. Inversely, M. denies a parallel between the Holocaust and any other history, but then goes on to state that conditions remain for a repetition. Her political cynicism, similar to that expressed by Marceline and Jean-Pierre in *Chronicle of a Summer* and a few years later by many of the Auschwitz survivors in Delbo's *The Measure of Our Days*, further erodes the uniqueness of the Holocaust by implying that even, or especially, an unprecedented event can become the model for further depredations.

"Les deux ghettos" demonstrates in condensed form the ambivalences of historical comparison in instances of intercultural memory: while the structure of the article seems to pull in the direction of equating past and present events, the parallelism of the structure provides a platform for differentiations and hesitations and an opportunity to assert historical difference. Even when these hesitations and distinctions express political cynicism, as in the case of M., they nonetheless testify to an ethical sensibility attuned to temporal unevenness and dislocation. The temporal structure of "return" (for the editors) or of potential return (for M. and X.) of past atrocities suggests a political failure to combat the "'objective' conditions" of the ghetto, but the perception of the unevenness amounts to an ethical intervention with implications for the politics of the future. In no sense can these complex and ambivalent formulations be subsumed under an abstract notion of universalism. Rather, the very act of comparison highlights unevenness and difference, for comparison is not the same as mere likening. Not universalization, but a multidirectional logic is at work.

To understand Duras's essay in its historical context, we must also take into account its venue. Edited by the anticolonial writer and municipal council member Claude Bourdet, a spokesperson for the non-Communist new Left, *France-Observateur* had been for years an active source for coverage sympathetic to the Algerian revolution and had recently dedicated many pages to the October 17 demonstrations.[18] Bourdet himself had been one of a handful of leftist and former resistant councilmen and assemblymen publicly calling for an investigation into the massacre. Front-page headlines in previous weeks had used many of the rhetorical commonplaces of the anticolonial movement (such as truth versus silence and oblivion), which also linked it to an emergent Holocaust memory: "La vérité sur les manifestations F.L.N" (The truth about the FLN demonstrations) (October 19, 1961), "Vous ne pouvez plus ignorer ça . . . " (You can no longer ignore that . . .) (October 26, 1961; with a photograph by the Jewish-Leftist journalist Elie Kagan of a wounded Algerian man), "Les silences de M. Papon" (The silences of Mr. Papon) (November 2, 1961). Even before the war, Bourdet had called attention to some of the salient connections between the struggles against fascism and colonialism that would be activated in the late 1950s and early 1960s. In a December 6, 1951, article protesting arbitrary detentions, closed trials, and obvious evidence of torture on the part of the French police in Algeria, Bourdet had asked, "Y a-t-il une Gestapo algérienne?" (Is there an Algerian Gestapo?). A little more than three years later, in an issue headlined "LA VERITE sur les tortures en Algérie . . . " (THE TRUTH on the tortures in Algeria . . .), Bourdet noted the return of torture in Algeria and returned to his earlier rhetoric in "Votre Gestapo d'Algérie" (Your Gestapo from Algeria).[19] At stake in these early examples is primarily memory of the occupation and its brutal repression of the French resistance—there is nothing in these articles by Bourdet to suggest a focus on the specificity of the Nazis' repression of Jews. He compares, for example, the site where the Gestapo tortured French resistors with the site where the police in Algeria did its dirty work, and he asks if there were no deputies who "desire that the world history of the future does not, with an identical scorn, confuse the Third Reich and the regime that emerged from the French Resistance" ("Y a-t-il" 6–7). Such broad antifascist rhetoric, trading on feelings of French national shame and patriotism, continues into the later stages of the war (as *Les belles lettres* also demonstrates), but was now joined by a new rhetoric that brought the specificity of the Nazi genocide closer to the surface: antiracism.[20]

Despite the echoes in Duras's article and other contributions to *France-Observateur* of Du Bois's essay on the Warsaw Ghetto and the techniques of *Chronicle of a Summer*, in France, the perception of "race" and the experience of racism became more and more prominent in the late stages of the war and, in particular, around the events leading up to and including October 17. This new focus of the anticolonial movement in the metropole overlaps with, but also differs significantly from mobilization around torture, especially in its relation to the Nazi genocide. While torture sparked memories of the Nazi occupation, it did not necessarily say anything specific about the Nazis' victims (even though many of those victims experienced the return of torture as prompting what Primo Levi called "the memory of the offense," a painful reminder of past trauma). The increasing racialization of public space in France during the war, however, drew attention to the victims of racism and led to frequent analogies between Algerians and Jews. A new sense of the Holocaust's specificity emerged, in other words, along with a new understanding of the stakes of the war and decolonization. To be sure, *Chronicle* already shows evidence of this new attention to "race," especially in the discussion that leads up to Marceline's unprecedented testimony. The circumstances of late 1961 then intensify this attention.

An article in the October 26 issue of *France-Observateur*, "Le racisme est collectif, la solidarité individuelle" (Racism is collective; solidarity individual), by the Algerian French writer Henri Kréa, brings recent events together with the two-decade-old past.[21] Like Duras's article, Kréa's short piece, based on interviews with Renault workers about the attitudes of the native French working class toward Algerians, also seems inspired in part by the format of the just-opened *Chronicle*, reviewed a few pages later. A photograph of Algerians at the Palais des Sports, one of the sites where thousands of demonstrators arrested on October 17 were being held, accompanies the article. The caption reads: "Cela ne vous rappelle rien? [Doesn't that remind you of something?]." A clear reference to the roundups of Jews during the occupation and, in particular, to the infamous July 1942 *rafle du Vel' d'Hiv'* in which thousands of "foreign" Jews were arrested by French police and held in a bicycle-racing stadium before being deported to Auschwitz, the photograph and caption link the Holocaust and the repression of Algerians through the trope of a gnawing but unspoken memory, a trope that captures the multidirectional intersection of two events that are caught between emergence and collective oblivion.

Like Duras's text, Kréa's article adds further dimensions to the relation among the different histories of racialization and warns against a too-easy parallelism. Asked to reflect on the project of inquiring about native French workers' attitudes toward their Algerian colleagues, an Algerian worker comments, "Many French workers still don't realize that a tragedy is unfolding between France and Algeria. The leaders are responsible; they keep quiet. And when they do speak or write something, they usually don't say anything. And no one listens. As far as racism, you won't have much trouble finding it; it's everywhere, even among those who cry while watching the film *Exodus*" (15). Referring to Otto Preminger's 1960 adaptation of Leon Uris's novel depicting the founding of Israel against the backdrop of the Holocaust and anti-Semitism, the Algerian worker reveals the fallacy of parallel histories even as he produces an association between the situations of Jews and Algerians in the twentieth century. Here is a vivid example of the non-zero-sum logic of memory at work. The very exposure of inequities in the recognition of different histories already contributes to a recalibration of public discourse: the powerful affective response to *Exodus* becomes the occasion for remarking the lack of such a response before the plight of Algerians and thus also prepares the grounds for such a response in the future.

France-Observateur's "reminder" of the roundup of Jews intends to awaken French citizens to the echo of the past in the present in order to mobilize them in opposition to government policy. This praiseworthy political intention masks and, in retrospect, reveals another relevant ethical issue—a void in the French public's engagement with the recent past. Although the implicit reference to the roundup of Jews in Paris indicates a nascent consciousness of the specificity of the Holocaust (recognized *in relation* to decolonization), no recognition registers French complicity with the Nazis in that roundup. This gap is in no way unusual—in the many mentions and intimations of the Vel' d'Hiv' roundup in late 1961 that I have found, the focus remains on Nazi policy and not French complicity. Instead of reading this gap as one more indication of France's inability to come to terms with its own history, however, I suggest that the Vel' d'Hiv' reference be read productively: as a step in a longer process of working through. Although French complicity is only registered in the text's political unconscious, the reference *holds the place* for a future explicit engagement. While insufficient as history and indicative of an early stage of public consciousness of the Holocaust and Vichy responsibility, this selective memory suggests that for contemporaries the primary link between the events lies instead in the racist ideology that underlies each.

The perception of a racial logic in decolonizing France not only registers a process that has only recently been studied in depth by historians. It also becomes a site of potential ethical engagement around the question of an earlier French complicity.

The frequent "reminders" of the Holocaust deployed in the fight against colonialism by *France-Observateur* and other anticolonial venues, such as the underground journal *Vérité-Liberté*, testify not so much to the universalization of the Holocaust's meanings as to the emergence of a notion of the Holocaust's specificity through its contact with the ongoing struggle over Algeria. In other words, the Holocaust does not simply become a universal moral standard that can then be applied to other histories; rather, some of those *other histories help produce a sense of the Holocaust's particularity*. At the same time, people impacted by the histories of colonialism and decolonization refer to this emergent understanding of the Holocaust as part of a *shared but not necessarily universal* moral and political project. Far from being a floating, universal signifier, the Holocaust emerges in its specificity as part of a multidirectional network of diverse histories of extreme violence, torture, and racist policy.

The conditions of possibility for bringing together Arab and Jewish histories in Algerian War–era France lie not in timeless or abstract notions of diasporic solidarity. Rather, just as for Du Bois and the Communist editors of *Jewish Life* similar analogies arose in response to a particular history, the cold war, the analogies that emerged around the events of October 17 bear witness to a particular context, albeit one that can never fully determine their shape. In *The Invention of Decolonization*, a meticulously documented account of French legal and political discourses during the endgame of the Algerian War, Todd Shepard demonstrates that not only did colonialism exacerbate the paradoxes of France's consensus ideology of republican universalism, but the very idea of decolonization also became the occasion for a reconfiguring of French identity along increasingly racialized grounds.

Struggling to extricate itself from an unwinnable situation, France backed away from a fundamental tenet of republican ideology: the meaninglessness of racial and ethnic difference. The first years of the war had seen the French state tinkering with its universalist ideology of radical equality to invent new forms of integration and make its colonial subjects fully French (Shepard 50). But even revised notions of universalism that could recognize certain differences in the name of creating equality—including, most surprisingly, varieties of "affirmative action" that the French deemed "exceptional promotion"—failed to answer the demands of the Algerian independence movement. Rather than addressing the paradox of how a state could be simultaneously colonialist and universalist, Shepard argues, France came to rely on a "common-sense" notion of racialized identity: "The French recognized that Algerians were so different, as a group, from other French citizens that they could not be accommodated within the French Republic. This was what the FLN had always proposed.... Yet until the final years of the Algerian War, French leaders energetically rejected this contention" (6). The recognition of difference came to function as a kind of fetish, covering over the traumatic realization that republican ideology itself was paradoxical at its heart: "Race and ethnicity appeared as meaningful markers to explain who could be considered French at a moment when definitions premised on legal codes or tradition proved weak" (2–3). The shift in perspective and policy marked by the "invention of decolonization," Shepard proposes, helped whitewash the uncomfortable fact that a regime dedicated to equality and universality could also annex and rule over foreign lands, and that shift had lasting effects on French politics and notions of identity.

The tensions that Shepard outlines between republican ideology and the fact of racial discrimination (in the sense of both the recognition of racial/ethnic difference as meaningful and of outright racism) have direct implications for thinking about the contemporary meaning of the events of October 1961, events that Shepard doesn't address directly, but that took place in the crucial period of transition during which French policy and attitudes began to shift. While the ideological and policy shifts Shepard describes had a dire impact on racialized minorities in both the short- and long-term, the ideological incoherence to which the shifts testified also created a space in which intellectuals and activists such as Duras, Bourdet, and Kréa could link the contemporary crisis to past events that had not yet received their due.

From Two to Three Ghettos: *The Stone Face*

The articles of Duras and other anticolonial intellectuals writing in 1961 register the shifts in French policy and ideology Shepard documents and represent a prime example of what I have been calling multidirectional memory: they respond to the French state's late colonial production of racialized identities by forging anamnestic solidarity among different, and differently oppressed, groups. However, rather than asserting a simple identity between analogous forms of racism—a move that would reproduce an antiracist universalism of the sort that was precisely in crisis at that moment—these works draw attention to asymmetries of experience. When Duras alters the tense of her questions to her Algerian Muslim and Polish Jewish informants and when Kréa includes evidence of the differential affective response to Jewish and Algerian Muslim histories, they neither mirror traditional French republican univeralism, nor the new racialized particularity of decolonizing France; instead, they provide a multifaceted, multidirectional response that seeks to find a space for ethics and politics outside of the dominant opposition between the particular and the universal. A similar work of differentiation against a backdrop of solidarity takes place in William Gardner Smith's novel *The Stone Face* (1963). Here, Duras's two ghettos morph into an even more complex juxtaposition of three ghettos. Yet, at the same time, the question of gender, a topic that remains implicit in Duras's short article, emerges in Smith's novel to trouble the relation between memory and politics. An extraordinary work of multidirectional generosity, *The Stone Face* also ultimately turns away from and risks "forgetting" some of its most crucial insights about complicity, solidarity, and the entanglement of collective memories.

Ignored for many years, *The Stone Face* has recently received deserved attention from important scholars such as the sociologist Paul Gilroy, the literary critic Kristin Ross, and the historian Tyler Stovall.[22] Yet, despite being the first novel to treat the events of October 17, 1961, and the only fictional work published in its immediate wake, *The Stone Face* remains outside the scope of most discussions of the memory of the massacre that focus on the national memories of France and Algeria. In *The Stone Face*, Smith, an African American novelist and journalist who had been living in

Paris since 1951, tells the story of Simeon Brown, a journalist and amateur painter who has left the United States to escape its endemic racism and, especially, the violent reactions it prompts in him. As a youth, Simeon lost an eye in a racist attack, and the patch he continues to wear bears witness to the persistent racist violence he suffers as an adult—always by individuals marked by an unfeeling, inhuman, "stone" face. Arrived in Paris, Simeon immediately enjoys relief from the pressures of American racism. He quickly enters into the expatriate life, which includes not only a host of African American artists, musicians, and intellectuals, but also white Americans and Europeans. Soon, Simeon becomes romantically involved with Maria, a beautiful young woman initially identified as a Polish exile. A series of chance encounters puts Simeon in contact with members of the Algerian community. As he learns more about the colonial history and violent decolonization unfolding around him through his relationships with Algerians, Simeon begins to question his initial impressions of France as a nonracist paradise. The second half of the novel focuses on Simeon's growing feelings of unease as he recognizes the hollowness of his newly privileged position in Paris and the dire fate of his Algerian friends. In the end, Simeon experiences the deterioration of his relationship with Maria, who is pursuing her dream of becoming a Hollywood movie star, and he throws his lot in with his Algerian friends: he becomes a witness and participant in the October 17 demonstration. Arrested after attacking a police officer during the demonstration and then quickly released from custody when police determine he is not Algerian, Simeon decides at the novel's end to return to the United States so that he can take part in the struggle for African American civil rights.

In *The Stone Face*, Smith provides a cutting portrait of African American expatriate life in Paris. The African American community in Paris circled around Richard Wright, whose attitude toward France is well captured by his unpublished assertion that "there is more freedom in one square block in Paris than there is in the entire United States of America" (qtd. in Stovall, "Fire" 186). However, as Stovall has argued, the freedom generated by the move to a new social context came with a price: the expatriates' privilege was at odds with the situation of France's colonial populations, in particular with that of Algerian workers in the metropole. The French-Algerian conflict created a crisis for the expatriates and revealed the contradictions of their unusual position in Paris as "privileged" people of color; ultimately, Stovall suggests, the community broke up in part because of tensions generated by the collapse of France's North African empire. Wright and others felt unable to speak out about the war despite their anticolonial convictions because they did not want to offend their French hosts; some, like James Baldwin, ended up leaving Paris during the war. Smith, by contrast, was one of the few to address the Algerian revolution head on and with great sympathy.[23] But, even more remarkably, Smith goes farther; he opens up the race question that linked and divided African Americans and Algerians by providing a reminder that such conflicts also took place against the backdrop of the recent Nazi genocide and occupation.

Complicities, or, Lumumba's Death

The Stone Face builds toward the climax of the October 17 demonstrations and depicts the repression of that evening in detailed terms that correspond closely to many other contemporary accounts. Smith narrates the events against a backdrop of generalized indifference that encompasses both Simeon's American expatriate friends, black and white, and the Parisian public: "Meanwhile, most of the city slept or went its carefree way. . . . Old-timers, some of whom had lived through the nightmare of the wartime German Occupation, or even the concentration camps, played cards or dominos or quatre-cents vingt-et-un in the old cafés" (202). The historical echoes that register in Simeon's focalized consciousness foreshadow his climactic realization of the apparent seamlessness of racism. On the evening of October 17, Simeon witnesses many scenes of anti-Algerian brutality, but one stands out: "A policeman was swinging his club over a woman who was holding a baby" (203). After intervening on behalf of the woman and child, Simeon finds himself held with thousands of demonstrators in "a gigantic sports stadium" (the Palais des Sports). While an Algerian addresses him as "frère," brother, a loudspeaker announces that "Algerians would remain in the stadium until room had been found for them in prisons, hospitals or camps in France; it added that agitators among them would be sent back to their '*douars* of origin'—to the concentration camps of the Algerian regions in which they had been born"

(205).[24] Lying down on the stadium ground, Simeon has the revelation toward which the book has been building:

> The pain in his eye had diminished somewhat, and before dropping off to sleep he thought: the face of the French cop, the face of Chris, of Mike, of the sailor, the face of the Nazi torturer at Buchenwald and Dachau, the face of the hysterical mob at Little Rock, the face of the Afrikaner bigot and the Portuguese butcher in Angola, and yes, the black faces of Lumumba's murderers—they were all the same face. Wherever this face was found, it was his enemy; and whoever feared, or suffered from, or fought against this face was his brother. (205–6)

Concatenating incidents of violence from multiple contexts, both personal and historical, this passage certainly seems to suggest the "universalizing argument" identified by Paul Gilroy (324) and captured in the title of the *New York Times* review of *The Stone Face*: "The Unvarying Visage of Hatred" (November 17, 1963, p. BR27). But what precisely is the universalizing argument in this passage and in the novel?

The passage presents a series of examples of the incarnation of the "face" that has haunted Simeon. The initial iterations of the face all recall perpetrators of racist or colonialist violence, but a shift takes place in the middle of the passage from faces given characterological status in the novel (the cop, Chris, Mike, and so on) to faces referred to as types (the Nazi torturer, the Afrikaner bigot, and so forth). A further shift heightens and reinforces this process of generalization and abstraction: the evocation of "the black faces of Lumumba's murderers." Here, however, questions arise. What happens when black faces are included as part of the abstract "face" that Simeon recognizes as his enemy? Does the inclusion of the "black" murderers of the Congolese anticolonial leader and prime minister signal a transcendence of race and colonialism or does the passage subsume those murderers within the series of racist perpetrators (as the "yes" might be read to indicate)? In either case, the strong drive toward universalism that takes place in this passage finds itself internally divided at the very point where one attempts to assign definitive meaning to the enemy "face." If the face is not a racist face, what is it? If it is, what does it mean to include colonized black people within its purview? Whether the passage indicates that racism has been transcended toward the "unvarying visage of hatred" or that the face of racism has been stripped of particular racial markings, the passage has rendered fraternity problematic. The friend/enemy (or brother/enemy) distinction that underwrites Simeon's revelation cannot withstand the force of the revelation itself: as the novel has emphasized through its contrast between complacent African American expatriates and locally victimized Algerians—and as it now reemphasizes through the example of Lumumba's murder—categories of belonging based on racial victimization or its transcendence are equally insufficient because ultimately self-divided.

As an alternative to interpretations based on transcendence or abstraction, I would propose a third reading of the passage: the turn that takes place through the inclusion of the events in the Congo—"yes, the black faces of Lumumba's murderers"—reveals *complicity* as Simeon's key discovery during his Paris sojourn. The concept of complicity offers a way of thinking about the iterations of the face that neither transcends race and racism, nor subsumes all of the figures into identical subject positions as racist perpetrators. The rhetoric of complicity suggests both a form of binding and a degree of distance: to be complicit is to be responsible (bound to certain events, processes, or people), but it is not identical to being guilty. Complicity suggests an *ethical* binding distinct from *legal* guilt, although they can surely overlap, as they do here. In this passage, Lumumba's murderers are both guilty and complicit: they are guilty of murder, to be sure, but their placement in the series of enemy faces highlights especially their complicity in the racist and colonial regimes Simeon has been pondering.[25] It thus recalls the complicity Simeon has remarked—or been forced to remark by his Algerian friends—in the members of the African American expatriate "colony" (as it is often called in the novel).[26] Early in the novel, as Simeon walks through the Left Bank, he hears someone "shout in thickly accented English: 'Hey! How does it feel to be a white man?' Simeon knew somehow that the words were for him and, turning, saw four Algerians sitting at a table of the Odéon Café" (55–56). As this classic scene of Althusserian interpellation *avant la lettre* is meant to illustrate, African Americans' unfamiliar privilege as "honorary" white people in Paris implicates them in France's own late colonial project, a project that is directed against other Others. To be complicit, as opposed to being guilty, implies at least a minimal distance from the center of events; according to the novel, African Americans in Paris are not perpetrators of the late colonial war, but they can be its complicit beneficiaries.

Since the interpellation in this case comes not from a state apparatus but from one of the "bad subjects" who has refused the universalizing address of the French state, Simeon's seemingly intuitive recognition that "the words were for him" also suggests that a recognition of complicity can be closely linked to—and may even be the condition of possibility for—solidarity across differences.

Seen in these terms, *The Stone Face* confirms critic Mark Sanders's argument that complicity is a key term for thinking about oppositional intellectual responsibility. As described by Sanders in his account of South African intellectuals and Apartheid, complicity comes in two forms: it encompasses both a "narrow sense" tied to specific events, and a "general sense" that acknowledges "a complicity in human-being as such."[27] These two senses represent not an option or choice, but rather, for Sanders, the very "aporia of responsibility," because the specificity of any particular cause always remains in tension with the general principles of justice: "Whenever justice is invoked, as it always is, in the name of a specific cause, there will be the risk of doing injustice. . . . Each concrete 'case' produces its own openings and limits of universalization" (6). The recognition of complicity cautions against an abstract universalism because—at least for the intellectual interested in justice, as Simeon certainly is—it inevitably sets particularizing and generalizing claims against each other. While agreeing with Sanders that a gap often remains between the particular and general senses of complicity, that gap or aporia functions, at least in Smith's novel, as a productive space of multidirectional memory. Although the novel contains a strong drive toward an abstract universalism—marked by the realization that all perpetrators share "the same face"—its foregrounding of complicity militates against such abstraction and leads instead to nonuniversalist analogies in which various particularities and generalities modify each other in multidirectional ways. Thus, for example, in the scenes discussed here acknowledgment of complicity shifts the meaning of both the particularity of "blackness" and the more general categories of race and justice. At the same time, the tension between the novel's avowed universalism and its insight into complicity also produces contradictions that arise around issues of gender and Jewishness.

While Simeon attempts to break with the complicity he sees around him, he can only do this through concrete acts of solidarity, not through occupying an abstract realm of justice. For instance, in the scene when Simeon first learns of Lumumba's murder, we learn that "Every black man in Paris had felt personally *involved*, personally outraged, by the overthrow of the Congolese premier. And they had felt equally concerned by his subsequent arrest" (171). But this feeling of generalized solidarity is immediately rendered tenuous by the newspaper's photographs depicting the triumphant enemies of Lumumba:

> With the exception of a couple of Belgian advisers, all the persons in the photographs were black.
> As he looked at the photograph, Simeon suddenly started with surprise. He stared at the picture in wonder.
> Those faces! Those *black* faces! (171–72)

In the evocations of Lumumba's death, recognition of complicity competes with the desire for solidarity. Both complicity and solidarity, however, are caught between the particular and the general: they are forms of binding premised on distinction. Without at least a minimal difference (between Africans and the diaspora, between Africans and colonialists, or between Africans and neocolonialists), neither solidarity nor complicity would name the feeling or the problem evoked by Lumumba's death.

This minimal distance becomes the occasion for acts of multidirectional memory. Indeed, the novel suggests that multidirectional memory might be the outcome of a recognition of a generalized complicity and of the need to resist particular complicities. Immediately following Lumumba's death (in early 1961), Simeon begins to see complicity everywhere around him:

> A decomposition was setting in. . . . The poison penetrated further into the people. One of its manifestations was a rash of chauvinism: ultra–right wing organizations, with strains of anti-Semitism and a white supremist [*sic*] ideology multiplied. . . . Most depressing of all to Simeon was the seeming indifference of the population to what was happening in Algeria, with the exception of the courageous minority. Everybody knew about the concentration camps and the tortures. Everybody knew about the filthy slums, the *bidonvilles*, in which hundreds of thousands of Algerians in France were obliged to live. But few cared enough to act or even to protest. *Wir sind die kleiner leuter* [*sic*]—"We are little people": this was the expression the Germans had used . . . to explain why they did nothing to stop the persecution of the Jews. It was also the attitude of most of the French. (173–74)

This passage not only depicts Paris during the run-up to the October 1961 massacre in historically and sociologically resonant terms (registering, for example, the rise of the OAS and new forms of policing in the metropole). It also stages an analogy between different forms of complicity in which, as in the passage on the "unvarying visage of hatred," the Nazi genocide once again takes on a prominent role. Simeon's ability to act in solidarity with Algerians derives from his multidirectional recognition of the generalized penetration of complicity's poison across social groups and historical periods. As Sanders remarks, the ability to oppose racist regimes derives from a tendency "to acknowledge, affirm, and generalize responsibility-in-complicity," while "striving to minimize acting-in-complicity" (12). As an African American in France exposed directly to colonial violence and to an unaccustomed privilege, Simeon is forced for the first time to recognize his own complicity in racism—what Sanders calls "the intimacy of psychic colonization" (x); this recognition allows him to take a critical perspective on other instances of complicity while broadening his sense of solidarity or "complicity in human-being as such."

Despite this broadened sense of complicity, solidarity, and responsibility, the ultimate result of this recognition, in narrative terms, is Simeon's decision to return to the United States in order to fight for a particular cause: African American civil rights (a return Smith himself did not undertake).[28] Thus, while the titles of the three sections that make up *The Stone Face* provide a condensed narrative of the progressive stages of Simeon's move from victimization to complicity to solidarity—"The Fugitive," "The White Man," and "The Brother"—the drive toward universalism cannot eliminate the residues of the particular. The lessons of this complicated scenario are not simple, as different evaluations of the novel's conclusion suggest. Ross, for instance, sees the novel as describing "a political awakening, a new political subjectivity taking shape through cultural contamination" (*May '68* 45). Gilroy, by contrast, believes that the novel turns away from its fundamentally diasporic ethics and cosmopolitan sensibility when Simeon decides to return "home." For Gilroy, the novel thus abandons the possibility of the political subjectivity described by Ross and marks a "capitulation to the demands of a narrow version of cultural kinship that Smith's universalizing argument appeared to have transcended" (*Against Race* 323–24). Stovall provides a reading somewhere between these two positions, suggesting that "Simeon's reaction to the Papon massacre . . . presents an international, diasporic perspective on racism, but it also implies that the struggle against racism shows the limits of exile as a political strategy" ("Fire This Time" 197). The distinctions between these critical positions testify to contradictions that Smith's novel registers without resolving. The novel remains caught in the aporia of responsibility, caught between the narrow and general senses of complicity. My reading of *The Stone Face* illuminates that aporia and ultimately confirms Sanders's insight, derived from Fanon and South Africa's Black Consciousness movement, that the general sense of complicity encompasses unconscious complicity and is linked to the problem of embodiment (Sanders 178–79). Instead of trying to banish the inevitable aporia of responsibility, it makes sense rather to learn what it means to live with it; in my terminology, that means adopting an approach attuned to multidirectionality instead of highlighting one side of the opposition between abstract universality and concrete particularity.

Dirty Jew: Gender and Jewishness

Perhaps with an eye to the tensions inherent in the concept of universalism—especially for a French colonial/postcolonial context in which republicanism is in crisis—Stovall aligns the significance of Smith's novel and the events it depicts with a *global* instead of universal perspective. As Stovall usefully comments in a short essay introducing *The Stone Face*, the transnational perspective of Smith's novel allows us to rethink the geographies of colonial history: "The Algerian War, and colonial history in general, is not just a bipolar relationship between *métropole* and colony, but part of a global history that both influenced and was influenced by people beyond the formal boundaries of empire. . . . [T]he Algerian War was a global event whose impact transcended the boundaries of both France and Algeria, an event that individuals interpreted according both to their understanding of imperial France and also in light of their own national and local histories."[29] As Stovall writes elsewhere, the war also "paved the way for a new, more sophisticated understanding of race and racial conflict as a global phenomenon," at least among some expatriates like Smith ("Fire This Time" 189–90). By allowing for a multipolar understanding of history and the circulation of memory, the framework of the global avoids some of the problems of the more overtly ideological terminology of the universal. But even as Stovall moves from the universal to the global, he still leaves certain particularities unexamined; the question of the boundaries and limits of interpretation reasserts itself.

In his brief discussions of the novel and its challenge to received notions of race and colonialism in postcolonial studies and African American writing, Stovall (like Ross, but unlike Gilroy) leaves out another of the ways the novel unsettles reified boundaries: its engagement with Jewish history.[30] By thematizing the Holocaust and anti-Semitism, Smith undoes the symmetry of various pairs that structure *The Stone Face*: France-Algeria, France-America, African America–Algerian France. This unsettling takes place through the figure of Simeon's lover Maria, who, although originally and repeatedly described as Polish, turns out in fact to be a Polish Jew. Maria, we learn, was sexually abused by a Nazi officer when she was a child and lost her family in a death camp. While the novel explicitly thematizes the various distinctions and solidarities of race and ethnicity, paying attention to the depiction of Maria, which has been underexplored in the criticism, reveals the way gender and sexuality mediate the novel's memory work along with race and ethnicity. Even more obviously than Marceline in *Chronicle of a Summer*, the youthful Maria does not fit the stereotypes of the Holocaust survivor that have since sedimented in collective consciousness (and not just because of her markedly Christian name!). It may be the discomfort produced by her lack of fit into the established categories of public memory that has led most scholars of the Holocaust, the Algerian War, and African American literature to overlook her presence or leave her character underexplored. Yet, whatever Maria's lack of fit within contemporary conceptions of the Holocaust survivor, the overlapping representations of Maria, Marceline, and M. (from Duras's article)—who are all deliberately staged in relation to colonized men and men of color—suggest that gender implicitly performed important work in helping negotiate the relation between a nascent public memory of the Holocaust and the transitional moment of decolonization.

Simeon's first sight of Maria emphasizes all the ways her body does not signify the concentrationary universe or mark her out as a racialized subject. Shortly after arriving in Paris, Simeon is sitting in a café with Babe, a more established member of the African American "colony," when a striking woman walks by:

> Simeon drew on his cigarette and was startled by the sight of a tall long-legged girl with dark glasses, short-cropped black hair and an impudent walk who was crossing the street toward them. What jolted him was the luminosity of the handsome girl, who must have been in her early twenties; an aura of smoldering energy, a sort of electric field surrounded her, her face and bare legs *glowed* with health. She was very much aware of her beautiful body, exaggerating its movements like a child playing with a new toy. (11)

Although, reading retrospectively, one might note the "electric field" and even Simeon's cigarette as displaced figures of the world of the camps, our initial perception of Maria, focalized through Simeon, emphasizes her beauty and health.[31] Nor does any hint of her past emerge when Babe identifies her for the smitten Simeon: "Name's Maria, she's Polish, come here on a trip from Poland to try to get into the movies and become another Brigitte Bardot" (11). Although Smith withholds information about Maria's past for the first third of the novel, Simeon soon realizes that the apparent luminosity and playfulness of Maria are masking some darker experience: "She was more than a child, Simeon thought. She was a prism of changing moods. Very often in her sleep she moaned and talked in Polish. Sometimes she screamed, then woke up" (68). Eventually Maria reveals her traumatic past to Simeon, although this revelation also comes in an unexpected moment—after Simeon asks her how many men she has slept with. She initially mentions two, but later goes on to reveal that "before you and before the other man there was the war and the labor camp where I was with my parents during the Occupation, and there was a German officer. . . . The German officer, the camp commander, liked me. I did what he wanted to keep me and my parents alive" (76). In her initial account of the camps, Maria never identifies herself as Jewish; even when the Nazi commandant turns on her, after receiving bad news from the home front, he is depicted as complaining, "You, you think you know something about suffering! What can you Poles know!" At the same time, however, the account of the camp selection, or "line-up," as the novel has it, and of the gas chambers to which Maria's parents are sent hints strongly at her Jewishness (77).

It is only in the context of anti-Semitic expressions by Simeon's Algerian friends that the novel explicitly reveals that she is Jewish. One day, Simeon is (again) sitting in a café discussing racism in the United States with Lou, a sympathetic white expatriate, while several Algerians listen in. When Maria returns from a shopping spree with a beautiful but expensive bracelet, she worries that she has been cheated by the salesperson, a speculation that leads to a first, unselfconscious anti-Semitic comment:

> Ben Youssef smiled. . . . [H]e seemed all innocence as he casually and unwittingly dropped his bomb: "Sure,'" he said, "probably some dirty Jew sold it to you."
> The words exploded full in their faces. Maria jerked her head up as though she had been slapped. . . . Simeon was stunned. These words, from one of the *Algerians*? Abruptly a whole mental and psychological structure he had built up since the day he had first talked with Hossein seemed to collapse.
> Maria's face was white with anger; all frivolity had gone.
> "I am dirty Jew" [*sic*], she said. (121–22)

Despite Maria's accented announcement, which probably comes as a surprise for many readers as it implicitly does for the Algerians, Simeon's most militant friend Hossein does not back away from Ben Youssef's words, but rather radicalizes them: he pronounces, "with sudden passion," that he hates Jews "'worse than I hate the French! Worse than I hate the colonialists!'" (123). In the discussion that ensues from the emergence of this forthrightly expressed prejudice, the members of this multinational café society debate and historicize anti-Semitism. While the authorial condemnation of this form of racism is clear, Smith also, as Paul Gilroy notes in one of the few discussions of this scene, "refuses closure" (*Against Race* 321). The narrative situates Hossein's prejudice within the contradictions of the anticolonial struggle in Algeria, where Jews mostly remained neutral or sided with the French, despite their long centuries in North Africa.

Several noteworthy features of the novel's portrayal of Maria may have contributed to the elisions and confusions that have attended her critical reception. Between her decidedly non-Jewish name and her persistent identification as Polish throughout the first half of the novel, Maria does not initially appear as Jewish. But once the details of her camp experience become known and she answers to Ben Youssef's unwitting anti-Semitic interpellation—with a phrase that echoes Fanon's famous discussion in *Black Skin, White Masks* of being called a "dirty nigger"—the initial withholding of information about her Jewishness calls out for analysis.[32] In fictional form, the novel traces the emergence of a differentiated understanding of the Nazi genocide; Ben Youssef's blunder produces an understanding of the Holocaust as part of a longer history of anti-Semitism targeting those interpellated as Jewish and not simply as "Poles"—although millions of non-Jewish Poles were also killed. As in *Chronicle of a Summer*, the emergence of that differentiated understanding takes place among multidirectional connections and tensions concerning the category of "race" in different historical and cultural contexts. Although staged as a competitive conflict over victimization (Jews are more or they are less oppressed than Algerians; Jews are more or they are less hated than colonialists), the underlying logic and ultimate effect of the novel's depiction of this conflict is to produce an open-ended map of overlapping regimes of racialization.

The multidirectional logic of the scene troubles the strongly universalist message of the novel and reveals its internal tensions. Once again, this complication happens because of the way Smith highlights the question of complicity. The scene where Maria's Jewishness is definitively revealed dialogically stages both the Algerians' complicity in an anti-Semitism that also remains alive in the metropole and the complicity of Jews in the oppression and exploitation of Arabs in Palestine and North Africa. The attempt by Lou, "the only 'pure' white person there," to mediate the tensions by declaring that "every oppressed group is oppressed in a different way and has a different history" is only superficially successful (124). Lou's comment suggests the inevitable complicity between particulars and the universal (every group shares the universality of having a particular history!), but its attempt to render differences analogous remains too symmetrical and ultimately abstract. The novel, however, does not present such a simplistic solution; rather, it highlights the painful asymmetries and unexpected complicities that result from those different histories. Despite Lou's reasonable explanations, Hossein is not appeased, and despite Ben Youssef's embarrassed apologies, Maria ends the chapter in silence.

More Close: Gender and Memory

The novel reveals the tensions and fissures of universalism not only in relation to Jewishness but also especially in relation to gender.[33] Yet, while Jewishness is an explicit, if ambivalent, presence in the novel, gender appears as the novel's not fully acknowledged unconscious. Gender difference becomes especially salient in the novel at many key moments of both cross-racial solidarity and intraminority conflict. For instance, the act that solidifies Simeon's nonordinary claim to fraternity with Algerians comes in his more traditionally coded attempt to protect a woman and child on the evening of October 17. But the ambiguities of gender and race cluster especially around the figure of Maria. On the one hand, when key elements of Maria's story of suffering emerge, Simeon's relationship with Maria seems to solidify. After she first tells him of the camps, Simeon is naturally moved: "Simeon was silent. He held her tight, feeling more close to her than ever. Perhaps they could understand each other, after all" (78). Later, after the ugly anti-Semitic scene, similar phrases reappear: "They did not talk, but Simeon felt very close to Maria and knew that she felt close to him" (126). In these scenes, heterosexual intimacy provides a figure for cross-ethnic solidarity. And yet, on the other hand, there is also unease here, perhaps signaled by the awkward formulation "more close," a phrase that suggests the difficult attempt to overcome the overdetermined differences of race and gender. Simeon and Maria's relationship is clearly doomed because of tensions over Simeon's involvement in the Algerian matter, and Maria eventually disappears from the story as she pursues her decidedly unpolitical dream of becoming a movie star. Despite her exit from the novel's central concerns, the text maintains sympathy with Maria and, as Gilroy suggests, "Simeon accepts her tale of suffering as compatible with rather than equivalent to the tradition of oppression that has induced him to flee" America (318). Nevertheless, she remains a troubling emblem of gendered and racialized difference, and the novel subordinates her story to those of other oppressed groups, primarily African Americans and Algerians.

Maria's ultimate lack of fit in the novel's production of cross-national solidarity becomes especially clear when, immediately after she and Simeon exchange letters of separation, she is replaced in the text by two

Algerian women whom Simeon meets at Ben Youssef's apartment (190–91). Djamila and Latifa share something of the history of suffering experienced by Maria; while she suffered under the Germans, they have been tortured and raped by the French.[34] Their presence in the novel allows Smith to reproduce graphic testimony of the sort that had circulated clandestinely in the late stages of the Algerian War—and which certainly would have been more than enough to get his book banned in France. But Djamila and Latifa also seem to serve another purpose. The novel contrasts them to Maria insofar as their suffering has emerged from a context of struggle—their resistance work with the FLN. As Simeon observes, despite their modesty, "these were the most emancipated of Moslem women. They had participated actively in a war. They would never wear the veil again" (193). While the Algerian women respond to their oppression by throwing off the veil and social conventions of gender, Maria seeks, figuratively, to put on a veil by becoming an actress and embracing such conventions:

Fame, wealth, her name in lights—yes, but most important, that would mean becoming someone else, that person, that legend on the screen. Acting would mean metamorphosis, it would wipe out the past, destroy memories. There would be no little Jewish girl named Maria whose body had been profaned by a monster in a concentration camp, no Maria who turned her eyes away as her parents went off to a horrible death. There would only be that person walking across a screen, living, loving and hating on the screen. (184)

The novel's implicit opposition between the Algerian women and Maria calls upon traditionally gendered binaries, such as those between activity and passivity, the public and the private, authenticity and masquerade. While differentiated from the obliviousness of the complacent Frenchmen sitting in cafes while Algerians are massacred in the streets, and while contextualized as a survival technique in the face of trauma, Maria's version of forgetting still functions to depoliticize the novel's account of the Nazi genocide. The horrors of the Nazi camps are analogized to (although never equated with) the violence of American racism and French colonialism. But the novel removes the Holocaust from the present of political action; it exists only in the past or in the form of a haunting memory in need of exorcism, while the violence of racism and colonialism requires action in the present.

The text's discursive erasure of Maria represents an aspect of the novel's closure that has not yet received critical attention. At the end, Simeon decides to return to the United States; this decision accompanies his realization that "America's Algerians were back there, fighting a battle harder than that of any guerillas in any burnt mountains. Fighting the stone face" (210). Conceptualizing African Americans as "America's Algerians" marks the political inversion traced by the novel. Earlier, after visiting the Goutte d'Or, an Algerian neighborhood in Paris that Simeon likens to Harlem (88), he tells Babe, "Seems to me that the Algerians are the niggers of France" (105). While once he had translated French social conditions and history into American terminology, Simeon's political maturity is marked by his final retranslation of American vocabulary into the terms of the French-Algerian War. But in this retranslation, what happens to the third terms that have also marked Simeon's sojourn in Paris, gender, Jewishness, and the Holocaust? Here a supplement to Gilroy's argument about *The Stone Face* arises. While, for Gilroy, Simeon's turning away from France and the Algerian crisis marks the novel's turning away from the cosmopolitan imagination that otherwise enlivens it, I argue that the novel's turning away from Maria and the legacy she represents is differently significant. The disappearance of Maria from the novel not only marks the marginalization of the Nazi genocide, which had previously mediated the relationship between Algerian and African American history; more importantly, it also facilitates a simplified, gendered opposition between authentic action in the present and an inauthentic relationship to the past.

It is important to distinguish Maria's desire to forget the trauma of the concentration camps, marked by her feminine-coded desire to disappear into the masquerade of her theatrical persona, from the text's own desire to forget Maria. Replacing Maria narratively with the Algerian women who "participated actively" in their "emancipat[ion]" by throwing off the veil supplements gendered binaries with a binary between the apolitical past and the political present and future. Such a polarization reoccurs in many progressive contemporary critics who decry the depoliticizing nature of memory in general and Holocaust memory in particular.[35] But it also obscures the critical, political role that memory has played throughout the novel (not to mention in the anticolonial milieu it documents): both through the flashbacks that contextualize Simeon's observations of racism in the Parisian present with his experiences of racism as a young man and adult in the United States and through the historical memory that allows Simeon to juxtapose French responses to the Algerian War on the eve of October 17 to earlier responses to the Nazi occupation.

But why is memory important to preserve and what is lost in forgetting its import? In a discussion of the very different conflicted legacies of communism in twentieth-century Europe, Fredric Jameson provides a suggestive starting point for answering this question: "The memory of that immense historical experienc[e] brooks no detour, even though there can be no reassuring way of 'coming to terms with it.' . . . There is no right way of dealing with the past—forgetfulness is no more therapeutic than a mesmerization by persistent trauma; but history is not made up of passing fashions which you are free to discard or replace."[36] Much the same can be said of the histories at stake in *The Stone Face* and, more generally, in 1960s France: even in the midst of the hot war of decolonization the recent, but comparatively distant, history of the Nazi genocide cannot simply be the object of a detour. The novel's apparent unease with Maria leads it to discard her a little too quickly. While, as Jameson aptly remarks, there is no right way of dealing with the past—nor should a novel be assigned the role of finding one—the novel can serve as an allegory of how the attempt to slough off the past inevitably leaves political tasks undone and opens up the possibility of a return of the unprocessed.

Observing with the enhanced vision of hindsight, we can see that the novel's detour around the problem of Maria points toward another unacknowledged problem of complicity even as it otherwise probes such problems with great insight. Despite all the analogizing between Algeria and Auschwitz in the journalistic and fictional texts surrounding October 17, a now glaringly obvious missing piece is the question of French complicity in the Nazi genocide. The analogy as it was articulated at the time took the form of a colonial comparison: the Nazis were to the French and the Jews as the French are today to the Algerians. This analogy obscures the fact that some of the French were also to the (French and foreign) Jews as the French are to the colonized of the Empire. Today that seems obvious, but it wasn't at the time. Not only was Papon's personal role during World War II unknown, but French society in general was in a state of denial about collaboration and the role of the Vichy regime—a state of denial that would only begin to be broken in the early 1970s by the combined force of Robert Paxton's history *Vichy France* and Marcel Ophuls's documentary *The Sorrow and the Pity*. My argument is not that Smith's novel bears the responsibility of addressing this French historical silence, but rather that we can see in its handling of Maria and the Nazi genocide some of the mechanisms of avoidance that can derail the always incomplete, but always necessary, process of coming to terms with the past. Despite its unique and impressive efforts to bring together multiple pasts—its active construction of a model of multidirectional memory linking African Americans, European Jews, and Algerian Muslims—the novel also retreats into a gendered vision of memory that strips its own memory work of its political valences: it risks feminizing recall of the past while associating political action with a masculinist transcendence of oppression.

Multidirectional Memory and the Universalization of the Holocaust

Like the political journalism of Duras and Kréa, Smith's novel seems at first to produce a universalist, antiracist narrative premised on analogies between different historical experiences of racial and colonial violence. Written by an expatriate author attentive to multiple national and transnational histories, *The Stone Face* would seem also to illustrate perfectly the globalization of memory—and especially the tendency of Holocaust memory to circulate far beyond its initial context and become a universal moral currency. Yet, in bringing together two or even three ghettos, Duras, Kréa, and Smith produce asymmetrical constellations that are more multidirectional than universalist. Not simply a terminological shift, the move from universalism to multidirectionality has serious implications for the ethics and politics of memory.

Sociologists have made the most forceful case for the link between the globalization and universalization of the Holocaust. The prominent cultural sociologist Jeffrey Alexander argues that sometime around 1961—the very moment we have been focusing on—the Nazi genocide of European Jews went from being perceived as a terrible wartime atrocity with limited implications to being an event uniquely suited to illuminating historical evil wherever it cropped up.[37] Thus, Alexander would most likely see the responses to October 17 that I highlight here as emerging exemplifications of what he calls moral universality, that is, of the way that the Holocaust serves as a template of cruelty that can foster understanding of the present and promote ethical and political action.[38] An equally ambitious attempt to develop a framework for thinking about the moral universality of the Holocaust can be found in Daniel Levy and Natan Sznaider's writings on "cosmopolitan" Holocaust memory.[39] For Levy and Sznaider, the forces of globalization have propelled memory of the Nazi genocide beyond the framework of the nation-state, which has until recently provided the primary reference point for collective memories. Like Alexander, although focused on a more international archive, Levy and Sznaider argue that a dialectic of particularity and universalism has accompanied the development of Holocaust memory in Germany, Israel, and the United States, and they claim that in the post–cold war era this memory has taken on global implications as a vehicle for claims to human rights and restitution. In an era of globalization, an abstract and decontextualized Holocaust memory "transcend[s] ethnic and national boundaries" and, at least in Europe, "is now considered in absolutely universal terms: it can happen to anyone, at anytime, and everyone is responsible" ("Memory Unbound" 88, 101). In "the abstract nature of 'good and evil' that symbolizes the Holocaust," Levy and Sznaider find "a moral touchstone in an age of uncertainty," which "contributes to the extra-territorial quality of cosmopolitan memory" and to the creation of "transnational solidarity" ("Memory Unbound" 102, 93). While Alexander and Levy/Sznaider are seeking to describe the status of Holocaust memory as it has developed since the early 1960s, their accounts also have a strong normative bent: they understand the globalization and universalization of the Nazi genocide as a progressive development that fosters solidarity and human rights.[40]

The response to the events of October 17 has provided an opportunity to address the set of interlocking terms that circulate in Alexander's and Levy/Sznaider's writings on Holocaust memory. I have sought to pry apart the too-easy collapse of the transnational, the global, and the comparative into the universal. In contradistinction to those who praise or criticize the universalization of the Holocaust, I have been arguing that the transnational circulation of the Holocaust is better understood as an aspect of memory's multidirectionality. While both Alexander and Levy/Sznaider offer insights into the global dynamics and moral claims of collective Holocaust memory, the perspective I have been offering here under the sign of multidirectional memory differs from theirs.[41] Although highlighting universality, globalization, and cosmopolitanism, these critics narrate the history of Holocaust memory solely from the perspective of supposedly autonomous changes in the Holocaust's meanings. They subsequently occlude the active role that other histories and memories have played in stimulating many of those changes. Their "universalist" arguments are thus decidedly local and even occasionally parochial. By overlooking Holocaust memory's dialogic interactions with the legacies of colonialism, decolonization, racialization, and slavery, they not only simplify the history of Holocaust memory, they also end up producing a notion of morality that remains too singular and abstractly universal. A more heterogeneous understanding of moral action that recognizes the importance of comparison and generalization while resisting too-easy universalization may not produce a global moral code, but it may produce the grounds for new transnational visions of justice and solidarity that do not reproduce the easily manipulated abstract code of "good and evil." As has grown especially clear in the post–9/11 moment, that code provides precisely the wrong framework for thinking about the legacies of political violence. A morality "beyond good and evil" would, in these circumstances, mean a morality that recognizes the danger of abstract categorization and singular moral templates. A multidirectional awareness of history's crosscutting echoes can help produce a vision that recognizes the aporia of responsibility—the difficult work of avoiding acting-in-complicity while remembering the generalized complicity in human being as such.

Texts contemporaneous with the October 17, 1961 massacre contribute to understanding how collective memory and complicity work in culturally complex contexts. They can help us see that the emergence of Holocaust memory in France was a multipart process in which a sense of the specificity of Jewish suffering under the Nazis was only later complemented by a more morally complex sense of the context in which the Holocaust unfolded in France. In anticolonial journalism of the time and in Smith's novel, we can also see how this history of Holocaust memory was itself folded into the ongoing history of decolonization that was shaking France in those years. As the Algerian War moved toward its end, the return of practices such as torture was joined by all-too-familiar racist processes of identification; together these two returns helped foster an increasing understanding of Jewish suffering in World War II. But that emerging memory also in turn served as a political resource, providing a vocabulary of human rights affronted that anticolonial activists could draw on to mobilize opposition to the late colonial state.

This intertwining of histories and memories leads to one further speculation: What if the bloody, Paris-centered events of October 17, which so obviously called up the Vel' d'Hiv' roundup for contemporaries, also sowed seeds for the belated awareness of French complicity during World War II? On the historical plane, this hypothesis must remain speculative. But looking retrospectively we can see that October 17 would later become the occasion for just such a reflection on complicity. In texts that view the 1961 massacre from a greater historical distance, such as Didier Daeninckx's *policier Meurtres pour mémoire*, Leïla Sebbar's novel for young adults *La Seine était rouge*, and Michael Haneke's film *Caché*, the retrospective view of October 17 develops the problematic of complicity present in *The Stone Face*, a problematic that has grown even more obviously salient because of the revelations about Papon's career that began emerging in the early 1980s. Recognizing the presence of complicity in these works also clarifies the way a belated ethics of memory attuned to questions of intergenerational transmission necessarily supplements the politics of memory that emerges in immediate struggles for decolonization. Paying attention to both the ethical and political dimensions of memory produces a sense of the "present" of any context as defined by multidirectional currents of history and layers of unevenly worked through historical time.

9

Hidden Children: The Ethics of Multigenerational Memory After 1961

The multidirectional solidarities found in texts and movements around 1961 were soon to become invisible because of the institutionalization of the Holocaust and colonialism as autonomous realms of history and discourse. But such solidarities have made a comeback in recent years, thanks, in no small part, to the "return" of October 17 in public discourse after the 1981 exposure of Maurice Papon's collaborationist past and after his 1997–98 trial for crimes against humanity. Recent interest in the October massacre has been part of a larger explosion of interest in the Algerian War era in France and elsewhere that has joined a longer-term fascination with the period of Vichy and the Nazi occupation. Such renewed interest appears at a moment of particularly vexed historical density in which multiple pasts circulate in volatile public forms. But the particular configurations and valences of such intersections have changed since the early 1960s.

While colonialism remains at the center of many of the current conflicts, the "hot" war of the Algerian revolution has been replaced by qualitatively different struggles over pedagogy, memory, and the writing of history. One event in the realms of law and politics has had particular resonance. Early in 2005, French parliamentarians passed a controversial law stipulating that "scholarly programs recognize in particular the positive role of the French presence abroad, especially in North Africa" (*La loi de 23 février 2005*). Although a year later President Chirac called for the voiding of the law and stated that "if the text divides the French, it must be rewritten," the very possibility of such legislation has served to instigate various counterdiscourses. Chirac's retraction came in the wake of both intellectual protest against the law's whitewashing of colonialism and, more immediately and just as pertinently, social unrest among immigrant and minority youth in the suburbs of France's large cities. Those fall 2005 protests from the margins captured the attention of the world and led many to wonder about the depth of the French crisis and France's inability to confront the legacies of colonialism and decolonization. Meanwhile, between the riots and the de facto voiding of the law, a group of prominent historians, including Pierre Vidal-Naquet and Pierre Nora, the initiator of the "lieux de mémoire" project, issued a petition titled "Liberté pour l'histoire." Concerned both by various forms of state intervention into the terrain of professional historians and by the increasing demands made by groups in civil society for a rewriting of history to reflect changing socio-political circumstances, the historians declare: "History is not a religion.... History is not morality.... History is not the slave of the present.... History is not memory.... History is not an object of law."[1] The petition generalizes the battle over the history and memory of colonialism; it calls for the abrogation not only of the February 23, 2005, law on the teaching of colonialism but also of a series of other laws concerning traumatic histories that the petition deems "unworthy of a democratic regime": the Gayssot law of July 13, 1990, concerning crimes against humanity (which outlaws Holocaust denial); the January 29, 2001, law recognizing the Armenian genocide; and the Taubira law of May 21, 2001, declaring slavery and the slave trade crimes against humanity.[2]

While other historians suggest that distinctions should be drawn between the law of February 23, 2005, and at least some of the other laws (notably the Gayssot law on Holocaust negationism), the "Liberté pour l'histoire" historians express an increasingly influential impatience with what the French call "le devoir de mémoire," the duty of memory, and a sense that the past has become subject to political and moralistic manipulation. Henry Rousso, for instance, the author of the definitive study of the memory of Vichy, has in recent years denounced what he understands as a now disproportionately Judeocentric understanding of the Vichy years, a "past that will not pass," as he titled his book with Eric Conan. Rousso has also written passionately about the problems that arise when historians are called before the courts as expert witnesses—a situation that, due to the very different procedures and criteria of truth, he believes can only leave the professional historian in an awkward, untenable position in relation to his or her métier.[3]

In a February 2006 interview in *Le Monde*, Pierre Nora ups the rhetorical ante.[4] Echoing Rousso's concerns and lamenting the current prominence of memory in French public discourse, Nora claims, "We have passed from a modest memory, which only demanded to make itself admitted and recognized, to a memory ready to impose itself by any means. I have elsewhere evoked a 'tyranny of memory'; it would be necessary today to speak of its *terrorism*. So much so that we are less sensitive to the suffering that it expresses than to the violence by which it wants to make itself heard" (9; my emphasis). Reaffirming the "basic principles" of history against this aggressive and "pathological" memory, Nora worries that contemporary society is "menaced by the rewriting of history from the point of view of the victims" (9). The problem with memory, for Nora as for the other "Liberté pour l'histoire" historians, is that is moralizes history, which "is not Manichean," and thus fosters social divisions:

> The real problem is less that of the competition or solidarity of victims than that of the conflictual incompatibility of memories. And before that serious and difficult problem I don't see any other possible response than an authority of reconciliation [*une autorité de conciliation*]. It can take two forms, non-coercive of course, but which suppose that both historians and politicians "pull themselves together." Political speech is indispensable, provided that it be courageous and without demagogy.... Reconciliation through history takes longer. But, ultimately, it is that which is needed, because memory divides and history alone unites. Historians are the best situated, between social pressure and intellectual expertise, to say to all—and for all—what the past authorizes and what it does not permit. (9)

While Nora and the other historians raise significant concerns about the public use of the past, Nora's interview also reveals that the stakes of current debates exceed the status of an academic discipline and involve rather the relations between identity, memory, and the state. Speaking against the backdrop of recent and ongoing social unrest among migrant and minority youth, Nora creates a chain of associations linking memory with the supposed pathology, irrationality, and violence of history's victims. His statements also implicitly acknowledge a crisis in the state's mechanisms of recognition and reconciliation. Against the state's weakness and the oppressed's divisiveness, Nora recommends the authoritative healing powers of historians.

Although Nora does not name the memory of October 17, 1961 as one of the targets of his complaint, many of its characteristics seem to correspond to the form of memory that troubles him. Promoted from below by movements of "victims" and their descendants, and stimulated by novelists' and filmmakers' acts of imagination, the memory of October 1961 has inserted itself aggressively into the French public sphere in the last twenty-five years. The argument I stake out here supports one of the elements of the "Liberté pour l'histoire" position: the idea that the state should not be in the business of writing history and that history cannot be legislated. But I break with the tenor of that document, as well as with the ideas put forward by Nora in the *Monde* interview, when it comes to the question of memory. In contrast to the historians, I argue that the forms of memory and countermemory produced by groups in civil society as well as by texts that circulate publicly play an essential role in opposing the homogenization and moralization of memory produced by the instrumentalization of the state.

In shifting our attention from "the suffering that [memory] expresses... to the violence by which it wants to make itself heard," Nora does put his finger on an important aspect of recent scholarly and imaginative approaches to October 17 and the Shoah: an emphasis on the means and modes of memory's *transmission*. As the postwar generations change, and fewer and fewer people have personal memory of the events of the period between the 1940s and the 1960s, the question of memory's transmission and mediation becomes as important as its content. The three texts I consider in this chapter turn as much on the passing down of memory as on the histories being transmitted. By staging the question of transmission through stories of intergenerational conflict, Didier Daeninckx's *policier Meurtres pour mémoire* (1984), Leïla Sebbar's novel for adolescents *La Seine était rouge: Paris, octobre 1961* (1999), and Michael Haneke's cinematic thriller *Caché* (2005) each ask us to reflect on the relation between multidirectional memory and what Marianne Hirsch has called "postmemory." Hirsch's term is meant to capture the specific relation of children to the traumatic events experienced by their parents—a relation that echoes through the texts explored here and that cannot be captured definitively by the concepts of either an impersonal history or a uniquely personal memory. Although rooted in intimate, familiar experience, postmemory has important implications for collective memory in an age of mass mediation and obsession with unresolved histories of violence. Analogizing her neologism to other recent "post" terms, such as postcolonial, postsecular, and postmodern, Hirsch writes:

Postmemory shares the layering of these other "posts," and their belatedness, aligning itself with the practice[s] of citation and mediation that characterize them, marking a particular end-of-century/turn-of-century moment of looking backward rather than ahead, and of defining the present in relation to a troubled past, rather than initiating new paradigms. Like them, it reflects an uneasy oscillation between continuity and rupture. And yet postmemory is not a movement, method or idea; I see it, rather, as a *structure* of inter- and trans-generational transmission of traumatic knowledge and experience. It is a *consequence* of traumatic recall but (unlike post-traumatic stress disorder) at a generational remove.[5]

Developed in the context of Holocaust studies, Hirsch's concept—as she recognizes—is itself susceptible to transmission across fields. As the texts explored in this chapter illustrate, the structure of postmemory emphatically manifests itself in postcolonial contexts such as the aftermath of the Algerian War. But these texts also encourage us to go one step farther. What Hirsch does not say—although her account does not exclude the possibility—is that postmemory may well constitute a particular version of memory's multidirectionality. Not only does the mediation and belatedness of postmemory recall the mediation and belatedness of all memory—its construction out of networks of spatially and temporally differentiated "moments"—but those characteristics of postmemory are precisely the points of entry for the multidirectional confluence of disparate historical imaginaries.

Most discussions of coming to terms with the past tend to assume a homology between collective memory and national or ethnic identity: scholars have provided numerous accounts or critiques of how Germans come to terms with German history, or how the French come to terms with French history. In *Multidirectional Memory*, I have been emphasizing that coming to terms with the past always happens in comparative contexts and via the circulation of memories linked to what are only apparently separate histories and national or ethnic constituencies. In sometimes subtle ways, the three texts I consider in this chapter call upon multiple contexts—including the Algerian War of Independence, World War II, the Algerian Civil War of the 1990s, the war on terrorism, and the plight of undocumented migrants in Europe—but the texts cannot be reduced to any of these contexts. Their complex and often enigmatic relation to context also represents their promise for thinking about an ethics of multidirectional remembrance in an age of postmemory.

For both rhetorical and epistemological reasons, Nora's assertion that current attempts to rewrite history from the perspective of the victims amount to a form of memory terrorism is troubling. Rather than turning away from Nora's challenge, however, I focus in this chapter on three works that seem to confirm his fears by deliberately staging memory as troubling, violent, or even terrorizing. Yet, these works' varied strategies of aggressively foregrounding the "haunting past" do not *produce* divisiveness but rather seek to uncover already existing, unresolved divisions. Their acts of uncovering hidden histories, traumas, and social divisions constitute the ethical dimension of multidirectional memory. They imply the need for an open-ended fidelity close to Alain Badiou's "ethic of truths."[6] For Badiou, ethics describes a particular type of response to an event that renders visible the previously hidden contradiction or "void" of a situation; ethical fidelity amounts to "a sustained investigation of the situation" in light of the event in order to "induce" a new subject who will construct a new truth and reconstruct the social situation (*Ethics* 67, 43). Badiou's suggestion that the ethical subject emerges out of the investigation of gaps in the present—and cannot be presupposed as prior to the investigation—proves particularly useful for a multidirectional ethics of memory.

As Daeninckx, Haneke, and Sebbar all suggest, the work of memory proceeds from the present when an individual is contingently "caught" on the contradictions of his or her situation and propelled into a search for the past, thus becoming a subject of fidelity and an agent of memory. As in *The Stone Face*, this movement from individual to subject and agent results from an interpellation, but here the interpellation seems to emerge neither from the state nor from a counterforce (such as the Algerians in Smith's novel); rather, the interpellation seems to arise from history itself, from the frequently overlooked or forgotten archive of the contemporary. On a first reading, it is easy to see that repressed personal and political events associated with October 1961 constitute the hidden void of the situation in all three texts discussed here. But if ethical fidelity entails reconfiguring individual and collective history around the revelation of that violence, these texts do not speak with one voice.

A single text inaugurated mainstream French literary engagement with the events of October 17: Didier Daeninckx's 1984 thriller, *Meurtres pour mémoire*. Daeninckx's often-discussed novel possesses a surprising narrative structure that suggests the need to think the specificity of multidirectional memory under conditions of postmemory—that is, of later generations' engagement with their parents' traumatic pasts. Helping to facilitate the reemergence of engagement with October 17 at a generational remove from the events, *Meurtres* sets the stage for Haneke's and Sebbar's works by asking us to think about what it means for histories to be hidden and what it means to bring them to light. Haneke's film joins *Meurtres* in exploring questions of memory especially through family narratives and, in particular, father/son relationships. Leïla Sebbar's novel for adolescents *La Seine était rouge: Paris, octobre 1961* similarly evokes the difficult transmission of memory between generations and, like the film, also raises questions about the different forms taken by the inheritance of a violent past. Anticipating *Caché*, *La Seine* engages centrally with questions of visibility and invisibility and is concerned with the role of film in producing ethical modes of memory. While Daeninckx's and Sebbar's novels each produce different ethical subjects of memory (and postmemory), Haneke's film presents no positive figure of the subject of fidelity. Rather, *Caché*'s staging of the terrorism of memory seeks to turn spectators into ethical subjects by instructing them in an ethics of multidirectional memory. Despite these differences, in all three cases an ethics emerges that seeks to foster not Nora's vision of societal unification via history but rather attentiveness to the multidirectional echoes that constitute the terrain of politics. Inspired by Sebbar's novel, I conclude by asking what it would mean for traumatic histories finally to receive a just burial.

Hard-boiled Memory: *Meurtres pour mémoire*

It is frequently remarked that Didier Daeninckx's 1984 novel *Meurtres pour mémoire* constitutes a milestone in the development of public consciousness about the massacre of October 17, 1961.[7] Written soon after the indictment of Maurice Papon for his anti-Jewish wartime activities, Daeninckx's novel brings traumatic and controversial histories into a popular format; concerned with the dark pasts of both Vichy and the Algerian War, *Meurtres pour mémoire* is, in the terms developed here, a decidedly multidirectional text. Moreover, *Meurtres* not only brings together the two histories that have concerned us in much of this book; it also brings together two *genres* that in the coming decades would be regularly employed in fictions of both the October events and the Nazi genocide. It joins a police thriller built on mystery, detection, and revelation with a plot of intergenerational historical transmission. Elements of both of those genres reappear, for instance, in Haneke's film and Sebbar's novel. Because, in the two decades between the massacre and the publication of Daeninckx's *policier*, little attention had been granted October 17 (despite Smith's novel and several works by Algerian writers that bear witness to the traces of the events), Daeninckx's choice of genres seems clearly motivated.[8] What better way to depict an event erased from public consciousness for the period of a generation than via a narrative that draws on intrigue and connects the fates of a parent and a child? Yet, things are not quite so simple.

Winner of the Grand Prix de la Littérature Policière and the Prix Paul Vaillant-Couturier in 1984, *Meurtres pour mémoire* does not provide exactly the plot one might expect given its deservedly canonical role in bringing the events of October 1961 to a popular audience. While in its social impact the novel has contributed to the outing of a "hidden" history—the massacre of Algerians in the streets of central Paris—as a narrative the novel works differently. The mystery one would have expected to be uncovered is in fact the starting point of the plot. *Meurtres* opens in the *bidonville* of Nanterre and follows the activities of several Algerians as they prepare for and take part in the unprecedented demonstrations in the center of Paris. By the end of the second chapter all of the characters through whom those events have been focalized are either dead—murdered outside the Bonne-Nouvelle metro station—or arrested and taken to the makeshift camps in sports stadiums at the edge of the city. None of these characters ever reappears during the course of the novel. But another plot is interwoven with the story of the demonstration, and it is this plot that announces the mystery at the heart of the thriller. Along with the brutal suppression of the demonstration, the opening chapters recount the last hours of the life of Roger Thiraud, a high school Latin and history teacher, who is himself deliberately gunned down outside his apartment during the demonstration, just steps away from where the Algerians are being massacred. The question of why this seemingly inconsequential figure has been assassinated in cold blood constitutes an important element of the novel's intrigue. In other words, Daeninckx's narrative treats the events of October 17 not as a hidden and repressed past, but as the occasion for another mystery. While the murder of Roger Thibaud during the demonstration facilitates the inclusion of several passages of exposition in which details are given about October 17 that at the time would not have been well known (thus earning the novel its deserved reputation for revelation), ultimately the massacre is only accidentally or contingently connected to the novel's plot.

In fact, besides the murder of Roger, there are at least two other mysteries at work in the novel. Immediately after presenting a capsule version of the events of October 17 (including the fictional death of Roger Thiraud), the narrative jumps ahead twenty years and in a short, half chapter recounts the last days of Thiraud's son Bernard—born two months after his father's death and himself murdered in cold blood in 1982 while visiting Toulouse. Bernard's murder marks a significant shift in the novel's narration. While the opening two and a half chapters employ an external narrator and shift between a set of character-bound focalizers (most of whom quickly end up dead), the remainder of the book (with the exception of one brief chapter) is narrated by the inspector Cadin, who is assigned the case of the younger Thiraud's murder and whose narration is marked by traits of the hard-boiled detective genre (black humor, irony, a certain machismo). At this point, it quickly becomes clear that the true mystery at the core of Cadin's inspection—and, thus, of the novel—is neither the murder of Bernard nor that of Roger, but rather the connection between them. Uncovering that connection necessitates a movement backward from 1982 to 1961 and ultimately to the 1940s and the period of

Nazi occupation and Vichy collaboration with genocide. Both Roger and Bernard have been killed in order to prevent the coming to light of crimes committed during the Holocaust by a high-ranking, Papon-like figure still active in the police force.

The tension between *Meurtre*'s historical impact (bringing October 17 to light) and its narrative means (revealing French complicity in the Holocaust) draws on the resources of the hard-boiled detective genre, which specializes in such indirection, and bears important implications for thinking about multidirectional memory as it passes across multiple generations. In the period between the end of World War II and the high point of decolonization in the early 1960s, the juxtaposition of the Holocaust past (however recent) with the ongoing conflict in the colonized world frequently registered in temporal asymmetry and anachronism—as texts such as "The Negro and the Warsaw Ghetto," *Chronicle of a Summer*, *Les belles lettres*, "The Two Ghettos," and *The Stone Face* testify. For texts produced in the last decades of the twentieth century and first decade of the twenty-first, anachronies remain prominent; now, however, both the Holocaust and decolonization have become "history" (however incomplete coming to terms with these histories remains). As both sets of events begin to recede in time, questions of generational transmission—or lack of transmission—take center stage. In order to address this transformation in individual and collective memory, artists and scholars engaged with the Holocaust in particular have in recent decades been exploring second- and third-generation stories and have sought aesthetic forms and analytic categories for these new memorial phenomena. Hirsch's term "postmemory" has proven especially useful for conceptualizing these largely post-1970s developments.

Meurtres pour mémoire's odd structural relation to "hidden" pasts confirms the intimate links between postmemory and multidirectional memory. Ultimately, the mystery at the heart of the novel is neither the events of October 17, 1961 (however hidden they may appear to the broad public), nor the events of the Holocaust (however "present" they may have come to be to that same public). Rather, the point of *Meurtres*—the mystery that it stages in order to resolve—is the *connection* between different eras and the persistence of the unresolved past in the present. Cadin's investigation into the fictional murders of Roger and Bernard Thibaud provides a materialization of the missing link between different crimes and different histories. In "real," historical terms, the investigation into these double murders embodies what had, in fact, just come to the attention of the French public, Maurice Papon's double guilt—on the one hand, for his heretofore unknown role in the deportation of Jews during the Nazi occupation and, on the other hand, for his publicly knowable, but mostly ignored activities in the late stages of French colonialism, including especially his particular role in the October massacre. The fictional means that Daeninckx employs to capture the many sides of Papon's brilliant career indicates, however, that the novel's aim extends beyond the particular indictment of one, albeit central, figure: like all detective work, Cadin's fictional murder investigation proceeds metonymically by moving from clue to clue and thus brings into view a wide swath of postwar French life. By making the discovery of homologies between eras the point of the narrative, Daeninckx provokes an engagement with larger problems of French complicity. Beyond memory of the events of the Nazi genocide and Algerian War, and beyond even the various kinds of links that have come to relate them in collective memory, what is at stake is the question of responsibility, and particularly *French* responsibility. French discourses contemporary to the October massacre made links back to the Nazi genocide, but did so without evoking French complicity, which had not yet been thematized in historical or political texts. Writing from a partial outsider's standpoint, William Gardner Smith did raise the question of complicity, although not specifically French complicity. Yet, we can now see how the links made in the immediate aftermath of the events between the Algerian War and World War II came to serve two decades later as the basis for an "investigation" of precisely those questions of complicity that had remained unasked.

In Daeninckx's narrative world, French complicity constitutes the ultimate crime and causal element of the intrigue (indeed, beyond the few Algerian characters evoked in the first two chapters of the novel, all of the characters are French). Bernard Thiraud must be murdered for the same reason as his father—for digging too deeply into the archives of World War II and particularly into the story of the deportation of Jews with the complicity of the French state. Thus, it is significant that as Cadin flips through the files Bernard had consulted in the archives of Toulouse, early in his investigation, he unknowingly comes upon a key text: Pierre Laval's 1942 recommendation "to not dismember Jewish families identified for deportation." As Laval wrote (and Daeninckx cites), "*because of the emotion produced by this barbaric measure, I have obtained agreement from the German army that children should not be separated from their parents and can thus follow them*" (64). Framed in the language of civility, Laval's truly "barbaric" order ensured that the Vichy government would eventually attain infamy for sending more Jews, and in particular Jewish children, to their deaths than the Germans had initially requested.[9] As secretary general of the prefecture of the Gironde during the occupation, Maurice Papon followed Laval's orders and took part in the deportation to the internment camp at Drancy, the way station for Auschwitz, of 1,600 Jews, of whom 130 were children under the age of thirteen. It is precisely in terms of the deportation of Jewish children that Daeninckx's roman à clef condemns André Veillut, the figure behind the murders of the Thirauds: "He scrupulously organized the transfer of Jewish families toward the internment center at Drancy. Neither by political conviction, nor by anti-Semitism, but simply in obeying the rules and in executing the orders of the hierarchy. . . . [T]he region that [he] covered came before all others in France in the deportation of Jewish children" (210–11). In describing Veillut as an exemplary figure of the banal, death-dealing bureaucrat made famous by Hannah Arendt in her account of Eichmann, Daeninckx provides a fictionalized version of the most widespread portrait of Papon as a nonideological perpetrator (albeit one that House and MacMaster, identifying Papon with far-right elements in the police and army, have recently contested [*Paris 1961* 33–60]). Whatever the historical accuracy of this veiled portrait of Papon, its purpose in the novel is clear: it creates the grounds for the novel's multidirectional linkage of different eras and different histories. When Bernard's girlfriend Claudine asks Cadin why Roger Thiraud had become involved in a case of deportations that took place when he was only a child, Cadin responds, "Roger Thiraud was born in Drancy—that's the link. It's sufficient" (211). The accidental link that connects Roger—and subsequently his son Bernard—to the history of French complicity parallels the contingent link that the novel establishes between October 17 (a "family" demonstration that included women and children) and the deportation of Jewish children. While Veillut's fictional career runs from World War II, through the period of the Algerian War, and well beyond—as did Papon's—Daeninckx highlights especially accidents of birth and family rather than ideological conviction.

The sideshadowing conventions of the hard-boiled detective genre—its tendency to expose a contingent or metonymical field of associations while "solving" a crime—allows Daeninckx to bring Algeria, Vichy, and many other contemporary issues into the same narrative frame without forcing them into a singular, causal narrative.[10] Such a focus on the contingent results not in a depoliticization of the questions of genocidal and colonial violence, but rather in an increasingly stringent ethical demand: by virtue of the accident of birth, national (and other) subjects inherit the imperative to investigate the multiple forms of violence that have been perpetrated in their name. While stories of victimized children can often lead to sentimentality, that is not the case here—perhaps in part because Daeninckx situates these stories amidst the ironic voice and black humor of the hard-boiled genre. Instead, in *Meurtres pour mémoire*, the foregrounding of children highlights the question of generation and intergenerational transmission. While Bernard seeks to follow through on research begun by his father, the novel attempts to reckon with two sets of crimes that long remained unaddressed; complicity and silence ensured that the crimes would continue to return in French society. Hence, the displaced temporality of the novel: while it addresses historical violence that took place in the 1940s and 1960s, the fictional violence it narrates (the murders of father and son) takes place in the 1960s and 1980s. The novel's layering of these two, temporally disjoined, yet overlapping series of violent acts ("real" and "fictional") on top of each other suggests two lessons about the importance of postmemory: first, that it can provide the narrative structure for a necessary, ethical reckoning with pasts that remain unprocessed; second, that such reckoning will frequently, if not always, require a multidirectional excavation of intersecting histories.

The novel thus also provides a kind of refutation *avant la lettre* of Nora's dictum about the "terrorism of memory": so long as memory remains muted, the novel suggests, violence will continue to unfold and revisit later generations. Given the tensions that continue to grip postcolonial France, such a critical lens might well be considered prophetic. Certainly, in any case, Daeninckx's narration of October 17 as part of a generational drama defined by hidden histories and unacknowledged complicity has had a shaping impact on the emergent canon of representations of the massacre, as both *La Seine était rouge* and *Caché* demonstrate. But, of course, the twenty years that would pass between *Meurtres* and these turn-of-the-millennium works would also produce new traumas and thus necessitate new forms of excavation and new narrative strategies. While Daeninckx's novel takes part in some of the conventions of postmemorial work—casting public history as the story of a father and son—the subject of memory it creates (Inspector Cadin) stands outside the network of intersecting individual and collective fates under investigation. Cadin's exteriority to—or, at least, distance from—the histories of the Algerian War and the Holocaust he uncovers stands in marked contrast to the central figures of *Caché* and *La Seine était rouge*, who are caught up, even if sometimes marginally, in the legacies of October 17. Together with the novel's conventional gender coding in which the male detective not only solves the case but wins the woman—the girlfriend of the victim, Bernard Thiraud, no less!—Cadin's exterior position as professional inspector marks the limits of hard-boiled memory. While the genre conventions of the hard-boiled narrative allow Daeninckx to "look awry" at the events of history—thus uncovering metonymical links of complicity in and between the Algerian War and World War II—those same conventions also serve to contain complicity through a traditionally heterosexual resolution that expels its taint outside the normative couple.[11]

Caché and the Ethics of Memory Terrorism

Michael Haneke's *Caché* (Hidden) draws on elements of *Meurtres*'s narrative structure. Like Daeninckx, Haneke builds a taut thriller in which mystery and history come together, but this time there is no outside position. Obsessed with surveillance and investigation, the film draws the position of the investigator into the crime. Haneke also seems to reverse the relationship Daeninckx establishes between foreground and background: now the events of October 17, 1961 do appear as the "hidden" history and not as the setting for another story of historical complicity. Yet, while Papon's massacre certainly was a secret in the early 1980s when Daeninckx penned his hard-boiled novel, by 2005 it had become an openly discussed theme of contemporary French history—which is not to say that its lessons, whatever they might be, had been assimilated by the state or the general public. The double reversal that marks *Caché* in relation to *Meurtres*—that it reverses the relationship between foreground and background but in a social setting that has itself been significantly transformed—suggests that, like Daeninckx's novel, Haneke's film is hiding more (or perhaps less) than it first appears.

A film structured around the return of the colonial repressed, *Caché* garnered three awards at the Cannes Film Festival in May 2005, just a few months after the passing of the controversial law that called for the teaching of the "positive aspects" of colonialism; the film opened in Paris that fall, in the immediate wake of the social unrest in the suburbs. Although clearly a timely film, *Caché* is also, in part, a film about the untimeliness of memory, about the disruptive "violence by which [memory] wants to make itself heard," to reprise Nora's terms. The story of Georges Laurent (Daniel Auteuil), a bourgeois, Parisian media intellectual terrorized by reminders of his childhood in the early 1960s, *Caché* takes part in recent reflection on the long-repressed events of October 17, 1961. In embracing the productivity of memory's violence, this French film, made by an Austrian director born in Germany during World War II, suggests the need for an ethic of remembrance attuned to situations marked by cultural difference. Organized around the impact of the return of the repressed on a bourgeois subject committed until the end to the disavowal of his complicity in late colonial violence, *Caché* also dramatizes the structure of violence, occulted knowledge, and trauma that Aimé Césaire called the *choc en retour*. Like Césaire, Haneke proves himself interested in exploring the ripple effects of late colonial brutality.

Caché's opening has quickly become famous: as the credits accumulate on the screen, a long stationary shot is trained on the exterior of a bourgeois urban home.[12] Soon we learn that we've been watching the first of what will become a series of surveillance videos sent to Georges and Anne Laurent.[13] As Libby Saxton remarks in a fine close reading of the opening, the knowledge that we are watching a video and not simply an establishing shot of a house also means that the opening shot is actually a close-up of a television screen and not a long shot of the façade.[14] This perspectival realignment, I would add, further produces a significant shift at the level of the film's narration: while the opening initially seems to be focalized through an external narrator, we come to realize that it represents the character-bound focalization of Georges. This movement from external narration to character-bound focalization allegorizes the internalization of the investigator's position that distinguishes *Caché* from *Meurtres*, where the "I" of the narrator rather establishes his exteriority to the histories at stake in the novel. The tension between external and character-bound focalization, as well as between narration and focalization, persists throughout the film and has significant implications for the film's work of memory. The effect of this opening trick is frequently remarked: it forces an identification both with those doing the surveillance and with Georges, and it puts into question the status of all further shots in the film, which now can be viewed, at least momentarily, as surveillance shots.[15] It also establishes the central mystery driving the plot—the question of who has sent the videos and why. The ultimately unresolved and apparently unresolvable question of the author/narrator of the videos suggests that an occulted realm of invisibility will persist, but the tension between focalization and narration also indicates that modes of visibility will be equally important in the film. Two modes of visibility thus emerge from the opening sequence: the invisible and inhuman position of the "hidden" camera, which interpellates viewers of the surveillance tapes, and the visible realm of the filmed/videotaped images, which harbors or "hides" ambiguous "clues" that spark investigation. Indeed, based on a reading of the film's baffling ending, *Caché*'s primary concern is with the synthesis or coexistence of these two modes: with invisible visibility, or, in other words, with that which is hidden in plain sight.

Perhaps most significant, the opening renders domesticity uncanny. Most of the surveillance shots target homes: the exteriors of the Laurent family's Paris home; the rural estate of Georges's mother; and the exterior and interior of the apartment of Majid (Maurice Bénichou), the Algerian man who, as a boy, had lived temporarily with Georges's family on the rural estate after his parents disappeared in the events of October 17, 1961. Early on, Georges realizes that the surveillance videos have something to do with Majid, and indeed they eventually lead him to the squalid apartment where the broken Majid lives. In this apartment the film's climactic scene takes place—the ambiguously motivated suicide of Majid in front of

Georges.[16] Although we know nothing of the intervening years of Majid's life, we will find out that forty years earlier the young Georges had had the recently orphaned Majid expelled from the Laurent family home shortly after he had found refuge there. This expulsion, the result of childhood jealousy and cruelty, represents the unexpiated individual crime at the center of the film's narrative, although, in the film's economy of guilt and responsibility, it also serves both to recall and displace the collective violence experienced by Majid's parents. Through association with the events of October 17, the expulsion and the adult Georges's unwillingness to take responsibility for it also appear to function as an allegory for the larger unwillingness of the French to face the crimes of the Algerian War era. Yet, as crucial as it is, the focus on October 17 in the film is contextualized within a larger comparative imaginary. This comparative recontextualization of October 17 becomes the film's challenge to viewers and the source of a potential ethics of multidirectional memory. In *Caché*, such an ethics involves undoing the viewer's identification with Georges and his gaze and translating surveillance into detection.[17]

One telling scene from the middle of the film illustrates the manner of this recontextualization. It draws the viewer's attention to multiple hidden histories in *Caché* and links them significantly to missing children and to the particular mode I have described as invisible visibility. As the anxiety produced by the menacing videos and the violent, childlike drawings that accompany them leads to the deterioration of the marriage of Georges and Anne (Juliette Binoche), their teenage son disappears. Assuming that this disappearance has something to do with the surveillance tapes, the worried parents argue about how to respond. Meanwhile, in the background of the scene a television embedded in a wall of bookshelves shows the evening news: images of the Iraq War flicker by, followed by a report on the Abu Ghraib torture trials; a portrait of the sadistic Charles Graner fills the television screen for several seconds before giving way to a report on Israeli violence in the Occupied Territories (see Figure 7). Through mise-en-scène, Haneke foregrounds framing and, especially, the interpenetration of different frames of reference. A television, surrounded by books and videotapes, framed by a movie camera: through this technique, which Haneke also uses elsewhere, the concatenation of media forms simultaneously embodies the specificity, overlap, and interference of different

FIGURE 7   Georges and Anne argue about their missing son while the television news reports on the Abu Ghraib torture scandal. Michael Haneke, *Caché* (2005). Author's collection.

histories as well as the vexed relationship between public and private space and between everyday life and extreme violence.[18]

Because of the centrality of the television in the scene, viewers are exposed to intimations of war, torture, and colonialism imported into the intimate realms of the bourgeois home, even as Georges and Anne remain oblivious to them. The double perspective fostered by the disjunction between the viewer's gaze and those of Georges and Anne splits the sutured point of view of the opening credit sequence in which the viewer's gaze is identified both with the surveillance and with Georges's simple "watching" of the video. In this later scene, viewers both see the links between particular individual and collective histories and see how the characters ignore those links. The film thus implies, as Césaire had a half-century earlier, that the condition of possibility for certain histories of imperial violence lies in a structural nonseeing on the part of bourgeois, metropolitan subjects. Via mise-en-scène, *Caché* suggests that postcolonial attempts to address unmastered colonial history find themselves perforce tied to various contemporary reassertions of empire as well as heterogeneous emanations of the past. The film also implies that that history will remain unmastered so long as it remains "unseen" and therefore outside the circuits of memory and responsibility. Furthermore, the scene helps us to understand how the memory of history's victims can come to seem "terrorist," as it does for Nora: the assertion of memory can itself appear violent or even traumatic when dominant society simply *doesn't see it coming*—when, as we've noted in our discussion of the *Discourse on Colonialism*, society lacks *Angstbereitschaft*. Through the staging of the double gaze in this scene, Haneke demonstrates, contra Nora, why ethics must turn on memory as well as history: social conflict can only be addressed through a discourse that weaves together past and present, public and private.

Hidden Children: Rereading *Caché* through the Papon Trial

But a question remains: Why stage this ethical problem around the figure of a missing child? Questions of genre and narrative link the film's form to its foregrounding of children and to the larger social context that makes children into a site of ethical comparison. *Caché* draws on the two narrative forms that are employed in *Meurtres pour mémoire* and that have appeared frequently in discussions of the October 17 massacre during the last two decades: because the events appear to have been summoned from hiding, writers, filmmakers, lawyers, and other social actors have turned frequently to *narratives of detection* and *narratives of intergenerational conflict and transgenerational transmission*.[19] Not only literary texts have approached the events through the double form of detection and transgenerational transmission; equally important have been the narratives created by social movements of second- and third-generation migrants and legal battles such as the Papon trial. Such literary and extraliterary narrative modes testify to anxieties about the transmission of memory at the familial and collective levels, and they draw attention to the failure of professional historians to uncover these particular hidden crimes. They also inevitably raise questions of comparison, since the various stories of detection tend to reveal more than one individual or collective history in the voids they uncover. *Caché*'s use of detection and intergenerational narratives remains more laconic and indirect in its comparative references than works such as those of Daeninckx or Sebbar or public spectacles such as the Papon trial. Its ethical charge lies in the pursuit of multivalent, multigenerational clues that it shares with these other texts and spectacles *and* with its rigorous refusal to produce a singular subject of memory and ethics.

A detour through the Papon trial will allow us to address the particular resonance of the child and intergenerational transmission in Haneke's film. In particular, it will allow us to offer a new reading of the film's enigmatic but crucial ending. The definitive entry of the October massacre into public memory itself occurred within the framework of another story: the 1997–98 trial of Maurice Papon for his role in the deportation of Jews to Nazi camps during World War II. It was this coming to terms with a genocidal past that gave rise to a "trial within the trial" in which Papon's responsibility for the October 1961 massacre also entered into the proceedings and thus into the public sphere. Papon's role in the deportation of approximately seventeen hundred Jews from Bordeaux had remained in the shadows until the sixteen-year process of bringing him to justice was begun in 1981 with publication of an exposé in *Le Canard enchaîné*. As the editors of the trial transcript write, the satirical Parisian newspaper "unveil[ed]" Papon's "hidden past [*le passé caché*]."[20] Ironically, it was the unveiling of this "hidden" element of a now well-known past (Vichy complicity) that allowed public discussion of a past that had been well known at the time (Papon's role in the Paris massacre) but had subsequently gone into hiding. In other words, the Papon trial became a meeting point for two "vectors of memory," as Nancy Wood might call them, that had until that point seemed to be pointing in opposite directions (with Vichy moving from hidden to visible and October 1961 moving from visible to hidden).[21]

The focal point of the October 17 subsection of the trial was the long testimony about the events leading up to, including, and surrounding the massacre by the historian Jean-Luc Einaudi, the author of *La bataille de Paris* and other relevant works. Throughout his testimony, which was given without notes (as required for all testimony in the trial), Einaudi bears witness to the multidirectional interweaving of the two histories at stake: the history of Nazi terror and Papon's complicity with it, which constituted the core of the trial, and the history of Papon's participation in the repression of Algerians in Algeria and France, the subject of Einaudi's particular testimony. For instance, Einaudi draws attention to the role of various crucial figures in both histories, including Paul Teitgen (*Le Procès* 1.235), the camp survivor whose famous resignation from his post during the Battle of Algiers is included in Delbo's *Les belles lettres*, and Edmond Michelet (1.229), a Dachau survivor who helped facilitate the publication of testimonies to torture during the Algerian War. Einaudi also points out how Papon's actions upon taking up his position as police prefect in Paris echo the recent past: "At the end of August 1958, he ordered roundups of North African workers, as he says in a communiqué. Do you know where he interned them? He interned them in the Vel' d'Hiv', which still existed, as well as in the Salle Japy, two places where Jews had been interned before being deported to Nazi extermination camps" (1.227). Besides pointing to the people and places that connect the two wars, Einaudi also ends his testimony by linking film and multidirectional memory. Referring to Jacques Panijel's clandestine film *Octobre à Paris*, commissioned by Pierre Vidal-Naquet and the other members of the Comité Maurice Audin, Einaudi clarifies that, beyond guilt and innocence, the stakes of the Papon trial are the production of a just collective memory through the unearthing of a hidden history:

This film, which speaks of the whole period of October 1961, ends with [the events at] the Charonne metro [in which nine Communist antiwar demonstrators were killed by the Parisian police]. It concludes with these words: "Are we finally going to realize that everybody is a kike [*un youpin*], that everybody is a dirty Arab [*bicot*], everybody?" This film was seized at the time of its first showing in Paris just as were magazines and books. M. Papon didn't want the truth to come out. Finally, that truth did appear. I have come here in memory of the Algerian victims, buried like dogs in a common grave reserved for unknown Muslims in the Thiais cemetery. Also, in memory of the dead of Charonne. (1.236)

As Einaudi's cinematic example and his own dedication of his testimony to the differently motivated martyrs of October 17 and Charonne indicate, the collective memory at stake in any account of October 1961 necessarily encompasses multiple histories, some of which have long been "buried" in the "common grave" of social oblivion.[22]

Einaudi's testimony was itself a dramatic event that contributed in no small measure to new interest in the still officially repressed history of October 17. So far as *Caché* is concerned, however, it is less the trial's explicit discussion of October 1961 than another of its features that is most suggestive: its staging of the discourses of *hidden children*, that is, of Jewish children given up by their parents, often to Christian families or schools, in order to shield them from the risk of deportation. As historian Annette Wieviorka has argued, the Papon trial signaled a shift in the contours of Holocaust memory:

> The Eichmann trial marked the advent of the witness. The Papon trial marked the double delegation of witnessing. The role of the witness was delegated first to the historians, who became witnesses for the prosecution, the defense, or the plaintiff. Everything there is to be said about this confusion of roles was said during the trial and in the works published immediately after the trial. But also—and this is what really interests me here—the Papon trial marked the delegation of witnessing to a new generation, that of the children who grew up during the war and for whom the memory of a traumatic past no longer resides in the recollection of particular events, about which nothing can be said, but in the irremediable shock those events created in their young lives.[23]

In the example of Einaudi we have already seen the first kind of delegation Wieviorka mentions, and in the examples of Nora and Rousso we have seen the anxiety this mixing of legal, public, and scholarly genres has produced for many disciplinary historians. Especially relevant to *Caché* is the generational translation that the trial marks, from the first-generation witnesses of the Eichmann trial to the "1.5" and second-generation witnesses of the Papon trial.[24] In earlier chapters, I have recontextualized the significance of the Eichmann trial for a history of Holocaust testimony by juxtaposing it with the contemporaneous testimonies included in Rouch and Morin's *Chronicle of a Summer* and Delbo's *Les belles lettres*. *Caché* and other October 17 texts help us to recontextualize the transformation of testimony Wieviorka describes by placing it within a larger discourse of trauma and the intergenerational transmission of memory.

Most striking for an analysis of *Caché*, the testimonies with the highest impact at the Papon trial, as Wieviorka clarifies, turn out not simply to be those of adults who had been children during the war, but those of the "hidden children [*enfants cachés*]." Among those, Esther Fogiel's testimony stands out. Fogiel had been raped and gruesomely mistreated by the family to which she was consigned by her soon-to-be-deported parents; in the mid-1960s, two decades after surviving her ordeal, Fogiel attempted suicide.[25] As Wieviorka remarks:

> Esther Fogiel is certainly an extreme case. Other children separated from their parents were fortunate to be welcomed into warmer environments. But her suffering, even her suicide attempt, are echoed to varying degrees in the experience of many who, as children, had to be hidden to escape persecution and who today are beginning to express themselves, notably in the newsletters of the hidden children associations [*associations d'enfants cachés*] that have been formed in France, the United States, Israel, Poland, and elsewhere. Esther Fogiel's testimony seems to be echoed in books such as Berthe Burko-Falcman's poignant novel, *L'enfant caché* [The hidden child]. While Holocaust survivor associations have seen their numbers dwindle drastically and worry about their future, associations of members of the second generation are flourishing. (148–49)

Besides Fogiel, other poignant testimonies by hidden children include those of Georges Gheldman, described by one trial observer as having "remained a child living in the memory of his separation from his mother," and Jacky Alisvaks, who remarked, "It's very difficult when one is a young boy and one is torn away from one's parents and forced to reconstruct a life, without knowing how."[26]

The connection between *Caché*, the Papon trial, and the discourses of hidden children help to clarify the film's penultimate scene as well as the closing credit sequence on the high school steps. Passing through the detour of the trial allows us to see how *Caché* echoes and transfigures the testimonies of Fogiel, Gheldman, Alisvaks, and other hidden children in the story of Majid, with his disappeared parents, mistreatment in refuge, and delayed suicide decades after the original trauma. Keeping in mind the discourse of hidden children that the Papon trial helped usher in, we can also read back to the final dream sequence involving Majid's separation from the Laurent family. That sequence can now be read as mediating between the violence of October 1961, the violence of World War II, and other contemporary forms of state violence. To set the context of the scene: returning home from work early after a disturbing encounter with Majid's son, who confronts Georges about Majid's suicide, Georges takes two sleeping pills—which he describes, suggestively, as *cachets* (tablets)—undresses, and lies down in his bed. The next scene is marked visually as Georges's dream of childhood, although its vividness and greater realism than some of the early such scenes also suggest the possibility that this is a remembrance. Shot from a perspective that has earlier been identified with the young Georges in one of his nightmares, we see the courtyard of the house where Georges grew up. An old-fashioned station wagon drives into the courtyard and we soon realize that we are seeing the scene in which Majid is being taken from the Laurent family after the presumed death of his parents at the hands of Papon's police. The young boy attempts to escape the couple that has come to take him to an orphanage or hospital and, even after being caught, continues to struggle against his captors and scream that he doesn't want to go. This sequence does more than provide a clue to the trauma in Majid's past—a trauma Georges remains utterly (even hyperbolically) unwilling to recognize consciously in the present. Coming at the end of the film, the scene is easily readable as the childhood of Georges and Majid, something that differentiates it from the other flashes of memory and dream that haunt Georges in the earlier parts of the film. But, at the same time, its dreamlike indeterminacy also leaves it open to further associations. Certainly, this scene of a child being snatched away from a safe domicile to be transported to a state institution echoes testimonies from the Papon trial, such as the testimonies of Jewish children separated by French police from their parents who were being deported to camps in the east. The "historical" colorization of the scene, the stone house, and the old station wagon allow this scene to reference the Vichy era as easily as 1961. Through this process of translation from trial to film, the stories of the hidden children receive further public resonance, while the more marginal events of October 17 find a socially sanctioned means of expression.

But the "free associative" quality of the dream sequence also encourages a further step. In the scene that follows and mirrors the opening, the closing credits roll as a stationary camera focuses on the steps outside what has earlier been identified as the high school of Pierrot, Georges's son. The school day has ended and streams of ethnically diverse teenagers emerge into the sun and make their way out onto the street. The camera remains absolutely stationary until the credits have finished and the screen fades to black. From its opening, the film has associated such stationary and "objective" points of view with the mysterious use of the surveillance camera. The final scene outside the school seems to suggest, hauntingly, that

FIGURE 8 Hidden children. Pierrot and Majid's son on the bottom left of the school steps. Michael Haneke, *Caché* (2005). Author's collection.

the process of surveillance will continue beyond the frame of the film.[27] Beyond that, however, the scene seems deliberately underdetermined, leaving viewers to wonder what purpose it might serve. In many theaters where *Caché* was shown, much of the audience had already left the house before this final scene reached its conclusion (at least in the three cities in the United States where I watched the film). But even for spectators with more patience, the scene remains opaque and its point unclear. Yet, while the wide-angle lens and static quality of the camera ensure a lack of particular focus in the scene, hidden within the frame is in fact an important clue to the film's meaning: the first onscreen encounter of Pierrot and Majid's son (see Figure 8). While many viewers seem to miss their presence on a first viewing, a second viewing reveals that the children are easily identifiable.[28]

The two sons have themselves played an uncertain role in the story that has just unfolded. Majid's unnamed son is one of the prime suspects for the surveillance that has menaced the Laurent family, yet he strongly asserts his innocence. His encounter with Pierrot hints at a possible complicity between the boys, representatives of the second or postmemory generation of the October 1961 events, although the nature and context of that complicity remains undeterminable, and it is difficult to tell whether the sons have met before. The apparent continuation of surveillance, meanwhile, suggests that the two boys still live within the same historical frames that have terrorized their parents, albeit in necessarily different ways.

Most significant, however, is their mode of appearance or nonappearance in this scene. Pierrot and Majid's son are both visible and invisible; they are hidden in plain sight. This mode of visibility constitutes a fundamental metaphor of the film and provides a further index of the film's participation in—and displacement of—the cultural discourse of "hidden children." The histories that *Caché* invokes are not in fact invisible, but, like the television news in the background or the two sons in the final scene, they are easily overlooked. Along with the unanswered question of who is responsible for the surveillance videos, the opaqueness of the children's easily missed encounter opens up the meaning of the film in suggestive ways. Because all readings of the encounter remain strictly and deliberately undecidable (Haneke has even withheld dialogue he claims to have written for the scene), the conclusion primarily functions as a stimulus to ethical questioning. What kind of responsible agent is the child? What kind of relationship do children have to the deeds and sufferings of their parents? What does it mean to suggest that larger social dramas of violence and retribution can be allegorized through the deeds of children and the familial inheritance of those deeds?

The opaque visibility of hidden children links *Caché* to at least two additional histories that, unlike October 1961, it does not explicitly address. The first history concerns the Papon trial and points toward the past; the second history concerns contemporary struggles and opens up questions about the future. The hidden children of the final scene and the "abduction" of Majid in the penultimate scene serve as links in a multidirectional chain connecting the Holocaust history recounted in the Papon trial, the events of October 1961, and a current ethical and political crisis. The rhetoric of "hidden children" has not remained fixed to the case of the Holocaust, although the genocide remains its primary context. It also surfaces in another contemporary French phenomenon: the organization of parents and teachers against the deportation of children belonging to undocumented migrant families. A 2006 article in *Le Monde* describes the

Réseau éducation sans frontières (Education Without Borders Network). Established in 2004, this network is committed to direct action to save children from deportation. *Le Monde* describes one of the typical participants: "Mother of three, Valérie Tranchand had never before been an activist. Two times she has taken a 'hidden child' [*enfant caché*] from the Victor Hugo High School under her wing. Civil disobedience? [She explained to her children that] 'One should respect the law, but not just any law. One can be led to disobey unjust laws.'"[29] The demand to disobey unjust laws, one of the most significant imperatives of post-Holocaust consciousness, can serve here to indicate how an ethic of comparison in which the past and present maintain a hold on each other can be translated into a political network with a practical program.

Irritating Ethics and Multidirectional Responsibility

Caché offers no explicit political agenda comparable to that of the Réseau éducation sans frontières. Rather, its ethical charge lies in the work of detection it forces on its viewers. The excessive demands for memory and justice it articulates are menacing because they promise no easy solution to questions of individual and collective responsibility. Rather, the film prompts us to scour the screen looking for clues and, simultaneously, to leave the frame of the image in search of relevant contexts. That combination of open aesthetic form and historical suggestiveness constitutes Haneke's ethical practice, and leads to a notion of fidelity whose scope is not determinable in advance. In contrast to Nora, who claims that "historians are the best situated . . . to say to all . . . what the past authorizes," Haneke uses memory as a lever to reopen questions of authority and responsibility. In *Caché*, history is an orphan and hidden children abound.

While the victimization of children haunts *Caché* and provides links to some of its hidden histories, the film and Haneke's oeuvre as a whole are equally concerned with the possibility that children can be perpetrators as well.[30] There is no sentimentality in Haneke's work; nor should the focus on Georges's childhood crime be taken as a way of minimizing or relativizing French colonial crimes. Insofar as Georges's participation in the expulsion of Majid from his familial house serves as an allegory of colonial violence, that allegory is a complex, multipart one. At a first level, Haneke's narration of the story through Georges's childhood act serves to irritate the viewer by raising the troubling question of the limits of moral responsibility and ethical agency. Much as viewers are put in the place of image-scouring detectives, we are also turned into ethical questioners invited to consider how we recognize responsible moral agents. Such questioning prompts further levels of evaluation. Rather than allowing us quickly and definitively to localize guilt in a clearly marked moral agent and thus take part in a process of blame that would facilitate distancing from responsibility and moral quandaries, *Caché* encourages a significant, although by no means infinite, expansion of ethical responsibility. For instance, it helps us to see that, however we evaluate Georges's role, the actual expulsion is in fact enacted by his parents, who, ambivalent as they may have been about the act, are nevertheless its responsible agents. The scene in which Georges visits his mother demonstrates the aftereffects of this responsibility; calm and bedridden, Georges's mother (Annie Girardot) refuses to return to the past when Georges mentions that he has had persistent dreams of Majid. Georges's mother seems to indict him for his callous act against Majid as a child via her oblique reference to Georges's knowledge of the sorry scenario, while simultaneously refusing to acknowledge or dwell upon her own implication in this history. Furthermore, the film suggests that the true crime may be not Georges's act as a child but his inability as an adult to recognize the profound effects of his actions on Majid's life, regardless of how one evaluates his responsibility as a child. In other words, his failing is one of memory and ethical imagination as much as it is of the lie he told as a boy (Georges uses the school slang "cafter" to describe this act). Reunited for the first time years later, after the appearance of the surveillance tapes, Majid rhetorically asks Georges, "What wouldn't one do to keep what one has?" His question resonates in the present as much as the past: Georges's refusal to come to terms with the past preserves his self-image as an ethical subject as much as his lie in the past preserved the ethnic sanctity of the nuclear family.

Both of these extensions of responsibility—to Georges's parents and to his adult self—turn on intergenerational as well as transgenerational links. That is, the film explores both the links of complicity between and across generations and the kinds of complicity that result from indirect forms of responsibility—precisely the forms that encompass the vast majority of citizens in any history of national shame. The film's ethically irritating casting of the story of October 1961 in terms of a childhood rivalry thus moves toward two fundamental indictments: it indicts subjects who may not in fact be legally responsible agents (because they were either "minors" or bystanders who played no active role) and it challenges notions of a statute of limitations (by opening the question of transgenerational responsibility). Such indictments maintain a fundamental distance from legal statutes and accusations; they imply ethical strictures and forms of fidelity that may exceed the law and thus more radically bring into question the state or situation they address. Furthermore, the focus on the responsibilities and victimization of children bears a lesson about the ethics of temporality: without the bond that links past and present—here embodied in the relation of the child to the adult—there can be no responsibility, no causal nexus within which to think justice. But the film also goes even further. By turning spectators into detectives confronted with an open-ended series of puzzles, *Caché* raises a series of questions that suggests, finally, that the scope of responsibility is multidirectional: Who is responsible for the surveillance videos? What is the meaning of the encounter between the two sons in the final scene? What are the limits of responsibility? How do the children in the film compare to the hidden children evoked in the trial or the young *sans papiers* who might be attending Pierrot's school? Drawing attention to "gray zones" of responsibility and complicity, these questions demand answers that exceed any linear model of causality and they complicate dualistic ethical models of self and other. When Haneke leaves the central mysteries of the film underdetermined, he allows the overdetermination of historical responsibility to come into view.[31] Georges is not the ethical subject of that multidirectional responsibility; rather, his failure to establish fidelity with the event that ruptured his childhood and much more—his failure to understand the event as a rupture, his failure even to recognize October 17 as an event—carves out in negative the space of a potential ethical subject to come.

La Place de la Concorde: Revisiting Sites of Memory in *La Seine était rouge*

Caché might be understood as conjuring the Oedipus myth in both its Sophoclean and Freudian versions. Its narrative structure follows that of the tragedy: a man is called to investigate a crime, but it turns out in the end that he may himself be the criminal he has been pursuing. Other elements of the Freudian version of the myth are scattered throughout the film: the threats (and actual acts) of violence and the intergenerational conflicts evoke the trauma of castration, while the awkward scenes between Georges and his mother, and between Pierrot and his mother, Anne, whom he suspects of infidelity, hint at unacknowledged desires. If the film plays with an Oedipal scenario, it does so without offering the kinds of resolution that both Sophocles and Freud provide. Georges's blindness comes not because he "sees" the depths of his crimes, as with the Greek tragic hero, but results rather from an interminable refusal to see (except in semi- or unconscious states). Nor is paternal authority successfully renegotiated, as in normative psychoanalysis; rather, the position of the father appears here in a terminal crisis of legitimation. Haneke does not grant the position of exteriority Daeninckx posits for the ethical subject of detection. If Haneke draws on Oedipus to suggest that no reconstruction of the white French subject is possible pending a further confrontation with questions of historical responsibility, Leïla Sebbar draws on another Sophoclean text to sketch the formation of a minority subject.[32] While, like *Meurtres* and *Caché*, Sebbar's *La Seine était rouge: Paris, octobre 1961* does take part in uncovering "hidden" histories, the novel's final appeal to the figure of Antigone also suggests the ethical imperative to cover over the dead, to reinstate the possibility of mourning.

Dedicated to the victims of the 1961 massacre, to the Comité Maurice Audin, and to a number of individuals who might be considered agents of multidirectional memory—including Daeninckx, Jean-Luc Einaudi, Elie Kagan, Jacques Panijel, and Paulette Péju—Sebbar's novel *La Seine était rouge: Paris, octobre 1961* self-consciously engages with questions of individual and collective memory. Like *Meurtres pour mémoire* and *Caché*, *La Seine était rouge* draws attention to the tense, if not broken, bonds between parents and children, and like those two works, it also explores those bonds in the name of an ethical project of remembrance. But unlike *Caché*, which only sketches sites of memory and ethical subjectivity by negation and implication, and unlike *Meurtres*, which reinstates a classic masculine subject, the hard-boiled detective, *La Seine* announces the birth of a new subject of memory, albeit one built on a figure of classical provenance and crafted at a site of dense historical traffic.[33]

The novel's mode of address, including its obviously pedagogical inspiration and its solicitation of identification with its teenage protagonist, marks it as a novel meant for an adolescent and young-adult readership, but it is by no means a simple or simplistic work. Sebbar employs a complex narrative structure and divides her relatively brief, 125-page novel into thirty-seven short chapters that bring together numerous different narrators and forms of focalization. The narrative is guided especially by the perspectives of three young characters: Amel, a sixteen-year-old *beur* girl growing up in Nanterre, and two friends in their twenties, Louis, a French filmmaker, and Omer, an Algerian journalist in exile. The book traces Amel's attempts to learn about the past from her reticent mother and grandmother, both of whom took part in the events of October 17 but continually put off Amel's request for information with the excuse that they will tell her on the "appointed day [*au jour dit*]."[34] Although Amel's mother Noria consistently rebuffs her daughter's desire for knowledge, she speaks freely to Louis, the son of a "porteuse de valise" (a French woman who provided material support to the FLN during the war), who is making a documentary film about the events. Instead of presenting the history of October 17 through direct narration or even through intergenerational transmission from mother and grandmother to daughter, the novel uses indirect means. Slightly more than one-third of the novel's chapters consist of "transcripts" from Louis's film in which Noria and a varied group of other eyewitnesses testify to their experiences on October 17 and in the days that followed. In addition, after having seen Louis's film—and receiving the story of her parents' experiences for the first time—Amel enlists Omer to join her as she traverses Paris looking for traces of the events. Revisiting sites mentioned in the film where significant events took place during the demonstrations, Amel and Omer also collect testimony of their own from Parisians whom they meet along the way.[35]

To make matters more complicated, the novel is by no means only interested in reconstructing the singular past of the police massacre, as its indirect, "inter-medial" style already suggests. Like Daeninckx, Haneke, and many others who have responded to the massacre, Sebbar clearly has her eye on a larger confluence of histories and memories. Besides providing a fragmented, but detailed, account of October 17 and its context, the novel also evokes numerous other histories, including the larger context of the Algerian War of Independence, World War II and the Holocaust, the French war in Indochina, Napoleon's invasion of Egypt, May 1968, and—perhaps most urgently—the Algerian Civil War of the 1990s. The pedagogical impetus of the narrative goes beyond even those multidirectional evocations; ultimately, it concerns itself with the very structures of collective memory. Written in the immediate wake of the 1997–98 Papon trial, the novel returns again and again to the question of memorialization as well as to the presence of particular monuments in Parisian space. From its dedication page to its surprising conclusion, *La Seine* highlights the interaction between agents and sites of memory. Indeed, despite its adolescent address, the novel might profitably be understood as a lesson for theorists of memory like Nora and Rousso, who have lately begun to recoil in front of the social force of the object of their analysis.

Sebbar's novel draws attention especially to various examples of what Nora famously termed *lieux de mémoire* (sites of memory), and it does so in ways that particularly recall World War II as well as modes of Holocaust remembrance. For Nora, the prominence of sites of memory in modernity marks the decline of a lived, collective memory passed down organically and continuously from generation to generation. As he writes in the famous introductory essay to the first volume of *Les lieux de mémoire*, "There are sites [*lieux*] of memory because there are no more environments [*milieux*] of memory."[36] While, in a sense, *La Seine* bears out Nora's claim—foregrounding the break between generations—it ultimately disposes with Nora's narrative of decline and suggests the possibility for new forms of remembrance in the interplay between sites and agents of memory. Even more clearly than *Meurtres*, *La Seine* exemplifies the structure Hirsch calls postmemory—an aesthetic she associates with children of Holocaust survivors and which she first developed in relation to *Maus*, Art Spiegelman's comic-book memoir of his survivor father. Like *Maus*, Sebbar's fictional work concerns the attempts of the second generation to reconstruct the stories of a reluctant generation of witnesses. It does so in a way that draws attention to the artificiality of that reconstruction by emphasizing the media (and mediation) of second-generation stories and by refusing to reconstruct a seamless narrative out of the mixed chronology of individual memory. Like the protagonists of many second-generation Holocaust stories, Amel and Louis perceive a significant gap between their experiences and life stories and those of their parents, which they attempt, with inevitably mixed success, to overcome.

Despite these and other similarities between *La Seine* and numerous texts of Holocaust postmemory, Sebbar also hints at significant differences between such texts. One of the most important motifs of *La Seine* is the recurrent visiting of *lieux de mémoires* by Amel, Louis, and Omer. These visits frequently result in the production of vernacular forms of countermemory, as Omer repeatedly inscribes the memory of the Algerian War alongside the official memory of state memorials. While, by the late 1990s, memory of World War II and the Nazi genocide had become widespread in French discourse and public space, the countermemories of Algerians and their descendants remain outside of the mainstream (as the gaps in Nora's monumental project attest). Thus, next to the "white marble plaque" on the Santé prison proclaiming that "in this prison on November 11, 1940 were imprisoned high school and university students who had responded to General de Gaulle's call and were among the first to stand up against the occupier," Omer spray paints in red: "1954–1962 In this prison were guillotined Algerian resistors who stood up against the French occupier" (28–29). Sebbar literalizes the partiality of official memory at the site of another memorial. At the Saint-Michel fountain, Omer's body blocks Amel's view of the inscription. Focalized through Amel, we read, "To the memory of the soldiers of the French forces of the interior and the inhabitants of the Fifth and . . . Arrondissements who on these sites . . . death in combat" (101). The incompletion of this memorial is soon supplemented by another red spray-painted message on the quai Saint-Michel: "Here Algerians fell for the independence of Algeria on October 17, 1961" (107). Inscribing memory of the Algerian War of Independence alongside official French war memory, *La Seine* does not engage in competitive memory and instead follows *Meurtres* in employing metonymical means: Omer's messages never cover over other sites, but rather take their place *alongside* them.[37]

This metonymical expansion of memory constitutes a multidirectional rhetoric that traverses *La Seine*, as can be seen in relation to a third memorial *détournement*, this time of the Place de la Concorde. The set of associations constructed around the simultaneously concrete and symbolic space of the Concorde also suggests interesting links between postmemory and multidirectional memory. In *Chronicle of a Summer*, Marceline's testimony from the midst of traffic in the Place de la Concorde peoples that chaotic, but seemingly innocent, public space with memories of deportation and humiliation. Just a year after Rouch and Morin filmed Marceline, the Concorde would become one of the sites of contemporary police violence. As Omer will write on the façade of the Hotel Crillon at Concorde, "Here Algerians were savagely beaten by prefect Papon's police on October 17, 1961" (81). Besides marking this Parisian landmark as a site of different histories of violence, Sebbar adds further metonymical and intertextual dimensions to the question of the "place" of the Concorde in public memory; she brings in modern Jewish history and the broader scope of colonialism by evoking photography (one of the key resources of postmemorial aesthetics) and a monument. Multiple—and sometimes accidental—associations render the Place de la Concorde an exemplary nexus of multidirectional memory and, ultimately, a "place" for the construction of counterdiscourses of memory and mourning.[38]

Through an ekphrastic and allusive use of photography, Sebbar evokes the Concorde as an "intersection" in a mobile network of collective memories.[39] In one of the testimonies from Louis's film, interposed immediately after Amel and Omer visit the Concorde, Amel's mother invokes a famous image: "We met Flora [Louis's mother] by accident, she told us that the Concorde was dangerous. Police were beating Algerians. The cops had machine guns. Her friend the photographer showed her photos of the Concorde metro station, a few weeks later I saw them. On the metro platform, men, Algerians, are penned in [*parqués*], hands on their heads, it's a roundup [*une rafle*], they're going to take them to the detention centers, like my father to the Palais des Sports" (79–80). Although inserted into a fictional narrative, the photograph Noria describes is easily identifiable as one of those taken by Elie Kagan, a Jewish photographer and journalist (see Figure 9).[40] Kagan, who survived the Nazi occupation in hiding, took many of the most reproduced photographs of that night and was later active in making the events of October 17 visible. In a notebook in the possession of his family, Kagan wrote a poetic text a few years after the massacre that reads Papon's brutality multidirectionally in light of the Vel' d'Hiv' roundup of Jews:

17 October 1961 [. . .]

Later they will call that hot day "Ratonnades à Paris." Arabs by the thousands, Concorde, Solférino, Rue de Lille, helmeted men. My fear, which surprises me.

October 61
July 42
October 61
July 42
Metro, cars crammed
Frenchmen, noses against the windows, indifferent,
They shoot, they kill, and then they quickly erase it. (Einaudi and Kagan 74)

Writing in the late 1960s, Kagan simultaneously captures the mood of 1961, which already read the events in relation to the Vel' d'Hiv' roundup, and draws on the experience of the aftermath of forgetting. But as his text demonstrates and as his appearance in Sebbar's novel confirms, multidirectional memory can emerge even out of the depths of oblivion.

Besides *La Seine*'s implicit reference to Kagan's Concorde photograph and his naming in the paratextual space of Sebbar's dedication, Kagan also appears in another of the testimonies included in Louis's film, this time by a French student whose Ukrainian Jewish mother tried to persuade him to stay away from the demonstration out of fear of the (to her) all-too-familiar violence that might erupt there (96). The student identifies himself as one of the small group of Frenchmen who assisted the FLN during the demonstration (and whose real-life counterparts make up some of the subjects of this book):

I was in the Solférino station that day, October 17, 1961. . . . Out of solidarity, certain people would be present. One of the orders for the [support] Network was to observe, to be a witness, not to participate directly. Photographer friends risked their lives, they took photos, Concorde, Solférino, Pont de Neuilly, Nanterre. One of them, especially, a friend of my parents, Elie Kagan, crossed Paris on his Vespa all the way to Nanterre where he knew that Algerians had been killed. I saw the photos of that tragic day. Overall, the journalists did not do their job. (95)

FIGURE 9   Elie Kagan's photograph, taken from the metro, of Algerian demonstrators attacked by police in the Concorde metro station. Courtesy of the Fonds Kagan/BDIC.

After contrasting Kagan's ethical "crossings" with mainstream journalism's failures, the student goes on to describe his own role in a scene that recapitulates one of Kagan's best-known image series: "When I arrived at Solférino, the station had been deserted. A man was sitting, all alone, on a bench, he was wounded in the head. Blood was flowing. He was dazed. I helped him. I took the metro with him" (96) (see Figure 10).[41] These references to Kagan's mobility (the mention of his Vespa is a common one in reports on October 17) and his and the student's metonymic association with traffic circles and metro stations stand as an emblem of the multidirectional traffic of memory circulating among and between the layers of Paris's urban text.[42]

In embedding references to well-known photographs—and a well-known Jewish photographer—in her narrative, Sebbar also evokes the affective power of one of the most prominent media associated with the articulation of belated postmemories. As Marianne Hirsch has been arguing for some time, photography is a privileged site for the intergenerational

Hidden Children 303

FIGURE 10 Elie Kagan's photograph of a young man assisting an Algerian demonstrator who has been bloodied by the police in the Solférino metro. Courtesy of the Fonds Kagan/BDIC.

transmission of the past: "It is the technology of photography, itself, and the belief in reference that it generates, that connects the Holocaust generation to the generation after. Photography's promise to offer an access to the event itself, and its easy assumption of iconic and symbolic power, makes it a uniquely powerful medium for the transmission of events that remain unimaginable" (107–8). Drawing on categories developed by Aleida Assmann, Hirsch argues that "postmemorial work . . . strives to *reactivate* and *reembody* more distant social/national and archival/cultural memorial structures by reinvesting them with resonant individual and collective forms of mediation and aesthetic expression" (111). Sebbar's novel, as well as the other texts explored in this chapter, follows the model Hirsch lays out here and interweaves the problematic of national and cultural memory with an intimate, familial narrative. In evoking Kagan and associating him with an immigrant Jewish milieu—not to mention activating memories of photographs that echo the roundups of Jews from twenty years earlier—Sebbar develops an approach that is both postmemorial and multidirectional.

In *La Seine*, the Place de la Concorde bears yet other levels of meaning that are significant for thinking through the articulation of postmemory with multidirectional memory. When Amel and Omer come upon the *place*, she attempts to provide him with a guided tour: "It's the Concorde, says Amel, and there is the obelisk and across there La Défense." But Omer resists Amel's neutral account of the city: "I'm not a tourist and about the obelisk, I don't give a damn. You [*Vous*] pillaged Egypt, Bonaparte the first and you are proud" (77). For Omer, the more than three-thousand-year-old obelisk is a reminder of Napoleon's campaign in Egypt and thus a metonymic sign commemorating France's "glorious" colonial past—a past into which he incorporates even the *beur* Amel—although in fact the obelisk was given to France by Mehmet Ali, the viceroy of Egypt, four decades later. Despite this anachronism, Omer's point highlights the significance of the campaign and the larger implications and longer-term legacies of the culture of imperialism. As Edward Said has written, the invasion of Egypt constituted a foundational moment for the Orientalist regime of power/knowledge: "The Napoleonic expedition, with its great collective monument of erudition, the *Description de l'Egypte*, provided a scene or setting for Orientalism, since Egypt and subsequently the other Islamic lands were viewed as the live province, the laboratory, the theater of effective Western knowledge about the Orient."[43] Omer's postcolonial gaze targets this theater of knowledge after it has been reimported to the metropole and has come to function as a point of orientation, even for subjects, like Amel, living under the continued impact of colonial legacies. Staging a confrontation with Orientalist knowledge at the site of intersecting histories—not only colonialism, the Nazi occupation, and Papon's police massacre mark the Concorde but also the revolutionary fervor of the French Revolution, which executed more than one thousand people at the very site where the obelisk now stands—Sebbar uses a metonymic, associative rhetoric to reveal the layered histories that define the inheritance of postmemory.

A final, anachronistic metonymy involving the Concorde suggests that a multidirectional and postmemorial agency can derive from the uncovering of the legacies of the past, but hints that that agency must also learn to put the past to rest. In the novel, Napoleon's campaign obsesses Louis, who, caught between the Orientalist lure of the East and his own skepticism about colonialism, would like to retrace the campaign with Amel in order to make a film.[44] In the end, Louis, Amel, and Omer meet accidentally in the famously cosmopolitan city of Alexandria—Amel having come with Omer and not, in the end, with Louis. In this brief final chapter, the two young men suggest how they would like to "narrate" Amel. While Louis wants to use her as a heroine for his film, Omer declares he will write her a play. His plot rewrites the novel we have just read as an updated version of a well-known Greek tragedy: "It's the story of a girl who digs a tomb for her brothers during the night, on a hill, she tries desperately, the ground is hard, soldiers watch over the body, the twin brothers, executed. The army has left the cadavers exposed on the square [*place*] of the village" (125). Omer's plot turns Amel into Antigone, seeking to do justice to the dead of October 17 by re-creating in memory their proper burial rites. Here, the novel insinuates an unremarked and accidental connection between Egypt, the Place de la Concorde, and the story of Antigone. While the Egyptian site of the obelisk's origins at the entrance to the Temple of Ramses II is today called Luxor, it was earlier known as Thebes. Thebes is, of course, also a different Greek city where the stories of Oedipus and Antigone unfold. Sebbar draws on this contingent chain of associations to reveal the work of both history and memory as a work of displacement. While an obelisk—and a place name—can be transported from one continent to another, thus radically altering its significance, the meaning of a stationary site itself undergoes displacement through the layering of histories that have traversed it. But none of those displacements reveals itself naturally—hence the need for an agent of remembrance and a metonymical rhetoric. Traversing Paris and ultimately the Mediterranean (although, significantly, not in the direction of Algeria!), Amel-as-Antigone serves as an agent at the level of the story and an embodiment of the text's metonymical rhetoric.

But questions remain that prove central to the particular pedagogy of postmemory in which Sebbar is engaged. Why, for instance, does Omer change the story of Antigone and leave *both* of her brothers unburied, whereas in Sophocles one brother has already received a proper burial and only the other remains forsaken? By altering the classic plot, Sebbar complicates the question of justice. In *Antigone*, the dilemma is posed starkly: "Creon will give the one / of our two brothers honor in the tomb;/ the other none."[45] As a declared enemy of the state, Polyneices cannot be buried; as the supposed upholder of the status quo, Eteocles receives a hero's funeral. Bucking the authority of the state, Antigone acts according to the higher morality of the family and justice. In *La Seine*, however, both brothers remain unburied; the task is thus marked as twice as difficult. In refusing to distinguish between the dead, Sebbar's multidirectional memory, which encompasses a range of histories and locations not linked by a historicist logic, reinforces the need for an ethics of memory that operates "beyond good and evil" (an ethics that is not in fact far from Antigone's). Emphasis on the two brothers also has an even more specific set of historical referents. Throughout the novel, attention is drawn not only to the French state's violence against Algerians on October 17, 1961, and to the longer *durée* of European colonialism and anti-Semitism, but also to a history of internecine violence that marked the struggle for Algerian independence and, by the 1990s, had emerged as a deadly truth about the postindependence Algerian state.[46] As Omer asserts to Amel, during a discussion of the Abrahamic legacy of sacrifice, a legacy he sees played out in the War of Independence and the civil war of the 1990s, "the gesture of slitting the throat is in us. Do you understand?" Although Amel refuses Omer's logic, responding that "we are not all throat cutters, I don't understand," the disturbing facts of counterviolence haunt the novel (63). Omer's "twin brothers," exposed on the village *place*, suggest the impossibility of cleanly assigning sides to the just and unjust: there are too many dead and the dead are, in fact, too closely related to each other (another echo of the larger Oedipus myth evoked here and in *Caché*).

In revisiting sites of memory, such as the Place de la Concorde, and reconfiguring monuments of cultural memory, such as *Antigone*, *La Seine était rouge* moves a step beyond *Caché* and creates the figure of an ethical subject of multidirectional memory. In Sebbar's hands, the *place* becomes the site of a "concord" of memories; that is, a site for the transformation of multiple histories of violence into a potentially peaceful future through the agency of a just and relational remembrance. "Relational" should be taken here as doubly significant: as meaning within the family, but within a family marked by historically resonant differences. The figure of Antigone, especially as recast in the novel's final scene, suggests that the violence to be overcome is internal to communities—whether the community be France or Algeria, or the united/divided, "transpolitical" space they represent together (to borrow concepts from Etienne Balibar and Paul Silverstein). The insistence on the need for an internal accounting and the placement of the agency for that accounting in the hands of Amel, a young, minoritized female subject of the postmemory generation, also distinguishes *La Seine* from *Meurtres*, where the subject of memory and investigation remains outside the complicity he uncovers, even if he remains henceforth attuned to the peeling layers of history that surround him.

Burying the Untombed Dead: The Ends of Multidirectional Memory

The turn to *Antigone* on the final page of Sebbar's novel raises a second question that bears implications for all of the texts under consideration here and indeed for the theorization of multidirectional memory in general. How do we understand the fact that, while so much of the discourse on October 17—including all of the texts explored here—has been about uncovering the hidden past, Sophocles's play involves the attempt to cover over the dead through a proper burial? Or, to reprise the terms with which we began, how does Sophocles's insistence on the law of burial correspond to the insistence of Pierre Nora and other historians that the discourse of memory has become so excessive that it threatens historical understanding and even poses a "terrorist" threat to society's coherence?

Antigone's description of the injustice she seeks to right has particular resonance, and poses a particular challenge, for the themes of this chapter:

Eteocles, with just entreatment treated,
as law provides [Creon] has hidden under earth
to have full honor with the dead below.

> But Polyneices' corpse who died in pain,
> they say [Creon] has proclaimed to the whole town
> that none may bury him and none bewail,
> but leave him unwept, untombed, a rich sweet sight
> for the hungry birds' beholding. (182)

Antigone—and the use made of it by Sebbar—bears a double lesson for the contemporary memory wars. First, the play insists that not only can the remembrance of the dead appear as terrorist, but that in certain circumstances it must assume a terrorizing position. As Sophocles and Sebbar clarify, it is the state that produces the dynamics of terror by refusing to recognize all of the dead. When the state instrumentalizes the law of mourning, claims of justice must emerge from "outlaw" agents of memory and postmemory. But, *Antigone* also insists and Sebbar implicitly confirms, the end of remembrance is the "just entreatment" of mourning. The outcome of fidelity to the catastrophic event, as Badiou's ethics also suggests, ought to be the transformation of the situation that served as the incubator of that catastrophe. When the catastrophes are multiple, as they so often are, the task becomes more difficult, but no less urgent. Pointing to the multidirectional legacies that intersect with and cluster around the massacre of October 17, 1961, Daeninckx, Haneke, and Sebbar seek not the endless uncovering of more and more layers of history, but an engagement with the fundamental situations that produce violence. By probing the uncomfortable overlap and complicities that mark histories of genocide and colonialism, they leave open the possibility of building new places of concord.

Epilogue: Multidirectional
Memory in an Age of
Occupations

Multidirectional Memory has sought to accomplish two central tasks: to renarrate important dimensions of post–World War II intellectual, cultural, and political history by revealing how coming to terms with the Nazi genocide of European Jews has always been intertwined with ongoing processes of decolonization; and to extrapolate the theoretical consequences of that newly understood intertwining for thinking about public memory and group identity. Toward those ends, the book has been both retrospective and forward-looking and has combined a revisionary gaze on the past with an optimistic sense of possibilities for the future.

Central to the possibilities I have sought to reveal and recommend has been the model of multidirectional memory, a model based on recognition of the productive interplay of disparate acts of remembrance and developed in contrast to an understanding of memory as involved in a competition over scarce public resources. The competitive model takes the scarcity of civic space—what I briefly evoked as "the real-estate development" model in my introductory discussion of Walter Benn Michaels—as the basis for its understanding of public memory. Thus, the Mall in Washington, DC becomes a staging ground for a zero-sum conflict over the relative presence of memory of slavery and the Holocaust in a highly nationalized context. The polemical thrust of my argument has been to reject the reductionism of the nation-centered, real-estate development model in favor of a more open-ended sense of the possibilities of memory and countermemory that might allow the "revisiting" and rewriting of hegemonic sites of memory.

Yet, if the contest of memories cannot be reduced to a battle over real estate, that does not mean that real estate and all it implies about symbolic, political, and economic power do not matter. Indeed, the possession of real estate can be one of the stakes in the contest of memories, as many of the most persistent political struggles around the globe attest. This project has already ventured far afield, but there are naturally many important areas I have not been able to address where overlapping legacies demand—and also might challenge—the multidirectional approach I have developed here. In the struggles of indigenous peoples around the world and in the Israeli-Palestinian conflict, to take two of the most obvious cases, conflicts of memory converge with contests over territory. There are no easy answers to political dilemmas such as these, but the solutions that are possible may well benefit from visions of solidarity such as the ones *Multidirectional Memory* makes visible. The rethinking of memory proposed here may not be able equally to address all dimensions of justice—particularly those that concern the redistribution of material resources—but it can contribute especially to rethinking questions of recognition and representation. As Nancy Fraser's work on "framing" justice suggests, questions about recognition and representation are crucial for establishing and contesting *what* form justice will take, *who* gets to count as a subject of justice, and *how* or under what jurisdiction justice will be adjudicated.[1]

For a scholar based in the United States, these difficult questions of what Fraser calls "abnormal justice" emerge especially when the claims of American Indians and the legacies of indigenous genocide are taken seriously because such claims and legacies break the frame of the nation-state and call for recognition of the United States's ongoing colonialist status.[2] As Jodi Byrd writes about confrontations with the past in the contemporary United States, "while twentieth-century genocides external to the American continent are avowed, those genocides intrinsic to American economic and territorial expansion—slavery and the removal and 'reservation' of American Indians—remain an essential abjection at the heart of

American identities."³ There can be no doubt that it has thus been "easier" (relatively speaking) for Americans to confront genocides elsewhere than to confront continuing dispossession of Indians—precisely because "real estate" is one of the factors involved—but it remains the case that memory's multidirectionality provides a critical resource, as Byrd also recognizes, for contesting that unequal distribution of attention. Byrd's nuanced discussion of the "competing discourses" on genocide that continue to circulate around American Indians balances the tense demands that arise when divergent memories converge (328). She simultaneously highlights the inevitability of comparison, the risk of comparison turning into equation, the ways that competitive models end up pitting "survivors against each other while reifying the oppressors' innocence and control," and the continued need to excavate and confront the legacies of Manifest Destiny (313).⁴ A multidirectional model helps keep all of these incommensurable risks and opportunities within the frame of justice. Confrontation with traumatic histories demands nothing less.

Just as it is important for scholars in the United States and other settler colonies to acknowledge the force of indigenous claims, it is also crucial for scholars of the Holocaust to acknowledge the ways their topic intersects with another ongoing conflict. Israel's occupation of Palestinian land has produced some of the most obvious—and often invidious—analogizing of the Nazi genocide in relation to political struggle. In this context, the Holocaust's invocation tends to take the form of a ritual trading of threats and insults. A typical—and relatively minor—exchange took place in February 2008 between Israeli and Palestinian spokespeople. After an Israeli defense official warned Palestinians that they would be subject to a "shoah" (disaster or Holocaust) if they continued firing rockets from the Gaza Strip into Israel, a Hamas official answered that Palestinians were faced with "new Nazis."⁵ Here we see in condensed form the typically spiraling logic of memory production and the tendency of "enemies" to share a language of suffering and retribution.

Frequently in the Israeli/Palestinian context the interlocked archives of genocide and colonialism explored in this book emerge with striking salience. Consider the strange story of the Israeli historian Benny Morris. In books such as *The Birth of the Palestinian Refugee Problem*, Morris has joined other contemporary critical historians in rewriting the myth of innocence that has accompanied narration of the founding of the State of Israel. But, while he used to be known as one of the most prominent "post-Zionist" scholars, in the last few years he has turned dramatically away from that appellation, publishing provocative defenses of Israel and condemnations of the Palestinians. Even as he has continued to uncover information about war crimes and crimes against humanity committed in 1948 by the Haganah, the precursor of the Israel Defense Forces, Morris has come to justify the "transferist" policy that he says originated with Israel's founding prime minister David Ben-Gurion. In an instantly infamous 2004 interview with the Israeli newspaper *Ha'aretz*, Morris claims:

Ben-Gurion was right.... Without the uprooting of the Palestinians, a Jewish state would not have arisen here.... There are circumstances in history that justify ethnic cleansing. I know that this term is completely negative in the discourse of the 21st century, but when the choice is between ethnic cleansing and genocide—the annihilation of your people—I prefer ethnic cleansing.... Even the great American democracy could not have been created without the annihilation of the Indians.[6]

Reflecting on contemporary politics, Morris suggests that "a cage has to be built for" the Palestinians, because "there is a wild animal there that has to be locked up" (Shavit). In a later reply to the outrage that followed these statements, Morris clarifies that his mention of the "cage" and of the genocide of Native Americans was a "slip" and that he does not currently support expulsions of Palestinians from Israel or the occupied territories. However, he still speculates in his more considered reply that "if in the future [Arabs from the territories or from the State of Israel] were to launch a massive violence against the State of Israel in combination with a broad assault on Israel by its neighbors, and endanger its survival, expulsions would certainly be in the cards."[7]

In his provocative interviews and writings of the post–9/11, post–Second Intifada, Iraq War era, Morris jumbles together extreme historical and contemporary violence, primitivist myths, and paranoid, apocalyptic fantasies. In addition, his discourse undergoes rapid shifts in perspective between the positions of victim, perpetrator, and bystander. The backdrop against which these shifts take place, however, is a consistent worldview: that of colonialism. Indeed, his discourse echoes the temporality and tropes Césaire identified as central to colonial discourse in 1950. Morris explicitly locates Israeli society and "the West" within a long history of colonial rule, and identifies in particular with those moments and figures of colonial history in decline: "the Roman Empire of the fourth, fifth, and sixth centuries," when "they let the barbarians in and they toppled the empire from within"; the Crusaders, who were the "vulnerable branch of Europe"; and the *pied noir* Albert Camus on the Algerian question— "he placed his mother ahead of morality. Preserving my people is more important than universal moral concepts" (Shavit). Situating himself and the fate of his country at such historical hinge points allows Morris to negotiate his ambivalent position as a revisionist historian (in the good sense), on the one hand, and an apologist for "ethnic cleansing" and political violence, on the other. To be sure, Morris speaks and writes from a context suffused with violence—that of the occupation as well as that of the suicide bombers. But the presence of contemporary violence alone cannot explain the phantasmatic excess of the discourse.

The category of multidirectional memory allows us to begin to approach the simultaneously political and psychic nature of the excess in such discourses because it insists that we take seriously the crosscutting nature of public memories. While memory wars such as those that continue to roil the Middle East can provoke despair at the reduction of politics to crude stereotypes and name calling, the uncomfortable proximity of memories is also the cauldron out of which new visions of solidarity and justice must emerge. Thus, crucially, even as Morris propounds a politics of separation, his own language betrays the mutual implication of histories and the complicities that colonial and genocidal violence inevitably create.[8] The unspeakable acknowledgment that "enemy" peoples share a common, if unequal, history is the utopian moment underlying the ideology of competitive victimization.

I draw two corollaries from the kinds of memory conflicts emblematized by the Israeli/Palestinian dispute. First, we cannot stem the structural multidirectionality of memory. Even if it were desirable—as it sometimes seems to be—to maintain a wall, or *cordon sanitaire,* between different histories, it is not possible to do so. Memories are mobile; histories are implicated in each other. Thus, finally, understanding political conflict entails understanding the interlacing of memories in the force field of public space. The only way forward is through their entanglement.

Notes

CHAPTER I

1. Walter Benn Michaels, "Plots Against America: Neoliberalism and Antiracism," *American Literary History* (summer 2006): 288–302; here 289–90. See also my response in "Against Zero-Sum Logic: A Response to Walter Benn Michaels," *American Literary History* (summer 2006): 303–11. Michaels's passage can be found in almost identical form in *The Trouble with Diversity: How We Learned to Love Identity and Ignore Inequality* (New York: Metropolitan, 2006), 55–56. Michaels makes some related points about the Holocaust, memory, and identity in his previous book *The Shape of the Signifier: 1967 to the End of History* (Princeton, NJ: Princeton University Press, 2004).

2. For a critical account of the memory boom, see Kerwin Lee Klein, "On the Emergence of *Memory* in Historical Discourse," *Representations* 69 (2000): 127–50. An earlier version of a related argument can be found in Charles Maier, "A Surfeit of Memory?" *History and Memory* 5, no. 2 (1993): 136–51. For sophisticated theoretical and cultural-historical discussion of the emergence of memory on a global scale and in relation to temporal, technological, and political change, see Andreas Huyssen, *Present Pasts: Urban Palimpsests and the Politics of Memory* (Stanford, CA: Stanford University Press, 2003). An excellent survey of recent work on memory, with an emphasis on sociology, can be found in Jeffrey K. Olick and Joyce Robbins, "Social Memory Studies: From 'Collective Memory' to the Historical Sociology of Mnemonic Practices," *Annual Review of Sociology* 24 (1998): 105–40. With the exception of Huyssen, none of these writings considers the kinds of intersecting, cross-ethnic, and transnational memories at stake in my study. Marita Sturken has explored the entanglement and negotiation of different memories, albeit within a national frame, in *Tangled Memories: The Vietnam War, the AIDS Epidemic, and the Politics of Remembering* (Berkeley: University of California Press, 1997). Memory is itself a historical category and does not remain stable over time. This book seeks to contribute to the theorization and historicization of memory in the late twentieth and early twenty-first centuries and thus engages primarily with work on modern memory practices. Important work on earlier periods includes Frances Yates, *The Art of Memory* (London: Routledge and

Kegan Paul, 1966); and Mary Carruthers, *The Book of Memory: A Study of Memory in Medieval Culture* (New York: Cambridge University Press, 1990).

3. See Richard Terdiman, *Present Past: Modernity and the Memory Crisis* (Ithaca, NY: Cornell University Press, 1993). In understanding memory as a form of working through, I am indebted especially to Dominick LaCapra's writings on trauma and Holocaust memory. Among other works, see his *History and Memory After Auschwitz* (Ithaca, NY: Cornell University Press, 1998). On remembrance as a form of social practice in the equally relevant contexts of Jewish studies and colonial/postcolonial studies, see, respectively, Jonathan Boyarin, *Storm from Paradise: The Politics of Jewish Memory* (Minneapolis: University of Minnesota Press, 1992); and Jennifer Cole, *Forget Colonialism? Sacrifice and the Art of Memory in Madagascar* (Berkeley: University of California Press, 2001).

4. Alon Confino and Peter Fritzsche, "Introduction: Noises of the Past," in *The Work of Memory: New Directions in the Study of German Society and Culture*, ed. A. Confino and P. Fritzsche (Urbana: University of Illinois Press, 2002), 5. Relatedly, Olick and Robbins clarify that collective memory is not a "thing," but rather comprises "distinct sets of mnemonic practices in various social sites" (112). Taking advantage of the semantic resources of the French language, Philippe Mesnard refers, in a work too little known in the English-speaking world, to "consciences de la Shoah." He thus suggests replacing the concept of memory with a phrase that combines the notions of "consciousness" and "conscience." See Philippe Mesnard, *Consciences de la Shoah: Critique des discours et des représentations* (Paris: Kimé, 2000).

5. For an exemplary and nuanced study that also knits together history, biography, and representation, see Susan Suleiman, *Crises of Memory and the Second World War* (Cambridge, MA: Harvard University Press, 2006).

6. For the belated emergence of Holocaust memory in different national contexts, see Peter Novick, *The Holocaust in American Life* (Boston: Houghton Mifflin, 1999); Tom Segev, *The Seventh Million: The Israelis and the Holocaust* (New York: Hill and Wang, 1993); and Annette Wieviorka, *The Era of the Witness*, trans. Jared Stark (Ithaca, NY: Cornell University Press, 2006). For the presence of Holocaust consciousness in the "third world," see William Miles, "Third World View of the Holocaust," *Journal of Genocide Research* 6, no. 3 (2004): 371–93.

7. On the globalization of Holocaust memory, see Huyssen, *Present Pasts*, especially his comments on the "globalization paradox" (13–14); and Daniel Levy and Natan Sznaider, *Holocaust and Memory in the Global Age*, trans. Assenka Oksiloff (Philadelphia, PA: Temple University Press, 2005). I return to Levy and Sznaider, as well as to the important work of Jeffrey Alexander on cultural trauma—*The Meanings of Social Life: A Cultural Sociology* (New York: Oxford University Press, 2003)—in Chapter 8.

8. In considering this era and this conjunction of histories, the work of scholars in postcolonial and African diaspora studies is essential. Both of these (already quite heterogeneous) fields have enormous literatures, and I mention only a few key texts here. Paul Gilroy's writings have been a particular inspiration. See especially his *The Black Atlantic: Modernity and Double Consciousness* (Cambridge, MA: Harvard University Press, 1993); and his *Against Race: Imagining Political Culture Beyond the Color Line* (Cambridge, MA: Belknap/Harvard University Press, 2002). Brent Hayes Edwards has continued and refined scholarship on diaspora. See *The Practice of Diaspora: Literature, Translation, and the Rise of Black Internationalism* (Cambridge, MA: Harvard University Press, 2003). For an excellent overview of colonial and postcolonial discourses, see Ania Loomba, *Colonialism/Postcolonialism*, 2d ed. (New York: Routledge, 2005). Robert Young's *Postcolonialism: An Historical Introduction* (Oxford, Eng.: Blackwell, 2001) provides a useful historical account of anticolonial writings and movements.

9. Elie Wiesel, *Against Silence: The Voice and Vision of Elie Wiesel*, ed. Irving Abrahamson (New York: Holocaust Library, 1985), 158. Claude Lanzmann, "The Obscenity of Understanding: An Evening with Claude Lanzmann," in *Trauma: Explorations in Memory*, ed. Cathy Caruth (Baltimore, MD: Johns Hopkins University Press), 206.

10. Steven T. Katz, "The Uniqueness of the Holocaust: The Historical Dimension," in *Is the Holocaust Unique?: Perspectives on Comparative Genocide*, 2d ed., ed. Alan S. Rosenbaum (Boulder, CO: Westview Press, 2001), 49–50.

11. The debate about uniqueness has generated an enormous amount of scholarly and polemical literature. On the side of uniqueness, some of the key figures are Yehuda Bauer, Katz, and Wiesel. Those who have challenged the claims of uniqueness include Ward Churchill, Ian Hancock, and David Stannard. For some representative contributions to this debate, see Rosenbaum, *Is the Holocaust Unique?*

12. Deborah Lipstadt, *Denying the Holocaust: The Growing Assault on Truth and Memory* (New York: Plume, 1994), 215.

13. Richard Golsan, *Vichy's Afterlife: History and Counterhistory in Postwar France* (Lincoln: University of Nebraska Press, 2000), 20–21.

14. Edward T. Linenthal, *Preserving Memory: The Struggle to Create America's Holocaust Museum* (New York: Viking, 1995), 267. Linenthal, who certainly recognizes the specificity of the Nazi genocide, does not, like some, argue that Holocaust memory functions only as a "screen memory," but rather provides a useful typology of different modes of memory.

15. David E. Stannard, "Uniqueness as Denial: The Politics of Genocide Scholarship," in *Is the Holocaust Unique?* ed. Alan S. Rosenbaum, 2d ed. (Boulder, CO: Westview Press, 2001), 250.

16. Samantha Power, *"A Problem from Hell": America and the Age of Genocide* (New York: Perennial, 2003), 503. As Dirk Moses points out, Power's study is also symptomatic of the phenomenon it describes, insofar as it refuses to recognize the possibility of the United States as a perpetrator of genocide and not simply a bystander. See A. Dirk Moses, "Conceptual Blockages and Definitional Dilemmas in the 'Racial Century': Genocides of Indigenous Peoples and the Holocaust," *Patterns of Prejudice* 36, no. 4 (2002): 7–35.

17. Fredric Jameson, *Postmodernism, or, The Cultural Logic of Late Capitalism* (Durham, NC: Duke University Press, 1991), xii–xiii.

18. For a succinct articulation of the relations between memory, narrative, and representation, see Mieke Bal's introduction to M. Bal, Jonathan Crewe, and Leo Spitzer, eds., *Acts of Memory: Cultural Recall in the Present* (Hanover, NH: Dartmouth College Press, 1998).

19. Michel Foucault, *The History of Sexuality: Volume 1: An Introduction*, trans. Robert Hurley (New York: Vintage, 1980), 12.

20. In a useful discussion of uniqueness discourse and questions of historical comparison, Moses makes a similar point; his focus, however, is not explicitly on questions of memory. See Moses, "Conceptual Blockages." See also Dan Stone, "The Historiography of Genocide: Beyond 'Uniqueness and Ethnic Competition,'" *History, Memory, and Mass Atrocity: Essays on the Holocaust and Genocide* (London: Vallentine Mitchell, 2006), 236–51.

21. James Young develops this point about the metaphorical charge of the Holocaust in his still extremely useful *Writing and Rewriting the Holocaust*. See James E. Young, *Writing and Rewriting the Holocaust: Narrative and the Consequences of Interpretation* (Bloomington: Indiana University Press, 1988). See also his excellent study of Holocaust memorialization, *The Texture of Memory: Holocaust Memorials and Meaning* (New Haven, CT: Yale University Press, 1994).

22. Miriam Hansen, "*Schindler's List* Is Not *Shoah*: The Second Commandment, Popular Modernism, and Public Memory," *Critical Inquiry* 22, no. 2 (1996): 13. Andreas Huyssen has made a similar claim: "The universalized 'never again' command and with it the instrumentalization of memory for political purposes have become a veil covering ongoing atrocities in our present world. The Holocaust is a screen memory." See Huyssen, "Trauma and Memory: A New Imaginary of Temporality," in *World Memory: Personal Trajectories in Global Time*, ed. Jill Bennett and Rosanne Kennedy (New York: Palgrave Macmillan, 2003), 19. My interest in thinking about competitive memory in relation to screen memory was first spurred by Gary Weissman. See his essential work on the contemporary American fascination with the Holocaust, *Fantasies of Witnessing: Postwar Efforts to Experience the Holocaust* (Ithaca, NY: Cornell University Press, 2004). For an excellent discussion of why screen memory is an inadequate frame for thinking about the Holocaust in relationship to aboriginal history in Australia, see Neil

Levi, "'No Sensible Comparison'?: The Place of the Holocaust in Australia's History Wars," *History and Memory* 19, no. 1 (2007): 124–56.

23. In the opening chapter of *Civilization and Its Discontents*, Freud attempts to find a metaphor for the preservative capacities of the mind. He evokes the famous image of Rome, with its layers of history preserved in ruins, but then goes on to remark that "destructive influences" analogous to trauma render the city a place of forgetting as much as a site of memory. Even barring such individual or collective traumas, we may not be as optimistic as Freud that in social life, as in mental life, "nothing which has once been formed can perish—that everything is somehow preserved and that in suitable circumstances . . . it can once more be brought to light." Yet, *Multidirectional Memory* takes inspiration from Freud in arguing that much more can be—and always is being—brought back to light than competitive models of memory suppose. See Sigmund Freud, *Civilization and Its Discontents*, trans. James Strachey (New York: W. W. Norton, 1962), 17–19.

24. For an extensive account of Freud's theories of memory that has influenced my own, see Terdiman's *Present Past*.

25. Sigmund Freud, "Screen Memories," *The Uncanny*, trans. David McLintock (New York: Penguin, 2003), 5–6.

26. R. Clifton Spargo makes this point eloquently in describing the approach to history of the contemporary trauma theory associated with Cathy Caruth and inspired by Freud: "What trauma theory proposes as a new mode of historiography is a forgetfulness full of memory, finding in our most basic structures of avoiding knowledge residues of history as trauma and in that sense also the implicit imperatives for subsequent acts of remembrance." See R. Clifton Spargo, *Vigilant Memory: Emmanuel Levinas, the Holocaust, and the Unjust Death* (Baltimore, MD: Johns Hopkins University Press, 2006), 257. Spargo's rich and challenging book also engages critically but appreciatively with Walter Benn Michaels and puts forward a concept of the "memory of injustice" that complements my concept of multidirectional memory.

27. Sigmund Freud, *The Psychopathology of Everyday Life*, trans. Anthea Bell (New York: Penguin, 2003), 45–46.

28. Hugh Haughton, "Introduction," in Freud, *Uncanny*, xix.

29. In an important study of West German Holocaust historiography, Nicolas Berg describes how discussion of the Holocaust in Germany (and elsewhere) has fluctuated between fears of "too much" and "too little" memory. Berg's decoding of these fears and his argument that there can be no perfect balance or just amount of Holocaust memory accord well with this study of multidirectional memory. Although I am more concerned with the "qualities" of memory than its "quantities," my understanding of memory as an associative process not easily contained by identity politics, instrumentalization, or zero-sum logics parallels Berg's account of memory's fluctuation, although I explore significantly different terrain. See Ni-

colas Berg, *Der Holocaust und die westdeutschen Historiker: Erforschung und Erinnerung* (Göttingen: Wallstein, 2003).

30. See, for example, Maurice Halbwachs, *On Collective Memory*, trans. Lewis A. Coser (Chicago: University of Chicago Press, 1992).

31. Avishai Margalit, *The Ethics of Memory* (Cambridge, MA: Harvard University Press, 2002), 51–52.

32. It is important to note that from the very moment that the postwar era began, World War II and Algerian struggles for independence have been linked. On May 8, 1945, a demonstration in the Algerian city of Sétif took place to mark the end of the war and call for decolonization. After several dozen *pied noirs* were killed in ensuing violence, the French army took part in reprisals that included the massacre of thousands (if not tens of thousands) of Algerians. At least in the formerly colonized world, the massacre has forever soldered together the liberation of Europe from fascism and the reluctance of that liberated Europe to let go of its own forms of extreme violence. On the Sétif massacre, see Yves Benot, *Massacres coloniaux: 1944–1950: La IVe République et la mise au pas des colonies françaises* (Paris: La Découverte, 2001 [1994]).

The recent historical echoes that have reawakened interest in Algeria and the Algerian War have also stirred the interest of other critics. For two different approaches that track Algeria's resonance for critical theory today, especially with respect to violence, justice, and torture, see David Carroll, *Albert Camus the Algerian: Colonialism, Terrorism, Justice* (New York: Columbia University Press, 2007); and Ranjana Khanna, *Algeria Cuts: Women and Representation, 1830 to the Present* (Stanford, CA: Stanford University Press, 2008).

33. Of course, comparison can—and often does—take competitive forms. Such forms show up with especially great frequency when questions of colonialism and "civilization" are at stake. A classic critique of such colonial comparisons can be found in Johannes Fabian, *Time and the Other* (New York: Columbia University Press, 1983). More recently, see Natalie Melas, *All the Difference in the World: Postcoloniality and the Ends of Comparison* (Stanford, CA: Stanford University Press, 2006). Harry Harootunian, who draws on Fabian, details other pitfalls of comparison, especially during the cold war and in relation to capitalist imperialism, in "Some Thoughts on Comparability and the Space-Time Problem," *boundary 2* 32, no. 2 (2005): 23–52. Harootunian argues that many contemporary approaches to comparison end up reifying time as space and proposes the importance of thinking the relationality of space-time along the lines of Bakhtin's chronotope, Henri Lefebvre's critique of everyday life, and Ernst Bloch's concept of nonsynchronicity. My concept of multidirectionality is also meant to draw attention to the inseparability of space and time in acts of remembrance—indeed to the interaction of multiple, nonsynchronous spaces and times. While my account

of multidirectionality acknowledges the potential for competitive comparisons, it seeks to unlock such competitive moments when they arise.

34. For a related view of comparison, with an emphasis on incommensurability, see Melas, *All the Difference in the World*. Emily Apter's *The Translation Zone: A New Comparative Literature* (Princeton, NJ: Princeton University Press, 2006) also offers a stimulating rethinking of comparative method. My interest in intraminority exchange overlaps with that of the contributors to Françoise Lionnet and Shu-mei Shih, eds., *Minor Transnationalism* (Durham, NC: Duke University Press, 2005). This book's methodology should also make clear my sympathy with Wai Chee Dimock's argument that national literatures need to be read "through other continents" and in relation to nonlinear temporalities, although I'm even less inclined than she is to hold onto adjectives such as "American." See *Through Other Continents: American Literature Across Deep Time* (Princeton, NJ: Princeton University Press, 2006).

35. Nancy Fraser, "Reframing Justice in a Globalizing World," *New Left Review* 36 (November–December 2005): 69–88.

36. The question of economic redistribution exceeds the "frame" of this book (which in no way should be taken as a judgment about the crucial nature of such a question). While matters of economic distribution may well involve zero-sum logics, questions of culture and politics work differently. More work needs to be done in coordinating the claims of these different realms.

37. Other accounts of justice I have found useful include Wai Chee Dimock, *Residues of Justice: Literature, Law, Philosophy* (Berkeley: University of California Press, 1996); and Iris Marion Young, *Justice and the Politics of Difference* (Princeton, NJ: Princeton University Press, 1990).

38. I return to Badiou and ethics in Chapter 9. See Alain Badiou, *Ethics: An Essay on the Understanding of Evil* (New York: Verso, 2002). See also my review of this book in *Critique* 43, no. 4 (2001): 478–84.

39. For a fascinating and timely discussion of how debates about Jewishness in Enlightenment Europe echo in the dilemmas of postcolonial societies such as India, see Aamir Mufti, *Enlightenment in the Colony: The Jewish Question and the Crisis of Postcolonial Culture* (Princeton, NJ: Princeton University Press, 2007).

40. Marianne Hirsch's concept of postmemory—a structure of generational memory that primarily describes the experiences of children of survivors of traumatic events—plays an important role in this final chapter. See her book *Family Frames: Photography, Narrative, and Postmemory* (Cambridge, MA: Harvard University Press, 1997), as well as the many essays on postmemory she has written since then.

I describe the figure of the child as an uneasy site of memory because I am aware of the dangers in the investment in such a figure. Queer theorists, including especially Lauren Berlant and Lee Edelman, have convincingly drawn attention to the potential of the figure of the child to reinstall sentimental normativity. While this risk remains significant, I would argue that the texts considered here emerge out of familial and cultural disruptions that they refuse to "normativize" through fetishistic disavowal. In these texts, in other words, the child marks a site of failed transmission and resistance to normativity. See Lauren Berlant, *The Queen of American Goes to Washington City: Essays on Sex and Citizenship* (Durham, NC: Duke University Press, 1997); and Lee Edelman, *No Future: Queer Theory and the Death Drive* (Durham, NC: Duke University Press, 2004).

41. On the "touching tales" that connect Turkish migrants in Germany to Jewish and other histories, see Leslie A. Adelson's rigorously argued book, *The Turkish Turn in Contemporary German Literature: Toward a New Critical Grammar of Migration* (New York: Palgrave MacMillan, 2005).

42. It is often mentioned that Bush and other administration and military personnel have been reading Alistair Horne's history of the Algerian War, *A Savage War of Peace: Algeria, 1954–1962* (New York: Viking, 1977). See, for instance, the extended discussion of analogies between Iraq and Algeria in Thomas Ricks's review of the reissuing of Horne's book: "Aftershocks: A Classic on France's Losing Fight with Arab Rebels Contains Troubling Echoes of Iraq Today," *Washington Post Book World*, November 19, 2006, T5. See also Ricks's surreal account of a seminar on the Algerian War at the Marine Corps' School of Advanced Warfighting: "SAW 7202–06: 'The French Army at War in Algeria, 1954–1962,'" *Washington Post*, April 28, 2006, A17.

CHAPTER 2

1. See the informative obituary by the English art historian Sarah Wilson in *The Independent*, September 18, 1998.

2. Kristin Ross, *Fast Cars, Clean Bodies: Decolonization and the Reordering of French Culture* (Cambridge, MA: MIT Press, 1996).

3. Kristin Ross, *May '68 and Its Afterlives* (Chicago: University of Chicago Press, 2002).

4. See the excellent standard biography: Elizabeth Young-Bruehl, *Hannah Arendt: For Love of the World*, 2d ed. (New Haven, CT: Yale University Press, 2004). See also the helpful chronology in Dana Villa, ed., *The Cambridge Companion to Hannah Arendt* (New York: Cambridge University Press, 2000).

5. In the last thirty years, the reception of Arendt's work has taken a number of interesting turns that make her oeuvre ever-more relevant to the project of decolonizing Holocaust memory. Starting with Ron H. Feldman's 1978 collection of Arendt's Jewish essays, *The Jew as Pariah*, and Elizabeth Young-Bruehl's 1982 biography, *Hannah Arendt: For Love of the World*, a new appreciation of the importance of Jewish history and politics entered into studies of Arendt's work. This work cul-

minated in the 1990s with critical studies by Dagmar Barnouw, Seyla Benhabib, and Richard J. Bernstein. At the same time, and from a slightly different angle, Margaret Canovan's illuminating 1992 study, *Hannah Arendt: A Reinterpretation of Her Political Thought*, produced a new vision of the centrality of *The Origins of Totalitarianism* to Arendt's political vision and significantly advanced understanding of Arendt's concept of totalitarianism, which had been buried for too long under cold war misunderstandings. See Hannah Arendt, *The Jew as Pariah: Jewish Identity and Politics in the Modern Age*, ed. Ron H. Feldman (New York: Grove Press, 1978); Dagmar Barnouw, *Visible Spaces: Hannah Arendt and the German-Jewish Experience* (Baltimore, MD: Johns Hopkins University Press, 1990); Seyla Benhabib, *The Reluctant Modernism of Hannah Arendt* (Thousand Oaks, CA: Sage, 1996); Richard J. Bernstein, *Hannah Arendt and the Jewish Question* (Cambridge, MA: MIT Press, 1996); Margaret Canovan, *Hannah Arendt: A Reinterpretation of Her Political Thought* (New York: Cambridge University Press, 1992); and Steven Ascheim, ed., *Hannah Arendt in Jerusalem* (Berkeley: University of California Press, 2001).

6. See Enrique Dussel, "Beyond Eurocentrism: The World-System and the Limits of Modernity," in *The Cultures of Globalization*, ed. Fredric Jameson and Masao Miyoshi (Durham, NC: Duke University Press, 1998), 3–31; and Ann Laura Stoler and Frederick Cooper, eds. *Tensions of Empire: Colonial Cultures in a Bourgeois World* (Berkeley: University of California Press, 1997).

7. From Dussel's world-systems perspective, Europe is not simply any part of the system, but "in fact, its *center*" (4). Some postcolonial critics might question this recentering of Europe, but Dussel's useful point is that the world-system is structured by hierarchies of wealth and power.

8. I derive the notion of cultural memory from Jan and Aleida Assmann, who use it to indicate the memory stored in canonical texts of culture. See, for instance, Jan Assmann, *Das kulturelle Gedächtnis* (Munich: C. H. Beck, 1999).

9. Recently, numerous scholars, such as Isabel Hull, Dirk Moses, Dan Stone, Enzo Traverso, and Jürgen Zimmerer, have taken inspiration from *Origins* to pursue with conceptual sophistication and in greater empirical detail the links between colonialism and genocide—a trend I return to in the conclusion of the next chapter. While drawing on the insights of such historians, my reading of Arendt eschews the empirical question of colonialism's relationship to the Holocaust in order to focus instead on the contributions and limits of her work to the conceptualization of multidirectionality and comparison. Such a consideration of Arendt's work necessitates interrogation of her very particular use of categories such as comprehension and the human. For a sense of the state of the rapidly changing field linking colonialism and genocide, see the interesting forum of leading historians and critics, "The German Colonial Imagination," *German History* 26, no. 2 (2008): 251–72; and A. Dirk Moses, ed., *Empire, Colony, Genocide: Conquest, Oc-*

cupation, and Subaltern Resistance in World History (New York: Berghahn, 2008), as well as the further references at the end of the next chapter.

10. Hannah Arendt, *The Origins of Totalitarianism*, new ed. (New York: Harcourt Brace Jovanovich, 1973).

11. Margaret Canovan, "Arendt's Theory of Totalitarianism: A Reassessment," *The Cambridge Companion to Hannah Arendt*, ed. Dana Villa (New York: Cambridge University Press, 2000), 25–43; here 26.

12. Arendt does not use terminology such as "the Holocaust" or even "the Nazi genocide," which would have been anachronistic at the time of her writing. Furthermore, her concept of what we today call the Holocaust is necessarily different from that which has followed a further half-century of research. Nevertheless, as I suggest below, Arendt was one of the first to grasp the distinctiveness of Nazi genocide and, even though her use of the concept of totalitarianism extends far beyond genocide, we are still justified in focusing on those elements in her account that correspond to contemporary understandings of the Holocaust (especially her discussion of the Nazi concentration and extermination camps). As will also become clear, Arendt's understanding of imperialism differs from the contemporary understandings generated in postcolonial studies. Conceptually and historically, her work occupies a middle zone between the older notion of imperialism as "the rivalry of the various imperial and metropolitan nation-states" and the more recent understanding of imperialism as "the relationship of metropolis to colony." I take this distinction from Fredric Jameson, "Modernism and Imperialism," in Terry Eagleton, Fredric Jameson, and Edward Said, *Nationalism, Colonialism, and Literature* (Minneapolis: University of Minnesota Press, 1990), 47. For a useful critical consideration of Arendt's account of colonialism, see Pascal Grosse, "From Colonialism to National Socialism to Postcolonialism: Hannah Arendt's Origins of Totalitarianism," *Postcolonial Studies* 9, no. 1 (2006): 35–52.

13. My description of the form of Arendt's historical representation of totalitarianism as a "disjunctive constellation" is deliberately meant to recall Walter Benjamin's "Theses on the Philosophy of History," a text that Arendt and her husband Heinrich Blücher smuggled out of France and discussed with other refugees in Lisbon as they awaited passage to the United States. See the account of this moment in Young-Bruehl (162). Arendt's intellectual connections to Benjamin are discussed by Richard Bernstein, Seyla Benhabib, and others. I return to the Benjaminian resonance of Arendt's work below.

14. Hannah Arendt, *Essays in Understanding, 1930–1954* (New York: Harcourt, Brace, and Co., 1994), 407.

15. Arendt also explicitly denies that she is a positivist or a pragmatist. See Arendt, *Essays*, 405.

16. Walter Benjamin, "Theses on the Philosophy of History," *Illuminations*, trans. Harry Zohn (New York: Schocken, 1968), 262. Translation modified.

17. On *homo sacer* and bare or naked life, see Giorgio Agamben, *Homo Sacer: Sovereign Power and Bare Life*, trans. Daniel Heller-Roazen (Stanford, CA: Stanford University Press, 1998). Agamben also discusses Arendt's writings on refugees and statelessness in *Means Without End: Notes on Politics*, trans. Vincenzo Binetti and Cesare Casarino (Minneapolis: University of Minnesota Press, 2000).

18. Foucault's notion of the biopolitical could be understood as itself partially deriving from Arendt, particularly her account in *The Human Condition* of the triumph of what she calls the social over the political. But, in typical fashion, Foucault never cites Arendt's influence. For a relevant version of Foucault's concept of biopolitics, see the conclusion to *The History of Sexuality, Vol. 1: An Introduction*, trans. Robert Hurley (New York: Vintage, 1980). On Arendt's concept of the social, see Arendt, *The Human Condition* (Chicago: University of Chicago Press, 1958); and Hannah Pitkin, *The Attack of the Blob: Hannah Arendt's Concept of the Social* (Chicago: University of Chicago Press, 1998).

19. For Agamben's views on the centrality of the Nazi camps and genocide to modern politics, see, besides *Homo Sacer*, also *Remnants of Auschwitz: The Witness and the Archive*, trans. Daniel Heller-Roazen (New York: Zone Books, 1999).

20. Dan Diner coins the term "counter-rationality" to name a perspective that neither "justifies" genocide as rational, nor removes it from human accountability by labeling it irrational. See Diner, *Beyond the Conceivable: Studies on Germany, Nazism, and the Holocaust* (Berkeley: University of California Press, 2000), 130–37.

21. Yehuda Bauer, *Rethinking the Holocaust* (New Haven, CT: Yale University Press, 2001), 45.

22. A similar point is made in Shiraz Dossa, *The Public Realm and the Public Self: The Political Theory of Hannah Arendt* (Waterloo, Canada: Wilfrid Laurier University Press, 1989), 34.

23. Jodi A. Byrd, "'Living My Native Life Deadly': Red Lake, Ward Churchill, and the Discourses of Competing Genocides," *American Indian Quarterly* 31, no. 2 (2007): 310–32; here 329.

24. In taking up the question of Arendt's depiction of race, I enter highly charged terrain. There is a clear divide on this question among Arendt's commentators. Robert Bernasconi, Shiraz Dossa, Anne Norton, and William Pietz are among those who have been quite critical of Arendt's racial politics, while scholars such as Canovan, Benhabib, and Young-Bruehl have defended Arendt against charges of racism and racial insensitivity. While I draw significantly on the latter scholars, I believe that Bernasconi, Dossa, Norton, and Pietz are correct in diagnosing some of Arendt's writings as racist. I don't believe that this disqualifies her contributions to thinking about imperialism, totalitarianism, or, indeed, race itself, but I do believe that the racialist features should not be ignored or excused—rather, they should be integrated into the analysis, as I try to do here. In addition

to work already cited, see William Pietz, "The 'Post-Colonialism' of Cold War Discourse," *Social Text* 19–20 (1988): 55–75; and Anne Norton, "Heart of Darkness: Africa and African Americans in the Writings of Hannah Arendt," in *Feminist Interpretations of Hannah Arendt*, ed. Bonnie Honig (Pittsburgh: University of Pittsburgh Press, 1995). Richard H. King and Dan Stone's anthology *Hannah Arendt and the Uses of History: Imperialism, Nation, Race, and Genocide* (Oxford, Eng., and New York: Berghahn, 2007), which was published after this chapter was written, collects several relevant essays that complement my own approach. See, in particular, King and Stone's useful summary of positions in the debate over Arendt's depiction of Africa in their "Introduction," *Hannah Arendt and the Uses of History*, ed. King and Stone, esp. 9–11; Robert Bernasconi's "When the Real Crime Began: Hannah Arendt's *The Origins of Totalitarianism* and the Dignity of the Western Philosophical Tradition," *Hannah Arendt and the Uses of History*, ed. King and Stone, 54–67; and Kathryn T. Gines's "Race Thinking and Racism in Hannah Arendt's *The Origins of Totalitarianism*," *Hannah Arendt and the Uses of History*, ed. King and Stone, 38–53.

25. See "On Some Motifs in Baudelaire," in Benjamin, *Illuminations*.

26. Not that we should discount the possibility of what LaCapra calls perpetrator trauma. As LaCapra points out, acknowledging that perpetrators can be traumatized by their deeds does not necessarily entail thinking of them as victims. See LaCapra, *History and Memory After Auschwitz* (Ithaca, NY: Cornell University Press, 1998), 41. I return to the issue of perpetrator trauma in the following chapter on Césaire.

27. For the citation from Conrad at the end of Arendt's passage, see Joseph Conrad, *Heart of Darkness*, 3d ed., ed. Robert Kimbrough (New York: W. W. Norton, 1988), 51. See also the discussion of Arendt's debt to the Conradian—and Hegelian—view of Africa as lacking history and culture in Richard H. King's fine book *Race, Culture, and the Intellectuals, 1940–1970* (Baltimore, MD, and Washington, DC: Johns Hopkins University Press and Woodrow Wilson Center Press, 2004), 116–17. King "confess[es] bafflement at how Arendt could have expressed such views" (117), but in my reading the ideas are structurally built into her account. While close to my reading in its attention to the links between the murder of Africans and the murder of Nazi inmates as well as in the foregrounding of the "paradox of Western humanism," King's analysis does not pursue the conceptualization that makes those links possible and also deeply problematic (118–19).

28. See Natalie Melas's related discussion of "imperial comparison" in *All the Difference in the World: Postcoloniality and the Ends of Comparison* (Stanford, CA: Stanford University Press, 2007), esp. 52–53.

29. In a theoretical regression from the fictional ur-text, while Conrad consistently refers to Europeans as phantoms and ghosts, in this passage Arendt describes Africans in those terms.

30. Canovan writes, "This kind of nationalism, which prided itself not on a people's worldly achievements but on their innate soul, is labeled 'tribal nationalism' by Arendt, linking it to her contrast between the rootless, 'natural' existence of 'savages' and the man-made world of civilization." As Canovan also points out, Jews are described in analogous fashion as "rootless" and "worldless" (*Hannah Arendt* 39, 44). Despite her occasional use of scare quotes to distance herself from Arendt's vocabulary, Canovan does not generally question the primitivist logic of these associations.

31. Edward Said develops the concept of a "*third* nature" as the goal of the "anti-imperialist imagination" in *Culture and Imperialism* (New York: Vintage, 1994). Playing off of the Marxist notion of "second nature" as capitalism's production of "a particular kind of nature and space," Said writes, "To the anti-imperialist imagination, our space at home in the peripheries has been usurped and put to use by outsiders for their purpose. It is therefore necessary to seek out, to map, to invent, or to discover a *third* nature, not pristine and pre-historical . . . but deriving from the deprivations of the present" (225–26).

32. I'm drawing here on Dominick LaCapra's ever-useful distinction between absence and loss. See "Trauma, Absence, Loss," in *Writing History, Writing Trauma* (Baltimore, MD: Johns Hopkins University Press, 2001). The distinction also plays an important role in my analysis of Schwarz-Bart and Phillips in Chapter 5.

33. David Lloyd's discussion of colonial trauma also links race, universality, and cultural difference in a way that describes Arendt perfectly: "Colonial violence is everywhere a racializing violence, producing its antagonists as objects of a biological and cultural judgment of inferiority. That judgment is based in the inevitably universalizing tendency of the narrative of development which at once legitimates colonial coercion in the name of its concept of humanity and, more importantly for my argument here, produces in relation to the colonized the effect of an incommensurability of cultures. This incommensurability of cultures, in denying the potential of the colonized culture for its own autonomous development, sets from within an absolute limit to the colonizer's claim to be the representative of a universally valid human history." See David Lloyd, "Colonial Trauma/Postcolonial Recovery?" *Interventions* 2, no. 2 (2000): 212–28; here 218–19.

34. Giorgio Agamben, *State of Exception*, trans. Kevin Attell (Chicago: University of Chicago Press, 2005), 87–88.

35. For a discussion of the "history, critique, and future viability of what has become known as Arendt's 'boomerang' thesis," see King and Stone, "Introduction," *Hannah Arendt and the Uses of History*, 2–9.

36. According to the *OED*, the figurative sense of boomerang emerges in 1845: "Your verbal boomerang slaps you on the nose." A second example is from 1870: "The boomerang of argument, which one throws in the opposite direction of

what he means to hit." The movement from physical violence to verbal aggression seems apposite to this discussion of discourses of genocide and imperialism.

CHAPTER 3

1. For an account of the dockworkers' strikes, see Alain Ruscio, *Les communistes français et la guerre d'Indochine, 1944–1954* (Paris: L'Harmattan, 1985), 240–65. On French political opinion regarding the war, see also Alain Ruscio, *La décolonisation tragique: Une histoire de la décolonisation française, 1945–1962* (Paris: Messidor, 1987), 52–60. More recently Ruscio has published, with commentary, a large collection of documents reflecting the long-term, but often ambivalent, engagement of the French Communist Party (PCF) with the colonial question. See Alain Ruscio, ed., *La question coloniale dans "l'Humanité" (1904–2004)* (Paris: La Dispute, 2005).

2. For these and other pertinent biographical facts, see the obituary in *Le Monde*, December 13, 2005. Shortly after painting *Riposte*, Taslitzky was sent by the Communist Party to Algeria to make a visual report on the situation there. Colonialism remained central to his oeuvre throughout his long life.

3. Césaire's text was originally published as *Discours sur le colonialisme* in 1950 by Réclame and then reissued by Présence Africaine in a revised version in 1955. The English translation by Joan Pinkham follows the 1955 version and was originally published in 1972, with a revised version appearing in 2000. In my discussion of Césaire, I will be referring, as appropriate, to all of these versions. Césaire left the Communist Party dramatically in 1956, publishing an open letter to French party leader Maurice Thorez that I discuss below. See Aimé Césaire, *Discours sur le colonialisme* (Paris: Réclame, 1950); Aimé Césaire, *Discours sur le colonialisme* (Paris: Présence Africaine, 1955); Aimé Césaire, *Discourse on Colonialism*, trans. Joan Pinkham (New York: Monthly Review, 2000); Aimé Césaire, *Lettre à Maurice Thorez* (Paris: Présence Africaine, 1956). In parenthetical references, I will cite the English version as *Discourse* and the French versions as *Discours* plus the date of publication (for example, *Discours* [1950]). I will cite the 1955 French version only for passages not included in the original Réclame edition.

4. It should be noted that Césaire does not use scare quotes around "coolies" and "nègres" in the French original (*Discours* [1950] 16).

5. See, especially, the impassioned polemic by a younger Martinican writer: Raphaël Confiant, *Aimé Césaire: Une Traversée Paradoxale Du Siècle* (Paris: Stock, 1993). See also the work of Jeannie Suk, who situates Césaire's paradoxes in a larger field of textual and political ambivalence: Jeannie Suk, *Postcolonial Paradoxes in French Caribbean Writing: Césaire, Glissant, Condé* (Oxford, Eng.: Clarendon, 2001).

6. See the account of the journal in A. James Arnold, *Modernism and Negritude: The Poetry and Poetics of Aimé Césaire* (Cambridge, MA: Harvard University Press, 1981), 71–101.

7. For biographical information and historical context, see Arnold, *Modernism;* and Clayton Eshelman and Annette Smith, "Introduction," in Aimé Césaire, *The Collected Poetry of Aimé Césaire*, trans. C. Eshelman and A. Smith (Berkeley: University of California Press, 1983), 1–31. For an evocative account of Martinique in this era, see David Macey, *Frantz Fanon: A Biography* (New York: Picador USA, 2001). For an account of transnational connections among black intellectuals in interwar Paris, see Brent Hayes Edwards, *The Practice of Diaspora: Literature, Translation, and the Rise of Black Internationalism* (Cambridge, MA: Harvard University Press, 2003).

8. For an introductory essay situating Césaire in relation to revolutionary anticolonial thought, see Robin D. G. Kelley, "A Poetics of Anticolonialism," in Aimé Césaire, *Discourse on Colonialism*, 7–28.

9. Georges Ngal, *"Lire . . . " le* Discours sur le Colonialisme *d'Aimé Césaire* (Paris: Présence Africaine, 1994), 38.

10. See *La gangrène* (Paris: Minuit, 1959). Césaire's text marks the shift in the history of decolonization: references to Algeria appear only in the 1955 edition. For an account of violence in Vietnam and Madagascar, as well as other colonial sites, including Algeria, during the period just before Césaire's book appeared, see Yves Benot, *Massacres coloniaux: 1944–1950: La IVe République et la mise au pas des colonies françaises* (Paris: La Découverte, 2001 [1994]).

11. Dominck LaCapra, *History and Memory After Auschwitz* (Ithaca, NY: Cornell University Press, 1998), 3n.

12. A return to origins and to a black essence is one of the tropes most frequently associated with negritude, which, in *Black Orpheus*, Sartre famously called "an antiracist racism." But in the *Discourse* Césaire seeks to distance himself from the ideas of regression and "the return to the pre-European past" ascribed to negritude, and he explicitly disavows in the *Discourse* that he ever held such views (44). Yet, as James Arnold suggests, "the facts are not quite so simple." Even if the author of *Notebook of a Return to the Native Land* "did not promote a back-to-Africa movement," "just as certainly he had written poetry that presented a pseudomythical alternative to the present, and that alternative can be seen as a return to ancient spiritual values" (178–79). In Mara De Gennaro's terms, Césaire's work combines two forms of "primitivism": both "an admiration of nonliterate cultures" and a "related tendency of modernists in the first half of the century to try to 'plumb the depths' . . . to expose an unknown and largely unknowable mode of natural or 'primitive' being" (59–60). Césaire's primirivism is, as De Gennaro argues, a form of humanism: he "appeal[s] to a supracultural state of commonality and interconnectedness that, in his view, transcends cultural particularities" (61). Césaire's ar-

ticulation of primitivism and humanism, of the natural and the human, recalls the terms of Arendt's genealogy of totalitarianism and the unsettling position of "'natural' human beings" within it. Ultimately, however, I would argue that primitivism does not play a significant role in the *Discourse* or in Césaire's articulation of genocide and colonialism, while it most certainly does play such a role in Arendt. See Mara De Gennaro, "Fighting 'Humanism' On Its Own Terms," *differences: A Journal of Feminist Cultural Studies* 14, no. 1 (2003): 53–73.

13. Césaire does not specify that his reference here is to *Emile* Faguet, but it seems likely given the context that he means this traditionalist literary critic who lived from 1847 to 1916. I have not been able to track down any more likely candidates.

14. René Depestre, "An Interview with Aimé Césaire," in Césaire, *Discourse on Colonialism*, 84.

15. The quotation in this sentence is from Jean Laplanche and Jean-Bertrand Pontalis, *The Language of Psychoanalysis*, trans. Donald Nicholson-Smith (London: Karnac, 1988), 387.

16. Sigmund Freud, "Fetishism," *Collected Papers*, vol. 5, ed. James Strachey (New York: Basic, 1959), 198–204.

17. Sigmund Freud, *Beyond the Pleasure Principle*, trans. James Strachey (New York: W. W. Norton, 1961), 41.

18. For the German, see Walter Benjamin, *Illuminationen* (Frankfurt: Suhrkamp, 1977), 260. For the English, see Benjamin, *Illuminations*, 262. For the French, see Walter Benjamin, *Ecrits français*, ed. Jean-Maurice Monnoyer (Paris: Gallimard, 1991), 346. It is indeed possible that Césaire was familiar with this text. As Monnoyer, the editor of Benjamin's French writings, points out, Pierre Missac translated Benjamin's theses as "Sur le concept d'histoire" in *Les temps modernes* 25 (October 1947): 623–34. (This version translates the key phrase as "choc" and not "choc en retour.") Césaire himself was the subject of a not-too-flattering review in *Les temps modernes* two issues later. See Etiemble, "Chronique littéraire: Le Requin and la Mouette, ou les Armes miraculeuses," *Les temps modernes* 27 (December 1947): 1099–1113.

19. See Freud, *Beyond the Pleasure Principle*, 36.

20. For an important consideration of such blockages to recognition, see A. Dirk Moses, "Conceptual Blockages and Definitional Dilemmas in the 'Racial Century': Genocides of Indigenous Peoples and the Holocaust," *Patterns of Prejudice* 36, no. 4 (2002): 7–35. The notion of "blockage" is also central to the passage from Benjamin on the *choc en retour*—although here again with a different valence. Benjamin understands blockage (*Stillstellung*, in German [260]; *bloquage*, in French [346]; "arrest" in English [262]) as an essential dimension of thought that leads to the formation of the constellation through the *choc en retour*.

21. The earliest French edition I have been able to find in the catalog of the Bibliothèque Nationale is *Jeunesse: suivi du Coeur des ténèbres*, trans. G. Jean Aubry and Andé Ruyters (Paris: Gallimard, 1925). This is a third edition.

22. Joseph Conrad, *Heart of Darkness*, 3d ed., ed. Robert Kimbrough (New York: W. W. Norton, 1988), 76.

23. Arendt's understanding of the development of racism does not ignore pre-imperialist notions of race. However, she strongly differentiates "race-thinking" from modern racism and sees no causal link between them. She writes that "there is an abyss between the men of brilliant and facile conceptions and men of brutal deeds and active bestiality which no intellectual explanation is able to bridge. It is highly probable that the thinking in terms of race would have disappeared in due time together with other irresponsible opinions of the nineteenth century, if the 'scramble for Africa' and the new era of imperialism had not exposed Western humanity to new and shocking experiences." While the insight into changes in thinking about race is crucial, the refusal to see any continuities is simplistic and the claim for the unique importance of the scramble for Africa seems idiosyncratic from a U.S. perspective in which race is at least as closely tied to slavery as to expansionism. See Hannah Arendt, *The Origins of Totalitarianism*, new ed. (New York: Harcourt Brace Jovanovich, 1973), 183. For a detailed critique of Arendt's distinction between race-thinking and racism with an emphasis on the U.S. and colonial contexts, see Kathryn T. Gines's "Race Thinking and Racism in Hannah Arendt's *The Origins of Totalitarianism*," in *Hannah Arendt and the Uses of History: Imperialism, Nation, Race, and Genocide*, ed. Richard H. King and Dan Stone (Oxford, Eng., and New York: Berghahn, 2007), 38–53.

24. Giorgio Agamben, *Homo Sacer: Sovereign Power and Bare Life*, trans. Daniel Heller-Roazen (Stanford, CA: Stanford University Press, 1998), 6.

25. Cathy Caruth, *Unclaimed Experience: Trauma, Narrative, and History* (Baltimore, MD: Johns Hopkins University Press, 1996), 1–9.

26. Ruth Leys, *Trauma: A Genealogy* (Chicago: University of Chicago Press, 2000), 266–97.

27. Leys also points out that Freud cites Tancred not "as an example of traumatic neurosis but as an example of the general tendency in even normal people to repeat unpleasurable experiences, and hence as an example of the repetition compulsion, or death drive" (293). By contrast, as David Quint remarks, Freud probably had not read Tasso; his account of Tancred and Clorinda is "borrowed secondhand from Goethe's *The Apprenticeship of Wilhelm Meister*." See David Quint, *Epic and Empire: Politics and Generic Form from Virgil to Milton* (Princeton, NJ: Princeton University Press, 1993), 404n. The issue, I believe, is less the "accuracy" of either Freud's or Caruth's readings, but rather what they make of the source texts.

28. Amy Novak, "Who Speaks? Who Listens? The Problem of Address in Two Nigerian Trauma Novels," Special Issue on "Postcolonial Trauma Novels," *Studies in the Novel* 40, nos. 1–2 (2008): 31–51. As Quint's fascinating discussion reveals, the story of Tancred and Clorinda is even more complex and suggestive than Freud, Caruth, and Novak acknowledge (cf. Quint 234–47).

29. Laura Brown, "Not Outside the Range: One Feminist Perspective on Psychic Trauma," in *Trauma: Explorations in Memory*, ed. Cathy Caruth (Baltimore, MD: Johns Hopkins University Press, 1995), 100–112.

30. For a critique of the "accident model" of trauma, see Nancy Van Styvendale, "The Trans/historicity of Trauma in Jeannette Armstrong's *Slash* and Sherman Alexie's *Indian Killer*," Special Issue on "Postcolonial Trauma Novels," ed. Stef Craps and Gert Buelens, *Studies in the Novel* 40, nos. 1–2 (2008): 203–23. Many of the essays in Craps and Buelens's important collection take up the problem of the accident model and draw on Brown and Fanon to provide alternatives. I assess the possibilities and limits of the postcolonial approach to trauma in my afterword to this special issue, "Decolonizing Trauma Studies: A Response," Special Issue on "Postcolonial Trauma Novels," ed. Stef Craps and Gert Buelens, *Studies in the Novel* 40, nos. 1–2 (2008): 224–34.

31. For trauma as a mode of living on, see David Lloyd, "Colonial Trauma/Postcolonial Recovery?" *Interventions* 2, no. 2 (2000): 219–20; Michael Rothberg, *Traumatic Realism: The Demands of Holocaust Representation* (Minneapolis: University of Minnesota Press, 2000), 138.

32. See LaCapra's discussion in *History and Memory After Auschwitz* (Ithaca, NY: Cornell University Press, 1998), 41.

33. Cathy Caruth, "Trauma and Experience: Introduction," *Trauma: Explorations in Memory*, ed. Cathy Caruth (Baltimore, MD: Johns Hopkins University Press, 1995), 11.

34. Frantz Fanon, "The Negro and Psychopathology," *Black Skin, White Masks*, trans. Charles Lam Markmann (New York: Grove Press, 1967 [1952]), 141–209. For a lucid and challenging discussion of Fanon from which I have benefited, see Pheng Cheah, "Crises of Money," *positions: east asia cultures critique* 16, no. 1 (spring 2008). Cheah's ultimate point is to suggest that theories of trauma—even ones, like Fanon's, developed in colonial contexts—are inadequate to the neocolonial relations of financial globalization.

35. See Bryan Cheyette's nuanced account of Fanon's writings on blacks and Jews. Using a method congruent with that employed here, Cheyette explores the "heterogeneous juxtapositions which bring together diasporic Jewry and the history of anti-Semitism with the colonial struggle and anti-Black racism." Bryan Cheyette, "Frantz Fanon and the Black-Jewish Imaginary," in *Frantz Fanon's Black Skin, White Masks: New Interdisciplinary Essays*, ed. Max Silverman (Manchester, Eng.: Manchester University Press, 2005), 74–99; citation from 75.

36. Sander Gilman, *The Jew's Body* (New York: Routledge, 1991).

37. Rosa Luxemburg, "The Junius Pamphlet: The Crisis in German Social Democracy," in *Rosa Luxemburg Speaks*, ed. Mary-Alice Waters (New York: Pathfinder, 1970), 269, 281. Cited in A. Dirk Moses, "Empire, Colony, Genocide: Keywords and the Philosophy of History," in *Empire, Colony, Genocide: Conquest, Occupation, and Subaltern Resistance in World History* (New York: Berghahn, 2008), 34.

38. Karl Korsch, "Notes on History: The Ambiguities of Totalitarian Ideologies," *New Essays* 6, no. 2 (fall 1942): 3. I have no evidence that Césaire read Luxemburg or Korsch, and Moses is the only scholar I know who has drawn attention to Luxemburg as a precursor of Césaire; I have seen no mention of Korsch as a precursor of Césaire. I was alerted to Korsch's argument by Enzo Traverso's *The Origins of Nazi Violence* (New York: New Press, 2003).

39. Robert Young, *White Mythologies: Writing History and the West* (New York: Routledge, 1991), 8. Young repeats this sentiment on page 125 and explicitly evokes the Holocaust at that point.

40. A stimulating critique of some of the important new work on German colonialism and the Holocaust can be found in Matthew P. Fitzpatrick, "The Pre-History of the Holocaust? The *Sonderweg* and *Historikerstreit* Debates and the Abject Colonial Past," *Central European History* 41 (2008): 1–27. See especially his discussions of Zimmerer and Hull (12–17). Fitzpatrick argues that genocide in the colonies and in Europe emerged out of different epistemologies, the former out of notions of "obdurate alterity" and the latter out of fears of "abject" pollution. But even with his skeptical approach to colonial-Holocaust continuities, Fitzpatrick does still grant colonialism a significant place in the Nazi genocide's genealogy.

41. Isabel V. Hull, *Absolute Destruction: Military Culture and the Practices of War in Imperial Germany* (Ithaca, NY: Cornell University Press, 2005), 332.

42. Isabel V. Hull, "Military Culture and the Production of 'Final Solutions' in the Colonies: The Example of Wilhelminian Germany," in *The Specter of Genocide: Mass Murder in Historical Perspective*, ed. Robert Gellately and Ben Kiernan (Cambridge and New York: Cambridge University Press, 2003), 141–62; here 143.

43. I have not been arguing that the colonial encounter had no significant effects on the concept of race, but rather that disparate and contradictory racial (as well as religious, national, and so on) discourses preceded and made possible that sometimes genocidal encounter. Modern imperialism rearticulated already existing forms of racism and race thinking. Recently, scholars of the early modern and medieval periods have been tracking the history of race in new ways. For the early modern period, see the lucid and accessible account in Ania Loomba, *Shakespeare, Race, and Colonialism* (New York: Oxford University Press, 2002). For a fascinating essay by a medievalist on the long history of "race," see Lisa Lampert, "Race, Periodicity, and the (Neo-) Middle Ages," *MLQ* 65, no. 3 (2004): 391–421.

44. Jürgen Zimmerer, "Colonialism and the Holocaust: Towards an Archaeology of Genocide," in *Genocide and Settler Society: Frontier Violence and Stolen Indigenous Children in Australian History*, ed. A. Dirk Moses (Oxford, Eng.: Berghahn Books, 2004), 53–54.

45. Jürgen Zimmerer, "The Birth of the *Ostland* Out of the Spirit of Colonialism: A Postcolonial Perspective on the Nazi Policy of Conquest and Extermination," *Patterns of Prejudice* 39, no. 2 (2005): 218.

46. Moses has also contributed to this project, drawing attention to "four different, even contradictory imperial and colonial logics" that were combined in Nazi genocide. In "Empire, Colony, Genocide," he identifies patterns of conquest that reach back to antiquity, "subaltern genocide" based on Nazi perceptions of Jews as "colonizers," notions of Jews as internal security threats, and depictions of Jews as traditional colonial Others (37–40).

CHAPTER 4

1. See "To the Nations of the World," in W. E. B. Du Bois, *The Oxford W. E. B. Du Bois Reader*, ed. Eric Sundquist (New York: Oxford University Press, 1996), 625. While the most famous articulation of "the problem of the twentieth century" comes in *The Souls of Black Folk*, Du Bois first formulated it in "To the Nations of the World," which was published as part of the *Report of the Pan-African Congress* of 1900. Future references will revert to the American spelling of "color." For the article on Warsaw, see W. E. B. Du Bois, "The Negro and the Warsaw Ghetto," *Jewish Life* (May 1952): 14–15. Future references to this text will be included parenthetically in the text. This article is reproduced in *The Oxford W. E. B. Du Bois Reader*, 469–73. Du Bois also briefly recounts his trip to Warsaw in a letter on September 27, 1949, to his benefactor Anita McCormick Blaine. See W. E. B. Du Bois, *The Correspondence of W. E. B. Du Bois*, vol. III, ed. Herbert Aptheker (Amherst: University of Massachusetts Press, 1978).

2. Theodor W. Adorno, *Prisms*, trans. Samuel Weber and Shierry Weber (Cambridge, MA: MIT Press, 1981), 34.

3. For an extended discussion of the various articulations and contexts of Adorno's writings on Auschwitz, see my "After Adorno: Culture in the Wake of Catastrophe," in Michael Rothberg, *Traumatic Realism: The Demands of Holocaust Representation* (Minneapolis: University of Minnesota Press, 2000).

4. Claude Lanzmann, "De l'Holocauste à *Holocauste*," *Au Sujet de Shoah* (Paris: Belin, 1990), 309. This and other important essays by and about Lanzmann and his film *Shoah* are now available in *Claude Lanzmann's Shoah: Key Essays*, ed. Stuart Liebman (New York: Oxford University Press, 2007).

5. Tzvetan Todorov, *Facing the Extreme: Moral Life in the Concentration Camps* (New York: Henry Holt, 1996), 40.

6. For more on the relationship between realism and antirealism in Holocaust studies, see the introduction to *Traumatic Realism*.

7. For an excellent survey of the full range of Du Bois's considerable writings on Jews, anti-Semitism, and Nazism, see Harold Brackman, "'A Calamity Almost Beyond Comprehension': Nazi Anti-Semitism and the Holocaust in the Thought of W.E.B. Du Bois," *American Jewish History* 88, no. 1 (2000): 53–93. For some of the best works by literary critics on the relationship of African Americans and Jewish Americans, see Emily Miller Budick, *Blacks and Jews in Literary Conversation* (New York: Cambridge University Press, 1998); and Adam Zachary Newton, *Facing Black and Jew: Literature as Public Space in Twentieth-Century America* (New York: Cambridge University Press, 1998). Eric Sundquist has published the most exhaustive and significant work on the relation of black and Jewish Americans to the Holocaust. See Eric Sundquist, *Strangers in the Land: Blacks, Jews, Post-Holocaust America* (Cambridge, MA: Belknap/Harvard University Press, 2005).

8. For a related discussion that focuses on race and interdisciplinarity in *The Souls of Black Folk*, see Russ Castronovo, "Within the Veil of Interdisciplinary Knowledge?: Jefferson, Du Bois, and the Negation of Politics," *New Literary History* 31 (2000): 781–804.

9. See the brief account of that year in Manning Marable, *W.E.B. Du Bois: Black Radical Democrat* (Boston: Twayne, 1986), 176–77. For the most complete studies of Du Bois during the this era, see Gerald Horne, *Black and Red: W.E.B. Du Bois and the Afro-American Response to the Cold War, 1944–1963* (Albany: State University of New York Press, 1986); David Levering Lewis, *W.E.B. Du Bois: The Fight for Equality and the American Century, 1919–1963* (New York: Henry Holt, 2000). *Jewish Life* published a selection from his 1949 New York address on peace; see W.E.B. Du Bois, "No More War!" *Jewish Life* (May 1949): 23–24. The full text is published as "Peace: Freedom's Road for Oppressed Peoples" in W. E. B. Du Bois, *W.E.B. Du Bois: A Reader*, ed. David Levering Lewis (New York: Henry Holt, 1995), 751–54. This reader also includes several other essays pertaining to the cold war.

10. Du Bois published a depressingly laudatory eulogy for Stalin; see "On Stalin," in *W.E.B. Du Bois: A Reader*, 796–97. For an important account of Du Bois's Stalinism, see William E. Cain, "From Liberalism to Communism: The Political Thought of W.E.B. Du Bois," *Cultures of United States Imperialism*, ed. Amy Kaplan and Donald Pease (Durham, NC: Duke University Press, 1993), 456–73. Unlike Césaire, Du Bois continued to defend Stalin even after Kruschchev's 1956 revelations; see Horne, *Black and Red*, 316–68.

11. Penny Von Eschen, *Race Against Empire: Black Americans and Anticolonialism, 1937–1957* (Ithaca, NY: Cornell University Press, 1997), 146.

12. Peter Novick, *The Holocaust in American Life* (Boston: Houghton Mifflin, 1999), 93. For further discussion of this era, see Lawrence Baron, "The Holocaust

and American Public Memory, 1945–1960," *Holocaust and Genocide Studies* 17, no. 1 (2003): 62–88.

13. For *Jewish Life*'s defense of Du Bois, see Dr. Harry F. Ward, "The Case of Dr. Du Bois," *Jewish Life* (July 1951): 23–25. On the *We Charge Genocide* campaign, see William L. Patterson, "Genocide against the Negro People," *Jewish Life* (January 1952): 11–13.

14. Du Bois to Proskauer, November 14, 1944. *The Correspondence of W. E. B. Du Bois*, 24–25. This is not to say that Du Bois was insensitive to Jewish suffering in Nazi Germany, but rather that he was always attuned to questions of political strategy. Already in 1936, Du Bois judged that "there has been no tragedy in modern times equal in its awful effects to the fight on the Jew in Germany." See "The Present Plight of the German Jew," *W.E.B. Du Bois: A Reader*, 81–82.

15. See, for example, Slavoj Zizek's provocative "A Leftist Plea for 'Eurocentrism,'" in Slavoj Zizek, *The Ticklish Subject: The Absent Centre of Political Ontology* (New York: Verso, 1999).

16. W. E. B. Du Bois, *Dusk of Dawn* (New York: Harcourt, Brace, and Company, 1940), 29–30.

17. W. E. B. Du Bois, *The Souls of Black Folks*, Norton Critical Edition, ed. Henry Louis Gates Jr. and Terri Hulme Oliver (New York: W. W. Norton, 1999), 148. *The Souls of Black Folk* has also been controversial for containing references to Jews that can be construed as anti-Semitic. See the editorial "Note on the Text" in *Souls* (xxxix–xli), which discusses changes Du Bois made in 1953 in response to perceptions of anti-Semitism in his book. The timing seems significant given the history under consideration here.

18. For an account of Du Bois's passport troubles and other experiences of cold war repression, see Horne, *Black and Red*, 212–18.

19. See *Warsaw: A Portrait of the City*, ed. Stefan Muszynski and Monika Krajewska (Warsaw: Arkady, 1984). This text has no pagination.

20. Russell Berman, "Du Bois and Wagner: Race, Nation, and Culture Between the United States and Germany," *German Quarterly* 70, no. 2 (1997): 128.

21. W. E. B. Du Bois, *The World and Africa: An Inquiry into the Part Which Africa Has Played in World History* (New York: Viking, 1947), 23. This passage is often used as evidence for the argument that the Nazi genocide simply repeated colonial violence on a new set of European victims (a version of the boomerang argument), but Du Bois came to a more nuanced view in "The Negro and the Warsaw Ghetto." For one example of that type of argument, see Robert Bernasconi, "When the Real Crime Began: Hannah Arendt's *The Origins of Totalitarianism* and the Dignity of the Western Philosophical Tradition,'" *Hannah Arendt and the Uses of History: Imperialism, Nation, Race, and Genocide*, ed. Richard H. King and Dan Stone (Oxford, Eng., and New York: Berghahn, 2007), 54–67.

22. Giorgio Agamben, *Remnants of Auschwitz: The Witness and the Archive*, trans. Daniel Heller-Roazen (New York: Zone Books, 1999), 85.

23. My discussion of the Warsaw Ghetto Monument draws on James Young's excellent study in *The Texture of Memory: Holocaust Memorials and Meaning* (New Haven, CT: Yale University Press), 155–84; on David Roskies's fascinating *Against the Apocalypse: Responses to Catastrophe in Modern Jewish Culture* (Syracuse, NY: Syracuse University Press, 1999), 297–302; on my own visit to the monument in 1997; and on Nathan Rapoport, *Nathan Rapoport: Sculptures and Monuments* (New York: Shengold Publishers, 1980).

24. In formulating a notion of double consciousness as a shared response of black and Jewish intellectuals to the extreme violence of modernity, I have been inspired by two of Paul Gilroy's important books. See Paul Gilroy, *The Black Atlantic: Modernity and Double Consciousness* (Cambridge, MA: Harvard University Press, 1993), esp. 187–223; Paul Gilroy, *Against Race: Imagining Political Culture Beyond the Color Line* (Cambridge, MA: Harvard University Press, 2000).

25. Indeed, the problem of race itself is also not what it was when Du Bois made his initial pronouncement. This does not mean that racism no longer plays a central role in contemporary regimes of power. Rather, as notions of race continuously shift, so does the role of racism. Michael Hardt and Antonio Negri locate these shifts as part of a transformation from modern sovereignty to what they call imperial or postmodern sovereignty: "The central moment of modern racism takes place on its boundary, in the global antithesis between inside and outside. As Du Bois said nearly one hundred years ago, the problem of the twentieth century is the problem of the color line. Imperial racism, by contrast, looking forward perhaps to the twenty-first century, rests on the play of differences and the management of micro-conflictualities within its continually expanding domain." See Michael Hardt and Antonio Negri, *Empire* (Cambridge, MA: Harvard University Press, 2000), 195.

26. See Walter Benjamin, "Theses on the Philosophy of History," *Illuminations*, trans. Harry Zohn (New York: Schocken, 1968).

CHAPTER 5

1. André Schwarz-Bart, *La Mulâtresse Solitude* (Paris: Seuil, 1972), 140. André Schwarz-Bart, *A Woman Named Solitude*, trans. Ralph Manheim (New York: Bantam, 1974), 150. Further references will be to the English translation unless otherwise noted.

2. Two fine discussions of the work of the Schwarz-Barts in the context of both the Holocaust and colonialism that have inspired my own are: Bella Brodzki, "Nomadism and the Textualization of Memory in André Schwarz-Bart's *La Mulâtresse Solitude*," *Yale French Studies* 83 (1993); Ronnie Scharfman, "Exiled from the

Shoah: André and Simone Schwarz-Bart's *Un plat de porc aux bananes vertes*," in *Auschwitz and After: Race, Culture, and "the Jewish Question" in France*, ed. Lawrence D. Kritzman (New York: Routledge, 1995). Most critical literature on the Schwarz-Barts concerns either the Holocaust or colonialism/postcolonialism. For a useful overview of Phillips's relationship to the Holocaust and Jewish history, see Wendy Zierler, "Caryl Phillips," *Holocaust Literature: An Encyclopedia of Writers and Their Work*, ed. S. Lillian Kremer, vol. II (New York: Routledge, 2002).

3. There is an enormous amount of work on "blacks and Jews." However, most of that work is focused on the U.S. context (see the references in the previous chapter). My work on Schwarz-Bart, Phillips, Du Bois, and others is meant to shift the discussion to a more comparative and transnational terrain—a terrain that I believe is relevant even when American black-Jewish relations are in question. An exception to the U.S.-centrism of most studies is Robert Philipson, *The Identity Question: Blacks and Jews in Europe and America* (Jackson: University Press of Mississippi, 2000).

4. Giambattista Vico, *New Science: Principles of the New Science Concerning the Common Nature of Nations*, trans. David Marsh, 3d ed. (London: Penguin, 1999), 333. Cited in Srinivas Aravamudan, "The Return of Anachronism," *MLQ* 62, no. 4 (2001): 331.

5. See the chapter, "Trauma, Absence, Loss," in Dominick LaCapra, *Writing History, Writing Trauma* (Baltimore, MD: Johns Hopkins University Press, 2001).

6. Gershom Scholem, "The Tradition of the Thirty-Six Hidden Just Men," in *The Messianic Idea in Judaism: And Other Essays on Jewish Spirituality* (New York: Shocken, 1971), 251–56, 251.

7. D. Mesher, "André Schwarz-Bart," *Holocaust Literature: An Encyclopedia of Writers and Their Work*, vol. 2, ed. S. Lillian Kremer (New York: Routledge, 2002), 1122–26, 1123.

8. Francine Kaufmann, *Pour relire Le Dernier des Justes* (Paris: Meridiens Klincksieck, 1986), 10–11, 24–27.

9. Schwarz-Bart, *The Last of the Just*, trans. Stephen Becker (New York: Atheneum, 1960), 3.

10. Whatever its status as historical explanation, the novel's historicism has provoked conflicting responses from literary critics. Sidra Ezrahi sees Jewish history subordinated to Christian history, while Alvin Rosenfeld sees the novel putting forth a model of spiritual resistance. See Sidra DeKoven Ezrahi, *By Words Alone: The Holocaust in Literature* (Chicago: University of Chicago Press, 1980), 133; Alvin H. Rosenfeld, *A Double Dying: Reflections on Holocaust Literature* (Bloomington: Indiana University Press, 1980), 69.

11. Lawrence Langer, *The Holocaust and the Literary Imagination* (New Haven, CT: Yale University Press, 1975), 252. This conundrum is also noted by Rosenfeld, *Double Dying*, 68–69.

12. Michel Salomon, "Jewishness and Negritude: An Interview with André Schwarz-Bart," *Midstream* (March 1967): 3–12; here 3.

13. Interestingly, in the same interview, Schwarz-Bart's wife Simone describes her youthful understanding of Jews as themselves an anachronistic people: "When I lived in the West Indies, I did not know what a Jew was. I thought that Jews were a people of the Bible who had existed in the very distant past and I had no ideas that there were still Jews today." Once she met Jews in Paris, however, she "immediately found many things in common" (5).

14. See Brodzki's discussion of this passage (228); she puts more emphasis than I do on disjunction in this passage and locates a sense of foreboding in the references to "the Western time line" and the waters, which will soon bring the slave hunters. On Schwarz-Bart's relationship to the tradition of *Kiddush haShem*, see Stanley Brodwin, "History and Martyrological Tragedy: The Jewish Experience in Sholem Asch and André Schwarz-Bart," *Twentieth Century Literature* 40, no. 1 (1990): 72–91.

15. On the different ways that dates function in discourse, see Aravamudan, "Return," 334–35. Aravamudan is referring to the work of James Chandler.

16. Although today the ruins of the Warsaw Ghetto have been almost entirely paved over, leaving only the monument that I discuss in the previous chapter on Du Bois, the description of visiting the plantation could easily describe a contemporary visit to one of the sites of the Nazi extermination camps, where often ashes and bone splinters do persist.

17. In the decades since the publication of Schwarz-Bart's novel, the memorialization of slavery in general and of the revolt described in *A Woman Named Solitude* has become more prominent in the Caribbean. For a consideration of this process, with a focus on Guadeloupe and Martinique, see Catherine A. Reinhardt, *Claims to Memory: Beyond Slavery and Emancipation in the French Caribbean* (New York: Berghahn, 2006). For Reinhardt's discussion of Solitude and the erection of a statue in her honor in 1999, see 149–53.

18. André Schwarz-Bart, "Pourquoi j'ai écrit *La Mulâtresse Solitude*," *Le Figaro littéraire*, January 26, 1967, 1, 8, 9. Translations from this text are my own. The reference to *Solitude* is not meant to indicate the 1972 novel but the entire series that was to include both the 1967 novel and the later text, as well as others. See also Scharfman's insightful discussion of this article (which she refers to as an interview).

19. Walzer uses the notion of "vicarious experience" in his discussion of how the story of Exodus has functioned as a powerful narrative in revolutionary political movements across the centuries. Already in the "Deuteronomic account of the covenant," we find the imperative "imaginatively to relive the moment of deliverance" from Egypt as the basis of Jewish identity. See Michael Walzer, *Exodus and Revolution* (New York: Basic Books, 1985), 84–85, 90. Walzer's book also led to a

polemical exchange with Edward Said, who wrote a critique of the book from a "Canaanite" perspective, over Zionism and the Palestinians.

20. Paul Berman has used the notion of the "almost the same," adopted from the French philosopher Vladimir Jankélévitch (and owing a debt to Freud), in a discussion of black-Jewish relations. Berman characterizes the intensity of relations between black and Jews as a product of their proximity and minor differences. See Paul Berman, "Introduction: The Other and the Almost the Same," *Blacks and Jews: Alliances and Arguments*, ed. Paul Berman (New York: Delta, 1994), 1–28.

21. It is interesting to juxtapose Schwarz-Bart's ruins with those of Walter Benjamin in his book on the *Trauerspiel*. For Benjamin, "allegories are in the realm of thoughts what ruins are in the realm of things," and "in allegory is the facies hippocratica of history that lies like a frozen landscape before the eyes of the beholder. History in everything that it has of the unseasonable, painful, abortive, expresses itself in that face. . . . [W]hat is expressed here portentously in the form of a riddle is not only the nature of human life in general, but also the biographical historicity of the individual in its most natural and organically corrupted form." Although allegory and the ruin are precisely historical in Benjamin's understanding, they are also associated with the kind of melancholy vision espoused by Schwarz-Bart. Benjamin is cited in Fredric Jameson, *Marxism and Form: Twentieth-Century Dialectical Theories of Literature* (Princeton, NJ: Princeton University Press, 1972), 71, 73.

22. For critical works that helpfully describe these and other aspects of Phillips's oeuvre in the texts I discuss, see Bryan Cheyette, "Venetian Spaces: Old-New Literatures and the Ambivalent Uses of Jewish History," *Reading the "New" Literatures in a Postcolonial Era*, ed. Susheila Nasta (Cambridge: D. S. Brewer, 2000); Stef Craps, "Linking Legacies of Loss: Traumatic Histories and Cross-Cultural Empathy in Caryl Phillips's *Higher Ground* and *The Nature of Blood*," *Studies in the Novel* 40, nos. 1–2 (2008): 191–202; Ashley Dawson, "'To Remember Too Much Is Indeed a Form of Madness': Caryl Phillips's *The Nature of Blood* and the Modalities of European Racism," *Postcolonial Studies* 7, no. 1 (2004): 83–101; Bénédicte Ledent, *Caryl Phillips* (Manchester, Eng.: Manchester University Press, 2002); Anne Whitehead, *Trauma Fiction* (Edinburgh: Edinburgh University Press, 2004), 89–116; Wendy Zierler, "Caryl Phillips," *Holocaust Literature: An Encyclopedia*, ed. S. Lillian Kremer (New York: Routledge, 2002); and Wendy Zierler, "'My Holocaust Is Not Your Holocaust': 'Facing' Black and Jewish Experience in *The Pawnbroker, Higher Ground*, and *The Nature of Blood*," *Holocaust and Genocide Studies* 18, no. 1 (2004): 46–67. For a fascinating discussion of works by Phillips other than those mentioned here, see Timothy Bewes, "Shame, Ventriloquy, and the Problem of the Cliché in Caryl Phillips," *Cultural Critique* 63 (2006): 33–60. Rebecca Walkowitz situates Phillips within the global circulation of world literatures as an example of what she calls "comparison literature." See "The Loca-

tion of Literature: The Transnational Book and the Migrant Writer," *Contemporary Literature*, Special Issue on "Immigrant Fictions" 47, no. 4 (2006): 527–45.

23. Caryl Phillips, *The European Tribe* (Boston and London: Faber and Faber, 1992 [1987]), 66–67.

24. Caryl Phillips, "On 'The Nature of Blood' and the Ghost of Anne Frank," *CommonQuest* (summer 1998): 4–7; here 6.

25. Diana Fuss, *Identification Papers* (New York: Routledge, 1995), 1, 5.

26. Eve Sedgwick, *Epistemology of the Closet* (Berkeley: University of California Press, 1990), 59, 61.

27. For an understanding of diaspora as premised not on the possibility of "return" to a lost home but on a discourse of hybridity and difference, see Stuart Hall, "Cultural Identity and Diaspora," *Identity: Community, Culture, Difference*, ed. Jonathan Rutherford (London: Lawrence & Wishart, 1990).

28. Interestingly, the model of Venice is only one of two "distinct genealogies of modern capitalism" identified by Arrighi, that which accords with capital's tendency to "becom[e] identified with particular states." The other model is "the Genoese diaspora 'nation,'" which "triumphed by *not* becoming identified with any particular state but by constructing world-encompassing, non-territorial business organizations." See Giovanni Arrighi, *The Long Twentieth Century: Money, Power, and the Origins of Our Times* (New York: Verso, 1994), 84.

29. The reference to the book review comes from Zierler's account of the critical reception of Phillips in "Caryl Phillips," 936–37. The second quotation comes from Cheyette, "Venetian Spaces," 63.

30. Caryl Phillips, *Higher Ground: A Novel in Three Parts* (New York: Viking, 1989), 60.

31. The work of William Gardner Smith, which I discuss in Chapter 8, also explores complicity and the difficult construction of solidarity between blacks, Jews, and, in his case, Arabs.

32. Caryl Phillips, *The Nature of Blood* (Boston and London: Faber and Faber, 1997), 3.

33. For a relevant and illuminating discussion of Othello in Shakespeare's source text that highlights the intersections between race, religion, and gender, see Ania Loomba, "*Othello* and the Racial Question," *Shakespeare, Race, and Colonialism* (New York: Oxford University Press, 2002), 91–111.

34. Susan Koshy, "Morphing Race into Ethnicity: Asian Americans and Critical Transformations of Whiteness," *boundary 2* 28, no. 1 (2001): 153–94; here 155.

35. Eva's own end, however, comes not in the camps or gas chambers, but in England, where she has gone in a delirious and deluded effort to reunite with a British soldier she met after the war. The uncanny presence of the survivor in immediate postwar England comes up against complete lack of understanding. The misunderstanding Eva meets is represented not only by the loutish behavior of

Gerry, the soldier, but also by the italicized narrative of Eva's sympathetic but baffled doctor (156–57, 172–73, 186).

36. In an essay on Toni Morrison's novel *Song of Solomon* I have described the relationship between intertextuality, trauma, and memory in terms that are also relevant for *The Nature of Blood.* See Michael Rothberg, "Dead Letter Office: Conspiracy, Trauma, and *Song of Solomon*'s Posthumous Communication," *African American Review* 37, no. 4 (2003): 501–16.

37. Cathy Caruth, "Trauma and Experience: Introduction," *Trauma: Explorations in Memory,* ed. Cathy Caruth (Baltimore, MD: Johns Hopkins University Press, 1995), 11.

38. Such indirect reference bears a resemblance to what, in a discussion of Holocaust memoirs, I have called "traumatic realism." See Michael Rothberg, *Traumatic Realism: The Demands of Holocaust Representation* (Minneapolis: University of Minnesota Press, 2000), chaps. 3 and 4.

39. See Eric Santner, "History Beyond the Pleasure Principle: Some Thoughts on the Representation of Trauma," in *Probing the Limits of Representation: Nazism and the "Final Solution,"* ed. Saul Friedlander (Cambridge, MA: Harvard University Press, 1992), 143–54.

CHAPTER 6

1. Qtd. in Tom Segev, *The Seventh Million: The Israelis and the Holocaust* (New York: Hill and Wang, 1993), 329–30.

2. Peter Novick, *The Holocaust in American Life* (New York: Mariner Books, 2000), 144.

3. Hannah Arendt, *Eichmann in Jerusalem: A Report on the Banality of Evil,* revised and enlarged edition (New York: Penguin, 1964), 16.

4. Annette Wieviorka, *L'ère du témoin* (Paris: Plon, 1998), 79. See now also the English translation: *The Era of the Witness,* trans. Jared Stark (Ithaca, NY: Cornell University Press, 2006). In a fascinating book on the Jean-François Steiner controversy of the mid-1960s, Samuel Moyn has recently argued, contra Wieviorka, that the reception of the Eichmann trial in France was delayed and relatively insignificant. Moyn's findings support my very different effort in this section of the book to decenter the trial's importance in favor of renewed attention to the context of decolonization. See Samuel Moyn, *A Holocaust Controversy: The Treblinka Affair in Postwar France* (Waltham, MA: Brandeis University Press, 2005).

5. Besides works mentioned in other notes, other important recent scholarship on Eichmann and the trial includes: David Cesarani, *Becoming Eichmann: Rethinking the Life, Crimes, and Trial of a "Desk Murderer"* (Cambridge, MA: Da Capo, 2004); David Cesarani, ed., *After Eichmann: Collective Memory and the Holocaust Since 1961* (New York: Routledge, 2005); and Lawrence Douglas, *The Mem-*

ory of Judgment: Making Law and History in the Trials of the Holocaust (New Haven, CT: Yale University Press, 2001).

6. Jeffrey Shandler, *While America Watches: Televising the Holocaust* (New York: Oxford University Press, 2000), esp. 127–32. Shandler takes the phrase "cinema vérité of due process" from an article in *The New Yorker*. Radio was probably an even more important medium than television at the time; it was through radio that most Israelis experienced the trial.

7. The first brief, but insightful discussion of the film in the context of the Holocaust by Joshua Hirsch appeared after this chapter was first written. See Joshua Hirsch, *Afterimage: Film, Trauma, and the Holocaust* (Philadelphia, PA: Temple University Press, 2003).

8. In an informative and illuminating essay, Steven Ungar considers a similar sequence of scenes, but does not situate it in relation to the history of Holocaust memory or the specificities of anticolonial discourse (although he mentions both in passing). See Steven Ungar, "In the Thick of Things: Rouch and Morin's *Chronique d'un été* Reconsidered," *French Cultural Studies* 14, no. 1 (2003): 5–22.

9. Edgar Morin, "Chronicle of a Film," in Jean Rouch, *Ciné-ethnography*, trans. and ed. Steven Feld (Minneapolis: University of Minnesota Press, 2003), 261. It is indeed true that no French film directly addressed the Algerian War until after its conclusion. Those that attempted to address it indirectly, such as Resnais's *Muriel*, were sometimes censored. See Benjamin Stora, *La gangrène et l'oubli: La mémoire de la guerre d'Algérie* (Paris: La Découverte, 1991), 38–45.

10. For a brilliant and detailed discussion of the tensions in the film's conception and production, with particular reference to debates about Bazin's phenomenological film theory, see Sam DiIorio, "Total Cinema: *Chronique d'un été* and the End of Bazinian Film Theory," *Screen* 48, no. 1 (2007): 25–43.

11. Quotations from the film will be taken from Jean Rouch, *Ciné-ethnography*, which includes a translation of the entire script which is more reliable than the English subtitles. For the original French version of the script, which also contains important supplementary materials, see Jean Rouch and Edgar Morin, *Chronique d'un été* (Paris: Interspectacles, 1962).

12. Paratextual materials suggest that up until this point in the film the filmmakers have deliberately muted the Holocaust's presence. A scene filmed early on in which Marceline describes her experiences has been edited out of the final version, although it is included in the script. This deliberate muting creates the sense, seemingly shared by the filmmakers, that the beginning of the film is "merely personal" while politics only emerges in the middle of the film. I would argue that these realms are more intertwined.

Rothman includes a fine close analysis of the scene with Jean-Pierre, but I disagree strongly with his unwarranted conclusion that "when Rouch films Marceline. . . . Symbolically, he builds a death camp for her, and for himself" (85). See also DiIorio's fine discussion of the construction of this scene out of film shot with two different camera technologies (34). As DiIorio points out, Rouch has actually edited out important references to Algeria here that help explain Jean-Pierre's bitterness. Jean-Pierre had been a member of the Jeanson network, many of whose members had been arrested a few months before shooting. See William Rothman, *Documentary Film Classics* (New York: Cambridge University Press, 1997).

13. Shortly after the making of *Chronicle*, Marceline Loridan and Jean-Pierre Sergent (their full names) made a film together on the Algerian revolution, *L'Algérie, L'Année Zéro*. Loridan also married the Dutch documentary filmmaker Joris Ivens and made twenty films with him around the world, including works opposing the Vietnam War and a twelve-hour film on China and the Cultural Revolution. In 2003, Marceline Loridan-Ivens directed her first feature film, *La petite prairie aux bouleaux*, the story of a Holocaust survivor who returns to Auschwitz after many years.

14. Drawing on a transcript of the rushes of the film, DiIorio makes a strong case that Rouch and Morin subtracted much of the political material they had filmed: "The tightly knit relationship between colonialism and occupation was systematically unraveled in the final cut. Political content was reduced to a spectral presence: it became the ghost which haunted this film and its protagonists" (36). While I agree with DiIorio that the final version of film does not include much in the way of radical political content, I nevertheless find the connections it does make between Algeria and Auschwitz politically significant for this moment in France, as I argue below. On the film's involvement with contemporary politics, see also Ivone Margulies, "*Chronicle of a Summer* (1960) as *Autocritique* (1959): A Transition in the French Left," *Quarterly Review of Film and Video* 21, no. 3 (2004): 173–85.

15. See James Clifford, *The Predicament of Culture: Twentieth-Century Ethnography, Literature, and Art* (Cambridge, MA: Harvard University Press, 1988), 139. For Rouch's own account of the museum during the war, see his essay "The Mad Fox and the Pale Master" (102–26). The head of the Musée de l'Homme resistance network for a time was another fascinating figure of multidirectional memory, Germaine Tillion, who died in 2008 at the age of 101. An anthropologist who had already worked before World War II in Algeria, Tillion was deported to Ravensbruck for her resistance activities. She went on to provide accounts of the camps, in books such as *Ravensbrück* (Neuchâtel: Editions de la baconnière, 1946), and of the Algerian War, in books such as *Les ennemis complémentaires* (Paris: Minuit, 1960). A moving tribute to Tillion's sense of justice can be found in Tzvetan Todorov, *Hope and Memory: Lessons from the Twentieth Century*, trans. David Bellos (Princeton, NJ: Princeton University Press, 2003).

16. Charlotte Delbo, *Auschwitz and After*, trans. Rosette Lamont (New Haven, CT: Yale University Press, 1995), 233–354. On *Auschwitz and After*, see Michael

Rothberg, *Traumatic Realism: The Demands of Holocaust Representation* (Minneapolis: University of Minnesota Press, 2000), 141–77. In Chapter 7, I will resituate Delbo's Auschwitz writings in relation to her opposition to the Algerian War.

17. Clifford's phrasing is quite close to the way that Rouch once described the scenes with Marceline: "All of a sudden an encounter [took] place between two unusual things that normally are not related, and a structure was created because of this meeting." Qtd. in Ellen Freyer "*Chronicle of a Summer*—Ten Years After," in *The Documentary Tradition*, 2d ed., ed. Lewis Jacobs (New York: W. W. Norton, 1979), 441.

18. Eaton describes Rouch's surrealism as "a surrealism as conveyed by the theme of the encounter." See Mick Eaton, "The Production of Cinematic Reality," in *Anthropology, Reality, Cinema: The Films of Jean Rouch*, ed. Mick Eaton (London: British Film Institute, 1979), 50. On Rouch and surrealism, see also Jeanette DeBouzek, "The 'Ethnographic Surrealism' of Jean Rouch," *Visual Anthropology* 2, nos. 3–4 (1989): 301–15; esp. 311–12; and Rouch's own comments in "The Mad Fox and the Pale Master" (102–26).

19. Resnais intended *Night and Fog* as an oblique commentary on the Algerian War, and its text was, in fact, written by a deportee, Jean Cayrol. But, unlike the scenes with Marceline, Cayrol's narration takes the form neither of personal testimony nor of testimony to the genocide of Jews, but rather of a poetic and political invocation of more generalized camp horrors.

20. Steven Feld, "Introduction," in Rouch, *Ciné-ethnography*, 14–15.

21. On voice and the Holocaust video archive, see Geoffrey Hartman, *The Longest Shadow: In the Aftermath of the Holocaust* (Bloomington: Indiana University Press, 1996), 144. Hartman has been one of the most consistently insightful commentators on the project of archiving video testimony.

22. Michel Marie, "Direct," in *Anthropology, Reality, Cinema: The Films of Jean Rouch*, ed. Mick Eaton (London: British Film Institute, 1979), 35.

23. Lawrence Langer, *Holocaust Testimonies: The Ruins of Memory* (New Haven, CT: Yale University Press, 1991), xii–xiii.

24. For a discussion of the editing of *Chronicle*, see Barry Dornfeld, "*Chronicle of a Summer* and the Editing of Cinéma-Vérité," *Visual Anthropology* 2, nos. 3–4 (1989): 317–31.

25. I am adapting Rouch's concept, which primarily refers to the kind of trance experienced by the cinematographer while filming possession ceremonies. This scene has, however, already been associated with "ciné-transe"; see DeBouzek, "'Ethnographic Surrealism,'" 305.

26. Joshua Hirsch also reads *Chronicle* as a precursor of *Shoah* and argues that it offers the first "representation of the witness as a bearer of traumatic memory" (68). However, because he does not consider discourses of decolonization he does not offer a new explanation of why *Chronicle* marks this emergence.

27. On Rouch's aesthetic ideology, see Eaton, "Production of Cinematic Reality."

28. Wieviorka does not suggest that it is only the Eichmann trial that matters. She also points to the publications of Wiesel and Schwarz-Bart, and to ongoing German trials (86–87).

29. Qtd. in Pierre Vidal-Naquet, *Mémoires: 2. Le trouble et la lumière (1955–1998)* (Paris: Seuil/La Découverte, "Points" 1998), 110.

30. Qtd. in Stora, *La gangrène et l'oubli*, 32; and Charlotte Delbo, *Les belles lettres* (Paris: Minuit, 1961), 81.

31. Jean Améry, *At the Mind's Limits: Contemplations by a Survivor on Auschwitz and Its Realities* (New York: Schocken Books, 1986), 23.

32. In 1961, the camp memoirist Delbo published her first book, *Les belles lettres*, which concerns the Algerian War. It is the subject of Chapter 7.

33. See Kristin Ross, *May '68 and Its Afterlives* (Chicago: University of Chicago Press, 2002), 49; and Maurice T. Maschino, "L'histoire expurgée de la Guerre d'Algérie," *Le Monde diplomatique* (February 2001).

34. See Hervé Hamon and Patrick Rotman, *Les porteurs de valises: La résistance française à la guerre d'Algérie* (Paris: Albin Michel, 1979), 398–99.

35. See Paul Clay Sorum, *Intellectuals and Decolonization in France* (Chapel Hill: University of North Carolina Press, 1977), 173. Neither Rouch nor Morin signed the manifesto, but they did sign a more moderate "Call to Opinion for a Negotiated Peace in Algeria," along with Merleau-Ponty, Ricoeur, Barthes, and others (Sorum, *Intellectuals*, 175). The manifesto will also play an important role in our subsequent discussion of Delbo.

36. Pierre Vidal-Naquet, *Face à la raison d'état: Un historien dans la guerre d'Algérie* (Paris: La Découverte, 1989), 83.

37. For a fascinating oral history that demonstrates the important role memory of the Nazi occupation and genocide played in motivating anticolonial resistance, see Martin Evans, *The Memory of Resistance: French Opposition to the Algerian War (1954–1962)* (Oxford, Eng.: Berg, 1997), 31–72. I am grateful to Joan Tumblety for this reference.

38. See David Macey, *Frantz Fanon: A Biography* (New York: Picador USA, 2001), 260–62. Mandouze ironically gave his memoir the same title as did Georges Bidault, himself a World War II resistance figure who went on to become one of the most infamous opponents of Algerian independence and defenders of "French Algeria." Bidault's memoir *D'une résistance à l'autre* was published in 1965 and emblematizes the fact that multidirectional resonances were by no means harnessed only on the side of anticolonial struggle. Gillo Pontecorvo's 1966 film *The Battle of Algiers* makes a similar point through the character of Colonel Mathieu, a former resistance fighter who now heads the counterinsurgency struggle in Algiers and who justifies the employment of torture with reference to the fact that he and

his men were themselves tortured by the Nazis. That this anticolonial film classic was directed by a Jewish, Communist, former resistance fighter whose earlier film *Kapo* (1959) treated the Nazi camps and whose later *Burn!* (1969) took up the Haitian revolution demonstrates once again that multidirectional memory is the matrix out of which various postwar struggles to come to terms with history and political actuality emerged. Given the multidirectional archive that this book seeks to construct, it is also worth mentioning that Pontecorvo got his start in cinema as the assistant to Joris Ivens, the radical Dutch documentarian who would later marry Marceline Loridan of *Chronicle of a Summer*!

39. Pierre Vidal-Naquet, *Assassins of Memory: Essays on the Denial of the Holocaust* (New York: Columbia University Press, 1992), 127.

40. For a convincing version of this argument that addresses the relationship between Camus's writings, the Holocaust, and the Algerian War, see Dominick LaCapra, *History and Memory After Auschwitz* (Ithaca, NY: Cornell University Press, 1998), 73–94. For more on Camus, colonialism, and the Holocaust, see the forthcoming work of Debarati Sanyal.

41. Henry Rousso, *Le syndrome de Vichy: 1944–198* (Paris: Seuil, 1987), chap. 2.

42. On this period, see Kristin Ross, *Fast Cars, Clean Bodies: Decolonization and the Reordering of French Culture* (Cambridge, MA: MIT Press, 1995). Ross, however, downplays the legacies of the Nazi occupation and genocide.

CHAPTER 7

1. See Primo Levi, "J'étais un homme" and Frantz Fanon, "De la violence," both in *Les Temps modernes* 181 (May 1961): 1533–69, 1453–93; for Eichmann and the massacre, see Robert Misrahi, "Le process Eichmann et la seconde naissance d'Israël," Jacques Vergès, "Lettre au Dr. Servatius sur la defense de Robert Lacoste," and T.M. [Les Temps modernes], "La 'Bataille de Paris,'" *Les Temps modernes* 186 (November 1961): 552–62, 563–65, and 618–20.

2. For an extended discussion of these dimensions of Delbo's work, see Michael Rothberg, *Traumatic Realism: The Demands of Holocaust Representation* (Minneapolis: University of Minnesota Press, 2000), 141–77. See also Thomas Trezise, "The Question of Community in Charlotte Delbo's *Auschwitz and After*," *MLN* 117, no. 4 (2003). Lawrence L. Langer, *The Age of Atrocity: Death in Modern Literature* (Boston: Beacon, 1978). Brett Ashley Kaplan, "Pleasure, Memory, and Time Suspension in Holocaust Literature: Celan and Delbo," *Comparative Literature Studies* 38, no. 4 (2001). Nicole Thatcher, *A Literary Analysis of Charlotte Delbo's Concentration Camp Re-Presentation* (Lewiston, NY: Edwin Mellen Press, 2000). Nicole Thatcher, *Charlotte Delbo: Une voix singulière* (Paris: L'Harmattan, 2003).

3. Charlotte Delbo, *Les belles lettres* (Paris: Minuit, 1961).

4. Delbo's statement that she let her manuscript sit to see if it would stand the test of time is reported in Lawrence L. Langer, "Introduction," trans. Rosette Lamont, *Auschwitz and After*, ed. Charlotte Delbo (New Haven, CT: Yale University Press, 1995), vol. x.

5. Kristin Ross, *Fast Cars, Clean Bodies: Decolonization and the Reordering of French Culture* (Cambridge, MA: MIT Press, 1995); Kristin Ross, *May '68 and Its Afterlives* (Chicago: University of Chicago Press, 2002).

6. Shoshana Felman and Dori Laub, *Testimony: Crises of Witnessing in Literature, Psychoanalysis, and History* (New York: Routledge, 1992).

7. There is no biography of Delbo. Thatcher includes brief biographical information in her books, cited above. The more extensive literature on Lefebvre has yet to make anything of his association with Delbo. Lefebvre's biographer, Remi Hess, remarks that Delbo "was the principal [administrative?] collaborator of Lefebvre in the 1960s and 1970s" and mentions that Delbo had been Lefebvre's student in the Lycée de Montargis in the early 1930s, but he dedicates only one footnote to her in his entire book. See Remi Hess, *Henri Lefebvre et l'aventure du siècle* (Paris: Éditions A.M. Métailié, 1988), 206–7n.

8. Charlotte Delbo, *Auschwitz and After*, trans. Rosette Lamont (New Haven, CT: Yale University Press, 1995), 132–33.

9. Charlotte Delbo, *Days and Memory*, trans. Rosette Lamont (Marlboro, VT: Marlboro Press, 1990), 111.

10. I have modified the translation according to the original. See Charlotte Delbo, *La mémoire et les jours* (Paris: Berg International, 1985), 133.

11. The massacre of scores of Algerians protesting a curfew in October 1961, mentioned in *Days and Memory*, is not discussed in *Les belles lettres*, which was published several months earlier. This massacre and its aftermath are the subject of the following chapters.

12. For information on publishing during the Nazi occupation, see Pierre Assouline, *Gaston Gallimard: A Half-Century of French Publishing*, trans. Harold J. Salemson (New York: Harcourt Brace Jovanovich, 1988). Assouline gives the date of Minuit's founding as 1941 (253).

13. In a subtle essay on the first volume of *Auschwitz and After*, Thomas Trezise has argued that Delbo disrupts genre conventions in her memoir as part of a larger questioning of communal consensus. See Trezise, "Community," 871.

14. Pieter Lagrou, *The Legacy of Nazi Occupation: Patriotic Memory and National Recovery in Western Europe, 1945–1965* (New York: Cambridge University Press, 2000), 304.

15. See Olivier Lalieu, *La déportation fragmentée: Les anciens déportés parlent de politique, 1945–1980* (Paris: La Boutique de l'Histoire, 1994), 149–62.

16. For further references to the invocation of the Nuremberg trials, as well as a translation of the passage from Le Meur that I have drawn upon, see Paul Clay So-

rum, *Intellectuals and Decolonization in France* (Chapel Hill: University of North Carolina Press, 1977), 153–54.

17. Ross, *Fast Cars,* 122.

18. Michael Warner, "Publics and Counterpublics," *Public Culture* 14, no. 1 (2002). See also Michael Warner, *Publics and Counterpublics* (New York: Zone, 2002).

19. I would distinguish this punctual temporality, which defines a *politics* of memory from a durational temporality, which defines an *ethics* of memory built on what Badiou calls fidelity and Ian Baucom might call accumulation. A durational ethics of memory is central to Chapter 9. See Alain Badiou, *Ethics: An Essay on the Understanding of Evil* (New York: Verso, 2002); and Ian Baucom, *Specters of the Atlantic: Finance Capital, Slavery, and the Philosophy of History* (Durham, NC: Duke University Press, 2005).

20. For a related critique of the dominance of the psychoanalytic model in theories of testimony, see Rosanne Kennedy and Tikka Jan Wilson, "Constructing Shared Histories: Stolen Generations Testimony, Narrative Therapy and Address," in *World Memory: Personal Trajectories in Global Time,* ed. Jill Bennett and Rosanne Kennedy (New York: Palgrave MacMillan, 2003), 119–39.

21. In a fine book on art, affect, and trauma, Jill Bennett also calls for a more "public" approach to testimony. Bennett's comments on the ethical dimensions of testimony stress the dialogic, face-to-face encounter of bearing witness. Her approach is thus closer to that of Felman and Laub than to that of Warner, since her notion of the public is modeled on conversation and not circulation (even though she is clearly interested in the latter as well). See Jill Bennett, *Empathic Vision: Affect, Trauma, and Contemporary Art* (Stanford, CA: Stanford University Press, 2005), 104–5.

22. My translations from the "Déclaration," the text of which can be found in Hervé Hamon and Patrick Rotman, *Les porteurs de valises: La résistance française à la guerre d'Algérie* (Paris: Albin Michel, 1979), 391–94.

23. Sorum, *Intellectuals,* 173–75; Hamon, *Porteurs de valises,* 303–18.

24. Delbo's invocation of such a ban in *Auschwitz and After* also locates its source in the state. See my discussion in Rothberg, *Traumatic Realism,* 147.

25. I am grateful to Wail Hassan for helping me with the Arabic.

26. On the contemporary context, see Naomi Klein, "'Never Before!': Our Amnesiac Torture Debate," *The Nation,* December 26, 2005, 12.

27. In a cogent consideration of the "national sentimentality" of U.S. liberal politics, Lauren Berlant offers a powerful critique of the deployment of testimony and rhetorics of pain and trauma by subaltern groups and their supporters. Berlant argues convincingly that "the pain and suffering of subordinated subjects is an ordinary and ongoing thing that is underdescribed by the traumatic identity form and its circulation in the state and law." With reference to Wendy Brown's related

critique of "wounded attachments," Berlant demonstrates how the trauma/testimony model resubordinates subjects to the state and sets artificial limits to the critique of oppression because it "assumes that the law describes what a person is, and that social violence can be located the way physical injury can be traced" (42). Finally, this model also insinuates a simplified notion of truth through testimony, which becomes conceptualized "as prelapsarian knowledge or a condensed comprehensive social theory" (43). I believe Berlant's claims are convincing within the framework of her argument—the use of testimony in a liberal state—but I am somewhat more sanguine about the importance of testimony in other contexts, such as that of the "state of exception" that defined the latter stages of the Algerian War and perhaps our own post–September 11 location in the "global war on terror." Nevertheless, the testimony model has obvious limits and is not capable of political transformation when detached from larger collective formations based on fidelity and solidarity. See Lauren Berlant, "The Subject of True Feeling: Pain, Privacy, and Politics," *Transformations: Thinking through Feminism*, ed. Sara Ahmed, Jane Kilby, Celia Lury, Maureen McNeil, and Beverley Skeggs (New York: Routledge, 2000), 33, 42, 43.

28. Qtd. in Mark Danner, *Torture and Truth: America, Abu Ghraib, and the War on Terror* (New York: New York Review, 2004), 248.

29. Danner, *Torture and Truth*, xiv.

30. The flickering image of torture, it must be admitted, has been a repeated one since the depredations of Abu Ghraib were revealed. Statistics demonstrate a sharp increase in instances of torture on (fictional) American television series. While work needs to be done on the meaning of those instances, it seems clear thus far that they do little to advance public debate or consciousness about the history and politics of torture; rather, they seem to function as part of a collective normalization and legitimation of torture. Hence, despite their omnipresence, they fail to produce a counter-image of the sort that the French activists attempted to produce. For an account of the new omnipresence of torture on American television, see the AP article, "Group: TV Torture Influencing Real Life," *New York Times*, February 11, 2007. *http://www.nytimes.com/aponline/arts/AP-TV-American-Torture.html*. Accessed on February 11, 2007.

31. As evidence of a backlash against the critique of colonialism, see the law passed on February 23, 2005, mandating attention in schools to the "positive" aspects of France's overseas presence. This law, along with the social unrest in the Paris suburbs, has opened up renewed discussion of France's colonial past, discussion that everywhere evokes the memory of Vichy and the Nazi occupation and that I return to in the next chapter. See the dossier, "La vérité sur la colonisation," in *Le Nouvel observateur* 2144 (December 8–14, 2005): 12–32.

32. For evidence supporting the claims about French public opinion and for a brief discussion of the Papon trial, see William Cohen's very useful essay on the

changing contours of French memory of torture in Algeria and of French understanding of its colonial projects. William B. Cohen, "The Algerian War and the Revision of France's Overseas Mission," *French Colonial History* 4 (2003). See also the evocative essay by David Prochaska, "That Was Then, This Is Now: The Battle of Algiers and After," *Radical History Review* 85 (2003).

33. Jim House and Neil MacMaster, *Paris 1961: Algerians, State Terror, and Memory* (Oxford: Oxford University Press, 2006), 26–27, 30.

CHAPTER 8

1. Jim House and Neil MacMaster, *Paris 1961: Algerians, State Terror, and Memory* (Oxford: Oxford University Press, 2006), 1. House and MacMaster's important book is the most authoritative account of the lead up to the October massacre and its aftermath.

2. As House and MacMaster write, "The key transitional period [for memory of the events] between October 1961 and February 1962 displaced the question of anti-Algerian violence and deferred the political effect of the 17 October events, a sign of the repression's very diffuse impact on the left" (*Paris 1961* 242).

3. Situating October 1961 in a transnational frame marked by race, gender, and generation helps to reveal why its memory has proven so provocative for a French public: the persistent importance of such social categories names a crisis in still powerful Republican ideologies of universalism and citizenship.

4. Despite its comprehensive scope and exemplary interdisciplinary methodology, House and MacMaster's *Paris 1961* makes no mention of Smith's novel. They also do not mention Haneke's film, but that work falls out of the primary chronological framework of their book, which stops in 2001 with the fortieth anniversary of the events. The book may have been in press before *Caché* appeared.

5. See Daniel Levy and Natan Sznaider, "Memory Unbound: The Holocaust and the Formation of Cosmopolitan Memory," *European Journal of Social Theory* 5, no. 1 (2002): 87–106; here 102.

6. In reconstructing the history—including the lead-up and aftermath—of the October 1961 events I have drawn on numerous studies and primary sources that are cited throughout this section and this chapter.

7. November also saw the publication of Paulette Péju's *Rattonades à Paris* (Paris: Maspero, 1961), which, much like Delbo's *Les belles lettres*, collected many key journalistic reports. It was immediately seized by the police, but has now been reprinted as *Rattonades à Paris* précédé de *Les harkis à Paris* (Paris: La Découverte, 2000).

8. In some of their chapter titles, House and MacMaster periodize memory of the events as follows: "The Marginalization of 17 October 1961 (1961–1968)"; "'Underground' Memories, 1962–1979"; "Emergent Memories, 1980–1997?"; "Ev-

er-Present Memories" (for the turn of the millennium and beyond). The reference to "underground memories" derives from Benjamin Stora.

9. House and MacMaster go on to write that "Sociologists and anthropologists working on inter-generational relations and memory transmission with Algerian migrant communities in France have found a wider pattern of 'reversal' of the usual model of memory transmission. This memory work was by definition a two-way inter-generational process engendered by the entrepreneurial memorial activities of the children and, latterly, grandchildren of Algerian migrants, often in conjunction with anti-racist associations, former anti-colonial activists, the far left, journalists, and, latterly, teachers and researchers. The memories of those people who did not experience the events are a mixture of inter-personally transmitted memories and memories acquired via some external medium (reading, radio, television)" (324–25). Here we can see that the emerging memories of October 1961 were multidirectional both because they were produced by multiethnic networks of memory carriers with varied ideologies and because the temporality of memory transmission did not flow in expected directions.

10. Nacer Kettane, *Le sourire de Brahim* (Paris: Denoël, 1985), 5, 9. The following year Mehdi Lallaoui's *Les Beurs de Seine* (Paris: Arcantère, 1986) appeared in the series "Mémoires et Identités," edited by T. Sbouaï. Panijel's film *Octobre à Paris* (1962) was immediately censored and since then has rarely been shown publicly (and never on television), although a pamphlet presenting the film also exists: Le Comité Maurice Audin and *Vérité-Liberté*, ed. *Octobre à Paris* (Paris: n.p., 1962). Scenes from the film have also been integrated into later documentaries such as *Drowning by Bullets*, also known as *Une journée portée disparue*, by Alan Hayling and Philip Brooks (1992). Although almost unwatched, Panijel's film has attained, through such forms of citation, status as a *lieu de mémoire*.

11. Michel Levine, *Les ratonnades d'octobre: Un meurtre collectif à Paris en 1961* (Paris: Ramsay, 1985); Jean-Luc Einaudi, *La bataille de Paris: 17 octobre 1961* (Paris: Seuil, 1991).

12. On the various trials, see Richard Golsan's extremely useful collection *The Papon Affair: Memory and Justice on Trial* (New York: Routledge, 2000). See also the trial transcript, Catherine Erhel, Mathieu Aucher, and Renaud de La Baume, eds., *Le Procès de Maurice Papon*, 2 vols. (Paris: Albin Michel, 1998). For a discussion of the commemorative plaque, see House and MacMaster, *Paris 1961*, 317–19.

13. Joshua Cole, "Remembering the Battle of Paris: 17 October 1961 in French and Algerian Memory," *French Politics, Culture, and Society* 21, no. 3 (fall 2003): 21–50; here 32.

14. My position is perhaps closest to Jim House, who, in his fine essay "Anti-racist Memories," shows how such connections have been deployed for more than a half-century by groups struggling to counter various forms of racism. However,

House, dedicated primarily to a historicizing analysis of October 17 memory, does not provide the same kind of historicization of Holocaust memory that he does for October 17. Drawing attention to multidirectional dynamics allows for a double historicization that demonstrates the shaping influence of the *interaction* of memories. See Jim House, "Antiracist Memories: The Case of 17 October 1961 in Historical Perspective," *Modern and Contemporary France* 9, no. 3 (2001): 355–68. In his book with MacMaster, House also mentions some of these connections, although without giving them too much emphasis. Nevertheless, House and MacMaster do end their book by calling for more comparative work. My project attempts to follow up on that call.

15. Jacques Buob and Alain Frachon, "'La France est malade de sa mémoire': Pierre Nora et le métier d'historien," in "Colonies: Un débat français," *Le Monde 2* (May–June 2006): 6–9.

16. Marguerite Duras, "Les deux ghettos," *France-Observateur*, November 9, 1961, 8–10.

17. Jean-François Revel, rev. of *Chronique d'un été*, *France-Observateur*, October 26, 1961, 26–27.

18. Today the magazine continues in a more mainstream guise as *Le Nouvel observateur*. *France-Observateur* provides most of my examples of coverage of the October 17 events in this section, but it was by no means the only media source that consistently linked current events with the recent Nazi past. Intensive coverage and similar analogies can also be found in *Vérité-Liberté*, as well as *Les Temps modens* and other leftist venues.

19. Claude Bourdet, "Y a-t-il une Gestapo algérienne?" *France-Observateur*, December 6, 1951, 6–8; and "Votre Gestapo d'Algérie," *France-Observateur*, January 13, 1955, 6–7.

20. Antiracist rhetoric and mobilization that drew upon analogies between anti-Jewish and anti-Algerian victimization were not new to this period, as House and MacMaster show. They draw attention in particular to the Mouvement contre le racisme and pour la paix (MRAP), an organization close to the French Communist Party with many Jewish members, which already in the early 1950s "sought to establish a direct parallel between French state practices under Vichy and those practiced by the French state against Algerians" (*Paris 1961* 197). But there does seem to be an intensification of such parallels around October 17 and a greater sense of the specificity of anti-Jewish persecution. Todd Shepard's argument in *The Invention of Decolonization*, discussed below, helps to explain why an intensification of references to race and racism might have taken place late in the war. The combination of these two historical accounts suggests both continuities and discontinuities between the pre-Algerian War and late war moments. My argument is that these valuable works of historical contextualization cannot render entirely readable the precise, comparative form references to race and rac-

ism took. The mobilization of solidarities across racialized identities remains in constant flux and takes shape only in dynamic, multidirectional movements. See Todd Shepard, *The Invention of Decolonization: The Algerian War and the Remaking of France* (Ithaca, NY: Cornell University Press, 2006).

21. Henri Kréa, "Le racisme est collectif, la solidarité individuelle," *France-Observateur*, October 26, 1961, 14–15.

22. William Gardner Smith, *The Stone Face* (New York: Farrar, Straus, and Co., 1963). On Smith's novel, see Paul Gilory, *Against Race: Imagining Political Culture Beyond the Color Line* (Cambridge, MA: Harvard University Press, 2000); Kristin Ross, *May '68 and Its Afterlives* (Chicago: University of Chicago Press, 2002); Tyler Stovall, "Preface to *The Stone Face*," *Contemporary French and Francophone Studies* 8, no. 3 (summer 2004): 305–27; Stovall, "The Fire This Time: Black American Expatriates and the Algerian War," *Yale French Studies* 98 (2000): 182–200. Smith also wrote an earlier novel about African American soldiers in early postwar Germany that works in fascinating ways with questions of race, nation, and gender. See Smith, *The Last of the Conquerors* (New York: Farrar, Straus, 1948). See Gilroy's discussion of this novel in *Against Race*.

23. See Stovall, "Fire," for an account of the impact of the Algerian War of Independence on African American expatriates. For more on the expatriates, see Stovall, *Paris Noir: African Americans in the City of Light* (New York: Houghton Mifflin, 1996); and Michel Fabre, *From Harlem to Paris: Black American Writers in France, 1840–1980* (Urbana: University of Illinois Press, 1991).

24. Although I have seen no other reports that French plans were openly announced in the sites where Algerians were held, Smith's account is otherwise accurate. Several hundred of the peaceful demonstrators were sent back to camps in their "*douars d'origine*"—camps that were indeed referred to as concentration camps by opponents of government policy.

25. Given the fact that Lumumba's murder followed his removal from power in a CIA-sponsored coup, his death might also be the occasion for a reflection on the complicity of Americans, but Smith foregrounds instead a "racial" complicity. Unrest in the Congo was also part of the context of decolonization alluded to in *Chronicle of a Summer*, much of which was filmed just before the coup.

26. Smith's use of "colony" to describe the expatriate community is not idiosyncratic, but it does take on additional resonance given the context of the French-Algerian War. For another use of "colony" outside the context of the war, see James Baldwin, "A Question of Identity," *Collected Essays* (New York: Library of America, 1998), 91–100.

27. Mark Sanders, *Complicities: The Intellectual and Apartheid* (Durham, NC: Duke University Press, 2002), 8. For more on complicity in the context of racism and the Holocaust, see Naomi Mandel's provocative study *Against the Unspeak-*

able: Complicity, the Holocaust, and Slavery in America (Charlottesville: University of Virginia Press, 2006).

28. Later in the 1960s, Smith moved to Ghana at the invitation of Kwame Nkrumah. But after the coup that removed Nkrumah from power in 1966, he returned to Paris, where he died in 1974.

29. Stovall, "Preface," 309. Stovall's "Preface" provides a short introduction to the republication of an excerpt from the novel (which depicts the October 17 massacre) and the first French translation of that same excerpt. In "The Fire This Time," Stovall provides a slightly more extensive discussion of the novel in an essay that includes a broad discussion of African American life in Paris during the Algerian War.

30. Stovall's silence on the Jewish and Holocaust-related dimensions of the novel is odd given that in his fine essay on expatriates and the Algerian War he does discuss the links between the October 17 massacre and the Nazi genocide by evoking the historical figure of Papon and Didier Daeninckx's novel *Meurtres pour mémoire*, which I discuss in the next chapter. See Stovall, "Fire," 196–97.

31. The ashes and smoke of cigarettes are a constant reminder of the Holocaust in the work of Art Spiegelman, for example, and the electric field recalls the electrified barbed wire that surrounded Nazi camps.

32. See Frantz Fanon, *Black Skin, White Masks*, trans. Charles Lam Markmann (New York: Grove Press, 1967), 109.

33. For a useful collection of essays on "Gender and Cultural Memory," see the special issue of *Signs* edited by Marianne Hirsch and Valerie Smith (28, no. 1 [fall 2002]).

34. Smith does not choose Djamila's name arbitrarily. Two of the most infamous cases of torture during the late 1950s and early 1960s involved women named Djamila: Boujhered and Boupacha. On Boupacha, see the previous chapter and also Ranjana Khanna's fascinating discussion of language, law, and transnational feminism in the Boupacha case, which was championed by Simone de Beauvoir and the lawyer Gisèle Halimi. In agreement with this book's project, Khanna is also attentive to the ways that "the ghosts of World War II" are part of the search for justice in the Algerian case. See Ranjana Khanna, "The Experience of Evidence: Language, the Law, and the Mockery of Justice," in *Algeria in Others' Languages*, ed. Anne-Emmanuelle Berger (Ithaca, NY: Cornell University Press, 2002), 107–38; here 129. See also the book that incorporates this essay, R. Khanna, *Algeria Cuts: Women and Representation, 1830 to the Present* (Stanford, CA: Stanford University Press, 2008).

35. See, for example, Alain Badiou's remarks on the Nazi genocide in *Ethics*, trans. Peter Hallward (New York: Verso, 2002); and Slavoj Zizek's in *Did Somebody Say Totalitarianism?* (New York: Verso, 2002).

356 Notes

36. Fredric Jameson, "Foreword: A Monument to Radical Instants," in Peter Weiss, *The Aesthetics of Resistance*, vol. 1, trans. Joachim Neugroschel (Durham, NC: Duke University Press, 2005), viii.

37. See Jeffrey Alexander, "On the Social Construction of Moral Universals: The 'Holocaust' from War Crime to Trauma Drama," *The Meanings of Social Life: A Cultural Sociology* (New York: Oxford University Press, 2003).

38. For an extended engagement with Alexander's work, see my "Multidirectional Memory and the Universalization of the Holocaust," in Jeffrey Alexander et al., *Remembering the Holocaust: A Debate* (New York: Oxford University Press, forthcoming 2009).

39. My discussion of the work of Levy and Sznaider draws both on their book *Erinnerung im globalen Zeitalter: Der Holocaust* and on an essay that provides an English-language sketch of their argument "Memory Unbound: The Holocaust and the Formation of Cosmopolitan Memory." Translations from the book are my own. An English-language version of the book has been published as *Holocaust and Memory in the Global Age* (Philadelphia, PA: Temple University Press, 2005).

40. The question of the "progressive" nature of Alexander's account is more complicated than it is for Levy/Sznaider, since Alexander sees the universalization of the Holocaust taking place only when a certain nationalist/progressive narrative has been abandoned. Yet, as I argue in "Multidirectional Memory and the Universalization of the Holocaust," Alexander's account remains progressive because it argues that the traumatic narrative that replaced the progressive one fosters the same kinds of human rights gains that Levy/Sznaider point to.

41. See also Aleida Assmann's discussion of Europe as a "community of memory." Assmann writes in response to Levy and Sznaider: "The Holocaust has not become a single universally shared memory, but it has become the paradigm or template through which other genocides and historical traumas are very often perceived and presented. The Holocaust has thereby not replaced other traumatic memories around the globe but has provided a language for their articulation." While I agree with this assessment, I believe Assmann leaves out the other side of the dialectic: the degree to which the emergence of the Holocaust as such a template took place in dialogue with other histories. Assmann's discussion of European memory in this lecture is surprisingly silent on the memory of colonialism and slavery. See Aleida Assmann, "Europe: A Community of Memory?" *German Historical Institute Bulletin* 40 (spring 2007): 11–25; citation from page 14.

CHAPTER 9

1. The petition was originally published in *Libération* on December 13, 2005; its text can be found on the website of *Le Nouvel observateur*. http://archquo.nouvelobs.com/cgi/articles?ad=societe/20051213.OBS8759.html. Accessed June 21, 2006.

2. The quotation from Chirac as well as basic information on the various laws mentioned here can be found in the special issue: "Colonies: Un débat français," *Le Monde 2* (May–June 2006): 3.

3. Rousso discusses many of these issues in a nuanced fashion in his very pertinent series of interviews with Philippe Petit. See Henry Rousso, *The Haunting Past: History, Memory and Justice in Contemporary France,* trans. Ralph Schoolcraft (Philadelphia: University of Pennsylvania Press, 2002). See also Eric Conan and Henry Rousso, *Vichy, un passé qui ne passe pas* (Paris: Fayard, 1994).

4. Jacques Buob and Alain Frachon, "'La France est malade de sa mémoire': Pierre Nora et le métier d'historien," in "Colonies: Un débat français," *Le Monde 2* (May–June 2006): 6–9.

5. Marianne Hirsch, "The Generation of Postmemory," *Poetics Today* 29, no. 1 (spring 2008): 103–28; here 106.

6. Alain Badiou, *Ethics*, trans. Peter Hallward (New York: Verso, 2002).

7. Didier Daeninckx, *Meurtres pour mémoire* (Paris: Gallimard, "Folio policier" 1984).

8. On the persistence of October 17 in the work of Algerian writers, see Seth Graebner, "Remembering 17 October 1961 and the Novels of Rachid Boudjedra," *Research in African Literatures* 36, no. 4 (winter 2005): 172–97.

9. See the discussion of the deportation of Jewish children in the classic historical study, Michael R. Marrus and Robert O. Paxton, *Vichy France and the Jews* (New York: Basic Books, 1981), 263–69.

10. My reference to "sideshadowing" is meant to evoke Michael André Bernstein's important book *Foregone Conclusions: Against Apocalyptic History* (Berkeley: University of California Press, 1994). Bernstein opposes sideshadowing to backshadowing, narratives in which future knowledge is projected back on earlier events to make them seem like part of a "necessary" progression. Sideshadowing emphasizes contingency over necessity and does not depict history as predetermined. My point here is that while the detective genre can harbor a powerful backshadowing impulse—since it seeks to uncover the necessary links that led to a crime—Daeninckx's deployment of the hard-boiled genre allows him to look sideways in order to survey contingent associations and layer multiple subplots into his narrative.

11. The Zizekian allusion to "looking awry" was suggested by my colleague Robert Rushing. I am grateful to him for his thoughts on the relationship between the hard-boiled genre and the kind of historical indirection deployed by Daeninckx. See his lively and illuminating psychoanalytic approach to detective fiction in *Resisting Arrest: Detective Fiction and Popular Culture* (New York: Other Press, 2007). See also Slavoj Zizek, *Looking Awry: An Introduction to Jacques Lacan through Popular Culture* (Cambridge, MA: MIT Press, 1992).

12. In describing the credits as "accumulating" on the screen I mean to echo Ian Baucom's argument for a philosophy of history that understands time as accumulating and not progressing. While Baucom is drawing on the work of Caribbean and Black Atlantic writers and thinkers coming to terms with the persistent haunting of slavery, his formulations are also valuable for the post-Holocaust/postcolonial contexts of *Multidirectional Memory* and are particularly apt for understanding questions of temporality, responsibility, and justice in *Caché*. See Ian Baucom, *Specters of the Atlantic: Slavery, Finance Capital, and the Philosophy of History* (Durham, NC: Duke University Press, 2006).

13. Almost all of Haneke's films include characters named Georges and Anne (or Georg and Anna, in the German-language films); many contain motifs of surveillance.

14. Libby Saxton, "Secrets and Revelations: Off-Screen Space in Michael Haneke's *Caché* (2005)," *Studies in French Cinema* 7, no. 1 (2007): 5–17; here 8.

15. I emphasize that identification is established with Georges and not Georges and Anne because, unlike the spectators and Georges, Anne has already viewed the tape at the point that the film begins. The distinction between the gazes of Georges and Anne is significant for the remainder of the film.

The theme of surveillance is also relevant to the colonial history that forms the background of *Caché*. Already in the middle of the nineteenth century, as Alexis de Tocqueville's 1847 "Rapport sur l'Algérie" demonstrates, French colonialism in Algeria was driven by the desire to "put under surveillance" the Algerian people, so as to "penetrate their techniques, their ideas, their beliefs, and . . . the secret to governing them" (Tocqueville cited in Paul Silverstein, *Algeria in France: Transpolitics, Race, and Nation* [Bloomington: Indiana University Press, 2004], 46–47).

16. Like so much else in the film, Majid's suicide is multiply significant. In particular, his self-inflicted slitting of the throat calls up the civil war that ripped apart Algeria during the 1990s following the cancelled elections of 1992. During the course of the decade, the violence between Islamists and government paramilitaries cost as many as one hundred thousand lives. A significant number of the victims had their throats cut. The figure of the cut, and the stain of blood it leaves on Majid's wall not only reminds viewers of a similar stain in Haneke's *The Seventh Continent* (1989) and gives the film its most dramatic image—used also in publicity posters—but also provides a figure for the ambiguous relation of France to Algeria, a relation that, as Etienne Balibar has remarked, hovers between "one nation" and "two." In other words, Majid's self-inflicted cut provides a figure for the wound that simultaneously differentiates Algeria and France from themselves and from each other, while also holding them together as what Paul Silverstein might call a "transpolitical" entity that is not one. See Etienne Balibar, "Algeria, France: One Nation or Two?" *Giving Ground: The Politics of Propinquity*, ed. Joan

Copjec and Michael Sorkin (New York: Verso, 1999), 162–72; and Silverstein, *Algeria in France*.

17. Max Silverman provides a persuasive account of the image and the gaze in *Caché*. In Silverman's suggestive reading, the film demonstrates how a society of bourgeois, Orientalist spectacle that is transfixed by the image can also potentially be undone by a de-Orientalized image and gaze. See Silverman, "The Empire Looks Back," *Screen* 48, no. 2 (2007): 245–49.

18. In *Der Siebente Kontinent* (*The Seventh Continent* [1989]), Haneke uses the radio much as he uses the television in *Caché*—to contextualize a private story in relation to public events. He also uses a similar television/bookshelf construction in the home of the main characters, Georg and Anna. When Georg begins the destruction of their house in preparation for the family's collective suicide, he begins by destroying the shelving surrounding the television (although not the television itself). "We have to do this systematically," he tells his wife. The systematic destruction continues to all of their other worldly possession, including, most shockingly, a giant aquarium filled with exotic fish, whose subsequent death Haneke films unhesitatingly, and all of their money, which is flushed down the toilet. In an interview on the DVD, Haneke remarks that both of these scenes elicited gasps from the audience during the film's initial screening. In *Benny's Video* (1992), Haneke again uses the television to insert public history into intimate contexts: this time news about the Balkan Wars and about skinheads attacking asylum-seekers in Germany. He also uses the same "framing" construction in Benny's bedroom, where the television (which plays a key role in the film) is housed in a bookshelf and surrounded with books and videos.

19. On detection, see Ranjana Khanna's nuanced essay on *Caché* in which she links the film to Poe's "Murders in the Rue Morgue." See Khanna, "From Rue Morgue to Rue des Iris," *Screen* 48, no. 2 (2007): 237–44.

20. See Catherine Erhel, Mathieu Aucher, and Renaud de la Baume, eds., *Le Procès de Maurice Papon*, 2 vols. (Paris: Albin Michel, 1998), 1.9. Future references to the trial transcript will be included in the text and will use the volume number followed by the page number.

21. See Nancy Wood, *Vectors of Memory: Legacies of Trauma in Postwar Europe* (London: Berg, 1999).

22. Unlike the events of October 17, the events at Charonne have not been the subject of collective forgetting. To the contrary, Charonne has been a primary site of memory for the French Left. While the relations between the memories of these two histories is complex—with Charonne often posed as a kind of screen memory blocking access to October 17—Einaudi's gesture here demonstrates how the better known events of Charonne can become a lever for evoking the other history as well. For a massively detailed and fascinating history of the events and memory of Charonne, including connections to October 17, see Alain Dewerpe, *Charonne, 8*

février 1962: Anthropologie historique d'un massacre d'État (Paris: Gallimard, 2006). The fact that Dewerpe is the son of one of the victims of the Charonne massacre, and his book thus a work of postmemory, is not irrelevant for this chapter.

23. Annette Wieviorka, *The Era of the Witness*, trans. Jared Stark (Ithaca, NY: Cornell University Press, 2006), 145.

24. The 1.5 generation is a category developed by Susan Suleiman in her fascinating book *Crises of Memory and the Second World War* (Cambridge, MA: Harvard University Press, 2006) to describe those who were young children during the events. The second generation, Marianne Hirsch's postmemory generation, was born after the events, but inherited a strong personal connection through familial transmission of stories and affects. Representatives of both of these generational groups testified during the Papon trial.

25. See Fogiel's testimony in Erhel, Aucher, and de la Baume, *Procès de Maurice Papon*, 1.838–41.

26. On Gheldman, see Eric Conan, *Le procès Papon: Un journal d'audience* (Paris: Gallimard, 1998), 95. For Alisvaks's testimony, see Erhel, Aucher, and de la Baume, *Procès de Maurice Papon*, 1.796.

27. A similar effect is produced, and in more explicit fashion, in *Funny Games*, where the ending essentially restages the beginning, but this time with a new set of victims. Unlike *Funny Games*, *Caché* can be read as having a more uplifting ending in which a new multicultural generation is seen emerging on the steps of the school—but this would ignore the menace also present in this final scene.

28. In an interview on the *Caché* DVD, Haneke confirms my sense that approximately half of the audience misses the presence of Pierrot and Majid's son in the final scene. What is significant is that this kind of visual ambiguity is built into the film, a result of choices about camera angle and the placement of extras. The film demands multiple viewings—and yet, even then, frustrates the desire for certainty.

29. Laetitia Van Eeckhout, "Mobilisation citoyenne contre les expulsions d'enfants," *Le Monde*, June 6, 2006. http://www.lemonde.fr/web/article/0,1-0@2-3226,36-784782,0.html. Accessed June 27, 2006.

30. Other films by Haneke that explore the victimization of children include *The Seventh Continent* and *The Time of the Wolf*. Films that raise questions about children and youths as perpetrators (and often victims as well) include especially *Benny's Video* and *Funny Games*. In *Benny's Video*, the eponymous teenager commits the random, unmotivated murder of a fellow teenager. In the wake of this act, he shaves his head, which results (as other characters comment) in his looking simultaneously like a concentration camp inmate and a neo-Nazi skinhead. This is among the only explicit references to Nazism in Haneke's oeuvre and it emphasizes the ambivalent legacies of fascism as they play out in subsequent generations.

31. *Caché* might be read productively through Clifton Spargo's notion of "the memory of injustice." Spargo writes, "How we think about history, the attention we pay to the injustice that is historical . . . actuates a space of critique within the present order. Among other things the memory of injustice, charted in its historical, systemic causations, provides an answer to the citizen who does not care because he cannot perceive himself to be causally responsible. It expands the principle of causation to a point where the subject accepts his positionality in a chain of causality." R. Clifton Spargo, *Vigilant Memory: Emmanuel Levinas, the Holocaust, and the Unjust Death* (Baltimore, MD: Johns Hopkins University Press, 2006), 261.

32. In an incisive short essay on *Caché*, Paul Gilroy points to the limits of the film's vision as its inability to move beyond the crisis of the white, bourgeois subject toward a fully imagined, alternative, nonwhite subject. In a clever and complementary argument, Mark Cousins suggests that the anxiety and potential ethical charge of the films are "offloaded" when its self-reflexive form becomes the subject of postviewing dinner conversation instead of the political question of colonial guilt. While I agree with Gilroy and Cousins that the film does not go so far as to stage a positive, alternative ethical and political project (as I will suggest *La Seine était rouge* does), I am somewhat more sanguine about the vision of an ethics-to-come sketched by Haneke. See Paul Gilroy, "Shooting Crabs in a Barrel," *Screen* 48, no. 2 (2007): 233–35; and Mark Cousins, "After the End: Word of Mouth and *Caché*," *Screen* 48, no. 2 (2007): 223–26.

33. My reading of Sebbar overlaps with two excellent essays on the novel by Anne Donadey and Dawn Fulton. The approach here differs, however, in situating *La Seine* primarily within the multidirectional traditions that are the focus of this book and in drawing attention to particular networks of association clustering around the photographs of Elie Kagan, the site of the Place de la Concorde, and the intertextual reference to Greek tragedy. See Anne Donadey, *Recasting Postcolonialism: Women Writing Between Worlds* (Portsmouth, NH: Heinemann, 2001), 28–33; and Dawn Fulton, "Elsewhere in Paris: Creolised Geographies in Leïla Sebbar's *La Seine était rouge*," *Culture, Theory & Critique* 48, no. 1 (2007): 25–38.

34. Leïla Sebbar, *La Seine était rouge: Paris, octobre 1961* (Paris: Thierry Magnier, 1999), 16.

35. Sebbar's interest in sites of memory associated with October 1961 contrasts significantly with Haneke's seeming avoidance of such sites. While recognizably set in Paris (glimpses of the significantly named Rue des Iris allows one to locate Georges's house precisely in the 13th arrondissement), *Caché* seems to mimic its protagonist's obliviousness to the history that surrounds him by refusing to make visible sites of historical violence. I am grateful to Manuel Rota for prompting me to focus on this aspect of the film.

36. Pierre Nora, "Entre Mémoire et Histoire: La problématique des lieux," *Les lieux de mémoire, I: La République*, ed. Pierre Nora (Paris: Gallimard, 1984), xvii.

37. Besides the general metonymical technique I find in both *La Seine* and Daeninckx's novel, Sebbar's interest in the layers of memory inscribed on and around public spaces seems to refer to two particular passages in *Meurtres pour mémoire*: one describing a wall in Toulouse covered with competing political graffiti; another, the final paragraph of the novel, in which Cadin and Claudine see a notice from the Nazi occupation uncovered by workers peeling off layers of posters in the Bonne-Nouvelle metro station (site of massacres on October 17, 1961) (159, 216). While the examples highlight competition and the blocking out of memory, the novel works to make the various messages visible—as does Sebbar's text.

38. Sebbar's strategies here might be likened to those of Patrick Modiano in his novel *La place de l'étoile*, which puns subversively on the relationship between the yellow star [*l'étoile jaune*] Jews were forced to wear during the occupation and the urban site, la Place de l'Etoile (the site of the Arc de Triomphe and, incidentally, another site through which Algerians passed during the night of October 17). Modiano's hybrid nonfiction work *Dora Bruder* is another obvious predecessor of Sebbar's novel insofar as it tells a story of postmemorial detection.

39. Sebbar's evocation of the Place de la Concorde as a site of "concord" between intersecting histories corresponds in interesting ways to the cultural-political significance of the site itself. As Maurice Agulhon reports in "Paris: A Traversal from East to West," an essay for the *lieux de mémoire* project, Concorde emerged in the postrevolutionary nineteenth century as a "neutralized" site: "The Place de la Concorde thus reflected a certain image of France, and it was incomprehensible that a square that was thus in a sense in the center of France should not also be the center of Paris. From this stemmed the idea that Paris was a city of halves, east and west, defined in relation to Concorde. . . . The antagonistic passions once associated with this central square were now buried in the past" (535). Sebbar, like Rouch and Morin before her, might be seen to revive some of those antagonistic passions, but she also does follow this historical narrative in making the *place* a site of potential concord. See Maurice Agulhon, "Paris: A Traversal from East to West," in *Realms of Memory: The Construction of the French Past: Volume III: Symbols*, ed. Pierre Nora, English-language edition ed. Lawrence Kritzman, trans. Arthur Goldhammer (New York: Columbia University Press, 1998), 523–52.

40. For a collection of Kagan's photographs from October 17, together with short biographical texts about him, see Jean-Luc Einaudi and Elie Kagan, *17 octobre 1961* (Arles, France: Actes Sud, 2001). The photograph mentioned here is found on pages 34–35 and is described as having been taken from the metro: "Elie Kagan gets into the metro. On the platform Algerians are penned in [*parqués*], machine guns in their backs. Up above, he notices the sign for the station: 'Con-

corde.' . . . His eye notes the tragic irony of the scene, the gulf between the sign and the facts" (36).

41. For this series of photographs, see Einaudi and Kagan, *17 octobre 1961*, 37–41.

42. Sebbar's interest in metro stations as sites of memory continues in her book of episodic "snapshots," *Métro: Instantanés* (Paris: Rocher, 2007). The entry titled "Octobre 2001, Solférino: L'Algérien" evokes October 17.

43. Edward Said, *Orientalism* (New York: Vintage, 1994 [1978]), 42–43.

44. The exact reason for Louis's obsession remains unclear. We know that he visited Egypt with his father at age ten (49), and, suggestively, that his father has Alexandrian Jewish friends, but the family's own connection to Egypt (professional? genealogical?) is not explained.

45. Sophocles, *Antigone*, trans. Elizabeth Wycoff, in *Greek Tragedies, Volume 1*, ed. David Grene and Richmond Lattimore (Chicago: University of Chicago Press, 1960), 181.

46. For examples of internecine and FLN violence, see pages 38, 42, 92. For references to the Algerian civil war of the 1990s, from which the character Omer has fled, see pages 22 and 52. Omer and Amel's discussion of the sacrifice of Abraham unites the two forms of violence (61–63).

EPILOGUE

1. See Nancy Fraser, "Reframing Justice in a Globalizing World," *New Left Review* 36 (2005): 69–88; and Nancy Fraser, "Abnormal Justice," *Critical Inquiry* 34 (2008): 393–422.

2. Abnormal justice describes situations in which "Even as they dispute substantive issues . . . the contestants also rehearse deep disagreements about who is entitled to address claims to whom concerning what; about where and how such claims should be vetted; and about who is obliged to redress them, if and when they are vindicated" (Fraser, "Abnormal Justice," 398).

3. Jodi A. Byrd, "'Living My Native Life Deadly': Red Lake, Ward Churchill, and the Discourses of Competing Genocides," *American Indian Quarterly* 31, no. 2 (2007): 318.

4. For more on the relation between the Holocaust and the genocide of indigenous peoples, see Lilian Freedberg, "Dare to Compare: Americanizing the Holocaust," *American Indian Quarterly* 24, no. 3 (2000): 353–80; A. Dirk Moses, ed., *Genocide and Settler Society: Frontier Violence and Stolen Indigenous Children in Australian History* (New York: Berghahn, 2004); and A. Dirk Moses, ed., *Empire, Colony, Genocide: Conquest, Occupation, and Subaltern Resistance in World History* (New York: Berghahn, 2008).

5. See Reuters, "Israeli Official Warns Palestinians of 'Shoah,'" *The New York Times*, February 29, 2008. *http://www.nytimes.com/reuters/world/international-palestinians-israel.html.* Accessed February 29, 2008.

6. Ari Shavit, "Survival of the Fittest: An Interview with Benny Morris," *Ha'aretz*, January 9, 2004. *http://www.haaretz.com/hasen/pages/ShArt.jhtml?itemNo =380986&contrassID=2.* Accessed June 23, 2008. For a short discussion of Morris's interview in the context of current Israeli politics, see Henry Siegman, "Israel: The Threat from Within," *The New York Review of Books,* February 26, 2004.

7. Benny Morris, "Right of Reply / I Do Not Support Expulsion," *Ha'aretz*, January 23, 2004. See also Benny Morris, "Der Zweite Holocaust," *Die Welt*, January 6, 2007. *http://www.welt.de/print-welt/article706570/Der_zweite_Holocaust.html.* Accessed December 1, 2007. Morris himself provided the English-language version, which is available at: *http://groups.yahoo.com/group/eejh/message/63915,* December 1, 2007. For an exposition of the politics of the discourse of the "second Holocaust," see Arye Naor, "Lessons of the Holocaust Versus Territories for Peace, 1967–2001," *Israel Studies* 8, no. 1 (2003): 130–52.

8. For an extended argument along these lines, see Gil Z. Hochberg, *In Spite of Partition: Jews, Arabs, and the Limits of Separatist Imagination* (Princeton, NJ: Princeton University Press, 2007).

Index

Aborigines. *See* indigenous peoples
Abu Ghraib torture scandal, 221–22, 283–84, 350n30
Adelson, Leslie A., 322n41
Adorno, Theodor W., 112–13, 124, 216, 334n3
Africa and Africans: Arendt's representation of, 37, 39–40, 51–53, 54–58, 60–62, 63–65, 80, 85, 88, 91, 326n24, 331n23; in Césaire, 70, 76, 86, 329n12; in *Chronicle of a Summer*, 179, 180, 182, 183–84; Conrad's representation of, 39–40, 55–57, 63, 83–85; Du Bois on, 119, 124; and genocide, 103–4; Luxemburg on, 96; in *Raft of the Medusa*, 67; Phillips on, 153,156, 159–60; Schwarz-Bart's depiction of, 145–46, 153; in *Stone Face*, 249–50, 251–52; in Tancred and Clorinda parable, 89, 94–95
African Americans: Du Bois on, 116, 120–21, 129–31; during cold war, 117; and the Holocaust, 1–2; in Paris, 247–48, 354n23; in Phillips's *Higher Ground*, 159–61; in Smith's *Last of the Conquerors*, 354n22; in Smith's *Stone Face*, 246–48, 250, 253, 256, 259, 261, 263. *See also* black-Jewish relations
Agamben, Giorgio: on bare life, 37, 45–46, 47, 54, 62–63, 86, 102, 325n17; on "biological continuum," 125–26; Eurocentrism of, 63, 102; on Nazi camps, 325n19
Agulhon, Maurice, 362n39

Alexander, Jeffrey, 263–65, 316n7, 356n40
Algerian Civil War (1990s), 272, 298, 363n46
Algerian War of Independence (1954–62): and African Americans, 247–48, 261, 354n23, 354n26, 355n29; and Charonne massacre, 232; in *Chronicle of a Summer*, 180, 183, 184, 194, 343n9; covered sympathetically in *France-Observateur*, 240; in Delbo, 26, 200, 206, 211, 215, 218; as global history, 254–55; and "invention of decolonization," 244–45; and May '68 uprising, 34; metropolitan resistance during, 25; and Papon, 234; and postmemory, 271; and post-World War II France, 201; related to Holocaust and World War II, 6, 17, 26, 134, 172, 179, 194–98, 204–5, 208–9, 244, 262, 277, 280, 298, 299, 320n32, 347n20, 355n30; related to Iraq War and "war on terror," 17, 28, 322n42; and torture, 192–93, 211, 223, 260, 266, 287 351n32. *See also* October 17, 1961 (police massacre)
Alleg, Henri, 193, 206
Alisvaks, Jacky, 289, 360n26
Althusser, Louis, 250
American Indians. *See* indigenous peoples
American Jewish Committee (AJC), 119
Améry, Jean, 17, 193
anachronism, 25, 136–37, 138, 140, 145–47, 150, 152, 157, 164, 276

anticolonialism: 40, 60, 161, 175–76, 317n8; among African Americans, 117, 248; among metropolitan intellectuals, 25–26, 34, 67, 69, 228, 233, 240–44, 246, 266, 346n17, 346–47n38; Césaire's contributions to, 24, 36, 40, 69–100; and *Chronicle of a Summer*, 184, 188, 192–98; and Delbo, 200, 201, 203, 212, 236; Du Bois's contributions to, 40; Fanon's contributions to, 24, 91–96; and Holocaust memory, 7; and humanism, 102; in *Stone Face*, 249, 261

Antigone (Sophocles), 296, 305–8
Apartheid, 251
Apter, Emily, 321n34
Aravamudan, Srinivas, 338n4, 339n15
Arendt, Hannah: 7, 23–24, 36–65, 69–73; on Africa, 51–58, 60–62, 63–65, 85–86; biography of, 38–39; on biopolitics, 47, 61, 325n18; on boomerang effect, 36, 63–65, 84–85, 106, 327n35; on colonial encounter, 54–58, 75, 77; on concentration camps, 58–61; concept of the human in, 47–48, 53–54; critical reception of, 39, 322–23n5, 323n9; on distinctiveness of Nazi genocide, 37, 44, 324n12; on Eichmann trial, 176–77, 278; *Eichmann in Jerusalem*, 176; *Human Condition*, 325n18; methodology of, 40–44, 101–3, 112, 324n15; *Origins of Totalitarianism*, 36–65; and progressive narrative, 43–44, 56, 58; on race, 52–58, 61–62, 63–65, 82, 325–26n24, 331n23; relation to Benjamin, 38, 43–44, 55, 56, 63, 80, 324n13; relation to Conrad's *Heart of Darkness*, 29, 37, 39–40, 55–58, 83, 85, 145, 326n27, 326n29; "Reply to Eric Voegelin," 42–44; on refugees, 44–47, 325n17; on rights, 40, 45–46, 61; "Social Science Techniques and the Study of Concentration Camps," 48–49; on totalitarianism, 41, 118, 330n12; on trauma, 54–55, 61, 90–91, 327n33; "We Refugees" 44–47

Arnold, A. James, 98, 329n6, 329n7, 329n12
Arrighi, Giovanni, 157, 341n28
Assmann, Aleida, 303, 323n8, 356n41
Assmann, Jan, 323n8
Assouline, Pierre, 348n12
Atlantic Civilization (Fougeron), 33–35, 37
Auschwitz (Nazi camp), 68, 141, 154, 182, 183, 200, 204–5, 208, 210, 218, 242, 278, 344n13

Badiou, Alain, 22, 272, 308, 321n38, 349n19, 355n35
Bakhtin, Mikhail, 320n33
Bal, Mieke, 318n18
Baldwin, James, 248, 354n26
Balibar, Etienne, 307, 358n16
bare life: 37, 45–47, 54, 58, 61, 62–63, 86, 102, 325n17
Barnouw, Dagmar, 323n5
Baron, Lawrence, 335n12
Battle of Algiers (Pontecorvo), 28, 346–47n38
Baucom, Ian, 349n19, 358n12
Bauer, Yehuda, 49–50, 51, 52, 317n11
Beauvoir, Simone de, 355n34
Ben-Gurion, David, 176, 197, 312
Benhabib, Seyla, 44, 323n5, 324n13, 325n24
Benjamin, Walter: 38; on civilization and barbarism, 56, 73, 80; on constellations, 43–44, 63, 106, 130, 324n13; on the Angel of History, 133; on ruins, 133, 340n21; on shock, 55, 80, 330 n20; "Theses on the Philosophy of History," 43, 56, 80, 324n13, 330n18
Bennett, Jill, 349n21
Benot, Yves, 320n32, 329n10
Berg, Nicolas, 319n29
Berlant, Lauren, 321–22n40, 349–50n27

Berman, Paul, 340n20
Berman, Russell, 124
Bernasconi, Robert, 325–26n24,
Bernstein, Michael André, 357n10
Bernstein, Richard J., 323n5, 324n13
Bewes, Timothy, 158, 340n22
Bidault, Georges, 346n38
biopolitics: Agamben's account of, 46, 62–63, 125–26; Arendt's account of, 47, 61, 325n18; Du Bois's critique of, 129, 131; Foucault's account of, 46, 125, 325n18
black-Jewish relations, 4, 25, 93–94, 117, 126, 132, 135–37, 148–50, 152, 153, 154, 157, 159, 162, 164, 169, 172, 332n35, 335n7, 338n3, 340n20
Blanchot, Maurice, 194
Bloch, Ernst, 320n33
Blücher, Heinrich, 324n13
boomerang effect: in Arendt, 23, 36, 59, 63–65, 69–70, 85, 91, 102; and Conrad, 82–85; and problem of origins, 106; in translation of Césaire, 23, 36, 69–70, 79
Boujhered, Djamila, 355n34
Boupacha, Djamila, 210, 221, 355n34
Bourdet, Claude, 230, 240–41, 245
Boyarin, Jonathan, 316n3
Brackman, Harold, 335n7
Breton, André, 72
Brodwin, Stanley, 339n14
Brodzki, Bella, 145, 147, 337n2, 339n14
Brown, Laura, 89, 332n30
Brown, Wendy, 349–50n27
Budick, Emily Miller, 335n7
Buelens, Gert, 332n30
Byrd, Jodi, 50, 310–11

Caché. See Haneke, Michael: *Caché*
Caillois, Roger, 100
Camus, Albert, 313, 347n40
Le Canard enchaîné (newspaper), 286
Canovan, Margaret, 41, 47–48, 52, 54, 60, 323n5, 325n24, 327n30
Caribbean: and Césaire, 71–72; migrants from, 22, 140, 143, 159, 162; and Phillips, 153, 159, 162; in Schwarz-Bart, 135, 146–48, 150–51, 153, 155; and slavery 135, 339n17
Carroll, David, 320n32
Carruthers, Mary, 316n2
Caruth, Cathy, 87–90, 91, 92, 94–95, 169, 319n26, 331n27, 332n28
Castronovo, Russ, 335n8
Cayrol, Jean, 345n19
censorship, 25–26, 72, 192–95, 197, 207, 209, 211, 212, 216, 222
Césaire, Aimé: 40, 69–107, 112, 114, 135, 175, 192; on anti-Semitism, 98–99; and Benjamin, 73, 80, 330n18, 330 n20; biography, 71–72, 329n7; and Communism, 70–71, 96–100, 118; concept of *choc en retour*, 23–24, 36, 70, 73, 79–80, 82–83, 85–86, 96, 102, 106, 281, 330n18; and Conrad's *Heart of Darkness*, 82–85; contributions to trauma theory, 87–88, 91, 96; and cosmopolitanism, 70–71, 99–100, 131; on disavowal, 73, 78–80, 91, 284; *Discourse on Colonialism*, 36, 69–91, 96–100, 328n3; on Jews, 100; *Lettre à Maurice Thorez*, 71, 98–100, 131, 328n3; on Nazism, 71, 73–77, 79, 81, 96–97, 98, 99–100; *Notebook of a Return to the Native Land*, 71–72, 329n12; and primitivism, 73, 75, 329–30n12; and progressive narrative, 70, 73, 80; on regression, 70, 73, 74–79, 81, 329n12; on return, 65, 74–77, 79–81, 85, 87; and surrealism, 72–73, 78, 187
Césaire, Suzanne Roussi, 72
Cesarani, David, 342n5
Chandler, James, 339n15
Charonne (1962 massacre), 232, 235, 287, 359–60n22
Cheah, Pheng, 332n34
Cheyette, Bryan, 160, 332n35, 340n22, 341n29
children: and ethics of memory, 297;

as Holocaust victims, 162, 194, 278, 288–89, 290, 357n9, 360n24; as perpetrators, 193–94, 360n30; and postmemory, 271, 279, 296, 298–99, 321n40; as responsible agents, 292, 295; sentimentality in representation of, 279, 321–22n40. *See also* hidden children

Chirac, Jacques, 268, 357n2

choc en retour. *See* Césaire, Aimé: concept of *choc en retour*

Christianity: and anti-Semitism, 140; and Du Bois, 127; and imperialism, 52, 79, 81, 124; and resistance to Nazism, 194, 288; Schwarz-Bart and, 139–40, 144, 338n10; and Tancred and Clorinda parable, 94–95

Chronicle of a Summer (Rouch and Morin): 25–26, 34, 178–98, 199–201, 240, 258, 276, 288; and Algerian War, 179, 180, 343n9, 344n14; as cinéma vérité, 25, 178, 180–81, 184, 188–90, 192, 194, 220, 343n10; and decolonization, 179, 180, 183–84, 192–98, 354n25; and Holocaust memory, 178, 180, 181–82, 184–87, 190–98, 343n7, 343n12; influence of, 180, 237, 241–42, 255; relation to *Hiroshima, Mon Amour*, 190; relation to *Night and Fog*, 184, 345n19; relation to *Shoah*, 190, 346n26; and surrealism, 187–88, 345n18; testimony in, 178, 184–87, 188–91, 192–97, 288, 300; "truth" in, 192–95

Chronique d'un été. See *Chronicle of a Summer*

Churchill, Ward, 317n11

cinéma vérité, 25, 178, 180–81, 188–90, 192, 194, 220

Cixous, Hélène, 28

Cliff, Michele, 27

Clifford, James, 187, 344n15, 345n17

Cohen, William, 350–51n32

cold war, 24, 112, 117–19, 121, 122, 128, 133, 244, 320n33, 323n5, 335n9, 336n18

Cole, Jennifer, 316n3

Cole, Joshua, 235

colonialism: Arendt on, 51–58, 60–62, 63–65, 75, 77, 85–86; Césaire on, 24, 69–91; and comparison, 262, 326n28; Fanon on, 24, 89, 91–94, 154–55, 257–58, 332n30, 332n34, 355n32; and Nazism, 23–24, 33–34, 36–37, 43, 52, 58, 63, 65, 73, 74, 76–77, 94, 97, 102, 104, 192; resistance to, 25, 67, 134, 172, 193, 194–95, 200, 201, 207, 209, 211, 215, 217–18, 220, 260, 346n37, 346n38. *See also* anticolonialism; decolonization; postcolonial studies; racism; torture

Comité Maurice Audin, 233, 287, 296, 352n10

communism, 70, 117, 121, 130, 262, 347n38. *See also* Communist Party (French [PCF]); Communist Party (American); Soviet Union; Césaire, Aimé; Du Bois, W. E. B.; Fougeron, André; Taslitzky, Boris

Communist Party (French [PCF]), 33, 66, 71, 96–99, 107, 114, 118, 194, 199, 208, 232, 287, 328n1, 328n3

Communist Party (American), 117–18, 244

comparison, 18–19, 27, 29, 35, 38, 49, 50, 64, 87, 96, 100, 119, 132, 152, 164, 187, 230, 240, 272, 311, 318n20, 320–21n33, 321n34, 323n9; and colonialism, 262, 326n28; "comparison literature," 170, 340n22; comparative imagination, 21, 65, 107; and ethics, 22, 265, 285, 293; and study of genocide, 101–3

competitive memory, model of, 3, 4, 5, 9, 10–11, 18, 114, 129, 156, 202, 229, 299, 309, 311, 318n22, 319n23

complicity: in Daeninckx's *Meurtres*, 277–80, 307; of French in colonial violence, 196, 277; of French in Holocaust, 196, 235, 236, 243–44, 262–63, 265–66, 286; in Haneke's *Caché*, 281, 291–92, 294–95; and

multidirectional memory, 27, 253, 265; in Phillips, 158, 160, 163; in Smith's *Stone Face*, 230, 246, 250–54, 258, 262, 341n31, 354n25; theory of, 251, 254, 265, 354n27
Conan, Eric, 269, 357n3, 360n26
concentration camps: in Agamben, 46, 102, 325n19; in Arendt, 37, 40, 45–46, 48, 54, 57, 58, 59, 324n12; in *Chronicle of a Summer*, 182, 184; in Delbo, 199, 204, 210, 218; in Du Bois, 124; in Fougeron, 33; in Haneke, 360n30; and Papon, 286; in Phillips, 160, 168; in Pontecorvo, 347n38; in Schwarz-Bart, 138, 141, 150; in Smith, 248, 252, 260, 261, 355n31; in Todorov, 113; use during Algerian War, 25, 193, 210, 252, 354n13
Confiant, Raphaël, 328n5
Confino, Alon, 4
Congo, 180, 182, 183, 184, 249–50, 252, 354n25
Conrad, Joseph: and Arendt, 37, 39–40, 55–58, 63, 73, 74–75, 85, 103–4, 145, 326n27, 326n29; and Césaire, 73, 74–75, 82–85, 105; *Heart of Darkness*, 37, 39–40, 55–58, 73, 74–75, 82–85, 326n29; and Morris, 29
Cooper, Frederick, 106
counterpublic, 202, 209, 214, 220–23
Cousins, Mark, 361n32
Craps, Stef, 332n30, 340n22
Cyprus, 165–66, 167–68

Daeninckx, Didier: 27, 233, 266, 270, 272, 273, 274–81, 285, 296, 298, 308, 355n30; on French complicity in Holocaust, 276, 277–78; and hard-boiled genre, 279–80, 357n10; and layers of memory, 362n37; *Meurtres pour mémoire*, 274–81; on October 17, 1961 massacre, 274–75
Danner, Mark, 222
Dawson, Ashley, 340n22
DeBouzek, Jeanette, 345n18, 345n25

Debray, Régis, 183
"Déclaration sur le droit à l'insoumission." *See* "Manifesto of the 121"
decolonization: age of, 34, 40, 96, 101, 107, 121, 172, 180, 320n32; and cinéma vérité, 188; and Fougeron, 33; and Holocaust memory, 7, 18, 20, 22, 67–69, 77, 178, 182, 187, 188, 192, 195, 197, 200–204, 205, 208, 230, 235, 239, 242–44, 255, 262, 265–66, 276, 309; and migration to metropolis, 136; and postcolonial politics, 153; and racialization, 228, 244–45, 353–54n20, 354n25. *See also* anticolonialism; colonialism; postcolonial studies
De Gennaro, Maria, 329–30n12
Delacroix, Eugène, 67, 69
Delanoë, Bertrand, 234
Delbo, Charlotte: 26, 34, 187, 193, 199–223, 236; on Algerian War, 199–223 *passim*; *Auschwitz and After*, 187, 199, 204–5, 210, 218, 219, 240, 344–45n16, 348n4, 349n24; *Les belles lettres*, 193, 199–223, 287, 288, 346n32 348n11, 351n7; biography, 203, 348n7; as counterpublic witness, 220–21, 223; *Days and Memory*, 199, 204, 205–6, 348n11; and documentary form, 199, 206, 347n2; and epistolary form, 200, 202, 207; and public sphere, 212–13, 215–17, 219–21, 222–23; relation to Henri Lefebvre, 203–4, 348n7; and testimony, 213–15, 219, 220–21; on torture, 211, 221–22
Derrida, Jacques, 28
Dewerpe, Alain, 360n22
diasporas: African, 71, 116, 121, 139, 142, 145–46, 252, 317n8, 329n7; Caribbean, 22, 143; Genoese diaspora, 341n28; overlapping black and Jewish, 23, 24, 107, 120, 134, 135, 136, 143, 149, 150–52, 153, 156, 164, 169, 244, 332n35; theory and critique of, 158, 166, 167, 253–54, 341n7; and trauma, 170

DiIorio, Sam, 343n10, 344n12, 344n14
Dimock, Wai Chee, 321n34, 321n37
Diner, Dan, 325n20
Donadey, Anne, 361n33
Dornfeld, Barry, 345n24
Dossa, Shiraz, 325n22, 325n24
Douglas, Lawrence, 342n5
Drowning by Bullets (Hayling and Brooks), 352n10
Du Bois, W. E. B.: 7, 22, 24, 25, 40, 107, 111–34, 157, 172, 175, 198, 338n3; and anti-Semitism, 336n17; and Benjamin, 133; and Communism, 70, 117–19, 244, 335n10; critique of uniqueness, 7, 116, 121; and double consciousness, 106, 128–31, 150, 171; *Dusk of Dawn*, 120; on Jews, 119, 120, 335n7; "The Negro and the Warsaw Ghetto," 111–34, 136, 147, 155, 171, 237, 241 339n16; persecution of by United States government, 117, 118, 336n18; on race and the color line, 104, 105, 111, 116, 125–26, 131–32, 153, 230, 337n25; on Sorrow Songs, 130; *Souls of Black Folk*, 120, 124, 125, 129–30, 131, 165, 335n8; visits to Germany, 115, 124; visits to Poland, 111, 115–16, 120, 122; on Warsaw Ghetto Monument, 127–31; *World and Africa*, 124, 336n21
Duras, Marguerite: 27, 230, 245, 246, 263; "Les deux ghettos," 236–40, 241, 242, 255; *Hiroshima, Mon Amour*, 190, 236
Dussel, Enrique, 39, 323n7

Eaton, Mick, 345n18, 346n27
Edelman, Lee, 321–22n40
Editions de Minuit (publisher), 206, 220, 348n12
Edwards, Brent Hayes, 317n8, 329n7
Egypt, 149, 298, 304, 305, 339n19, 363n44
Eichmann, Adolf, 176–77, 209, 342n5
Eichmann trial, 22, 25–26, 172, 176–80, 191, 192, 195, 200–201, 220, 288, 342n4, 342n5, 346n28, 347n1
Einaudi, Jean-Luc, 233–34, 286–87, 288, 362n40, 363n41
ethics: Badiou's theory of, 22, 272, 308, 321n38, 349n19, 355n35; and children, 285, 292, 294; and complicity, 244, 250; and fidelity, 22, 224, 272–73, 293, 308, 349n19; and mourning, 296, 308; and multidirectional memory, 22, 27, 29, 172, 223, 228, 229–30, 236, 240, 246, 263–66, 272, 279, 281, 283, 286, 297, 306, 349n19; and testimony, 219, 349n21
ethnographic surrealism, 187–88, 345n18
Eurocentrism, 24, 39, 53, 69, 70, 77, 78, 87, 90–91, 99, 105, 106, 112, 323n7
Evans, Martin, 346n37
everyday life: 181, 183, 203–204, 237, 284, 320n33
Ezrahi, Sidra DeKoven, 151–52, 338n10

Fabian, Johannes 64, 320n33
Fabre, Michel, 354n23
Faguet, Emile, 75, 330n13
Fanon, Frantz: 72, 101, 102, 194, 199, 254; on black-Jewish relations, 23, 92–94, 332n35; on colonial trauma, 24, 89, 91–94, 96, 332n30, 332n34; and racist gaze, 154–55, 257–58, 355n32
Feld, Steven, 345n20
Feldman, Ron H., 322n5
Felman, Shoshana, 202, 213–15, 219, 349n21
Fitzpatrick, Matthew P., 333n40
Flaherty, Robert, 180
Fogiel, Esther, 288–89, 360n25
forgetting, 13, 77, 196, 201, 205, 213, 219, 221, 228, 229, 260, 301, 319n23, 359n22
form, problems of: in Delbo, 199–201, 202–3, 206–7, 211–13, 222; in Du Bois and Rapoport, 128–31, 150; in Schwarz-Bart, 149–50
Foucault, Michel: on "biological continuum," 125; and biopolitics,

46, 125, 325n18; and "the repressive hypothesis," 11
Fougeron, André, 33–36, 37, 66, 70, 96, 114, 118, 176
France-Observateur (magazine), 200, 236–38, 240–44, 353n18
Fraser, Nancy, 19–21, 310, 363n1, 363n2
Freedberg, Lilian, 363n4
French laws concerning history, 267–68, 350n31
Fritzsche, Peter, 4
Freud, Sigmund: on disavowal, 78; on identification, 155–56; on memory, 68, 319n23, 319n24; on Oedipus, 296; on return of the repressed, 79; on screen memory, 12–14, 16; on trauma, 78, 81, 88, 90, 94, 319n23, 319n26, 331n27
Front de Libération Nationale (FLN), 26, 194, 209, 215, 217, 227, 228, 231, 236, 241, 245, 260, 297, 301, 363n46
Fulton, Dawn, 361n33
Fuss, Diana, 155

genocide, comparative study of, 10, 70, 102–7, 318n16, 318n20, 323n9, 346n46, 363n4
Géricault, Théodore, 66–67, 69
Gerlach, Christian, 104
Gheldman, Georges, 289, 360n26
Gilman, Sander, 94
Gilroy, Paul: on black and Jewish diasporas, 317n8, 337n24; on *Caché*, 361n32; on *The Stone Face*, 246, 249, 253, 255, 257, 259, 261
Gines, Katherine T., 326n24, 331n23
Golsan, Richard, 9, 352n12
Graebner, Seth, 357n8
Griaule, Marcel, 183
Grosse, Pascal, 324n12
Guadeloupe, 135, 144, 146, 154, 339

Halbwachs, Maurice, 14–15, 320n30
Halimi, Gisèle, 355n34
Hall, Stuart, 341n27

Hancock, Ian, 317n11
Haneke, Michael: and Abu Ghraib scandal, 283; *Benny's Video*, 359n18; *Caché*, 17, 27, 28, 230, 266, 270, 273, 274, 280–95, 296, 298, 308, 351n4, 358n16, 359n17, 359n18, 360n28, 361n31, 361n32, 361n35; complicity as theme in, 266, 294–95; *Funny Games*, 360n27; and "hidden children," 288–89, 292–93; and modes of visibility, 282, 291–92; and October 17, 1961 massacre, 230, 280, 281, 282–83; and Papon Trial, 285–89; and question of responsibility, 293–95; *Seventh Continent*, 358n16, 359n18, 360n30; and surveillance, 280, 281–82, 291, 358n13; *Time of the Wolf*, 360n30
Hansen, Miriam, 12
Hardt, Michael, 337n25
harkis, 231–32
Harootunian, Harry, 320n33
Hartman, Geoffrey, 345n21
Haughton, Hugh, 13
Hausner, Gideon, 191
Heart of Darkness (Conrad), 37, 39–40, 55–58, 73, 74–75, 82–85, 326n29
Hegel, G. W. F., 5–6, 58, 161, 326n27,
Heidegger, Martin, 38, 44
Herero and Nama, genocide of, 103
Hess, Remi, 348n7
hidden children, 288–90, 292–93, 295
Hiroshima, Mon Amour (Resnais and Duras): 190, 236
Hirsch, Joshua, 343n7, 345n26
Hirsch, Marianne, 271, 276, 298, 302–4, 321n40, 355n33, 360n24
Hitler, Adolf, 49, 67–69, 76, 77, 79–80, 81, 102, 125, 149
Hochberg, Gil Z., 364n8
Hochhuth, Rolf, 176
Holocaust (events): as counter-rational, 325n20; deportation of Jews from France, 278, 286; distance from United States of, 16; as irrational, 50. See also genocide, comparative study

of; Nazism; Vel' d'Hiv' roundup; Vichy regime; Warsaw ghetto; Warsaw ghetto uprising
Holocaust memory: and the American Left, 118; and depoliticization, 261; and the Eichmann trial, 176–78, 190–91; emergence and history of, 6, 7, 17, 22, 27, 112, 153, 172, 176–78, 190–91, 200–201, 229, 288, 316n6; in France, 26, 265; and gender, 255; globalization of, 230, 263–65, 316n7; relation to other histories and memories, 2–3, 9, 148, 179, 192, 197, 200, 204, 229, 236; as screen memory, 12–16; as shared memory, 15
Holocaust studies, 22, 53, 70, 87, 101–7, 112–15, 122, 128, 132, 213, 219, 271
Holocaust survivors: as anticolonial activists, 134; and competitive memory, 311; French associations of, 208, 289; gendered identity of, 237, 255; public identity of, 177, 189–91, 195, 196; testimony by, 25, 168, 176–78, 185–87, 189–91, 192, 193, 202, 204, 218
homo sacer. See Agamben, Giorgio; bare life
Horne, Alistair, 322n42
Horne, Gerald, 335n9, 335n10, 336n18
House, Jim, 224, 227–28, 231, 232, 233, 235, 278, 351n1, 351n2, 351n4, 351n8, 352n9, 352n12, 352–53n14, 353n20
Hull, Isabel V. 103–4, 105–6, 323n9, 333n40
human, concept of the: in Agamben, 102; in Arendt, 36, 37, 41, 44–45, 47–48, 51, 53–54, 56, 57–59, 60–61, 62, 64, 65, 102, 323n9, 330n12; in Césaire, 36, 37, 85, 86, 102, 330n12
humanism, 62, 101–2, 326n27, 329–30n12
Husserl, Edmund, 44
Huston, Nancy, 28
Huyssen, Andreas, 315n2, 316n7, 318n22

identification, 120, 148–49, 154–57, 159, 161, 164, 169, 171, 282, 283, 297, 358n15
identity: and memory, 2–7, 11, 18, 20, 21, 87, 132, 139, 158, 191, 236, 269, 271, 309, 315n1, 319n29, 339n19
indigenous peoples: and boomerang effect, 65; and discourse of uniqueness, 8, 50; and genocide, 97, 100, 196, 312, 318n16, 363n4; and multidirectional memory, 28; and screen memory of Holocaust, 12, 318n22; and struggles over territory, 310–11
Indochina. See Vietnam
interpellation, 250–51, 257, 272–73
Iraq War (2003–), 28, 172, 222, 283, 312, 322n42
Israel, 25, 163, 165, 167, 176–77, 191, 243, 343n6
Israeli/Palestinian conflict, 28–29, 283, 310–13

Jameson, Fredric: on confronting history, 262; on imperialism, 81–82, 324n12; on periodization, 10
Jankélévitch, Vladimir, 340n20
Jeanson, Francis, 194, 206, 209, 210, 215–6, 220, 344n12
Jerusalem Delivered (Tasso), 88–90, 94–96, 331n27
Jewish Life (magazine), 111, 115–20 *passim*, 126, 244, 335n9, 336n13
Jews: in Algeria, 257; in Césaire, 100; emigration to Palestine, 38; in Europe, 22–23, 44, 120; in Soviet Union, 119; as targets of Nazis, 41; in the United States, 117–18, 120. *See also* black-Jewish relations
justice: 321n37, 355n34; in *Caché*, 293, 295, 358n12, 361n31; and complicity, 251–52; Du Bois on, 130; Fraser's theory of, 19–21, 310, 363n2; in *La Seine était rouge*, 305–8; and

multidirectional memory, 5, 19–21, 22, 29, 265, 310–11, 313

Kaplan, Brett Ashley, 347n2
Kaufmann, Francine, 139, 142
Katz, Steven T., 8, 317n11
Kelley, Robin D. G., 329n8
Kennedy, Rosanne, 349n20
Kettane, Nacer, 233
Khanna, Ranjana, 320n32, 355n34, 359n19
King, Richard, 326n24, 326n27
Klein, Kerwin Lee, 315n2
Klein, Naomi, 349n26
Korsch, Karl, 96–97, 333n38
Koshy, Susan, 166–67
Kréa, Henri, 230, 242–43, 245, 246, 263

Lacan, Jacques, 170
LaCapra, Dominick: on absence and loss, 151, 169, 327n32; on acting out and working through, 152, 316n3; on Camus, 347n40; on historical vs. structural trauma, 137, 151; on perpetrator trauma, 90, 326n26, 332n32; on regression, 75, 78; on return of the repressed, 79, 81
Lagrou, Pieter, 208
Lalieu, Olivier, 208
Lallaoui, Mehdi, 352n10
Lampert, Lisa, 333n43
Langer, Lawrence, 141, 189, 204, 348n4
Lanzmann, Claude, 8, 113, 190, 334n4
Laplanche, Jean, 78, 330n15
Laub, Dori, 202, 213–15, 349n21
Laval, Pierre, 278
Ledent, Bénédicte, 159, 161, 162
Lefebvre, Henri, 181, 203, 320n33, 348n7
Le Meur, Jean, 209–10, 348n16
Lewis, David Levering, 121, 335n9
Levi, Neil, 318–19n22
Levi, Primo, 102, 168, 187, 199, 242
Levine, Michel, 233
Lévi-Strauss, Claude, 72
Levy, Daniel, 231, 264–65, 316n7, 356n39, 356n40, 356n41
Leys, Ruth, 89–90, 331n27
"Liberté pour l'histoire" (petition), 268–70
Liberty Leading the People (Delacroix), 67
lieux de mémoire, 235, 268, 298, 299, 362n39. *See also* memory: sites of
Linenthal, Edward T., 9, 12, 317n14
Lionnet, Françoise, 321n34
Lipstadt, Deborah, 9 50
Lloyd, David, 327n33, 332n31
Loomba, Ania, 317n8, 333n43, 341n33
Loridan-Ivens, Marceline: collaboration with Jean-Pierre Sergent, 344n13; marriage to Joris Ivens, 344n13, 347n38; *Petite prairie aux bouleaux* (film), 344n13; testimony in *Chronicle of a Summer*, 181–92 passim, 195, 197, 237, 240, 242, 255, 300, 343n12, 345n19
Lumumba, Patrice, 184, 249–50, 252, 354n25
Luxemburg, Rosa, 96–97, 333n38
lynching, 100, 120

Macey, David, 329n7, 346n38
MacMaster, Neil, 224, 227–28, 231, 232, 233, 235, 278, 351n1, 351n2, 351n4, 351n8, 352n9, 352n12, 353n14, 353n20
Maier, Charles, 315n2
Mandel, Naomi, 354n27
Mandouze, André, 194–95, 346n38
"Manifesto of the 121," 194, 209, 215–16, 346n35
Marceline. *See* Loridan-Ivens, Marceline
Marable, Manning, 335n9
Margalit, Avishai, 15
Margulies, Ivone, 344n14
Marie, Michel, 189
Marrus, Michael R., 357n9
Martinique, 71–72, 339n17
May '68 uprising, 34, 201, 298
Melas, Natalie, 320n33, 321n34, 326n28
memory: as associative process, 12–13;

definition of, 3–4; globalization of, 230, 263–65, 316n7; vs. history, 268; individual vs. collection versions of, 14–16; sites of, 4, 235, 268, 297, 298, 299, 306, 310, 361n35, 363n42; and the state, 268–70; "terrorism" of, 269, 272, 273, 279, 285, 307–8. *See also* competitive memory; Holocaust memory; multidirectional memory

Ménil, René, 72
Mesher, D., 138
Mesnard, Philippe, 316n4
Michaels, Walter Benn, 1–7 *passim*, 9, 12, 20, 87, 309, 315n1, 319n26
Michelet, Edmond, 287
Miles, William, 316n6
Missac, Pierre, 330n18
Modiano, Patrick, 362n38
Le Monde (newspaper), 76, 200, 210, 269, 292–93, 357n2
Monnoyer, Jean-Maurice, 330n18
Morin, Edgar: and Algerian War, 346n35; appearance in *Chronicle of a Summer* of, 180, 181, 183; concept of cinéma verité of, 181, 189; essay on *Chronicle of a Summer* by, 182, 190; and theory of everyday life of, 181; on torture, 193. *See also Chronicle of a Summer*
Morris, Benny, 29, 311–13, 364n7
Morrison, Toni, 342n36
Moses, A. Dirk, 102, 318n16, 318n20, 323n9, 330n20, 333n38, 334n46, 363n4
Mouvement contre le racisme et pour la paix, 353n20
Moyn, Samuel, 342n4
Mufti, Aamir, 321n39
Muhammad, Khalid, 1–7 *passim*, 9, 11, 19
multidirectional memory: archive of, 18; as collective memory, 15–16; and complicity, 251; conceptualization of, 3–7, 11–12, 35–36, 309; deferral, displacement and, 228–29; as ethical practice, 229–30, 272, 273, 283, 306; as global phenomenon, 28; and justice, 19–21, 29, 310, 311; and

"memory of injustice," 319n26; and postmemory, 271, 300, 304; and "repressive hypothesis," 11; and screen memory, 14–16; as shared memory, 15; and struggles over territory, 310; vs. competitive memory, 3, 10–12, 17–18, 21, 228–29, 309, 319n23, 321n33; vs. universalization, 263–65

Musée de l'Homme, 180, 183, 185, 344
Muselmann, the, 54

Nanterre, 237, 274, 297, 301
Naor, Arye, 364n7
Napoleon, 298, 304, 305
narrative fetishism, 170
Nazism: and biopolitics, 125–26; and colonialism, 23–24, 33–34, 36–37, 43, 52, 58, 63, 65, 73, 74, 76–77, 94, 97, 102, 104, 192; and critique of humanism, 101; discussion of in Communist circles, 118; French myth of resistance to, 196; and return of the repressed, 79–80; in Taslitzky, 67–69
Negri, Antonio, 337n25
Newton, Adam Zachary, 335n7
Nietzsche, Friedrich, 45, 211
Night and Fog (Resnais), 184, 188, 345n19
Ngal, Georges, 73
Nkrumah, Kwame, 355n28
Nora, Pierre: and *lieux de mémoire*, 299; suspicion of memory, 235, 268–70, 272, 273, 279, 281, 285, 288, 293, 298, 307
Norton, Anne, 325n24
Novak, Amy, 89, 90, 95, 332n28
Novick, Peter, 118, 176–77, 191, 316n6

October 17, 1961 (police massacre): contemporary response to, 199, 227–31, 232–33, 236–45, 262, 265–66, 351n2, 353n18, 353n20; in Daeninckx's *Meurtres*, 274–80, 362n37; events of, 26, 227, 231–32, 348n11, 351n1; and French universalism, 351n3; in

Haneke's *Caché*, 280–83, 285, 288, 289–90, 291–92, 295, 296, 361n35; Kagan's photographs of, 300–304, 362–63n40; memory of, 26, 27, 205, 227–31, 233–36, 270, 351–52n8, 352n9, 353n14; Papon's role in, 223, 231, 234–35, 267, 286–87, 355n30; relation to memory of Charonne, 359–60n22; in Sebbar's *La Seine*, 296–302, 306–8; in Smith's *Stone Face*, 246–49, 253, 259, 262, 354n24, 355n29

Octobre à Paris (Panijel), 233, 287, 352n10

Oedipus myth, 296, 305, 306

Olick, Jeffrey K., 315n2, 316n4

Ophuls, Marcel, 263

Orientalism, 50, 304–5, 309n17

Organisation Armée Secrète (OAS), 26, 231, 253

Othello (literary character), 156–58, 164–68, 169, 341n33

Ozick, Cynthia, 168

Panijel, Jacques, 233, 287, 296, 352n10

Palestinians, 168, 258, 311–12, 340n19. *See also* Israeli/Palestinian crisis

Papon, Maurice: and *Caché*, 285–90, 292; and deportation of Jews, 9, 223, 262, 267, 274; and massacre of Algerians, 9, 26, 223–24, 227, 231, 241, 254, 300, 304; and *Meurtres pour mémoire*, 276–79. *See also* Papon trial

Papon trial, 9, 27, 223, 234–35, 236, 267, 285–89, 290, 292, 298, 350n32, 352n12, 360n24

Paris, 26, 38, 71–72, 98, 140, 143, 180, 181, 186, 187, 188, 199, 205, 227, 231, 232, 234, 243, 247–48, 250, 252–53, 261, 362n39; black diaspora in, 355n29; depiction in *Caché*, 361n35; depiction in *La Seine était rouge*, 297–98, 300–302; depiction in *Stone Face*, 247–48, 250, 252–53, 261; massacre of Algerians in, 227, 231–32, 274; fall 2005 uprising in suburbs of, 268, 281, 350n31

particularity: *See* universal/particular dialectic

Paxton, Robert O., 263, 357n9

Patterson, William L., 336n13

Péju, Paulette, 296, 351n7

Pétain, Marshal Philippe, 72

Phillips, Caryl, 24–25, 107, 134, 153–72, 175; and anachronism, 136–37; and Anne Frank, 154; *Atlantic Sound*, 168; *Cambridge*, 158; critical reception of, 159, 340n22, 341n29; *Crossing the River*, 158; *European Tribe*, 153–58, 159, 163, 164, 165, 169; *Higher Ground*, 159–63; and black-Jewish relations, 153, 154–56, 157, 159, 161–63, 164, 338n2; *Nature of Blood*, 163–70; and Othello, 156–58, 164, 165–68; on race, space, and diaspora, 105, 157–58, 167–68; relation to Schwarz-Bart, 153, 166–67, 170–71; and "stratified minoritization," 167; and trauma, 169–70

Philipson, Robert, 338n3

Pietz, William, 64–65, 325–26n24

Place de la Concorde (Paris), 185–86, 189, 190, 300–302, 304–5, 306, 361n33, 362n39

politics: Agamben's conception of, 46, 62–63, 102, 125, 325n19; Arendt's conception of, 38, 39, 41, 45, 46, 52, 60, 322n5; of decolonization, 188, 236; of "framing," 21; and human rights, 229; of memory, 3–4, 9, 11, 26, 29, 36, 113–14, 172, 179, 202–3, 208, 221, 223, 229–30, 232, 263, 319n29; of Middle East, 177, 312–13, 364n6, 364n7; racial, 118, 166–67, 325n24; relation to ethics, 22, 266, 273, 349n19; and testimony, 203, 215, 222, 349–50n27. *See also* anticolonialism; biopolitics; decolonization

Pontalis, Jean-Bertrand, 78, 330n15

Pontecorvo, Gillo, 28, 346–47n38

postmemory: and children, 27, 291, 298, 360n22; definition of, 271,

321n40, 360n24; and justice, 308; and photography, 302–4; relation to multidirectional memory, 271, 273, 276, 279, 300, 305
postcolonial studies, 22, 62, 94, 101, 106, 114, 115, 118, 132, 255, 316n3, 317n8, 324n12
Power, Samantha, 10, 318n16
Prochaska, David, 351n32
Proskauer, Joseph, 119
psychoanalysis, 12–14, 77–79, 89, 91, 170, 202, 213–15, 296, 349n20, 357n11
public sphere: challenges to, 179, 202, 215, 216, 218, 220, 223; and decolonization, 192, 195, 206, 242, 270, 286; and Holocaust memory, 27, 134, 176–79, 191, 197, 200; and the Left, 126; and memory, 2–3, 5, 202–3, 221, 362n37; and power, 21

Quint, David, 94–95, 331n27, 332n28

racism: and anti-Semitism, 1–2, 92–94, 140, 229, 230, 242–43, 246, 257, 260, 352n35, 352–53n14; and decolonization, 192, 241–42, 245, 353–54n20; discussed by Arendt, 54, 58, 61, 63, 64, 91, 325n24, 331n23; discussed by Césaire, 76–77, 98; discussed in *Chronicle of a Summer*, 182, 183; discussed by Du Bois, 115, 116–18, 122, 124–25, 131; discussed by Fanon, 92–94; discussed by Phillips, 157, 170–71; discussed by Smith, 247, 248–50, 253, 254, 257, 260, 261–62; history of, 333n43, 337n25; and Negritude, 329n12; and trauma, 89
Raft of the Medusa (Géricault), 66–67
Rapoport, Nathan, 24, 122, 127–31, 147, 337n23
recognition, 3, 5–7, 10, 19–21, 60, 64, 152, 228, 236, 243, 245, 270, 310, 330n20
reconciliation, 235, 236, 269–70
redistribution, 20, 310, 321n36

refugees, 39, 44–47, 54, 57–58, 61, 72, 159, 163, 165, 167, 325n17
Reinhardt, Catherine A., 339n17
representation; and the Holocaust, 113, 129, 131, 170, 189, 190, 202, 216; and memory, 4, 10, 35–36, 43, 316n5, 318n18; political, 19–20, 310
Réseau éducation sans frontières (Education Without Borders Network), 292–93
resistance: to colonialism, 25, 67, 134, 172, 193, 194–95, 200, 201, 207, 209, 211, 215, 217–18, 220, 260, 346n37, 346n38; to Nazism, 25, 33, 68, 127–28, 130, 147, 166, 172, 177, 183, 194–95, 196, 199, 201, 206, 208, 209, 218, 240–41, 344n15, 346–47n38; to racism, 23, 24–25, 111–12, 115, 126, 130, 131, 134, 153, 161, 166, 167
Resnais, Alain, 184, 190, 236, 343n9, 345n19
Ricks, Thomas, 322n44
Riposte (Taslitzky), 66–69, 328n2
Robbins, Joyce, 315n2, 316n4
Rosenfeld, Alvin, 338n10, 338n11
Roskies, David, 128–29, 130, 337n23
Ross, Kristin: on the Algerian War, 201, 204; on anticolonialism and May '68, 201; on 1950s, 34, 347n42; on *The Stone Face*, 246, 253, 255; on torture, 211
Rothman, William, 343–44n12
Rouch, Jean: and Algerian War, 346n35; appearance in *Chronicle of a Summer* of, 180, 181, 184; concept of cinéma verité of, 181, 188–89, 192, 194; as ethnographic filmmaker, 180; and the Musée de l'Homme, 344n15; surrealism of, 187, 190, 345n18. See also *Chronicle of a Summer*
Rousso, Henri, 196, 268–69, 288, 298, 357n3
ruins, 24, 107, 114, 123, 126, 127, 131–32, 133, 135, 136, 146–48, 152–53, 172, 319n23, 339n16, 340n21

Ruscio, Alain, 328n1
Rushing, Robert, 357n11

Said, Edward, 304, 327n31, 340n19
Salomon, Michel, 142
Sanders, Mark, 251, 253, 254
Santner, Eric, 170
Sanyal, Debarati, 347n40
Sartre, Jean-Paul, 93, 194, 210, 329n12
Saxton, Libby, 281
Scharfman, Ronnie, 148, 337n2, 339n18
Scholem, Gershom, 144
Schwarz-Bart, André, 24–25, 135–52, 153, 154, 171, 172, 337–38n2; and anachronism, 136–37, 146–48; and Benjamin, 340n21; on Caribbean diaspora, 22, 143, 148–49, 155; confusion of absence and loss in, 151–53, 327n32; and controversy, 139; discourse of vicitimization, 151–52, 166; on Jewish identity, 143, 148–49, 156, 161; "Jewishness and Negritude," 138, 142–43; juxtaposition of Warsaw and Caribbean, 104, 133, 135, 157; *Last of the Just*, 135, 137, 138–44, 170, 187; "Pourquoi j'ai écrit La Mulâtresse Solitude," 138, 148–50, 339n18; *Un plat de porc aux bananes vertes*, 135, 142; and problem of form, 149–50; on slavery, 146, 148–49; *Woman Named Solitude*, 135, 137, 144–48, 339n17
Schwarz-Bart, Simone, 135, 148, 338n2, 339n13
screen memory, 12–16, 196, 317n14, 318n22, 359n22
Sedgwick, Eve, 156
Sebbar, Leïla: and Antigone, 305–8; evocation of Elie Kagan's photographs, 300–304; *Métro*, 363n42; and October 17, 1961 massacre, 296–302, 306–8; and Place de la Concorde, 300–305, 362n39; and postmemory, 298–300, 302–8; *La Seine était rouge*, 27, 266, 270, 273, 274, 296–308, 361n33

Segev, Tom, 176, 191, 316n6
Sergent, Jean-Pierre, 182–83, 187, 240, 343–44n12, 344n13
Shandler, Jeffrey, 178, 191, 343n6
Shepard, Todd, 244–45, 246, 353–54n20
Shih, Shu-mei, 321n24
Shoah (Lanzmann), 190, 334n4, 345n26
Shylock (literary character), 157
sideshadowing, 279, 357n10
Siegman, Henry, 364n6
Silverman, Max, 359n17
Silverstein, Paul, 307, 358–59n16
Smith, Valerie, 355n33
Smith, William Gardner, 27, 134; biography of, 246–47, 355n28; depiction of October 17, 1961 massacre, 246–49, 253, 259, 262, 354n24, 355n29; engagement with complicity, 250–54, 277, 341n31, 354n25; on gender and memory, 259–61; *Last of the Conquerors*, 354n22; portrait of African American expatriates, 247–48, 250, 354n26; references to Nazism and Holocaust, 249, 252–53, 255–58, 261–63, 265; *The Stone Face*, 230, 246–63, 351n4
Solitude (legendary figure of Guadeloupe), 146, 166, 167, 339n17
Sophocles, 296, 306–308
Sorum, Paul Clay, 346n35, 348n16
Sorrow and the Pity, The (Ophuls), 263
South Africa, 28, 52–53, 63–64, 251, 254
sovereignty, 46–47, 62, 86, 125, 337n25
Soviet Union, 105, 117, 128
Spargo, R. Clifton, 319n26, 361n31
Spiegelman, Art, 298, 355n31
SS (*Schutzstaffel*), 33, 35, 58–59, 61, 68, 185
Stalinism, 8, 43, 98–99, 117, 128, 129, 130, 335n10
Stannard, David E., 10, 12, 317n11
Steiner, Jean-François, 342n4
Stoler, Ann Laura, 106
Stone, Dan, 318n20, 323n9, 326n24, 327n35

Stora, Benjamin, 193–94, 195–96, 343n9, 352n8
Stovall, Tyler, 246, 247–48, 253–55, 354n23, 355n29, 355n30
Sturken, Marita, 315n2
Suk, Jeannie, 328n5
Suleiman, Susan, 316n5, 360n24
Sundquist, Eric, 335n7
surrealism, 72–73, 78, 187, 345n18
Sznaider, Natan, 231, 264–65, 316n7, 356n39, 356n40, 356n41

Tancred and Clorinda, parable of, 88–90, 94–96, 331n27, 332n28
Taslitzky, Boris, 66–70, 77, 96, 114, 118, 176, 328n2
Tasso, Torquato, 88–90, 94–96, 331n27
Teitgen, Paul, 193, 211, 287
Témoignage chrétien (Christian Witness [group]), 194
Témoignages et Documents (journal), 194
Les Temps modernes (journal), 199, 200, 210, 330n18, 347n1
Terdiman, Richard, 3, 316n3, 319n24
territory, conflicts over, 310
testimony: in anticolonial activism, 194–95; in *Chronicle of a Summer*, 178, 184–87, 188–91, 192–97, 288, 300; counterpublic testimony, 220–21; critiques of testimony, 349n20, 349–50n27; in Delbo, 213–15, 219; in Eichmann trial, 25–26, 176–78, 191, 192, 195, 201; Felman and Laub's theory of, 202, 213–15, 219, 349n21; Fortunoff Video Archive, 215, 345n21; in Papon trial, 286–89, 360n25, 360n26
Thatcher, Nicole, 347n2, 348n7
Thorez, Maurice, 328n3
Tillion, Germaine, 344n15
Tocqueville, Alexis de, 358n15
Todorov, Tzvetan, 113, 344n15
torture: in Abu Ghraib and "war on terror," 28, 221–23, 283–84, 349n26, 350n30; during Algerian War, 17, 25–26, 134, 192–93, 195, 205, 207, 208, 209, 210, 211, 216, 221, 223, 231, 239, 241, 252, 260, 266, 287, 320n32, 346–47n38, 351n32, 355n34; as ethical problem, 221; in Indochina, 76; in Madagascar, 74; as link between colonialism and Holocaust, 17, 195, 211, 216, 228, 242, 244, 266
trauma: "accident model" of, 332n30; Caruth on, 87–89, 90–91, 319n26; in *Chronicle of a Summer*, 181–82, 187–88, 189, 197; and colonial encounter, 55, 58, 61, 75, 80–81, 327n33; cultural trauma, 316n7; and disavowal, 78; Fanon on, 91–94, 332n34; Leys on, 89, 331n27; of perpetrators, 59, 88–89, 90, 92, 326n26; and postmemory, 271, 273, 288; and screen memory, 12, 16; structural vs. historical, 137, 151–53, 161, 169–70; and testimony, 202, 214–15, 345n26, 349–50n27; "traumatic realism," 342n38
trauma theory, 24, 87, 89, 91, 94, 133, 319n26
Traverso, Enzo, 323n9, 333n38
truth: conception of in cinéma vérité, 25, 181, 192; criteria of, 269; and decolonization, 25, 192–95, 203, 206, 241; and ethics, 272; and memory, 14; and testimony, 213, 220, 350n27; "truth cure," 193, 203, 206
Trezise, Thomas, 347n2, 348n13
Tropiques (literary journal), 72

Ungar, Steven, 343n8
uniqueness, discourses of: 7–11, 14, 36–37, 42, 49–52, 96, 101, 105, 106, 119, 121, 127, 129, 138, 148, 152, 170, 171, 178, 179, 184, 191, 230, 240, 317n11, 318n20
universal/particular dialectic, 21, 27, 29, 97–99, 101, 112, 128, 130–31, 132, 230, 244, 246, 251–52, 254, 258, 264–65
universalism, 26, 36–37, 62, 95–96, 99–100, 240, 244–46, 249, 251, 259,

263–64, 351n3
universalization, 27, 68, 81, 229–30, 240, 244, 249, 251, 263–65, 356n40

Van Styvendale, Nancy, 332n30
Vel' d'Hiv' roundup, 68, 242, 243, 266, 287, 301
Venice, 156–58, 165, 341n28
Vérité des Travailleurs (journal), 194
Vérité-Liberté (journal), 194, 195, 200, 244, 352n10, 353n18
Vérités Anticolonialistes (journal), 194
Vérités Pour (journal), 194
Vertov, Dziga, 180
Vichy regime: consequences for Martinique of, 72; connected to October 17, 1961 massacre, 233–35, 243, 274, 279, 286, 290, 350n31, 353n20; memory and legacies of, 196, 201, 262–63, 267–69; persecution of Jews in 9, 276, 278, 357n9
Vico, Giambattista, 136, 147
Vidal-Naquet, Pierre, 194–95, 206, 216, 268, 287
Vietnam, 33, 66, 74, 76, 193, 195, 205, 236, 298, 329n10, 344n13
Voegelin, Eric, 42–43
Von Eschen, Penny, 117

Wagner, Richard, 124
Walkowitz, Rebecca, 170, 340n22
Walzer, Michael, 149, 339–40n19
Warner, Michael, 202, 209, 212–15, 220, 222, 349n21
"war on terror," 26, 172, 222, 224, 229, 272
Warsaw ghetto: 339n16; Du Bois's visit to, 24, 104, 111–33, 136, 147, 171, 241, 276; in Duras's "Deux Ghettos," 237–41; in writings of Phillips, 153; in writings of Schwarz-Bart, 135, 136,
146–47, 167, 171
Warsaw Ghetto Monument (Rapoport), 111, 122, 127–31, 147, 337n23
Warsaw ghetto uprising, 111, 127, 147, 167
We Charge Genocide (political campaign), 118, 336n13
Weissman, Gary, 318n22
West Indies: *See* Caribbean
Whitehead, Anne, 340n22
Wiesel, Elie, 8, 135, 168, 187, 214, 317n11, 346n28
Wieviorka, Annette: on Eichmann trial, 177, 191, 288, 342n4; on emergence of Holocaust survivor, 191; on French Holocaust memory, 196, 316n6, 346n28; on hidden children, 288–89; on Papon trial, 288
Wilson, Sarah, 322n1
Wilson, Tikka Jan, 349n20
Wood, Nancy, 286
Wright, Richard, 247–48

Yates, Frances, 315n2
Young, Iris Marion, 321n37
Young, James E.: on Holocaust as metaphor, 318n21; on Warsaw Ghetto Monument, 128, 130, 337n23
Young, Robert, 101–2, 317n8, 333n39
Young-Bruehl, Elizabeth, 322n4, 322n5, 324n13, 325n24

zero-sum logic, 3, 9, 11, 18, 20, 21, 134, 309, 315n1, 319n29, 321n36. *See also* competitive memory
Zierler, Wendy, 338n2, 340n22, 341n29
Zimmerer, Jürgen, 104–6, 323n9, 333n40
Zionism, 38, 142, 177, 178, 312, 340n19
Zizek, Slavoj, 336n15, 355n35, 357–58n11

Cultural Memory in the Present

Jacob Taubes, *Western Eschatology*

Jean-François Lyotard, *Enthusiasm: The Kantian Critique of History*

Frank Ankersmit, Ewa Domanska, and Hans Kellner, eds., *Re-Figuring Hayden White*

Stéphane Mosès, *The Angel of History: Rosenzweig, Benjamin, Scholem*

Ernst van Alphen, Mieke Bal, and Carel Smith, eds., *The Rhetoric of Sincerity*

Alexandre Lefebvre, *The Image of the Law: Deleuze, Bergson, Spinoza*

Samira Haj, *Reconfiguring Islamic Tradition: Reform, Rationality, and Modernity*

Diane Perpich, *The Ethics of Emmanuel Levinas*

Marcel Detienne, *Comparing the Incomparable*

François Delaporte, *Anatomy of the Passions*

René Girard, *Mimesis and Theory: Essays on Literature and Criticism, 1959–2005*

Richard Baxstrom, *Houses in Motion: The Experience of Place and the Problem of Belief in Urban Malaysia*

Jennifer L. Culbert, *Dead Certainty: The Death Penalty and the Problem of Judgment*

Samantha Frost, *Lessons from a Materialist Thinker: Hobbesian Reflections on Ethics and Politics*

Regina Mara Schwartz, *Sacramental Poetics at the Dawn of Secularism: When God Left the World*

Gil Anidjar, *Semites: Race, Religion, Literature*

Ranjana Khanna, *Algeria Cuts: Women and Representation, 1830 to the Present*

Esther Peeren, *Intersubjectivities and Popular Culture: Bakhtin and Beyond*

Eyal Peretz, *Becoming Visionary: Brian De Palma's Cinematic Education of the Senses*

Diana Sorensen, *A Turbulent Decade Remembered: Scenes from the Latin American Sixties*

Hubert Damisch, *A Childhood Memory by Piero della Francesca*

Dana Hollander, *Exemplarity and Chosenness: Rosenzweig and Derrida on the Nation of Philosophy*

Asja Szafraniec, *Beckett, Derrida, and the Event of Literature*

Sara Guyer, *Romanticism After Auschwitz*

Alison Ross, *The Aesthetic Paths of Philosophy: Presentation in Kant, Heidegger, Lacoue-Labarthe, and Nancy*

Gerhard Richter, *Thought-Images: Frankfurt School Writers' Reflections from Damaged Life*

Bella Brodzki, *Can These Bones Live? Translation, Survival, and Cultural Memory*

Rodolphe Gasché, *The Honor of Thinking: Critique, Theory, Philosophy*

Brigitte Peucker, *The Material Image: Art and the Real in Film*

Natalie Melas, *All the Difference in the World: Postcoloniality and the Ends of Comparison*

Jonathan Culler, *The Literary in Theory*

Michael G. Levine, *The Belated Witness: Literature, Testimony, and the Question of Holocaust Survival*

Jennifer A. Jordan, *Structures of Memory: Understanding German Change in Berlin and Beyond*

Christoph Menke, *Reflections of Equality*

Marlène Zarader, *The Unthought Debt: Heidegger and the Hebraic Heritage*

Jan Assmann, *Religion and Cultural Memory: Ten Studies*

David Scott and Charles Hirschkind, *Powers of the Secular Modern: Talal Asad and His Interlocutors*

Gyanendra Pandey, *Routine Violence: Nations, Fragments, Histories*

James Siegel, *Naming the Witch*

J. M. Bernstein, *Against Voluptuous Bodies: Late Modernism and the Meaning of Painting*

Theodore W. Jennings, Jr., *Reading Derrida / Thinking Paul: On Justice*

Richard Rorty and Eduardo Mendieta, *Take Care of Freedom and Truth Will Take Care of Itself: Interviews with Richard Rorty*

Jacques Derrida, *Paper Machine*

Renaud Barbaras, *Desire and Distance: Introduction to a Phenomenology of Perception*

Jill Bennett, *Empathic Vision: Affect, Trauma, and Contemporary Art*

Ban Wang, *Illuminations from the Past: Trauma, Memory, and History in Modern China*

James Phillips, *Heidegger's Volk: Between National Socialism and Poetry*

Frank Ankersmit, *Sublime Historical Experience*

István Rév, *Retroactive Justice: Prehistory of Post-Communism*

Paola Marrati, *Genesis and Trace: Derrida Reading Husserl and Heidegger*

Krzysztof Ziarek, *The Force of Art*

Marie-José Mondzain, *Image, Icon, Economy: The Byzantine Origins of the Contemporary Imaginary*

Cecilia Sjöholm, *The Antigone Complex: Ethics and the Invention of Feminine Desire*

Jacques Derrida and Elisabeth Roudinesco, *For What Tomorrow . . . : A Dialogue*

Elisabeth Weber, *Questioning Judaism: Interviews by Elisabeth Weber*

Jacques Derrida and Catherine Malabou, *Counterpath: Traveling with Jacques Derrida*

Martin Seel, *Aesthetics of Appearing*

Nanette Salomon, *Shifting Priorities: Gender and Genre in Seventeenth-Century Dutch Painting*

Jacob Taubes, *The Political Theology of Paul*

Jean-Luc Marion, *The Crossing of the Visible*

Eric Michaud, *An Art for Eternity: The Cult of Art in Nazi Germany*

Anne Freadman, *The Machinery of Talk: Charles Peirce and the Sign Hypothesis*

Stanley Cavell, *Emerson's Transcendental Etudes*

Stuart McLean, *The Event and Its Terrors: Ireland, Famine, Modernity*

Beate Rössler, ed., *Privacies: Philosophical Evaluations*

Bernard Faure, *Double Exposure: Cutting Across Buddhist and Western Discourses*

Alessia Ricciardi, *The Ends Of Mourning: Psychoanalysis, Literature, Film*

Alain Badiou, *Saint Paul: The Foundation of Universalism*

Gil Anidjar, *The Jew, The Arab: A History of the Enemy*

Jonathan Culler and Kevin Lamb, eds., *Just Being Difficult? Academic Writing in the Public Arena*

Jean-Luc Nancy, *A Finite Thinking*, edited by Simon Sparks

Theodor W. Adorno, *Can One Live after Auschwitz? A Philosophical Reader*, edited by Rolf Tiedemann

Patricia Pisters, *The Matrix of Visual Culture: Working with Deleuze in Film Theory*

Talal Asad, *Formations of the Secular: Christianity, Islam, Modernity*

Dorothea von Mücke, *The Rise of the Fantastic Tale*

Marc Redfield, *The Politics of Aesthetics: Nationalism, Gender, Romanticism*

Emmanuel Levinas, *On Escape*

Dan Zahavi, *Husserl's Phenomenology*

Rodolphe Gasché, *The Idea of Form: Rethinking Kant's Aesthetics*

Michael Naas, *Taking on the Tradition: Jacques Derrida and the Legacies of Deconstruction*

Herlinde Pauer-Studer, ed., *Constructions of Practical Reason: Interviews on Moral and Political Philosophy*

Jean-Luc Marion, *Being Given: Toward a Phenomenology of Givenness*

Theodor W. Adorno and Max Horkheimer, *Dialectic of Enlightenment*

Ian Balfour, *The Rhetoric of Romantic Prophecy*

Martin Stokhof, *World and Life as One: Ethics and Ontology in Wittgenstein's Early Thought*

Gianni Vattimo, *Nietzsche: An Introduction*

Jacques Derrida, *Negotiations: Interventions and Interviews, 1971–1998*, ed. Elizabeth Rottenberg

Brett Levinson, *The Ends of Literature: Post-transition and Neoliberalism in the Wake of the "Boom"*

Timothy J. Reiss, *Against Autonomy: Global Dialectics of Cultural Exchange*

Hent de Vries and Samuel Weber, eds., *Religion and Media*

Niklas Luhmann, *Theories of Distinction: Redescribing the Descriptions of Modernity*, ed. and introd. William Rasch

Johannes Fabian, *Anthropology with an Attitude: Critical Essays*

Michel Henry, *I Am the Truth: Toward a Philosophy of Christianity*

Gil Anidjar, *"Our Place in Al-Andalus": Kabbalah, Philosophy, Literature in Arab-Jewish Letters*

Hélène Cixous and Jacques Derrida, *Veils*

F. R. Ankersmit, *Historical Representation*

F. R. Ankersmit, *Political Representation*

Elissa Marder, *Dead Time: Temporal Disorders in the Wake of Modernity (Baudelaire and Flaubert)*

Reinhart Koselleck, *The Practice of Conceptual History: Timing History, Spacing Concepts*

Niklas Luhmann, *The Reality of the Mass Media*

Hubert Damisch, *A Childhood Memory by Piero della Francesca*

Hubert Damisch, *A Theory of /Cloud/: Toward a History of Painting*

Jean-Luc Nancy, *The Speculative Remark (One of Hegel's Bons Mots)*

Jean-François Lyotard, *Soundproof Room: Malraux's Anti-Aesthetics*

Jan Patočka, *Plato and Europe*

Hubert Damisch, *Skyline: The Narcissistic City*

Isabel Hoving, *In Praise of New Travelers: Reading Caribbean Migrant Women Writers*

Richard Rand, ed., *Futures: Of Derrida*

William Rasch, *Niklas Luhmann's Modernity: The Paradox of System Differentiation*

Jacques Derrida and Anne Dufourmantelle, *Of Hospitality*

Jean-François Lyotard, *The Confession of Augustine*

Kaja Silverman, *World Spectators*

Samuel Weber, *Institution and Interpretation: Expanded Edition*

Jeffrey S. Librett, *The Rhetoric of Cultural Dialogue: Jews and Germans in the Epoch of Emancipation*

Ulrich Baer, *Remnants of Song: Trauma and the Experience of Modernity in Charles Baudelaire and Paul Celan*

Samuel C. Wheeler III, *Deconstruction as Analytic Philosophy*

David S. Ferris, *Silent Urns: Romanticism, Hellenism, Modernity*

Rodolphe Gasché, *Of Minimal Things: Studies on the Notion of Relation*

Sarah Winter, *Freud and the Institution of Psychoanalytic Knowledge*

Samuel Weber, *The Legend of Freud: Expanded Edition*

Aris Fioretos, ed., *The Solid Letter: Readings of Friedrich Hölderlin*

J. Hillis Miller / Manuel Asensi, *Black Holes / J. Hillis Miller; or, Boustrophedonic Reading*

Miryam Sas, *Fault Lines: Cultural Memory and Japanese Surrealism*

Peter Schwenger, *Fantasm and Fiction: On Textual Envisioning*

Didier Maleuvre, *Museum Memories: History, Technology, Art*

Jacques Derrida, *Monolingualism of the Other; or, The Prosthesis of Origin*

Andrew Baruch Wachtel, *Making a Nation, Breaking a Nation: Literature and Cultural Politics in Yugoslavia*

Niklas Luhmann, *Love as Passion: The Codification of Intimacy*

Mieke Bal, ed., *The Practice of Cultural Analysis: Exposing Interdisciplinary Interpretation*

Jacques Derrida and Gianni Vattimo, eds., *Religion*